THE LAST CAMPAIGN

THE LAST CAMPAIGN

SHERMAN, GERONIMO
AND THE WAR FOR AMERICA

H. W. BRANDS

THORNDIKE PRESS
A part of Gale, a Cengage Company

Copyright © 2022 by H. W. Brands.
All photographs are courtesy of the Library of Congress.
Map on pages 6–7 by John Burgoyne.
Thorndike Press, a part of Gale, a Cengage Company.

LIBRARY OF CONGRESS CIP DATA ON FILE.
CATALOGUING IN PUBLICATION FOR THIS BOOK
IS AVAILABLE FROM THE LIBRARY OF CONGRESS.

ISBN-13: 979-8-88578-686-7 (hardcover alk. paper)

Published in 2023 by arrangement with Doubleday, an imprint of The Knopf Doubleday Publishing Group, a division of Penguin Random House LLC.

Printed in Mexico
Print Number: 1   Print Year: 2023

CONTENTS

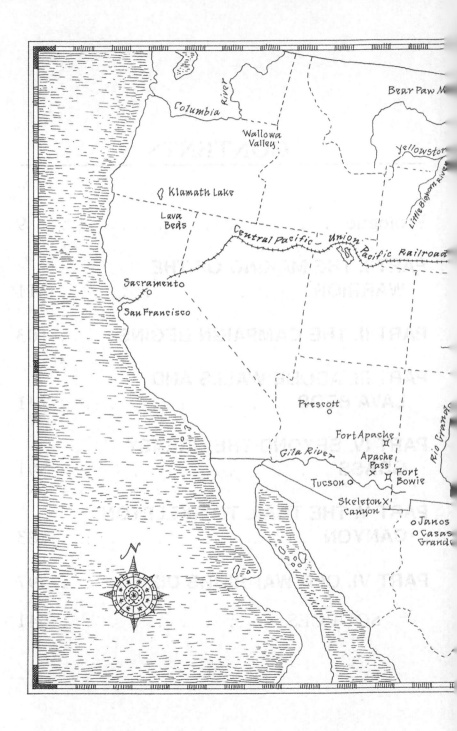

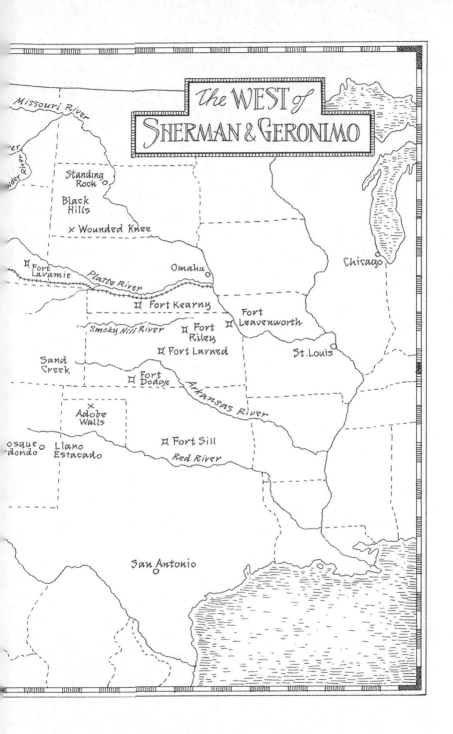

The WEST of SHERMAN & GERONIMO

Missouri River

...er
...nder River

Standing Rock

Black Hills

× Wounded Knee

Fort Laramie

Platte River

Omaha

Chicago

Fort Kearny

Smoky Hill River

Fort Riley

Fort Leavenworth

Fort Larned

St. Louis

Sand Creek

Fort Dodge

Arkansas River

× Adobe Walls

...osque ...dondo

Llano Estacado

Fort Sill

Red River

San Antonio

PROLOGUE

The war for America likely commenced early in the human history of the Americas. Indeed, it might have grown out of conflict already under way when the first East Asian hunters or fishers arrived in ice-age North America. This was no pleasure trip; the food-seekers almost certainly had been driven from home by enemies, or by hunger their enemies kept them from allaying. They knew life as a struggle: against nature for the resources required for human sustenance, and against other humans who stood in their way.

They were not individualists; singly they couldn't have survived the first winter. Their unit was the clan or the tribe, large enough to reproduce but small enough to relocate in response to setbacks and opportunities. To each tribe, other tribes — later arrivals from the old world, or splinters from the first comers — were competitors, presumptive enemies.

The enemies, while threatening the tribes

from without, enforced coherence within. As generations passed, the tribes developed folkways that distinguished them from their enemies. The languages of different tribes grew mutually unintelligible. Their origin stories assigned to each tribe first place in creation's plan. Strength and skill in defending the tribe in war against enemies became the hallmark of tribal leadership. The heroes of a tribe were its greatest warriors and became its leaders.

Alliances emerged, the better to wage war on non-allies. Weaker tribes were scattered, enslaved, absorbed. In a few spots, after the cultivation of food plants took hold, empires were built on the backs of tribes that couldn't get out of the way.

By then the climate had changed and the oceans risen, and the new world was cut off from the old. Memories of the old world had faded and died. Yet in the old world tribes competed and fought just as they did in the new world, just as humans always had. And when, after five hundred generations of separation, a few tribes from the old world discovered a novel route to the new, they joined the war they found in progress there.

■ ■ ■ ■

PART I
THE MAKING OF
THE WARRIOR

■ ■ ■ ■

1

"I was born in No-doyohn Canyon, Arizona, June, 1829," Geronimo recalled from the distance of old age. "In that country, which lies around the headwaters of the Gila River, I was reared. This range was our fatherland; among these mountains our wigwams were hidden; the scattered valleys contained our fields; the boundless prairies, stretching away on every side, were our pastures; the rocky caverns were our burying places."

Geronimo's people, the Apaches, had not always lived near the Gila River. Their language was of the Athabaskan family, revealing roots far to the north, among the tribes of the Northwest Coast. The Apaches had migrated to the desert and mountains of the Southwest, probably under compulsion, for life was harder there. They reached the Gila River a few centuries before Geronimo's birth, perhaps around the time Columbus reached the West Indies.

Geronimo was the fourth in a family of

eight children. They were four boys and four girls. "As a babe I rolled on the dirt floor of my father's tepee, hung in my *tsoch*" — cradle — "at my mother's back, or suspended from the bough of a tree," he said. "I was warmed by the sun, rocked by the winds, and sheltered by the trees as other Indian babes." As he grew, he learned. "My mother taught me the legends of our people; taught me of the sun and sky, the moon and stars, the clouds and storms. She also taught me to kneel and pray to *Usen*" — God — "for strength, health, wisdom, and protection. We never prayed against any person, but if we had aught against any individual we ourselves took vengeance. We were taught that Usen does not care for the petty quarrels of men."

Other lessons came from his father. "My father had often told me of the brave deeds of our warriors, of the pleasures of the chase, and the glories of the warpath," Geronimo said. He and his brothers emulated what they heard. "We played that we were warriors. We would practice stealing upon some object that represented an enemy, and in our childish imitation often perform the feats of war. Sometimes we would hide away from our mother to see if she could find us, and often when thus concealed go to sleep and perhaps remain hidden for many hours."

With age came responsibility. "When we were old enough to be of real service, we went to the field with our parents not to play, but to toil. When the crops were to be planted we broke the ground with wooden hoes. We planted the corn in straight rows, the beans among the corn, and the melons and pumpkins in irregular order over the field. We cultivated these crops as there was need." Plots were modest in size. "Our field usually contained about two acres of ground. The fields were never fenced. It was common for many families to cultivate land in the same valley and share the burden of protecting the growing crops from destruction by the ponies of the tribe, or by deer and other wild animals."

The crops set a rhythm for life. "Melons were gathered as they were consumed. In the autumn, pumpkins and beans were gathered and placed in bags or baskets; ears of corn were tied together by the husks, and then the harvest was carried on the backs of ponies up to our homes. Here the corn was shelled, and all the harvest stored away in caves or other secluded places to be used in winter."

Another essential came free from nature. "We did not cultivate tobacco, but found it growing wild. This we cut and cured in autumn, but if the supply ran out, the leaves from the stalks left standing served our purpose. All Indians smoked — men and women." Where other tribes smoked pipes, the Apaches preferred cigarettes, with the tobacco typically rolled in oak leaves. "No boy was allowed to smoke until he had hunted alone and killed large game — wolves and bears. Unmarried women were not prohibited from smoking, but were considered immodest if they did so. Nearly all matrons smoked."

More labor went into a favorite beverage. "Besides grinding the corn (by hand with stone mortars and pestles) for bread, we sometimes crushed it and soaked it, and after it had fermented made from this juice a *tiswin*, which had the power of intoxication, and was very highly prized by the Indians. This work was done by the squaws and children."

Nature provided the medicines the Apaches employed against disease and injury. "The Indians knew what herbs to use for medicine, how to prepare them, and how to give the medicine," Geronimo said. "This they had been taught by Usen in the beginning, and each succeeding generation had men who were skilled in the art of healing." Belief informed the healing. "In gathering the herbs, in preparing them, and in administering the medicine, as much faith was held in prayer as in the actual effect of the medicine. Usually about eight persons worked together in making medicine, and there were forms of prayer and incantations to attend each stage of the process. Four attended to the incantations and four to the preparation of the herbs."

Four was a number sacred to the Apaches.

In later years outsiders would call Geronimo a medicine man. He never claimed the title for himself, although necessity made him proficient in certain of the healing arts. "Some of the Indians were skilled in cutting out bullets, arrow heads, and other missiles with which warriors were wounded," he said. "I myself have done much of this, using a common dirk or butcher knife."

The boy continued to grow. "When I was about eight or ten years old, I began to follow the chase, and to me this was never work. Out on the prairies, which ran up to our mountain homes, wandered herds of deer, antelope, elk, and buffalo, to be slaughtered when we needed them. Usually we hunted buffalo on horseback, killing them with arrows and spears. Their skins were used to make tepees and bedding; their flesh, to eat."

The buffalo were formidable, but deer were wary. "It required more skill to hunt the deer than any other animal. We never tried to approach a deer except against the wind. Frequently we would spend hours in stealing upon grazing deer. If they were in the open, we would crawl long distances on the ground, keeping a weed or brush before us, so that our approach would not be noticed. Often we could kill several out of one herd before the others would run away. Their flesh was dried and packed in vessels, and would keep in this condition for many months. The hide of the deer was soaked in water and ashes and the hair removed, and then the process of tanning continued until the buckskin was soft and pliable. Perhaps no other animal was more valuable to us than the deer."

The forests and valleys contained many turkeys. "These we would drive to the plains, then slowly ride up toward them until they were almost tired out. When they began to drop and hide we would ride in upon them and by swinging from the side of our horses, catch them. If one started to fly we would ride swiftly under him and kill him with a short stick, or hunting club. In this way we could usually get as many wild turkeys as we could carry home on a horse."

Rabbits were stupid but quick. "Our horses were trained to follow the rabbit at full speed, and as they approached them we would swing from one side of the horse and strike the rabbit with our hunting club. If he was too far away we would throw the stick and kill him. This was great sport when we were boys, but as warriors we seldom hunted small game."

The streams abounded with fish, but the Apaches let them be. "Usen did not intend snakes, frogs, or fishes to be eaten," Geronimo explained. "I have never eaten of them."

Eagles were hunted for their feathers. "It required great skill to steal upon an eagle, for besides having sharp eyes, he is wise and never stops at any place where he does not have a good view of the surrounding country."

Courage was needed in hunting bears and mountain lions. "I have killed many bears with a spear, but was never injured in a fight with one," Geronimo said. "I have killed several mountain lions with arrows, and one with a spear. Both bears and mountain lions are good for food and valuable for their skin. When we killed them we carried them home on our horses. We often made quivers for our arrows from the skin of the mountain lion. These were very pretty and very durable."

The men of Geronimo's family displayed their courage most clearly as warriors. "My grandfather, Maco, had been our chief," he said. "I never saw him, but my father often told me of the great size, strength, and sagacity of this old warrior. Their principal wars had been with the Mexicans. They had some wars with other tribes of Indians also, but were seldom at peace for any great length of time with the Mexican towns." Geronimo would follow in his grandfather's footsteps against the Mexicans.

"Maco died when my father was but a young warrior, and Mangas Coloradas became chief of the Bedonkohe Apaches," Geronimo continued. "When I was but a small boy my father died, after having been sick for some time. When he passed away, carefully the watchers closed his eyes, then they arrayed him in his best clothes, painted his face afresh, wrapped a rich blanket around him, saddled his favorite horse, bore his arms in front of him, and led his horse behind, repeating in wailing tones his deeds of valor as they carried his body to a cave in the mountain. Then they slew his horses, and we gave away all of his other property, as was customary in our tribe, after which his body was deposited in the cave, his arms beside him. His grave is hidden by piles of stone. Wrapped in splendor he lies in seclusion, and the winds in the pines sing a low requiem over the dead warrior."

After his father's death, Geronimo took responsibility for his mother. "She never married again, although according to the customs of our tribe she might have done so immediately after his death. Usually, however, the widow who has children remains single after her husband's death for two or three years; but the widow without children marries again immediately. After a warrior's death, his widow returns to her people and may be given away or sold by her father or brothers. My mother chose to live with me, and she never desired to marry again. We lived near our old home and I supported her."

Geronimo came of age at seventeen, in 1846. "I was admitted to the council of the warriors. Then I was very happy, for I could go wherever I wanted and do whatever I liked. I had not been under the control of any individual, but the customs of our tribe prohibited me from sharing the glories of the warpath until the council admitted me. When opportunity offered, after this, I could go on the warpath with my tribe. This would be glorious. I hoped soon to serve my people in battle. I had long desired to fight with our warriors."

He had another reason for being happy. "Now I could marry the fair Alope, daughter of No-po-so. She was a slender, delicate girl, but we had been lovers for a long time. So, as soon as the council granted me these privileges I went to see her father concerning our marriage. Perhaps our love was of no interest to him; perhaps he wanted to keep Alope with him, for she was a dutiful daughter; at any rate he asked many ponies for her. I made no reply, but in a few days appeared before his wigwam with the herd of ponies and took with me Alope. This was all the marriage ceremony necessary in our tribe."

Geronimo set up a tepee not far from his mother's. "The tepee was made of buffalo hides and in it were many bear robes, lion hides, and other trophies of the chase, as well as my spears, bows, and arrows. Alope had made many little decorations of beads and drawn work on buckskin, which she placed in our tepee. She also drew many pictures on

21

the walls of our home. She was a good wife, but she was never strong. We followed the traditions of our fathers and were happy. Three children came to us — children that played, loitered, and worked as I had done."

As a young man, Geronimo knew little of the world beyond his own people. Their battles were with neighboring tribes and Mexicans. Of the larger war for America, against the powerful tribe rising in the East, they were unaware. "During my minority we had never seen a missionary or a priest," he recalled. "We had never seen a white man."

2

William Sherman's parents arrived in Ohio when much of the state was still occupied by Indians. The Shawnee chief Tecumseh was trying to organize the tribes of the region into a confederacy against the whites, with the goal of throwing them back across the Appalachian Mountains. Tecumseh's efforts amid the War of 1812, when he joined forces with Britain, struck terror into the hearts of many settlers, but they elicited respect from Charles Sherman, William's father. He tried to talk his wife into naming a son for the great chief. She put him off by insisting on her brothers' names for their first two male children. But his persistence paid. "When I came along, on the 8th of February, 1820, mother having no more brothers, my father succeeded in his original purpose, and named me William Tecumseh," Sherman remembered. His father favored the Indian name, and the boy grew up as Tecumseh, or "Cump."

The family, though large — with eleven children — lived in comfortable circumstances in Lancaster, Ohio. Charles Sherman was an attorney and then a judge on the Ohio supreme court. Judges in those days rode circuit, regularly taking Charles Sherman away from home. "I recall him, returning home on horseback, when all the boys used to run and contend for the privilege of riding his horse from the front door back to the stable," Sherman said. "On one occasion, I was the first, and being mounted rode to the stable; but 'Old Dick' was impatient because the stable-door was not opened promptly, so he started for the barn of our neighbor Mr. King; there, also, no one was in waiting to open the gate, and, after a reasonable time, Dick started back for home somewhat in a hurry, and threw me among a pile of stones, in front of preacher Wright's house, where I was picked up apparently a dead boy. But my time was not yet, and I recovered, though the scars remain to this day."

Real calamity struck the Shermans when Cump was nine. "News had come that father was ill unto death, at Lebanon, a hundred miles away," Sherman recalled. "Mother started at once, by coach, but met the news of his death about Washington" — Ohio — "and returned home. He had ridden on horseback from Cincinnati to Lebanon to hold court, during a hot day in June. On the next day he took his seat on the bench, opened court in the forenoon, but in the afternoon, after recess, was seized with a severe chill and had to adjourn the court. The best medical aid was called in, and for three days with apparent success, but the fever then assumed a more dangerous type, and he gradually yielded to it, dying on the sixth day."

Deprived of his father at about the age Geronimo was deprived of *his* father, Sherman found his life turned inside out. The three oldest children were almost adults and could fend for themselves. But the younger ones, save the three youngest, were more than their mother could support. "The rest of us were scattered," Sherman said.

His care fell to the family of Thomas Ewing, a distinguished neighbor. Ewing would shortly be elected to the Senate, and later would serve as secretary of the Treasury and of the Interior. Ewing paid Sherman's tuition at the Lancaster Academy, where the boy studied Greek, Latin and French, besides more pedestrian subjects. Ewing laid plans for his surrogate son, without consulting the lad. "I was notified to prepare for West Point, of which institution we had little knowledge, except that it was very strict, and that the army was its natural consequence," Sherman recalled. Competition for places in the military academy wasn't fierce in Ohio; indeed, some of the state's spots went unfilled. But Ewing's stature as a senator didn't hurt Sherman's chances. "During the autumn of 1835 and spring of 1836 I devoted myself chiefly to mathematics and French, which were known to be the chief requisites for admission to West Point." His work was rewarded, and in the spring of 1836 he received, through Ewing, a letter of appointment as a cadet.

In his sixteen years, Sherman had never traveled far from Lancaster, and his journey to West Point opened his eyes. "I left Lancaster about the 20th of May in the stagecoach for Zanesville," he said. "There we transferred to the coaches of the Great National Road, the highway of travel from the West to the East. The stages generally travelled in gangs of from one to six coaches, each drawn by four good horses, carrying nine passengers inside and three or four outside." In three days of continuous travel, they reached Frederick, Maryland. "There we were told that we could take rail-cars to Baltimore, and thence to Washington; but there was also a two-horse hack ready to start for Washington direct. Not having full faith in the novel and dangerous railroad, I stuck to the coach, and in the night reached Gadsby's Hotel in Washington City."

The nation's capital was still being carved from the wilderness, but it was like nothing

Sherman had ever seen. "I hunted up Mr. Ewing and found him boarding with a mess of senators at Mrs. Hill's, corner of Third and C Streets, and transferred my trunk to the same place. I spent a week in Washington, and think I saw more of the place in that time than I ever have since in the many years of residence there. General Jackson was President, and was at the zenith of his fame. I recall looking at him a full hour, one morning, through the wood railing on Pennsylvania Avenue, as he paced up and down the gravel walk on the north front of the White House. He wore a cap and an overcoat so full that his form seemed smaller than I had expected. I also recall the appearance of Postmaster-General Amos Kendall, of Vice-President Van Buren, Messrs. Calhoun, Webster, Clay, Cass, Silas Wright, etc."

Heading north from Washington, Sherman visited Baltimore, Philadelphia and New York. He overcame his fear of railroads on the way. The last leg of his journey was by steamboat up the Hudson. The vessel, operated by and named for Cornelius Vanderbilt, who was amassing what would become one of America's great fortunes, encountered heavy traffic on the river, going to and from the Erie Canal, which, among other things, was making the Vanderbilt fortune possible.

West Point didn't impress Sherman, nor did he impress West Point. His had not been the idea to attend, and he hardly knew what he was getting into. Nothing in his life so far gave him or anyone who knew him reason to believe he had the talents of a soldier, notwithstanding his Indian warrior's name. The military academy — which insisted on "Sherman" rather than "Cump" — was for him, as for the other cadets, a passage from youth to adulthood, conveniently at government expense. "At the Academy I was not considered a good soldier, for at no time was I selected for any office, but remained a private throughout the whole four years," he remembered. "Then, as now, neatness in dress and form, with a strict conformity to the rules, were the qualifications required for office, and I suppose I was found not to excel in any of these." All the same, he discovered that he was smart, able to do well in the classroom. "I always held a respectable reputation with the professors, and generally ranked among the best, especially in drawing, chemistry, mathematics, and natural philosophy." Yet his inattention to rules counted against him. "My average demerits, per annum, were about one hundred and fifty, which reduced my final class standing from number four to six" — out of forty-three.

28

3

When Sherman saw Andrew Jackson through the fence at the White House, the president might have been pondering the fate of America's Indian tribes. The fame that had propelled Jackson to the presidency followed his stunning victory over British forces at New Orleans at the end of the War of 1812, but before that he had been known as an Indian fighter. Orphaned in the Carolinas during the Revolutionary War, Jackson moved to Nashville in 1790, when Tennessee was still the western district of North Carolina. It was also home to various Indian tribes who disputed the invasion of their lands by white settlers. Many of the settlers, including Jackson, were Scots-Irish immigrants and their children, a tribe accustomed to fighting for what they sought in life. Jackson became the leader of the Tennessee branch of the tribe, elected major general of the Tennessee militia.

In that capacity he defended the Tennessee

settlements against Indian raids, not to mention against the duplicity of the federal War Department in Washington. After the start of the War of 1812, the War Department appealed to Jackson to raise a force of Tennessee militia and lead them to Louisiana, in preparation for an attack by the British. The Tennesseans rallied to Jackson's call, winning for themselves and their descendants the nickname "Volunteers." But after the summons to the Mississippi proved premature, Washington ordered Jackson to dissolve his force; the government would no longer fund their upkeep. Jackson refused to abandon his men hundreds of miles from home. Instead he paid for their provisions from his own pocket and marched them back to Tennessee as a group. On the way someone remarked of Jackson that he was as tough as a hickory limb, and "Old Hickory" he became.

Tecumseh had been in the area preaching Indian resistance to whites and had acquired a following among the Creeks. A band of Creeks known as Red Sticks descended on a white community at Fort Mims above Mobile Bay, slaughtering hundreds, including women and children. Jackson was summoned to track down and punish the killers. He gathered his Tennesseans and formed an alliance with several hundred Indian enemies of the Red Sticks, including Cherokees, Choctaws and some Creeks. Jackson's force cornered the

Red Sticks at Horseshoe Bend in the Tallapoosa River and delivered a bloody defeat. While still Old Hickory to the Tennesseans, he became Sharp Knife to the Indians.

Jackson's was a turbulent spirit, and recognizing kindred souls among his fellow frontiersmen, he judged that peace would never come to the region until whites and Indians were separated. He knew the whites weren't going to abandon the communities they had created; of the Scots-Irish it was said that they kept the Sabbath and anything else they laid hold of. The only solution, therefore, was the removal of the Indians to a part of the country beyond the frontier of settlement.

The idea didn't originate with Jackson. Every president starting with George Washington had worked to separate whites from Indians, typically by moving tribes out of the path of white settlement. James Monroe in 1825 explicitly asked Congress for authorization to remove tribes from the eastern states to the federal territories of the West. Removal would be for the Indians' own good, Monroe said. "Without a timely anticipation of and provision against the dangers to which they are exposed, under causes which it will be difficult if not impossible to control, their degradation and extermination will be inevitable."

Jackson's reputation as an Indian fighter gave him credibility Monroe lacked on Indian

31

policy. And another half decade of growth in the white population made resolution of the tensions resulting from white pressure on Indian lands more imperative. "The condition and ulterior destiny of the Indian tribes within the limits of some of our States have become objects of much interest and importance," Jackson told Congress in his first annual message. "It has long been the policy of Government to introduce among them the arts of civilization, in the hope of gradually reclaiming them from a wandering life. This policy has, however, been coupled with another, wholly incompatible with its success. Professing a desire to civilize and settle them, we have at the same time lost no opportunity to purchase their lands and thrust them farther into the wilderness. By this means they have not only been kept in a wandering state, but been led to look upon us as unjust and indifferent to their fate. Thus, though lavish in its expenditures upon the subject, Government has constantly defeated its own policy, and the Indians in general, receding farther and farther to the west, have retained their savage habits."

Some Indians, however, had taken the government at its word and adopted white ways. These were the so-called "civilized tribes" — the Cherokees, Choctaws, Chickasaws, Creeks and Seminoles. Yet they insisted on retaining their tribal governments, pro-

32

claiming themselves sovereign nations within the states in which they resided. This was a problem for the states, for it prevented enforcement of state laws within the boundaries claimed by the tribes. And it was a problem for the Constitution. "The Constitution declares that 'no new State shall be formed or erected within the jurisdiction of any other State' without the consent of its legislature," Jackson said. The assertions of the tribes directly contradicted the Constitution on this point.

At present the matter was most acute in Georgia and Alabama. But the principle applied to all the states. "There is no constitutional, conventional or legal provision which allows them" — Georgia and Alabama — "less power over the Indians within their borders than is possessed by Maine or New York. Would the people of Maine permit the Penobscot tribe to erect an independent government within their State? And unless they did, would it not be the duty of the General Government to support them in resisting such a measure? Would the people of New York permit each remnant of the Six Nations" — of the Iroquois confederacy — "within her borders to declare itself an independent people under the protection of the United States? Could the Indians establish a separate republic on each of their reservations in Ohio?" Of course not. "And if they were so disposed, would it be the duty of this Government to protect them in the attempt?" Again, of course not, for in doing so, the government would destroy the states it was created to protect.

Resolution of the problem lay in the relocation of the tribes in question, Jackson said. If the Indians insisted on living separately from whites, subject to their own laws rather than the laws of the states, they needed to move beyond the boundaries of the states — to the federal lands across the Mississippi.

Jackson urged Congress to approve a program to facilitate the relocation. "I suggest for your consideration the propriety of setting apart an ample district west of the Mississippi, and without the limits of any State or Territory now formed, to be guaranteed to the Indian tribes as long as they shall occupy it, each tribe having a distinct control over the portion designated for its use. There they may be secured in the enjoyment of governments of their own choice, subject to no other control from the United States than such as may be necessary to preserve peace on the frontier and between the several tribes."

Jackson hoped to avoid compulsion. "This emigration should be voluntary, for it would be as cruel as unjust to compel the aborigines to abandon the graves of their fathers and seek a home in a distant land." But the tribes must understand the consequences of remaining. "They should be distinctly informed that if they remain within the limits of the States, they must be subject to their laws. In return for their obedience as individuals, they will without doubt be protected in the enjoyment of those possessions which they have improved by their industry." Jackson would welcome this outcome. "Submitting to the laws of the States, and receiving, like other citizens, protection in their persons and property, they will ere long become merged in the mass of our population."

Yet Jackson supposed the Indians would not welcome it. They wanted to retain their tribal identities. And so emigration was the only route. It would be for their own good, as the history of other Indian tribes demonstrated. "Their present condition, contrasted with what they once were, makes a most powerful appeal to our sympathies," Jackson said. "Our ancestors found them the uncontrolled possessors of these vast regions. By persuasion and force they have been made to retire from river to river and from mountain to mountain, until some of the tribes have become extinct and others have left but remnants to preserve for a while their once terrible names. Surrounded by the whites with their arts of civilization, which by destroying the resources of the savage doom him to weakness and decay, the fate of the Mohegan, the Narragansett, and the Delaware is fast over-taking the Choctaw, the Cherokee, and the Creek. That this fate surely awaits them if they remain within the limits of the States does not admit of a doubt. Humanity and national honor demand that every effort should be made to avert so great a calamity."

Jackson had a knack for making enemies, among whites as much as among the Indians he fought. His political foes were gathering into what would become the Whig party; they opposed nearly everything Jackson advocated. Edward Everett of Massachusetts was an orator for the ages — to wit, the ages his speeches often seemed to last. Decades hence Everett would wax eloquent for two hours at the dedication of the Gettysburg cemetery, only to be eclipsed by Abraham Lincoln's two-*minute* address. Everett now rose in the House of Representatives to condemn Jackson's removal plan; the speech made a small book when published. "The evil, sir, is enormous; the violence is extreme; the breach of public faith deplorable; the inevitable suffering incalculable," said Everett of Jackson's scheme. Everett implored his colleagues, "Do not stain the fair fame of the country. It has been justly said it is in the keeping of Congress on this subject. It is more wrapped up in this policy, in the estimation of the civilized world, than in all your other doings. Its elements are plain and tangible and few. Nations of dependent Indians, against their will, under color of law, are driven from their homes into the wilderness. You cannot explain it; you cannot reason it away. The subtleties which satisfy you will not satisfy the severe judgment of enlightened Europe. Our friends there will view this measure with sorrow, and our enemies alone with joy. And we ourselves, sir, when the interests and passions of the day are past, will look back upon it with self-reproach and a regret as bitter as unavailing."

Not for the last time, easterners like Everett showed greater sympathy for Indians than did westerners like Jackson. Jackson's message, and the comments of other westerners then and later, suggested why this was so: most of the Indians of the East had been nearly annihilated generations earlier, leaving no threat to the lives and property of Everett and his neighbors. To the people of the West, the Indians were a continuing threat. Neither Everett nor his neighbors had lost a wife or child to an Indian raid; many westerners had.

Because the East was more populous than the West, its relative influence was greater in the House than in the Senate. Jackson's bill passed the latter comfortably but the former by a mere four votes, of nearly two hundred cast. Yet a victory was a victory, and in May 1830 he signed the Indian Removal Act, which authorized the president to create an

37

Indian Territory west of the Mississippi, from which the eastern tribes might claim parcels. On these tracts the tribes could live according to their own laws, free of the hindrance of any states. The law also appropriated half a million dollars to pay costs of emigration incurred by the tribes.

Within months Jackson was pleased to report the first treaties signed under the new law's auspices. The president congratulated the leaders of the Choctaws and Chickasaws for their wisdom in accepting the government's offer of subsidized resettlement. "In negotiating these treaties, they were made to understand their true condition, and they have preferred maintaining their independence in the Western forests to submitting to the laws of the States in which they now reside," Jackson said. He hoped the other eastern tribes would follow their lead. "Humanity has often wept over the fate of the aborigines of this country, and philanthropy has been long busily employed in devising means to avert it, but its progress has never for a moment been arrested, and one by one have many powerful tribes disappeared from the earth. To follow to the tomb the last of his race and to tread on the graves of extinct nations excite melancholy reflections. But true philanthropy reconciles the mind to these vicissitudes as it does to the extinction of one generation to make room for another."

Jackson acknowledged that relocation was hard. "Doubtless it will be painful to leave the graves of their fathers," he said. But many others had made similar hard choices. "What do they more than our ancestors did or than our children are now doing? To better their condition in an unknown land our forefathers left all that was dear in earthly objects. Our children by thousands yearly leave the land of their birth to seek new homes in distant regions." The Indians, moreover, were receiving free land and government assistance to get there. "How many thousands of our own people would gladly embrace the opportunity of removing to the West on such conditions! If the offers made to the Indians were extended to them, they would be hailed with gratitude and joy."

Whatever white settlers might have thought of the terms of the Removal Act, even the Indians who accepted relocation as inevitable did not hail the prospect with gratitude and joy. "We were hedged in by two evils, and we chose that which we thought the least," wrote George Harkins, a Choctaw chief, in an open letter to the American people. "We could not recognize the right that the state of Mississippi had assumed, to legislate for us. Although the legislature of the state were qualified to make laws for their own citizens, that did not qualify them to become law-makers to a people that was so dissimilar in manners and customs as the Choctaws are to the Mississippians." Leaving home would be painful, but staying put, under prospective circumstances, would be worse. "We as Choctaws rather chose to suffer and be free."

The Cherokees challenged the Jackson program in court. The Cherokees' origins lay in the vicinity of the Great Lakes, home of the Iroquois, whose language family the Cherokees shared. They moved south, fighting their way into what would become the Carolinas and Georgia, and arrived in the latter place about the time the English got to Virginia. Their descendants in Jackson's day denied the premise of the Removal Act: that if Indians remained within the boundaries of states, they must be subject to the laws of those states. The Supreme Court, headed by John Marshall, a committed foe of nearly all things Jacksonian, found in the Cherokees' favor in 1832 in *Worcester v. Georgia*. The tribe, Marshall said, constituted a nation beyond the reach of Georgia law.

Jackson didn't actually say what editor Horace Greeley ascribed to him in response to the verdict: "John Marshall has made his decision; now let him enforce it." Yet Jackson behaved as though he had. He lifted not a finger to protect the Cherokees as Georgians continued to press upon the Cherokee lands. Or rather, his protection was limited to

Cherokees inclined to accept the terms of the Removal Act, however grudgingly. The act drove a wedge through the tribe — and the other southeastern tribes. In the case of the Choctaws and the Chickasaws, the accommodationists were in the majority. Among the Cherokees the division was more equal, and more bitter for its balance. A chief called Major Ridge led the accommodationists; John Ross headed the rejectionists. Ridge contended that the sheer weight of the non-Indian population made trying to hold out in Georgia suicidal. Against a few tens of thousands of Cherokees were arrayed more than a million whites. And the demographic disadvantage got worse every year. If the Cherokees tried to remain in Georgia, they would simply be swept from the face of the earth.

John Ross rejected Ridge's argument as defeatist, and he rejected the Removal Act as immoral. Even as Ridge and other chiefs signed a treaty with the government and relocated their part of the tribe to the Indian Territory, Ross and his followers remained stubbornly in place. Their resistance outlasted Jackson, who retired in 1837, but it didn't stop Jackson's successor, Martin Van Buren, from enforcing the Ridge treaty and insisting on the removal of the Ross faction. The resulting march, amid the rain and snow of winter, proved a disaster. Of some sixteen

41

thousand men, women and children who left Georgia, prodded by the rifles of federal troops, four thousand died of exposure and disease on what came to be called the Trail of Tears.

The debacle did nothing to heal the division among the Cherokees. The Ridge group blamed Ross for not conceding the inevitable before it was too late. The Ross group blamed Ridge for selling out his people via the treaty with the government. The anger of the Ross faction ran so deep that some of their number murdered Ridge, intensifying the division the more.

4

William Sherman witnessed how the removal question played out among the Seminoles. Like the other tribes, the Seminoles split, with part of the tribe granting the irresistibility of white settlement and concluding that, if they were going to move west, they should do so at once, before all the good land was taken. Other Seminoles determined to remain in their Florida homeland, counting on the region's difficult terrain and vegetation, and their own wiliness and determination, to keep the whites at bay.

Sherman was sent to Florida not long after graduation from West Point. Florida was a sultry place, and the pursuit of the Seminoles was a desultory business, leaving Sherman and his fellow officers time for fishing and hunting. A local named Ashlock served as guide. "He soon initiated us into the mysteries of shark-spearing, trolling for red-fish, and taking the sheep's-head and mullet," Sherman recounted. "These abounded so that we could at any time catch an unlimited quantity at pleasure. The companies also owned nets for catching green turtles. These nets had meshes about a foot square, were set across channels in the lagoon, the ends secured to stakes driven into the mud, the lower line sunk with lead or stone weights and the upper line floated with cork. We usually visited these nets twice a day, and found from one to six green turtles entangled in the meshes. Disengaging them, they were carried to pens, made with stakes stuck in the mud, where they were fed with mangrove-leaves, and our cooks had at all times an ample supply of the best of green turtles." Sherman and his comrades got a sense of why the Seminoles liked Florida and didn't want to leave.

Occasionally business beckoned. "One day, in the summer of 1841, the sentinel on the housetop at Fort Pierce called out, 'Indians! Indians!' " Sherman recalled. "Everybody sprang to his gun, the companies formed promptly on the parade-ground, and soon were reported as approaching the post, from the pine-woods in rear, four Indians on horseback. They rode straight up to the gateway, dismounted, and came in. They were conducted by the officer of the day to the commanding officer, Major Childs, who sat on the porch in front of his own room. After the usual pause, one of them, a black man named Joe, who spoke English, said they had been sent in by Coacoochee (Wild Cat), one of the most noted of the Seminole chiefs, to see the big chief of the post." The population of Seminoles included escaped slaves from white-owned plantations, and some Seminoles held black slaves of their own. Joe apparently was a free man. "He gradually unwrapped a piece of paper, which was passed over to Major Childs, who read it, and it was in the nature of a 'Safe Guard' for Wild Cat to come into Fort Pierce to receive provisions and assistance while collecting his tribe, with the purpose of emigrating to their reservation west of Arkansas. The paper was signed by General Worth, who had succeeded General Taylor, at Tampa Bay, in command of all the troops in Florida."

Major Childs asked where Coacoochee was.

"Close by," Joe answered. He explained that the chief wanted to know if Major Childs would honor the pass.

Childs said he would. Coacoochee ought to come in.

Joe said he could go and get him.

Childs offered help. "Major Childs ordered me to take eight or ten mounted men and go out to escort him in," Sherman said. "Detailing ten men to saddle up, and taking Joe and one Indian boy along on their own ponies, I started out under their guidance."

All went well at first, but Coacoochee was not soon found. "We continued to ride five or six miles, when I began to suspect treachery," Sherman said. The army veterans in Florida had warned that the Seminoles were deceitful. Sherman questioned Joe, who assured him they were almost there. They kept riding.

"At last we approached one of those close hammocks, so well known in Florida, standing like an island in the interminable pine-forest, with a pond of water near it," Sherman said. "On its edge I noticed a few Indians loitering, which Joe pointed out as the place. Apprehensive of treachery, I halted the guard, gave orders to the sergeant to watch me closely, and rode forward alone with the two Indian guides. As we neared the hammock, about a dozen Indian warriors rose up and waited for us. When in their midst I inquired for the chief, Coacoochee. He approached my horse and, slapping his breast, said, 'Me Coacoochee.' "

Sherman looked the chief over. "He was a very handsome young Indian warrior, not more than twenty-five years old, but in his then dress could hardly be distinguished from the rest." Sherman explained that he had been sent by his own chief, Major Childs, to escort Coacoochee to the fort.

Coacoochee said he wanted to talk. Sherman should dismount.

"I told him that I had no 'talk' in me, but that, on his reaching the post, he could talk as much as he pleased with the 'big chief,' Major Childs," Sherman recounted.

Coacoochee didn't respond to this, and the other Indians didn't push him. "They all seemed to be indifferent and in no hurry; and I noticed that all their guns were leaning against a tree," Sherman recalled. He sensed trouble, which he tried to avert. "I beckoned to the sergeant, who advanced rapidly with his escort, and told him to secure the rifles, which he proceeded to do. Coacoochee pretended to be very angry, but I explained to him that his warriors were tired and mine were not, and that the soldiers would carry the guns on their horses. I told him I would provide him a horse to ride, and the sooner he was ready the better for all."

Coacoochee conceded the point. "He then stripped, washed himself in the pond, and began to dress in all his Indian finery, which consisted of buckskin leggins, moccasins, and several shirts. He then began to put on vests, one after another, and one of them had the marks of a bullet, just above the pocket, with the stain of blood. In the pocket was a one-dollar Tallahassee Bank note, and the rascal had the impudence to ask me to give him silver coin for that dollar. He had evidently killed the wearer, and was disappointed because the pocket contained a paper dollar instead of one in silver. In due time he was dressed with turban and ostrich-feathers, and mounted the horse reserved for him, and thus we rode back together to Fort Pierce."

Major Childs greeted him and invited him to sit on the porch. The chief did so, and a conversation ensued. Coacoochee said he was weary of the war. He would gather his people for relocation, he said. But they were scattered over a large area and would take a month to come together. In the meantime they would require rations, which the major should provide.

"All this was agreed to, and a month was allowed for him to get ready with his whole band (numbering some one hundred and fifty or one hundred and sixty) to migrate," Sherman recounted. "The 'talk' then ceased, and Coacoochee and his envoys proceeded to get regularly drunk, which was easily done by the agency of commissary whiskey. They stayed at Fort Pierce during the night, and the next day departed. Several times during the month there came into the post two or more of these same Indians, always to beg for something to eat or drink, and after a full month Coacoochee and about twenty of his warriors came in with several ponies, but with none of their women or children."

Sherman's commandant had expected as much. "Major Childs had not from the beginning the least faith in his sincerity; had made up his mind to seize the whole party and compel them to emigrate," Sherman said.

"He arranged for the usual council, and instructed Lieutenant Taylor to invite Coacoochee and his uncle (who was held to be a principal chief) to his room to take some good brandy, instead of the common commissary whiskey. At a signal agreed on I was to go to the quarters of Company A, to dispatch the first-sergeant and another man to Lieutenant Taylor's room, there to seize the two chiefs and secure them; and with the company I was to enter Major Childs's room and secure the remainder of the party. Meantime Lieutenant Van Vliet was ordered to go to the quarters of his company, F, and at the same signal to march rapidly to the rear of the officers' quarters, so as to catch any who might attempt to escape by the open windows to the rear. All resulted exactly as prearranged, and in a few minutes the whole party was in irons. At first they claimed that we had acted treacherously, but very soon they admitted that for a month Coacoochee had been quietly removing his women and children toward Lake Okeechobee and the Everglades, and that this visit to our post was to have been their last."

Coacoochee concluded the game was up. He summoned the families, and together they were packed off to their new homes. "This was a heavy loss to the Seminoles," Sherman observed. "But there still remained in the Peninsula a few hundred warriors with their families scattered into very small parcels, who were concealed in the most inaccessible hammocks and swamps. These had no difficulty in finding plenty of food anywhere and everywhere. Deer and wild turkey were abundant, and as for fish there was no end to them."

From the perspective of the 1870s, Sherman reflected on the way things had turned out. "Florida was the Indian's paradise, was of little value to us, and it was a great pity to remove the Seminoles at all, for we could have collected there all the Choctaws, Creeks, Cherokees, and Chickasaws, in addition to the Seminoles. They would have thrived in the Peninsula, whereas they now occupy lands that are very valuable, which are coveted by their white neighbors on all sides, while the Peninsula of Florida still remains with a population less than should make a good state."

5

Before Geronimo met any white Americans or came to think of them as enemies of the Apaches, he spent years fighting Mexicans. In Geronimo's youth, the northern reaches of Mexico formally encompassed the Arizona homeland of the Apaches. Yet even after Mexico in the 1840s relinquished what became the American Southwest — the region stretching from the Sabine River on the eastern border of Texas to the Pacific coast of California — the Apaches for years encountered Mexicans more often than Americans.

The encounters were typically hostile. The Apaches considered Mexican settlements fair game for raiding — for horses and guns, among other things — and the Mexicans fought back, building forts from which soldiers sallied forth to track and kill Apaches. The struggle was long and brutal, with the Mexican government paying bounties for Apache scalps, and Apaches killing Mexicans on sight lest they themselves be killed.

Occasionally truces were called. Geronimo remembered one from the early 1850s. "Being at peace with the Mexican towns as well as with all the neighboring Indian tribes, we went south into Old Mexico to trade," he said. "Our whole tribe" — the Bedonkohe Apaches — "went through Sonora toward Casas Grandes, our destination, but just before reaching that place we stopped at another Mexican town called by the Indians 'Kas-ki-yeh.' " The Mexicans called it Janos, and it was in northern Chihuahua state. "Here we stayed for several days, camping just outside the city. Every day we would go into town to trade, leaving our camp under the protection of a small guard so that our arms, supplies, and women and children would not be disturbed during our absence."

Previous truces hadn't held for long, and this one didn't either. "Late one afternoon, when returning from town, we were met by a few women and children who told us that Mexican troops from some other town had attacked our camp, killed all the warriors of the guard, captured all our ponies, secured our arms, destroyed our supplies, and killed many of our women and children," Geronimo said. "Quickly we separated, concealing ourselves as best we could until nightfall, when we assembled at our appointed place of rendezvous — a thicket by the river. Silently we stole in one by one: sentinels were placed, and, when all were counted, I found that my aged mother, my young wife, and my three small children were among the slain."

The slaughter of his family hit Geronimo like nothing before — or after, as things turned out. He was stunned. "There were no lights in camp, so without being noticed I silently turned away and stood by the river. How long I stood there I do not know."

Eventually the survivors had to decide what to do. "When I saw the warriors arranging for a council I took my place," Geronimo said. "That night I did not give my vote for or against any measure, but it was decided that as there were only eighty warriors left, and as we were without arms or supplies, and were furthermore surrounded by the Mexicans far inside their own territory, we could not hope to fight successfully. So our chief, Mangas Coloradas, gave the order to start at once in perfect silence for our homes in Arizona, leaving the dead upon the field.

"I stood until all had passed, hardly knowing what I would do," Geronimo said. "I had no weapon, nor did I hardly wish to fight, neither did I contemplate recovering the bodies of my loved ones, for that was forbidden. I did not pray, nor did I resolve to do anything in particular, for I had no purpose left. I finally followed the tribe silently, keeping just within hearing distance of the soft noise of the feet of the retreating Apaches. The next morning some of the Indians killed a small amount of game and we halted long enough for the tribe to cook and eat, when the march was resumed. I had killed no game, and did not eat. During the first march as well as while we were camped at this place I spoke to no one and no one spoke to me — there was nothing to say."

For two days and three nights they marched, stopping only to eat. Finally, near the border with the United States, they allowed themselves to rest. Geronimo broke his fast and his silence. "I took some food and talked with the other Indians who had lost in the massacre," he said. But they couldn't fathom his grief. "None had lost as I had, for I had lost all."

A few days later they reached their homes. Geronimo's grief flared again. "There were the decorations that Alope had made, and there were the playthings of our little ones. I burned them all, even our tepee. I also burned my mother's tepee and destroyed all her property."

In his loss, he found a new purpose. "I was never again contented in our quiet home. True, I could visit my father's grave, but I had vowed vengeance upon the Mexican troopers who had wronged me, and whenever I came near his grave or saw anything to remind me of former happy days, my heart would ache for revenge upon Mexico."

Geronimo's revenge required the cooperation of other Apaches. Mangas Coloradas, recognizing the intensity of Geronimo's hatred of the Mexicans, appointed him envoy to other Apache bands. He went first to the Chokonen, or Chiricahua, band. "Cochise, their chief, called a council at early dawn," Geronimo remembered. "Silently the warriors assembled at an open place in a mountain dell and took their seats on the ground, arranged in rows according to their ranks. Silently they sat smoking. At a signal from the chief I arose and presented my cause."

"Kinsmen," said Geronimo to the Chiricahua warriors, "you have heard what the Mexicans have recently done without cause. You are my relatives — uncles, cousins, brothers. We are men the same as the Mexicans are — we can do to them what they have done to us. Let us go forward and trail them. I will lead you to their city. We will attack them in their homes. I will fight in the front of the battle. I only ask you to follow me to avenge this wrong done by these Mexicans. Will you come?"

The warriors indicated their assent.

"Remember the rule in war," Geronimo continued. "Men may return or they may be killed. If any of these young men are killed, I want no blame from their kinsmen, for they themselves have chosen to go. If I am killed no one need mourn for me. My people have all been killed in that country, and I, too, will die if need be."

None demurred.

Geronimo returned to the Bedonkohe village. He reported his success to Mangas Coloradas, who next sent him to speak to the Nedni Apaches. They responded similarly.

"It was in the summer of 1859, almost a year from the date of the massacre of Kaskiyeh, that these three tribes were assembled on the Mexican border to go upon the warpath," Geronimo recalled. He relived the moment in his memory. "Their faces were painted, the war bands fastened upon their brows, their long scalp-locks ready for the hand and knife of the warrior who could overcome them." The scalp-locks were a taunt at the Mexican policy of bounties for scalps; the scalps would be easy to take, if the Mexicans could get close enough. The war party had made provision for their dependents. "Their families had been hidden away in a mountain rendezvous near the Mexican border. With these families a guard was posted, and a number of places of rendezvous designated in case the camp should be disturbed."

They were lightly laden, allowing stealthy, swift travel. "None of us were mounted, and each warrior wore moccasins and also a cloth

56

wrapped about his loins. This cloth could be spread over him when he slept, and when on the march would be ample protection as clothing. In battle, if the fight was hard, we did not wish much clothing. Each warrior carried three days' rations." They would supplement the rations with game killed along the march. "We traveled in three divisions: the Bedonkohe Apaches led by Mangas Coloradas, the Chokonen Apaches by Cochise, and the Nedni Apaches." They walked from before dawn until after dark and covered forty or forty-five miles per day.

As the raid was Geronimo's idea, he took the lead. Concealment was paramount. "We followed the river courses and mountain ranges because we could better thereby keep our movements concealed," he said. In Sonora they bypassed settlements, again to avoid attention, until they approached Arispe, which Geronimo had chosen as a target. "When we were almost at Arispe we camped, and eight men rode out from the city to parley with us. These we captured, killed and scalped." The goal was to lure the rest of the troops out of the town.

"The next day they came." The Mexican soldiers eschewed a general engagement, preferring to skirmish and test the strength of the invaders. Yet in the afternoon, Geronimo and the Apaches scored a success. "We captured their supply train, so we had plenty of provisions and some more guns."

The Apaches rested overnight. "Early the next morning the warriors were assembled to pray — not for help, but that they might have health and avoid ambush or deceptions by the enemy," Geronimo said. The Mexicans marched out in force at around ten o'clock. "There were two companies of cavalry and two of infantry," Geronimo recalled. "I recognized the cavalry as the soldiers who had killed my people at Kaskiyeh. This I told to the chieftains, and they said that I might direct the battle." Geronimo appreciated the gesture. "I was no chief and never had been, but because I had been more deeply wronged than others, this honor was conferred upon me, and I resolved to prove worthy of the trust."

He had never led warriors in battle, but he had paid attention in past engagements, and he possessed a keen tactical sense. "I arranged the Indians in a hollow circle near the river, and the Mexicans drew their infantry up in two lines, with the cavalry in reserve. We were in the timber, and they advanced until within about four hundred yards, when they halted and opened fire." Geronimo let the initial salvos pass, with the Apaches still concealed by the trees. Then, while the Mexicans were reloading, he mounted the attack. "I led a charge against them, at the same time sending some braves to attack their rear." His stored hatred drove him forward. "In all the battle I thought of my murdered mother, wife, and babies — of my father's grave and my vow of vengeance, and I fought with fury. Many fell by my hand, and constantly I led the advance. Many braves were killed."

The battle raged for two hours. Finally the guns fell silent and the shouting died away. "Four Indians were alone in the center of the field — myself and three other warriors," Geronimo said. "Our arrows were all gone, our spears broken off in the bodies of dead enemies. We had only our hands and knives with which to fight, but all who had stood against us were dead." Unexpectedly two Mexican soldiers appeared from another part of the battlefield. "They shot down two of our men and we, the remaining two, fled toward our own warriors. My companion was struck down by a saber, but I reached our warriors, seized a spear, and turned. The one who pursued me missed his aim and fell by my spear. With his saber I met the trooper who had killed my companion and we grappled and fell. I killed him with my knife and quickly rose over his body, brandishing his saber, seeking for other troopers to kill. There were none."

His comrades recognized in Geronimo a war leader of courage and prowess. "Over the bloody field, covered with the bodies of

Mexicans, rang the fierce Apache war-whoop," he recalled. "Still covered with the blood of my enemies, still holding my conquering weapon, still hot with the joy of battle, victory, and vengeance, I was surrounded by the Apache braves and made war chief of all the Apaches."

He savored the moment, then let his fellows take their prizes. "I gave orders for scalping the slain."

6

Sherman became a war chief a short while later, after participating in events that made Mexico's Apache problem America's Apache problem. The removal program that had sent Sherman to Florida to catch Coacoochee and the Seminoles had envisioned the American West — the land beyond the Mississippi — as a region where Indians might live unbothered by whites for decades. The region was vast, far from the present frontier of settlement, and apparently good for nothing that mattered to most whites. But this vision underestimated the growth of the American population and the acquisitiveness of certain American leaders. James Polk became president in 1845, after a campaign promising the annexation of Texas, which had broken away from Mexico, and the acquisition of Oregon, then in dispute with Britain. Texas was indeed annexed, and part of Oregon was acquired. Polk's appetite grew, and he demanded California from Mexico. When Mexico refused, Polk sent American troops to a disputed strip along the Texas-Mexico border. Mexican forces took the bait, killed several Americans, and gave Polk his casus belli. Opposition Whigs distrusted Democrat Polk and doubted his explanation of events, but Congress as a whole voted him the war declaration he wanted.

Sherman was assigned to an American contingent that sailed around South America to California. He hoped to see battle, if only as relief from the tedium that afflicted army life in peacetime. But the ocean journey took six months, and by the time Sherman's ship reached Monterey, the modest fighting California experienced had ended. "Everything on shore looked bright and beautiful, the hills covered with grass and flowers, the live-oaks so serene and homelike, and the low adobe houses, with red-tiled roofs and whitened walls, contrasted well with the dark pine-trees behind, making a decidedly good impression upon us who had come so far to spy out the land," Sherman wrote of the arrival. "Nothing could be more peaceful in its looks than Monterey in January, 1847."

The locals hardly registered that a war was on. "We found the people of Monterey a mixed set of Americans, native Mexicans, and Indians, about one thousand all told. They were kind and pleasant, and seemed to have nothing to do, except such as owned ranches in the country for the rearing of horses and cattle. Horses could be bought at any price from four dollars up to sixteen, but no horse was ever valued above a doubloon or Mexican ounce (sixteen dollars). Cattle cost eight dollars fifty cents for the best, and this made beef net about two cents a pound, but at that time nobody bought beef by the pound, but by the carcass."

California remained quiet during the next several months, even while American forces invaded central Mexico and seized Mexico City. Sherman became an aide to Colonel Richard Mason, the military governor of the American occupation. "I remember one day, in the spring of 1848, that two men, Americans, came into the office and inquired for the Governor," Sherman recollected. "I asked their business, and one answered that they had just come down from Captain Sutter" — John Sutter, a Swiss national who had a ranch and trading post on the Sacramento River — "on special business, and they wanted to see Governor Mason in person." Sherman escorted them into Mason's office and left.

Several minutes later Mason opened the door and called to Sherman to come into the office. "I went in, and my attention was directed to a series of papers unfolded on his table, in which lay about half an ounce of placer gold," Sherman said, referring to flakes

of the kind retrieved from streambeds by pan-
ning.

"What is that?" asked Mason.

Sherman fingered the material. "Is it gold?"
he offered.

Mason asked if Sherman had ever seen native gold.

Sherman said he had, in Georgia a few
years earlier. But it was in finer pieces, almost
grains. He added that the question could be
settled by easy tests. He put a flake in his
mouth, and the acid of his saliva served only
to increase its luster. This was consistent with
gold. He sent the office clerk to find an ax
and a hatchet. Using the ax as an anvil and
the back of the hatchet as a hammer, he
pounded the flake. Rather than shattering, as
iron pyrite or mica would have done, it flat-
tened out, as gold does. Sherman concluded
that it was indeed gold, and Mason concurred. Sherman later remarked, with the
advantage of hindsight, "That gold was the
first discovered in the Sierra Nevada, which
soon revolutionized the whole country, and
actually moved the whole civilized world."

It also revolutionized American relations
with the Indians of the Southwest. Although
neither Sherman nor Mason nor anyone else
in California knew it at the time the two men
walked into Mason's office, American and
Mexican negotiators had just concluded a
treaty ending the war and transferring Cali-

fornia to the United States. The transfer alone would have made Geronimo's Apaches and the other indigenous peoples of the Southwest an issue for the American government eventually. Sooner or later, Americans would have found their way to the region in appreciable numbers. But the gold discovery guaranteed that their arrival came sooner rather than later — *much* sooner. The news the two men brought to Mason leaked to California and then to the world, and the world responded by rushing to the goldfields. Scores of thousands of gold-seekers poured into California to lay hands on their share of the bonanza. In doing so they set in motion events that changed the lives of the Indians of the Southwest almost beyond recognition.

The tribes of California felt the impact first and most dramatically. Those who lived in the Sierra Nevada had long known of the gold there, but they placed little value on it. When they learned that white people *did* value it, greatly, and would pay for it in trade goods the Indians valued, some of the Indians took up baskets and sifted gold from the sand and gravel much as the white prospectors did with their metal pans. Their presence was initially ignored by the newcomers, but as the supply of claims diminished under the demand of the immigrants, the Indians were elbowed aside and their proceeds stolen. When they resisted, they were removed by force. When they fought back, they were murdered and their villages burned. The human capacity for self-justification, ever present in American relations with the Indians, took extreme form in California. Peter Burnett, the first civilian governor of territorial California, pontificated, "The white man, to whom time is money, and who labors hard all day to create the comforts of life, cannot sit up all night to watch his property. And after being robbed a few times, he becomes desperate, and resolves upon a war of extermination. That is the common feeling of our people who have lived upon the Indian frontier. The two races are kept asunder by so many causes, and having no ties of marriage or consanguinity to unite them, they must ever remain at enmity. That a war of extermination will continue to be waged between the races until the Indian race is extinct must be expected. While we cannot anticipate this result but with painful regret, the inevitable destiny of the race is beyond the power or wisdom of men to avert."

The California newcomers were too busy hunting for gold to wage the organized war of extermination Burnett forecast, settling instead for informal campaigns, ad hoc reprisals and extemporaneous violence that had much the same effect. Thousands of Indians were killed; even more perished from disease and displacement.

7

The consequences of the gold rush spread far beyond California. The sudden peopling of California triggered demand there for admission to the Union as a state; because the Californians proposed to bar slavery, their statehood petition touched off a fight in Congress between the free states of the North and the slave states of the South. The fight wasn't resolved until the passage of the Compromise of 1850, including California's admission and a toughened Fugitive Slave Act. The compromise appealed to the politicians in Washington who passed it, but it outraged many in both the North and South. Antislavery groups in the North assailed the Fugitive Slave Act as compelling complicity in the capture and return of poor souls simply trying to claim their freedom; fire-eaters in the South condemned the admission of free-state California as a surrender of the Senate to the abolitionist aggressors of the North.

The anger touched off by the 1850 compromise made future compromises between North and South all but impossible; a breakup of the Union appeared alarmingly probable. And it seemed to come closer when Congress passed the Kansas-Nebraska Act of 1854, which repealed the section of the 1820 Missouri Compromise that had forbidden slavery in the upper part of the Louisiana Purchase. Kansas Territory became a battleground where advocates of slavery competed with opponents to gain a political majority prior to the writing of a constitution for a state of Kansas. Opposing militias roamed the territory, killing each other and laying waste to each other's settlements. John Brown led one antislavery group, which seized five proslavery settlers in the dead of night and hacked them to pieces with broadswords. Brown escalated his war against slavery in 1859 by staging a raid on a federal arsenal at Harpers Ferry, Virginia, with the goal of distributing weapons to slaves in the vicinity who would rise up against their masters and violently claim their freedom. The raid failed and Brown was tried and executed, but his courage on the way to the gallows thrilled Northern abolitionists, who hailed him as a martyr. The Brown raid and especially the Northern reaction to it made many white Southerners fear for their future and their very lives so long as they remained within the Union. The nomination of Abraham Lincoln as the candidate of the antislavery Republican party, and then his election as president, proved more than the South could bear: seven states bolted the Union and formed the Confederate States of America. Four more slave states joined them after fighting broke out at Fort Sumter, South Carolina, and Lincoln called for 75,000 volunteers to suppress the rebellion.

Sherman answered Lincoln's call in his own way. Sherman had left the army following his 1850 marriage to Ellen Ewing, the daughter of his foster father. Thomas Ewing was then a member of Zachary Taylor's cabinet, and the president, the vice president and numerous other dignitaries attended the Washington wedding. Determined to provide for his wife, and the children who soon began arriving, in the manner to which Ellen had been accustomed, Sherman resigned his army commission to work for a St. Louis bank. The bank sent him back to California to manage its San Francisco branch, but the branch failed amid a financial crisis there. Sherman was transferred to New York, only to have the crisis follow him and take down the New York branch as well. He left the banking business in favor of a law practice, which didn't suit him, and then the superintendency of a military academy in Louisiana, which did. But Louisiana's secession reminded him where his loyalty lay, and he returned north to offer his services again to the army.

He fought at the first battle of Bull Run, where he performed more ably than most of his comrades in that Union defeat. He was posted to Kentucky, a crucial border state — that is, a slave state that remained loyal to the Union. But the stress of having to do too much with too little, the meddling of politicians in what he considered military affairs, and a chronically edgy personality pushed him to the breaking point. He was given a leave of absence; upon his return he was attached to the command of Ulysses Grant, who was gaining a reputation as a determined and successful fighter. Grant and Sherman won a bloody victory at Shiloh before proceeding to a complicated and lengthy, but finally successful, siege of Vicksburg.

Grant's reward for Vicksburg was command of all Union armies; Sherman's was the command of Union forces in the western theater. Grant took on Robert E. Lee in Virginia; Sherman marched through Tennessee and Georgia.

Sherman captured Atlanta and there revealed the grim lesson the war was teaching him. The city fathers asked him to rescind an evacuation order he had issued, lest it cause suffering to the civilian population. Sherman responded that suffering was the *point* of his evacuation order, and of his approach to war.

"War is cruelty," he said. "You cannot refine it; and those who brought war on our country deserve all the curses and maledictions a people can pour out. I know I had no hand in making this war, and I know I will make more sacrifices today than any of you to secure peace. But you cannot have peace and a division of our country." The United States would become like Mexico, forever at war. The path to peace was through acknowledgment of the folly of secession, Sherman said. "Once admit the Union, once more acknowledge the authority of our National Government, and instead of devoting your houses and streets and roads to the dread uses of war, I and this army become at once your protectors and supporters, shielding you from danger, let it come from what quarter it may."

Until then, the war must rage. The people of the South must feel its costs, and must recognize the greater costs to come if they continued to fight. The suffering of Atlanta was part of the lesson. "You might as well appeal against the thunderstorm as against these terrible hardships of war," Sherman said. "They are inevitable, and the only way the people of Atlanta can hope once more to live in peace and quiet at home is to stop this war, which can alone be done by admitting that it began in error and is perpetuated in pride." He sent the delegation away. "Now, you must go, and take with you the old and feeble; feed and nurse them, and build for them in more quiet places proper habitations to shield them against the weather until the mad passions of men cool down and allow the Union and peace once more to settle on your old homes at Atlanta."

8

The Civil War compelled many of the Indian tribes to choose between the competing white tribes. Most based their decisions on simple geography: tribes still living in the North sided with the North, those in the South with the South. In both these cases, doing otherwise would have been foolhardy. Despite the policy of Indian removal, remnants of various tribes still existed east of the Mississippi, yet not in sufficient numbers to challenge the armies of the Union or the Confederacy. For the Iroquois of New York *not* to have avowed allegiance to the Union might have led to their utter and final destruction. The few thousand Cherokees, Choctaws and Seminoles who had managed to evade removal might similarly have been crushed by Confederate troops. In the case of the southern tribes, their practice of holding black slaves added to their incentive to ally with the Confederacy.

Deciding between North and South was

more complicated for the tribes of the West. The Indian Territory — reduced to Oklahoma, after the statehood of Arkansas — abutted the Confederate states of Arkansas and Texas, and in that territory some of the tribes held slaves. Yet the territory also abutted the Union states of Missouri and Kansas, and other tribes did *not* hold slaves.

A more salient question was which side was going to win. This had been the crucial question for the Indian tribes in every war among the whites, going back to colonial days. In the French and Indian War, tribes on the frontier of European settlement placed their bets on whether the French or the British would prevail. In the American Revolutionary War, they chose between the Americans and the British. Likewise in the War of 1812. The dominant line of reasoning was that if a tribe or part of a tribe chose the side that turned out to be the loser, they would suffer for the choice. On the other hand, if they chose the winner, they might benefit.

In fact, tribes that chose the loser typically did suffer, but so, often, did tribes that chose the winner. The American victory in the Revolutionary War removed the restraining arm of Britain upon the Americans' expansion into the Ohio Valley. In the decades after the war, settlers poured into the valley, displacing dozens of tribes. The War of 1812 had no clear winner overall, but its outcome left the tribes of the Mississippi Valley likewise at the mercy of the Americans. Andrew Jackson received crucial assistance from Cherokees and Creeks in the war, but such gratitude as he felt didn't keep him from leading the postwar effort to drive them across the Mississippi, along with those Indians who had opposed him.

The tribes of the Indian Territory split on the allegiance question during the Civil War, and sometimes changed course midstream. John Ross and his Cherokee followers sided with the Confederates at first, on the slavery issue as much as anything else. But the arrival of Union troops prompted a reconsideration, and Ross cast his lot with the Union. Other Cherokees stuck with the South to the bitter end — bitter for the Confederates, and doubly so for the Confederate Cherokees, who now bore the onus of rebellion in addition to the racial and cultural inferiority long imputed to them by whites.

For the tribes beyond the Indian Territory, questions of allegiance weren't pressing. No one expected the tribes of the Great Plains or the Southwest to take part in the fighting, which with rare exceptions happened far away. Many of the tribes enjoyed a respite during the war, as federal troops were withdrawn from the frontier to fight the rebels in the South.

Yet like nearly every other gift the Indians received from the government, this one came with a catch. Troops on the frontier had often protected Indians from white settlers, and the departure of the troops signaled to the settlers that they could invade Indian land, steal Indian property and even kill Indians without worrying about government sanction. Further, the same exigencies that required the redeployment of the troops caused a suspension of annuity payments promised to various tribes in exchange for previous cessions of land.

The Dakotas, or Santee Sioux, of Minnesota felt the double cost of federal inattention. This eastern branch of the Sioux nation had been living on treaty terms with the American government for a decade when the Civil War broke out, and during that time their complaints had accumulated. "The whites were always trying to make the Indians give up their life and live like white men — go to farming, work hard and do as they did — and the Indians did not know how to do that, and did not want to anyway," recalled Big Eagle, a Dakota chief. "Many of the whites always seemed to say by their manner when they saw an Indian, 'I am much better than you,' and the Indians did not like this." Rivalries among the Dakotas aggravated the complaints against the whites. "There was a white man's party and an Indian party," Big

Eagle said. "We had politics among us, and there was much feeling." Specific grievances brought the general dissatisfaction to a head. White settlers didn't honor the boundaries of the Dakota reservation, the annuity payments didn't arrive on time or in full, and the federal Indian agents and traders the Dakotas dealt with were corrupt and hard-hearted. Another Dakota chief, Little Crow, led a delegation to Washington to complain, but to little effect. Minnesota had been a federal territory at the time of the treaty-making, but it was now a state, with its own elected officials. Those officials answered to Minnesota's voters, who did not include the Dakotas. In any event, with the Union careening toward civil war, Washington had much to worry about besides complaining Indians.

The Dakotas' situation grew worse after the war began. The war for the Union taking priority with Washington, the treaty payments fell further behind, and the grafting by the agents and traders became more egregious than ever. The payments had provided basic necessities, and without them, the Dakotas slowly starved. The principal agent refused to offer help; one trader was heard to have said the Indians should eat grass or their own dung.

Little Crow had been a moderate among the Dakotas, inclined toward accommodation rather than confrontation. From his time in the East, he knew what the Dakotas and other tribes were up against: a powerful, aggressive nation with a hundred times the population of the Indians. Yet he couldn't simply watch his people die. And when younger Dakota men, less knowledgeable, less patient and more eager to prove themselves as warriors, demanded an effort to redress the wrongs their tribe had suffered, he let himself be persuaded.

The whites' distraction afforded the perfect opportunity. "The war with the South was going on then, and a great many men had left the state and gone down there to fight," Big Eagle said. A Union recruiting force came to western Minnesota to find volunteers, and accepted mixed-race young men. "The Indians now thought the whites must be pretty hard up for men to fight the South, or they would not come so far out on the frontier and take half-breeds." The resistance-minded Dakota plotted among themselves. "It began to be whispered about that now would be a good time to go to war with the whites and get back the lands," Big Eagle said. "It was believed that the men who had enlisted last had all left the state, and that before help could be sent, the Indians could clean out the country, and that the Winnebago, and even the Chippewa, would assist the Sioux. It was also thought that a war with the whites would cause the Sioux to forget the troubles among themselves and enable many of them to pay off old scores."

Big Eagle reluctantly — or so he claimed afterward — cast his lot with the insurgents. "Though I took part in the war, I was against it," he said. "I had been to Washington and knew the power of the whites and that they would finally conquer us. We might succeed for a time, but we would be overpowered and defeated at last." By this point, Little Crow didn't want to hear such defeatism. "Little Crow told some of my band that if I refused to lead them to shoot me as a traitor who would not stand up for his nation, and then select another leader in my place," Big Eagle said.

The campaign began swiftly and brutally. Dakota warriors commenced by killing the trader Andrew Myrick, the one who had told them to eat grass. His corpse was later found with his mouth stuffed with grass. They burned the post of the Indian agent. They fell upon settlers, stabbing and bludgeoning men, women and children, and burning their homesteads.

What began as reprisal grew into a campaign of terror across western Minnesota, with the goal of expelling the white settlers. More than six hundred white men, women and children were killed, and others were taken captive. The stories related by survivors magnified the effect of the killings. "The

daughter of Mr. Schwandt, *enceinte*" —
pregnant — "was cut open," said Justina
Kreiger, a German immigrant. "The child
was taken alive from the mother, and nailed
to a tree. The son of Mr. Schwandt, aged
thirteen years, who had been beaten by the
Indians until dead, as was supposed, was
present and saw the entire tragedy. He saw
the child taken alive from the body of his
sister, Mrs. Waltz, and nailed to a tree in the
yard. It struggled some time after the nails
were driven through it!"

The slaughter and the stories produced the
result the Dakotas desired. Tens of thousands
of settlers dropped their plows, gathered their
children and moveable property, and fled
western Minnesota for the eastern part of the
state. The dream of the Dakota revanchists of
reclaiming their homeland appeared within
reach.

But as Little Crow had feared, the whites
prepared a counterattack. He tried to stave it
off by writing a letter to Henry Sibley,
formerly governor of Minnesota and now
commander of the state's militia. "Dear Sir,"
Little Crow wrote. "For what reason we have
commenced this war, I will tell you. It is on
account of Major Galbraith" — the Indian
agent. "We made a treaty with the Government. We beg for what little we do get, and
then can't get it till our children was dying
with hunger. It was with the traders that

Mr. A. J. Myrick told the Indians they could eat grass or their own dung." Little Crow acknowledged that the young men of his tribe had been the most eager for war, but he had made their cause his own. "I have done this myself." He added, "I have a great many prisoner women and children," and he invited Sibley to make an offer for their freedom.

Sibley made no offer but instead a demand. "You have murdered many of our people without any sufficient cause," he wrote. "Return me the prisoners under a flag of truce, and I will talk to you like a man."

Little Crow retained the captives, and Sibley and the Minnesotans prepared for war. They were constrained by the existing war for the Union, which had first claim on the able-bodied men of the state. Governor Alexander Ramsey insisted that the federal draft be suspended in Minnesota; Abraham Lincoln, amid the first serious invasion of the North by Confederate forces — the invasion that culminated in the battle of Antietam — was unwilling to grant a formal waiver but allowed that if temporary exigencies delayed the draft in Minnesota, he would look the other way. The harder question was what the Minnesotans would fight with. They lacked weapons, and the War Department in Washington was loath to part with any.

Minnesotans howled against the delay. Minnesota newspapers cried for protection for people and property; Minnesota officials condemned Lincoln for ignoring a state that had helped put him in the White House. Henry Sibley meanwhile declared that time was wasting to cleanse Minnesota of the wretches who had done the evil deeds. "Let us exterminate these vermin while we have them together," Sibley said.

The War Department eventually found some weapons, and Lincoln sent an army detachment under General John Pope, lately the loser at the second battle of Bull Run. The Minnesotans would have preferred a more distinguished protector, but they took solace from the determination Pope conveyed. "The horrible massacres of women and children and the outrageous abuse of female prisoners, still alive, call for punishment beyond human power to inflict," he wrote to Sibley. "There will be no peace in this region by virtue of treaties and Indian faith. It is my purpose utterly to exterminate the Sioux if I have the power to do so and even if it requires a campaign lasting the whole of next year. Destroy everything belonging to them and force them out to the plains, unless, as I suggest, you can capture them. They are to be treated as maniacs or wild beasts, and by no means as people with whom treaties or compromises can be made."

The campaign required far less than a year. The Dakota attacks had succeeded on account of their surprise and the lack of organized resistance by the whites. Once the whites girded properly for battle and counterattacked, the Dakota campaign fell to pieces. Little Crow fled to Canada, the hostages were released, and hundreds of Dakota warriors were taken prisoner.

At this point the demands of the Minnesotans turned to retribution. Pope oversaw trials of the Dakota prisoners, which lasted several weeks. More than three hundred were convicted of murder or rape and were sentenced to death.

Lincoln did not normally intervene in the operation of military courts, but he was troubled by the large number of death sentences in this case, and he decided to investigate. "Please forward, as soon as possible, the full and complete record of these convictions," he wrote to Pope. "And if the record does not fully indicate the more guilty and influential of the culprits, please have a careful statement made on these points and forwarded to me."

Pope complied even while defending the verdicts. "The only distinction between the culprits is as to which of them murdered most people or violated most young girls," he wrote to Lincoln. "All of them are guilty of these things in more or less degree." Pope warned that the citizens of Minnesota were besides themselves with anger. He wasn't sure he could control them should justice not be delivered. "If the guilty are not all executed," he said, "I think it nearly impossible to prevent the indiscriminate massacre of all the Indians — old men, women, and children."

Governor Ramsey echoed Pope's warning. "I hope the execution of every Sioux Indian condemned by the military court will be at once ordered," he telegraphed to Lincoln. "It would be wrong upon principle and policy to refuse this. Private revenge would on all this border take the place of official judgment on these Indians."

Lincoln couldn't ignore the warnings. If the Minnesota militia or irregulars turned on the Dakotas collectively, there was little he could do about it. He lacked the troops to defend the tribe, and he knew that Congress, amid the war against the Confederacy, would never support him in raising new troops for such a purpose.

Still, his conscience wouldn't let the matter go. He spent weeks poring over the cases of the convicted Dakotas and in December delivered his own verdict. "Anxious to not act with so much clemency as to encourage another outbreak, on the one hand, nor with so much severity as to be real cruelty on the other, I caused a careful examination of the records of trials to be made, in view of first ordering the execution of such as had been proved guilty of violating females," he told the Senate, which was pressing Lincoln on the matter. "Contrary to my expectations, only two of this class were found. I then directed a further examination, and a classification of all who were proven to have participated in *massacres,* as distinguished from participation in *battles.* This class numbered forty, and included the two convicted of female violation. One of the number is strongly recommended by the commission which tried them for commutation to ten years' imprisonment. I have ordered the other thirty-nine to be executed."

The executions were carried out, minus another one Lincoln spared, on hearing additional evidence. No vigilante massacre of Dakotas ensued, but some Minnesotans held Lincoln's clemency against him. After the president's reelection victory in 1864, Alexander Ramsey, by then a senator, visited the White House. "President in fine spirits, talks of the results of the election, majority in several states," Ramsey recorded in his diary. "Said his in Minnesota in 1860 was 10,000 and now only 7,000. I jocularly remarked that if he had hung more Indians, we should have given him his old majority. He said, 'I could not afford to hang men for votes.' "

9

Lincoln had less control over the fate of
hundreds of Cheyennes and Arapahos
camped along Sand Creek in eastern Colorado Territory. Until a few years previous,
Colorado had been a region whites rarely
visited. Fur trappers — the mountain men —
hunted beaver on the streams, but to the
Indians the trappers and partnering fur traders typically seemed an asset rather than a li-
ability, in that they brought trade goods that
could be purchased by the Indians for a few
pelts. The heavy migration to Oregon and
California skirted north, where the crossing
of the Rockies was easier. But the situation
changed when gold was discovered near what
overnight became Denver. Suddenly Colorado was a destination for tens of thousands
of whites, who were as grasping there as they
were wherever gold occurred. Federal troops
kept peace until the Civil War, when they
departed, leaving the Cheyennes, Arapahos
and others to their own devices.

Colorado acquired territorial status on the eve of the Civil War, and when that war began, the territorial governor, John Evans, issued a call for militia volunteers to replace the departed federal troops. Three regiments answered the governor's call. John Chivington, a Methodist minister, became the commanding colonel of the Third Colorado Regiment.

Evans wasn't happy when a delegation of Cheyennes and Arapahos requested a conference to arrange a peace treaty. He knew that the War Department in Washington had its eye on every healthy man for possible service against the Confederates; a peace treaty in Colorado might well be followed by a summons of the Colorado militia. The governor rejected the Indian overture at once. "What shall I do with the Third Colorado Regiment if I make peace?" he was reported to have said. "They have been raised to kill Indians, and they must kill Indians."

John Chivington eagerly endorsed the governor's verdict. "Kill and scalp all!" the pastor-colonel exhorted his troops. "Little and big — nits make lice!"

The regiment marched off, looking for Indians. They found several hundred Cheyennes and Arapahos in a village on Sand Creek. These Indians had not engaged in recent raids or violence, and they thought they were safe under the protection of the government.

John S. Smith was in the camp when Chivington and the Third Colorado arrived in late November 1864. Smith had lived among the Indians of the plains for three decades and had married into the Cheyenne band. He was fluent in Cheyenne and often served as an interpreter for the federal Indian agent.

The events of November 29 subsequently prompted an investigation. "How many Indians were there in the camp?" a questioner asked Smith.

"I think about 500 — men, women and children," Smith replied.

"What number of warriors or men?"

"About 200."

"What time in the day or night was the attack made?"

"Between daybreak and sunrise," Smith said.

He was asked to describe the attack in his own words.

"As soon as the troops were discovered, very early in the morning, about daybreak, the Indians commenced flocking to the head chief's lodge," Smith said. The head chief was Black Kettle, a Cheyenne. "He ran out his flag. He had a large American flag which was presented to him, I think, by Colonel Greenwood some years ago, and under this American flag he had likewise a small white flag."

"Was it light, so that the flags could be clearly seen?"

"Yes, they could be plainly seen," Smith said.

"How long was this before any firing was heard?"

"A very few minutes. They were but a short time coming into camp after they were first discovered. They came on a charge. When I first saw them they were about three-quarters of a mile from the camp, and the flag was run up by Black Kettle."

Smith paused, but was urged to continue.

"The firing commenced on the northeast side of Sand Creek," Smith said. "That was near Black Kettle's lodge. The men, women and children rushed to the upper end of the village, and ran to the lodge of another chief at the other end, War Bonnet."

"Were the Indians armed?"

"Some of them were. Some of them left their arms in their lodges. Some few picked up their bows and arrows and lances as they left their lodges. The younger men did."

"Did they form in any battle array, or with a view to oppose the charge?"

"No, sir," said Smith. "They just flocked in a promiscuous herd — men, women and children together. The bed of Sand Creek ran right up; there was little or no water in it at this place. Then they came to some breaks in the banks about where the troops overtook them, and the slaughter commenced, I suppose about three hundred yards above the main village. White Antelope was the first Indian killed, within a hundred yards of where I was in the camp at the time."

Smith paused, perhaps re-envisioning the scene. The Indians defended themselves but the attackers were relentless. "They fought them from very early in the morning," he said of the Indians, "until about eleven o'clock that day before they all got back together in camp. The troops then returned to the Indian village, followed the Indians up the creek two or three miles firing on them, then returned back to the Indian camp, and destroyed everything there was there — the entire village of one hundred lodges."

Smith had a child who was caught in the attack. "I had a son there, a half-breed," he told the investigators. "He gave himself up. In this stampede of the Indians he started to go with them, but when he found there was a fair show he turned around and came back to our camp where the troops were. I made several efforts to get to the troops, but was fired on myself by our own troops. My son stayed in the camp of our soldiers one day and a night, and then was shot down by the soldiers."

Smith himself was nearly killed. "My life was threatened, and they had to put a guard around me to save my life."

Smith was asked how many Indians were killed in the attack.

"I think about seventy or eighty, including men, women and children," he said. "Twenty-five or thirty of them were warriors, probably, and the rest women, children, boys and old men."

Were any barbarities inflicted on the dead?

"The worst I have ever seen," Smith said.

He was asked to describe them.

"All manner of depredations were inflicted on their persons. They were scalped, their brains knocked out. The men used their knives, ripped open women, clubbed little children, knocked them in the head with their guns, beat their brains out, mutilated their bodies in every sense of the word."

Other witnesses corroborated Smith's story, and elaborated. James Connor was a member of a unit of New Mexico militia that became attached to Chivington's regiment. Connor was informed that the regiment was seeking hostile Indians and so was surprised when Chivington led them toward the Sand Creek village, which was known to be filled with friendly Indians. "I was aware that they" — the Indians — "were resting there in fancied security under promises held out to them of safety." Connor recalled the numbers of soldiers and of Indians. "The command of Colonel Chivington was composed of about one thousand men," he said. "The village of the Indians consisted of from one hundred to one hundred and thirty lodges and, as far as I am able to judge, of from five hundred to six hundred souls, the majority of which were women and children." Connor described the aftermath of the attack. "In going over the battleground the next day, I did not see the body of a man, woman or child but was scalped, and in many instances their bodies were mutilated in the most horrible manner. Men, women and children's private parts were cut out, etc. I heard one man say that he had cut out a woman's private parts and had them for exhibition on a stick. I heard another man say he had cut the fingers off an Indian to get the rings on the hand. . . . I heard of one instance of a child a few months old being thrown in the feed-box of a wagon, and after being carried some distance left on the ground to perish. I also heard of numerous instances in which men had cut out the private parts of females and stretched them over the saddle bows, and wore them over their hats while riding in the ranks." Connor added pointedly, "All these matters were a subject of general conversation, and could not help being known by Colonel J. M. Chivington."

10

Among the Indian tribes, the Apaches had a peculiar vantage on the Civil War, for their homeland was occupied at different times by armies of both the North and the South. Much of New Mexico Territory, comprising the modern states of New Mexico and Arizona, wasn't considered particularly valuable by either side, being too barren or mountainous. But the southern portion was prized for its potential as a railway corridor to the Pacific. Indeed, its value in this regard was what had caused it to be appended — as the Gadsden Purchase — to the territory taken by the United States from Mexico in the war between those two countries. For the Confederacy, the region was vital to its hopes of expansion westward from Texas. Consequently the region became vital to the Union, to keep the Confederacy bottled up.

Actual fighting between Union and Confederate troops in New Mexico was limited. The climactic battle took place at Glorieta Pass, southeast of Santa Fe, in the early spring of 1862. The outcome was a tactical draw but a strategic defeat for the Confederates, whose attenuated supply line compelled a retreat, eventually to Texas.

Thereafter the heaviest fighting in the territory was between Apaches and Union soldiers. Some of the Mescalero Apaches had bet on a Confederate victory and conducted bloody raids against settlements of Unionists; the withdrawal of the Confederates left the Mescaleros vulnerable to a vengeful James Carleton, the Union commander for New Mexico. "All Indian men of that tribe are to be killed whenever and wherever you can find them," Carleton ordered Kit Carson, a veteran scout and currently an army colonel. "The women and children will not be harmed, but you will take them prisoners, and feed them at Fort Stanton until you receive other instructions about them. If the Indians send in a flag and desire to treat for peace, say to the bearer that when the people of New Mexico were attacked by the Texans, the Mescaleros broke their treaty of peace, and murdered innocent people, and ran off their stock; that now our hands are untied, and you have been sent to punish them for their treachery and their crimes; that you have no power to make peace; that you are there to kill them wherever you can find them; that if they beg for peace, their chiefs and twenty of their principal men must come to Santa Fe to have a talk here; but tell them fairly and frankly that you will keep after their people and slay them until you receive orders to desist from these headquarters; that this making of treaties for them to break whenever they have an interest in breaking them will not be done any more; that that time has passed by; that we have no faith in their promises; that we believe if we kill some of their men in fair, open war, they will be apt to remember that it will be better for them to remain at peace than to be at war." Carleton concluded, "I trust that this severity, in the long run, will be the most humane course that could be pursued toward these Indians."

Carleton wouldn't be the last to discover that Apaches were difficult to find when they didn't want to be found, and his ferocious-sounding policy did the tribe only middling damage. Part of the reason was that many of the Apaches still considered Mexicans to be their primary foes. Geronimo scarcely noticed the blue-coated newcomers to the Apache lands, so consuming did his hatred of Mexicans remain. "All the other Apaches were satisfied after the battle of Kaskiyeh, but I still desired more revenge," Geronimo recalled. "For several months we were busy with the chase and other peaceful pursuits." Yet peace, for Geronimo, lacked the savor of war. "Finally I succeeded in persuading two other warriors, Ah-koch-ne and Ko-deh-ne, to go with me to invade the Mexican country."

The three headed south, traveling as light as Apache warriors usually did. "We entered Mexico on the north line of Sonora and followed the Sierra de Antunez Mountains to the south end of the range. Here we decided to attack a small village. I do not know the name of this village."

They waited overnight. "At daylight we approached from the mountains. Five horses were hitched outside. We advanced cautiously, but just before we reached the horses the Mexicans opened fire from the houses. My two companions were killed. Mexicans swarmed on every side; some were mounted; some were on foot, and all seemed to be armed."

Geronimo wondered if he had walked into a trap. But he had little opportunity to ponder the question. "Three times that day I was surrounded, but I kept fighting, dodging, and hiding," he said. "Several times during the day while in concealment I had a chance to take deliberate aim at some Mexican, who, gun in hand, was looking for me. I do not think I missed my aim."

He hoped the night would be his friend. "With the gathering darkness I found more time to retreat toward Arizona," he said. But

96

his foes were determined. "The Mexicans did not quit the chase. Several times the next day mounted Mexicans tried to head me off; many times they fired on me, but I had no more arrows, so I depended upon running and hiding, although I was very tired." He hadn't eaten since before the fight began, nor had he taken any rest. "The second night I got clear of my pursuers, but I never slackened my pace until I reached our home in Arizona. I came into our camp without booty, without my companions, exhausted, but not discouraged."

Not all in the band shared his indifference to failure. The wives and children of his dead companions had to be cared for by the rest of the tribe. "Some of the Apaches blamed me for the evil result of the expedition," Geronimo said. Yet he offered neither apologies nor explanations. He simply kept quiet. "Having failed, it was only proper that I should remain silent." His hatred for the killers of his family remained. "My feelings toward the Mexicans did not change. I still hated them and longed for revenge. I never ceased to plan for their punishment." Yet his plans found few takers. "It was hard to get the other warriors to listen to my proposed raids."

He kept trying, and finally recruited another pair of warriors. He mapped out a different strategy. "On our former raid we had gone

97

through the Nedni Apaches' range into Sonora. This time we went through the country of the Cho-kon-en and entered the Sierra Madre Mountains." Once more they kept to the mountains until Geronimo spied a likely target: a village at the foot of the mountains. Again he planned a dawn attack.

And again the plan went awry. "That night Mexican scouts discovered our camp and fired on us, killing one warrior," Geronimo said. He and his remaining comrade fled into the mountains. In the morning they saw a column of Mexican cavalry coming from the south. The soldiers appeared laden for a long journey. "We followed their trail until we were sure that they were headed for our range in Arizona, then we hurried past them and in three days reached our own settlement." The Mexican horse soldiers were only hours behind. They attacked on arrival. "Their first volley killed three small boys. Many of the warriors of our tribe were away from home, but the few of us who were in camp were able to drive the troops out of the mountains before night. We killed eight Mexicans and lost five: two warriors and three boys." The Mexicans retreated southward, but the Apaches sent four warriors to follow them. Only after the Mexicans had crossed the international border back into Mexico did the warriors let them go. "We were quite sure they would not return soon," Geronimo said.

Yet he was not through with them. The Mexican invasion of Apache country seemed to Geronimo's fellow warriors to require a response. Two dozen agreed to join him in another raid on Mexico. After but a few days' march they caught up with the Mexican column. Or it might have been another group of soldiers; to Geronimo the difference was immaterial. "There was only one company of cavalry in this command, and I thought that by properly surprising them we could defeat them," he recalled. Geronimo laid an ambush. "This was at a place where the whole company must pass through a mountain defile. We reserved fire until all of the troops had passed through; then the signal was given. The Mexican troopers, seemingly without a word of command, dismounted, and placing their horses on the outside of the company, for breastworks, made a good fight against us. I saw that we could not dislodge them without using all our ammunition, so I led a charge." The Indians converged on the Mexicans from all sides, fighting with knives and spears. "I raised my spear to kill a Mexican soldier just as he leveled his gun at me. I was advancing rapidly, and my foot slipping in a pool of blood, I fell under the Mexican trooper. He struck me over the head with the butt of his gun, knocking me senseless."

Luckily for Geronimo, a warrior right

behind him killed the Mexican with a spear thrust. The Apaches proceeded to annihilate the Mexicans. The Apache war cry resounded across the field, and the scalp knives swiftly did their work.

The Apaches tended to their dead and wounded. Geronimo, at first thought dead, was discovered to be merely unconscious. "They bathed my head in cold water and restored me to consciousness," he recalled. "Then they bound up my wound, and the next morning, although weak from loss of blood and suffering from a severe headache, I was able to march on the return to Arizona. I did not fully recover for months, and I still wear the scar given me by that musketeer."

The campaign sated most of the Apaches' desire for revenge. "We had lost so heavily that there really was no glory in our victory," Geronimo said. "No one seemed to want to go on the warpath again that year."

But the next year he was at it again. With a dozen comrades he returned to Mexico, this time entering Chihuahua, the state east of Sonora. They encountered a pack train and made an attack. The drivers fled, leaving the mules and their loads behind. Geronimo and the others dumped the bacon in the loads — Apaches finding pig flesh distasteful — and started with mules and the rest of the cargo back toward home.

They didn't get far. The drivers had alerted

the Mexican authorities, who sent out troops. "It was at daybreak and we were just finishing our breakfast," Geronimo said. "We had no idea that we had been pursued or that our enemies were near until they opened fire. At the first volley a bullet struck me a glancing lick just at the lower corner of the left eye and I fell unconscious. All the other Indians fled to cover. The Mexicans, thinking me dead, started in pursuit of the fleeing Indians. In a few moments I regained consciousness and had started at full speed for the woods when another company coming up opened fire on me. Then the soldiers who had been chasing the other Indians turned, and I stood between two hostile companies, but I did not stand long. Bullets whistled in every direction and at close range to me. One inflicted a slight flesh wound on my side, but I kept running, dodging and fighting, until I got clear of my pursuers. I climbed up a steep canyon, where the cavalry could not follow. The troopers saw me, but did not dismount and try to follow."

Geronimo and his comrades had agreed that in case they got separated, they would meet in the Santa Rita Mountains of Arizona. They did so, three days later. From there they made it home, empty-handed. "We had not even a partial victory to report. I again returned wounded, but I was not yet discouraged," Geronimo said. "Again I was blamed by our people, and again I had no reply."

The situation grew worse. Geronimo's wounds kept him in the village while the other warriors went hunting, or on a trade mission to the Navajo country, to acquire blankets. "One morning just at daybreak, when the squaws were lighting the camp fires to prepare breakfast, three companies of Mexican troops who had surrounded our settlement in the night opened fire. There was no time for fighting. Men, women, and children fled for their lives. Many women and children and a few warriors were killed, and four women were captured. My left eye was still swollen shut, but with the other I saw well enough to hit one of the officers with an arrow, and then make good my escape among the rocks. The troopers burned our tepees and took our arms, provisions, ponies and blankets."

The outlook was grim. The Mexican attack revealed the weak point of the Apaches and most other tribes. Winter was approaching, and without food, shelter, weapons for defense and hunting, and horses for transport, the band would be hard-pressed simply to survive. "It was a long, long time before we were again able to go on the warpath against the Mexicans," Geronimo said.

■ ■ ■ ■

PART II
THE CAMPAIGN
BEGINS

■ ■ ■ ■

11

The implacability Sherman showed Atlanta fueled the most fearsome campaign in the history of American warfare until then: his deliberately destructive march from Atlanta to the sea. In a message to Grant, Sherman proposed to cut a swath through Georgia, depriving the Confederacy of essential provisions and driving home the cost of continuing the rebellion. "The utter destruction of its roads, houses and people will cripple their military resources," he said. "I can make the march, and make Georgia howl."

Sherman made the march, and Georgia howled. By the time he reached the sea at Savannah, the Confederacy was doomed. Grant's Virginia campaign of maneuver against Lee had become a matter of attrition, and Sherman's trail of smoke and ruin made plain that the South must soon surrender lest the destruction grow still worse. At Appomattox, Lee acknowledged the inevitable and signed the surrender that brought the war to an end.

Just as the end of the Revolutionary War had left the Indians at the mercy of the victorious Americans, so the end of the Civil War left them to face the victorious Union army. One great advantage the whites had over the Indians in most of the long struggle between the former and the latter was that the whites were unified while the Indians were divided. Tecumseh had understood this, had tried to unify the Indians, and had failed. Occasionally the whites fell out among themselves: during the wars between the British and French in colonial times, during the Revolution, and again during the Civil War. But these were the exceptions, and each ended with whichever group of whites had won presenting, again, a solid front against the Indians.

In 1865 the odds against the Indians were greater than they had ever been. The Union army had been tested in battle, with officers like Sherman having mastered the brutal art of war. Westward expansion, largely stifled by the conflict between North and South, resumed with a vengeance. And the Indians continued to struggle with disease, dislocation and the other disruptive forces that sapped their strength and numbers. In 1865 the total population of Indians in the United States was fewer than four hundred thousand, and falling. The population of non-Indians was over thirty million, and growing rapidly.

And yet against these odds the Indians fought as they had never fought before. At least some of them did, giving Sherman and the Union army all they could handle. The last campaign for America began; where and how it would end was what the fighting would determine.

Sherman should have been happy at the close of the Civil War. He was a great man, second only to Grant among the heroes at arms among the victors. His scorched-earth approach had won over its critics by breaking the will of the South; some called him a military genius — even if more than a few of those thought him an evil genius.

Yet happiness didn't come easily to Sherman. His mind worked faster than most other people's, and more relentlessly. When he was compelled to suffer knaves and fools — a large group, in his thinking — his temper often got the better of him. He respected Grant and Lincoln, and felt Lincoln's death, at the hand of John Wilkes Booth, as a personal blow. He confided in his younger brother John, a senator from Ohio, but distrusted other politicians and deemed Washington a nest of intrigue and incompetence. He kept his distance from the capital whenever he could.

No sooner had the grand review in Washington of the victorious Union army ended than Sherman gathered his wife and their younger children and headed west. They visited Chicago, where he spoke at a benefit for soldiers' families strapped by the war. They dropped down to South Bend, Indiana, to see two of the older children, who attended school there. They looped to Ohio to see members of his and Ellen's families. They wended through Kentucky and Tennessee en route to St. Louis, where he took command of the postwar army of the trans-Mississippi West.

"My thoughts and feelings at once reverted to the construction of the great Pacific Railway, which had been chartered by Congress in the midst of war, and was then in progress," Sherman recalled of his first days in his new post. And well might his thoughts and feelings have turned to the railroad. The Civil War had taught Sherman — and every other general on both sides — the value of railroads to military campaigns. The North's dominance in railroads translated into dominance on the battlefield, because it allowed the North to mobilize resources more effectively than the South did.

Sherman had a second reason for cherishing railroads. As a Californian in the 1850s he had experienced the emotional distance between the West Coast and the East, which was a direct consequence of the time required to travel between the two regions. This feeling of distance had inspired secessionist mutterings in California during the first part of the war. Some of the mutterers conceived a connection with the Confederacy; others fancied an independent Pacific republic, funded by the gold from California's mines and perhaps the silver from neighboring Nevada.

The Pacific Railway Act of 1862 took dead aim at this secessionist thinking, and hit the target. The measure funded the construction of a transcontinental railroad, whose mere promise — of shrinking a four-month overland journey, or a four-week trip by steamer and Panama portage, to a four-day hop in the comfort of a railroad car — killed the secession movement outright. California at once became the most loyal of Union states; its residents began planning trips back to their eastern hometowns.

"I put myself in communication with the parties engaged in the work, visiting them in person, and assured them that I would afford them all possible assistance and encouragement," Sherman said of the crews building the Union Pacific, the eastern partner in the construction. The company appreciated the attention. "Dr. Durant, the leading man of the Union Pacific, seemed to me a person of ardent nature, of great ability and energy, enthusiastic in his undertaking, and determined to build the road from Omaha to San Francisco," Sherman wrote. In fact, the Union Pacific would build to a meeting point with the Central Pacific, which had started in California and was working east. "He had an able corps of assistants, collecting materials, letting out contracts for ties, grading, etc., and I attended the celebration of the first completed division of sixteen and a half miles, from Omaha to Papillon." Sixteen miles wasn't nothing, but it was a tiny fraction of the distance to be covered. "When the orators spoke so confidently of the determination to build two thousand miles of railway across the plains, mountains, and desert, devoid of timber, with no population, but on the contrary raided by the bold and bloody Sioux and Cheyennes, who had almost successfully defied our power for half a century, I was disposed to treat it jocularly," Sherman said. But Thomas Durant was quite serious, and his earnestness rubbed off on Sherman.

Sherman recommended that the army create a new military Department of the Platte, headquartered at Omaha. It would be responsible for protecting the construction crews of the Union Pacific and their handiwork, and likewise guarding the crews and work of the Kansas Pacific, a subsidiary of the Union Pacific that was building west from Kansas City toward a junction with the Union Pacific at a point yet to be determined. The troops would also secure the telegraph lines erected beside the tracks.

This was a major task. "During the years 1865 and 1866," Sherman reflected, "the Great Plains remained almost in a state of nature, being the pasture-fields of about ten million buffalo, deer, elk, and antelope, and were in full possession of the Sioux, Cheyennes, Arapahoes, and Kiowas, a race of bold Indians, who saw plainly that the construction of two parallel railroads right through their country would prove destructive to the game on which they subsisted, and consequently fatal to themselves."

When the army approved Sherman's recommendation, he decided to survey his new department. In the spring of 1866 he left St. Louis and traveled to Fort Riley, on the route of the Kansas Pacific in central Kansas, and then to Fort Kearny, Nebraska, in the path of the Union Pacific. "There seems to be little or no emigration to Colorado or New Mexico over this road," he wrote to Grant regarding the overland trail. "But emigrants are taking up homesteads in the valley for thirty and forty miles above Riley. I came over the railroad to a point 87 miles from Kansas City and found construction parties laying rail at the rate of 1/2 mile per day. The superintendent says he will have 100 miles completed by June 1, but it will take into the fall to get the rails laid to Riley, 136 miles from the Missouri River."

Fort Kearny had a good location but little else. "Kearny is made up of a set of old dilapidated frame buildings standing in the middle of a vast plain without a tree, except on the islands of the Platte, about a mile distant," Sherman recorded. "It is a lonely desolate place, but convenient, as near it unite all the roads west, from Leavenworth, Atchison, Nebraska City and Omaha." He didn't think the neighborhood would ever support a large population. "There is no stone, timber or coal at or near Kearny. The ground looks fertile and produces good grass, but the drought of summer and severity of winter will prevent its being an inviting country to the emigrant."

Yet the advance of the railroad would make life easier at Fort Kearny, as at Fort Riley. Thomas Durant showed Sherman what his company was capable of doing. "I have been around to the machine and workshops of the Union Pacific Railroad, which are certainly on a large scale, exhibiting both the ability and purpose to push their work," Sherman wrote to Grant. "The company has on hand here enough iron and ties to build 50 miles of road, and Mr. Durant assured me that he has contracted for enough for 150 miles of road. Already 80 miles of road are done, and he expects to complete the first hundred miles by the middle of June, and the second hundred miles in all 1866. This will make a continuous railway to a point 5 miles beyond Fort Kearny." The Kansas Pacific was making comparable headway, to Sherman's pleasure. "With railroads completed to Forts Kearny and Riley, our military question of supplies is much simplified," he told Grant. Provisioning the western forts had always been an expensive headache. The railroads would make it cheap and almost easy. "I hope the President and Secretary of War will continue as hitherto to befriend these roads as far as the law allows," Sherman said.

Supply was essential to the success of Sherman's mission. Almost anywhere in the West was a hardship posting for most of Sherman's soldiers, and the forts on the plains were the worst. "Some of the posts out on the Plains are really enough to make men desert, built years ago of upright cottonwood poles, daubed with mud, and covered with mounds of earth, as full of fleas and bed-bugs as a full sponge is of water," he observed. "Were it not for the intensely bitter winds of winter which force men to go in such holes, or perish, no human being, white man, Indian, or negro would go inside. Still, if there is no help for it, our officers and men will endure them; but we can help it, and must." Sherman knew the army was in a belt-tightening mode after the flush days of the Civil War, but he argued that some cuts were less prudent than others. "If it becomes necessary to save the money, the War Department should stop all other expenses and give our troops on that bleak and dreary frontier at least clean houses, however coarse. When stone can be had the troops must build of that; but there are stretches of hundreds of miles without stone, or any building materials whatever, and there is no alternative but to buy boards and haul them out." Even Congress could see that. "We cannot expect troops to be worth anything if we winter them in holes, and force them to fight with rats, bed-bugs and fleas for existence."

12

During the Civil War, Sherman had dealt with Northern merchants who profited handsomely from the war, even when their profits involved buying and selling — of contraband Southern cotton, for example — that put his soldiers and their mission at risk. He discovered a similar dynamic during another tour, of eastern Colorado and Wyoming in the autumn of 1866. He explained the situation to a commiserating Grant, whose summary treatment of merchants in the Civil War had landed him in political trouble. Sherman wrote of a farmer named Craig, proprietor of a thriving operation on the Huerfano River, a tributary of the Arkansas. "He has thoroughly proven the ability to produce," Sherman said of Craig. "But then comes the more difficult problem of consumption. Who is to buy his corn? The miners of Colorado, in the mountains two hundred miles distant, will take some, but the cost of hauling is enormous. The few travelers and stage companies will buy a little. But he and all situated like him look to our military for a market, and that is the real pressure for garrisons and an Indian war." The Indians were blamed for the troubles, but they weren't the instigators. "The Utes are harmless and peaceable, and the Cheyennes and Arapahoes are off after the buffaloes, God only knows where," Sherman said. Nonetheless, Craig and his ilk demanded a campaign against them.

Sherman refused to oblige. "I don't see how we can make a decent excuse for an Indian war," he said. "I have traveled all the way from Laramie without a single soldier or escort. I meet single men, unarmed, traveling along the road as in Missouri. Cattle and horses graze loose far from their owners, most tempting to a starving Indian, and though the Indians might easily make a descent on these scattered ranches, yet they have not done so, and I see no external signs of a fear of such an event." This didn't stop the whites from claiming fear and demanding that Sherman defend them. "All the people are clamorous for military protection. I received at Puebla a petition to that effect signed by so many names that I could not help answering that the names to the petition exceeded in number the strength of any of our small garrisons."

Yet for all Sherman's recognition that whites were to blame, he knew he wouldn't forever be able to resist their demands for military action. They controlled the territorial press, they possessed the vote in territorial elections, and they had the ear of officials in Washington. The Indians had no such connections and influence. The whites would precipitate or simply fabricate Indian attacks and demand that the army come to their defense. Congress would press the War Department, which would call on Sherman to act. Sherman had experienced enough of politics during the Civil War to know that congressional demands for action often outstripped the necessary appropriations; he supposed the same would happen now, and he and the army would be blamed. Worse, he'd be compelled to put his soldiers into situations where they couldn't defend themselves. The whole situation reminded him why he despised politics.

He offered a solution. "I propose the coming year (with your consent and with that of the Secretary of the Interior, in whose control these Indians are supposed to be) to restrict the Sioux north of the Platte west of the Missouri river and east of the new road to Montana, which starts from Laramie to Virginia City by way of Forts Reno, Philip Kearny, C. F. Smith etc.," Sherman wrote to Grant in November 1866. "All Sioux found outside of these limits, without a written pass from some military commander defining clearly their object, should be dealt with summarily. In like manner, I would restrict the Arapahoes, Cheyennes, Comanches, Kiowas, Apaches and Navajos south of the Arkansas and east of Fort Union."

Sherman explained the benefits of his plan. "This will leave for our people exclusively the use of the wide belt east and west between the Platte and the Arkansas, in which lie the two great railroads and over which passes the bulk of travel to the mountain territories." Separation of whites and Indians must come sooner or later, as it had in other parts of the country. "As long as these Indians can hunt the buffalo and antelope within the described limits, we will have the depredations of last summer — and worse yet, the exaggerations of danger raised by our own people, often for a very base purpose." Sherman had learned the value of transport and communication during the Civil War, and he considered them equally vital in the postwar West. "It is our duty and it shall be my study to make the progress of construction of the great Pacific railways that lie in this belt of country as safe as possible, as also to protect the stage and telegraph lines against any hostile bands. But they are so long that to guard them perfectly is an impossibility unless we can restrict the Indians as herein stated."

What Sherman was proposing was a new set of reservations, but without the treaty negotiations that had accompanied the establishment of previous reservations. Sherman wanted the government simply to announce the policy and let him and his soldiers enforce it.

Grant supported Sherman's recommendation. As much as Sherman, Grant had come to value railroads during the Civil War. "The protection of the Pacific railroad, so that not only the portion already completed shall be entirely safe, but that the portion yet to be constructed shall in no way be delayed either by actual or apprehended danger, is indispensable," Grant wrote to Edwin Stanton, the secretary of war. "Aside from the great value of this road to the country benefited by it, it has the strongest claims upon the military service as it will be one of its most efficient aids in the control of the Indians in the vast regions through which it passes."

Emigrants to the West couldn't wait for the railroad to be completed. Prospectors had struck gold in Montana during the Civil War, and when the fighting's end freed hundreds of thousands of young males for new adventures, a sizable fraction headed for the new diggings. Their route followed the Oregon and California Trail across the plains to western Wyoming, where it angled north through the valley of the Powder River and around the eastern base of the Bighorn

Mountains to Bozeman Pass and Virginia City. In doing so, it crossed the hunting ground of the western Sioux, or Lakotas, the most powerful tribe of the plains. The Lakotas had leveraged control of the fur trade of the upper Missouri to forge alliances with American traders who furnished guns, ammunition and, crucially, smallpox vaccine that enabled the Lakotas to dominate and destroy their Indian neighbors as almost no other American tribe ever had.

Yet power is a comparative concept, and many of the Lakotas, observing what had happened to their eastern cousins in Minnesota in 1862, and their Cheyenne and Arapaho neighbors at Sand Creek in 1864, resigned themselves to a retreat to territory away from the routes of the whites. The Lakota realm had not always been as large as it was in the 1860s; the Lakotas could learn again to live with less.

Yet some Lakotas resisted violently. Red Cloud, a leader of the Oglala band, was almost the same age as Sherman, and had been fighting even longer. He let all who would listen know he intended to keep fighting, more fiercely than ever. "Friends," he told a council of the Plains tribes, "it has been our misfortune to welcome the white man. We have been deceived. He brought with him some shining things that pleased our eyes; he brought weapons more effective than our own: above all, he brought the spirit water that makes one forget for a time old age, weakness and sorrow." These items were a snare to Indians, and would lure them from the path that had made the Indians strong. "If you would possess these things for yourselves, you must begin anew and put away the wisdom of your fathers," Red Cloud said. "You must lay up food, and forget the hungry. When your house is built, your storeroom filled, then look around for a neighbor whom you can take at a disadvantage, and seize all that he has! Give away only what you do not want; or rather, do not part with any of your possessions unless in exchange for another's." The Lakotas had come to a moment of truth. "My countrymen, shall the glittering trinkets of this rich man, his deceitful drink that overcomes the mind, shall these things tempt us to give up our homes, our hunting grounds, and the honorable teaching of our old men? Shall we permit ourselves to be driven to and fro, to be herded like the cattle of the white man?"

When the whites built forts to guard the Bozeman road, Red Cloud urged a final stand. "Hear ye, Lakotas!" he declared. "When the Great Father at Washington sent us his chief soldier" — General William Harney — "to ask for a path through our hunting grounds, a way for his iron road to the mountains and the western sea, we were told that they wished merely to pass through our country, not to tarry among us, but to seek for gold in the far west. Our old chiefs thought to show their friendship and good will, when they allowed this dangerous snake in our midst. They promised to protect the wayfarers. Yet before the ashes of the council fire are cold, the Great Father is building his forts among us. You have heard the sound of the white soldier's ax upon the Little Piney. His presence here is an insult and a threat. It is an insult to the spirits of our ancestors. Are we then to give up their sacred graves to be plowed for corn? Lakotas, I am for war!"

Red Cloud's followers attacked the posts on the Bozeman road and the provisioners who supplied them. Soldiers from the forts sallied out in response, inflicting casualties and provoking further attacks. When tempers at Fort Philip Kearny, one of the Bozeman posts, had reached the boiling point, Red Cloud laid a trap to deliver a devastating blow.

Sherman first learned of Red Cloud's design, and its terrible success, in a message from the commander at Fort Phil Kearny. "I have had today a fight unexampled in Indian warfare," Colonel Henry Carrington said. "My loss is ninety-four killed. I have recovered forty-nine bodies, and thirty-five more are to be brought in in the morning." A whole company, led by William Fetterman, had been wiped out. Carrington blamed overwhelming odds. "The Indians engaged were nearly three thousand," he said. He pleaded for reinforcements. "Give me two companies of cavalry at least, forthwith, well-armed, or four companies of infantry." They must be dispatched at once. "Any remissness will result in mutilation and butchery beyond precedent."

Sherman discounted Carrington's numbers for the alarm they conveyed. In fact, eighty-one officers and men had been killed in Red Cloud's attack, and the Indian force was closer to one thousand than to three thousand. All the same, Sherman was shaken and puzzled by the disaster. "I do not yet understand how the massacre of Colonel Fetterman's party could have been so complete," he wrote to Grant. Sherman supposed poor decisions had been made, by Fetterman or Carrington or both. But misjudgments were part of military life, and Sherman was determined that his troops not be sacrificed again. "We must act with vindictive earnestness against the Sioux, even to their extermination, men, women and children," he told Grant. "Nothing less will reach the root of this case."

The next day Sherman telegraphed to Grant's adjutant at the War Department, explaining that heavy snow on the plains was hampering his investigation of the Fetterman affair. But he was already preparing a reprisal. "The Indians must be pursued and punished," Sherman said. "I will see if the two new colored regiments now organizing in General Hancock's department" — Winfield Scott Hancock's Department of the Missouri — "can be made available by April 1. If not, I may have to ask some help from General Grant. Please ascertain of him if he has any troops he could spare this spring, as we must not overlook this case, but must pursue and punish at all hazards."

Sherman's investigation uncovered bloody details and reckless disregard of orders. "Knowing your anxiety to hear something definite and comprehensible of the Fort Phil Kearney matter, I have had a copy made of a letter from a sergeant there to a clerk in this office, which seems to explain the case fully," Sherman wrote to Grant. The sergeant's letter described skirmishes during the two weeks before the disaster — the baiting of the trap. In one skirmish, two officers were killed and scalped. The day of the attack itself began with sniping at a timber train bringing in firewood. Fetterman, disdainful of the Lakotas' fighting ability and eager to prove his own, gathered a company and galloped out of the fort.

The question of orders had become crucial to the investigation; Colonel Carrington was saying he had ordered Fetterman not to go too far, lest he outrun available reserves. The sergeant corroborated Carrington's account. "Upon their leaving the fort, the colonel gave orders for the detachment to protect the train but to remain in supporting distance of the garrison. But contrary to these orders they pursued the Indians, who immediately left the train without inflicting any damage, for some six miles, to the main force of the enemy, which lay in ambush. The Indians, perceiving as I suppose that they had the advantage in numbers, immediately rushed from their places of concealment and succeeded in cutting our men off from any communication with the post, and the scene which followed you and all others may imagine, but I cannot describe it as not a man was left to tell the tale. All were butchered and scalped, their bodies gashed, chopped with knives and tomahawks, stripped of every article of clothing and then perhaps while in the agonies of death shot through and through with arrows. Poor Sergeant Morgan was shot through the breast and scalped; his body was full of arrows."

Carrington, not yet knowing what had befallen Fetterman's column, had sent out a second detachment in support. "Captain Powell followed their trail across a high bluff into a valley, where to the surprise and mortification of his command he found not those brave and noble hearts who a few hours previous had left the fort with buoyant spirits thirsting for revenge, but eighty-four mangled and disfigured corpses lying naked on the ground." Powell had sent a report back to Carrington with a request for wagons to transport the dead. "The report went like a death knell to the heart of every soldier," the sergeant said. "We could hardly believe it until the arrival of Captain Powell's detachment and the return of the wagons bringing forty-five dead bodies. The remaining thirty-six were not brought in until the next morning."

The garrison at the fort feared worse was yet to come. "The snow is deep and the weather so intensely cold that the guards have to be relieved every half hour," the sergeant said. But vigilance was more necessary than ever. "The men are sleeping in their clothes, and accoutrements on. Indian signals have been seen, and we don't know what hour the post may be attacked." The soldiers longed for reinforcements, to save their own lives and avenge their slaughtered comrades. "We want men and arms on these plains to exterminate this accursed race of savages. We are fighting a foe that is the devil."

The sergeant closed on a personal note: "Please write soon and pray God to hasten the day when I shall get out of this horrible place. Good-bye; this may be my last letter."

13

The blasts of winter impeded the sending of
reinforcements, which Congress was anyway
reluctant to fund. Sherman dropped talk of
exterminating the Sioux, in favor of a broadly
defensive strategy. "All the troops in the
departments of Dakota, Platte, and Missouri,
embracing Indian country, have been and are
now being placed in position to afford the
protection to the telegraph and mail routes
across the plains, as well as to the four
principal roads by which the emigrants travel
or merchants send their goods destined to
the mountain territories," Sherman explained
to Grant in March 1867. "These troops will
occupy posts readily built but designed for
defence by a fraction of the garrison, while
the balance can operate as escorts or expeditions between the posts." The soldiers' mission was peacekeeping and law-enforcing.
"Commanding officers of these posts or stations will act against all people who violate
the laws of Congress, or who endanger the

lives or property of our people, be they white, black, or copper-colored," Sherman said. He acknowledged that the West wasn't the East. "When there are no courts or civil authorities to hold and punish such malefactors, we must of necessity use the musket pretty freely." But only against active wrongdoers. "Peaceful people — whites, blacks or Indians — will be left to be dealt with by the civil authorities and agents."

Sherman said that some of the Indians appeared determined to fight; he was prepared to deal with them. "General Hancock, in the Department of the Missouri, has organized a special force of about fifteen hundred (1,500) men, mostly of the Seventh Cavalry (a new regiment) and some infantry drawn from the inner posts, with which he will proceed in person to the country of the Cheyennes and Kiowas, below the Arkansas, and will then confer with them to ascertain if they want to fight, in which case he will indulge them," Sherman told Grant. "If, however, they will assure him that they will remain at peace, subject to their treaties and agents, he will not disturb them, but impress on them the imprudence of assuming an insolent manner and tone when they visit our posts, and he will impress on them that it is to their interest to keep their hunting parties and their young warriors off our main lines of travel, where their presence gives the occasion for the many rumors which so distract our people."

A larger force, under General Christopher Augur, would defend the region along the Platte against the Red Cloud band of Lakotas, who needed to be taught a lesson for their treatment of the Fetterman company. "No mercy should be shown these Indians, for they grant no quarter, nor ask for it," Sherman told Grant. Yet Sherman was staying Augur's hand for the moment, because Congress was talking about appointing commissioners to investigate the causes of the conflict on the plains and to seek a remedy. "I have instructed him to delay actual hostilities until these commissioners have exhausted their efforts and reported to him their inability to influence the conduct of the hostile Sioux by pacific measures."

Defensive warfare offended Sherman's martial sensibilities, and although compelled to it for the present, he rejected the concept as a long-term strategy. "Defensive measures will not answer against Indians," he told Grant. "We are tied down to long routes, and our detachments are necessarily small, hardly enough to build shelters and gather firewood, the materials for which have to be hauled two and three hundred miles, while the Indians move hundreds and thousands of miles, taking along with them their ponies, lodges, wives and children. They are thus enabled at one time to attack or molest our roads at one point, and in a month or so make their appearance at another, hundreds of miles distant. Our troops must get among them, and must kill enough of them to inspire fear, and then must conduct the remainder to places where Indian agents can and will reside among them and be held responsible for their conduct." The arithmetic of plains warfare made a merely defensive approach unsustainable. "If fifty Indians are allowed to remain between the Arkansas and Platte, we will have to guard every stage station, every train, and all railroad working parties," Sherman said. "In other words, fifty hostile Indians will checkmate three thousand soldiers." This must not be tolerated. "Rather get them out as soon as possible, and it makes little difference whether they be coaxed out by Indian commissioners or killed."

The agents Sherman wrote of were a sore subject for him and for every army officer in the West. The agents were civilians, and answered to the Indian Bureau, an office of the Interior Department, rather than to the War Department. The agents granted licenses to traders who sold supplies to the tribes with which the government had treaties; these supplies included arms and ammunition, often of the latest design. The arrangement suited the agents and the traders but angered the soldiers who found themselves outgunned by the Indians they were supposed to control. "We the military are held responsible for the peace of the frontier, and it is an absurdity to attempt it if Indian agents and traders can legalize and encourage so dangerous a traffic," Sherman wrote to Winfield Hancock. Sherman had received a written statement from several Indian agents on the upper Arkansas reminding him that they were authorized by Congress to carry on their trade in weapons. Sherman, declaring the agents' statement "an outrage upon our rights and supervision of the matter," told Hancock, "I now authorize you to disregard that paper and at once stop the practice, keeping the issues and sales of arms and ammunition under the rigid control and supervision of the commanding officers of the posts and districts." For the record — Sherman sent Grant a copy — he delivered an implicit ultimatum to the administration in Washington: "If the Indian agents may without limit supply the Indians with arms, I would not expose our troops and trains to them at all, but would withdraw our soldiers, who already have a herculean task on their hands."

Grant backed Sherman, calling his suspension of the arms sales "just right." Grant told War Secretary Stanton, "I will instruct him to enforce his order until it is countermanded by the President or yourself." Grant supported Sherman's ultimatum as well. "We have treaties with all tribes of Indians from time to time. If the rule is to be followed that all tribes with which we have treaties and pay annuities can procure such articles" — arms and ammunition — "without stint or limit, it will not be long before the matter becomes perfectly understood by the Indians, and they avail themselves of it to equip perfectly for war. They will get the arms either by making treaties themselves or through tribes who have such treaties."

Grant expected the Indian Bureau and the Interior Department to object, but he didn't care. In fact, he raised the stakes by calling for a military takeover of the Indian Bureau. Blaming the existing arrangement for the Fetterman massacre and subsequent attacks by Red Cloud's warriors, Grant told Stanton, "They show the urgent necessity for an immediate transfer of the Indian Bureau to the War Department, and the abolition of the civil Indian agents and licensed traders. If the present practice is to be continued, I do not see that any course is left open to us but to withdraw our troops to the settlements and call upon Congress to provide means and troops to carry on formidable hostilities against the Indians until all the Indians or all the whites on the Great Plains and between the settlements on the Missouri and the Pacific slope are exterminated."

■ ■ ■

Grant and Sherman had distinguished reputations as soldiers, and when they spoke on military matters, people listened. But the Indian Bureau had patrons in Washington, chiefly members of Congress whose reelection campaigns counted on the support of people like those awarded Indian agencies and trading rights. Nor was the Interior Department willing to give up the Indian Bureau without a fight.

Lewis Bogy headed the Indian Bureau, and as soon as he heard what Sherman and Grant were demanding, he lit a backfire. The agents and traders weren't the problem, Bogy said; the soldiers were. "One of the greatest difficulties, and indeed I think the greatest difficulty, I encounter in administering the affairs of this bureau is the constant interference on the part of the military with all Indian affairs," he asserted. "The commanders of the different forts throughout the whole Indian country claim and exercise the right of controlling the Indian agents and of issuing orders in relation to the trade with the Indians by the licensed traders. From observation both in this bureau and as a citizen of the West" — Bogy was from Missouri — "I am and have been for years satisfied that this was the cause of most of our

Indian wars." Besides being counterproductive, Bogy said, the army's overreach was illegal. The Indian Bureau had been created by Congress and given the mandate its agents were attempting to carry out in the West. "The military should be made to understand that they are in that country merely as a police to aid the agent in the discharge of his duties and not to control him. The law regulates the trade with Indians, and no military commander should be allowed to interfere."

Bogy dismissed as unfounded and uninformed Sherman's objection to arms sales. "The Indian has to depend upon the chase for his subsistence and that of his wife and children," he said. "Arms and ammunition are of absolute necessity. He will, therefore, if possible and no matter at what cost, procure them." Allegations by army officers that the Indians were stockpiling weapons for war was ludicrous. Their nomadic lifestyle made this impossible, Bogy said. "No Indian will buy two guns. One, he will and ought to have. Nor will he lay up any large quantity of powder, as he has no means of keeping it. He needs one gun and a little powder, and this is his only means of subsistence."

Bogy also rejected Sherman's plan for the removal of Indians from the railway corridor between the Platte and the Arkansas. He argued artfully, claiming to support Sherman's end goal. "That the belt of country lying between the Platte River on the north and the Arkansas River on the south should be opened to the whites by the removal of the Indians now occupying it is a necessity which cannot be doubted," Bogy affirmed. "The fact that railroads are now being built through this country, and that it is the highway for the thousands of emigrants going to our western territories, imposes on the government the necessity of affording to them complete protection. To effect this object the removal of the Indians from this strip of country is therefore an absolute necessity. On this subject, I agree with the view expressed by General Sherman."

Bogy then added, "But I entirely dissent from the position he assumes in his report as to the mode of accomplishing this object." Sherman might try to dictate to the Indians, but they would never obey. At least, a substantial number would not obey, but instead would resist. "And will not this resistance lead to trouble and war with them, in which the lives of thousands of persons will be sacrificed, the railroads now already being far advanced in the country destroyed, the profitable trade of the prairies even with these very Indians themselves annihilated, and the government involved in millions of dollars of expense?" asked Bogy rhetorically.

Bogy advised working with the Indians

rather than dictating to them. "Cannot a policy be adopted which will effect the same object without involving the disasters above enumerated?" He thought it could. "There is one fact which cannot be denied by anyone acquainted with Indians; it is that their chiefs are all superior men — they are always their best men. No one becomes a chief until he has proven his valor in war and wisdom in council. These chiefs control their different tribes with the exception of a few bad men found among them, as among us. With proper means, I am satisfied that these chiefs can all be made to see and fully understand their position and the necessity imposed upon the government of securing this belt of country to the whites."

Bogy supposed tact and material goods might persuade the Indians to agree to a treaty setting the boundaries where Sherman desired. In any event, the American government must not overturn nearly a century of policy toward the Indians. "It is too late to abandon the system of treaties with Indians," Bogy said. Inducements worked better than threats with Indians, as with other people. "Annuities ought to be increased and stock — cattle, sheep and horses — given to them to raise. It is of little consequence to this government if a few hundred thousand dollars more or less per annum be expended, provided these people are kept quiet, and at the same time means of subsistence be furnished to them to support themselves for the few years which in all probability they will yet exist."

Bogy couldn't provide closer cost estimates, but he knew how to get them. "My idea is to appoint separate commissions of first rate men to visit each state and territory having an Indian population, with instructions to these commissioners to master the Indian subject in the state or territory they are sent to — that is, ascertain the number of Indians, their status socially, and in every other way find out if they can be aggregated on one or two reservations; select the section of country where this reservation should be; how much should be paid annually to them in the way of annuity until they can support themselves; what kind of goods should be furnished, if any; how much stock of cattle and sheep; and indeed to master the subject fully and thoroughly, and report the result of their labors, say next fall, for final action." The recommendations of the commissioners should form the basis of a comprehensive and definitive settlement with all the Indians.

Bogy suggested launching the commission program with the tribes Sherman sought to remove from the path of the railroads. A council should be called, inviting the tribal leaders to meet with appointed commissioners. Time was of the essence. "This council should be held this spring, as it is of absolute necessity if we desire to withdraw these Indians from this line of road," Bogy said. He was writing for the benefit of Orville Browning, his boss as secretary of the interior, but also for the members of Congress who would have to be persuaded to fund the commission. "Permit me therefore to request you to lay this communication before the two houses of Congress at as early a day as possible, so as to obtain action during this session," he concluded.

14

Bogy's commission plan had an ally within the camp of the War Department — in fact, in the office of the commanding general. Ely Parker was a senior aide to Grant, having been at the general's right hand since the Civil War. He was also a Seneca Indian, born to Seneca parents on the Seneca reservation in western New York State. His father, a Christian convert and Baptist minister, insisted that his children be educated in Christian schools, where Ely excelled. The young man read law for three years, only to be frustrated by a change in the code of the New York bar, preventing Indians from becoming lawyers. He turned to engineering and studied at Rensselaer Polytechnic Institute before joining a team updating the Erie Canal. His engineering proficiency won him a job with the federal government, which sent him to Galena, Illinois, where he met and befriended a washed-out army officer named Ulysses Grant.

The Civil War relaunched Grant's career but initially stymied Parker's. Hearing of Lincoln's call for volunteers, Parker judged that the government needed good engineers more than ever, and he went to Washington to offer his services. His hopes rose when he secured an interview with William Seward, the secretary of state and a fellow New Yorker. But they fell when Seward met him and learned he was an Indian. "Mr. Seward in a short time said to me that the struggle in which I wished to insist was an affair between white men, and one in which the Indian was not called to act," Parker recalled. " 'The fight must be settled by white men alone,' he said."

Seward explained that bringing Indians into the war would benefit the South, where more Indians lived. This was small comfort to Parker, who saw military service as a demonstration of his — and his people's — loyalty to the Union.

Before long, Seward's objections were overrun by the war. The Confederacy enlisted Indian troops, and the Union War Department decided to counter. It recruited Indian troops, and it sent a messenger to Parker explaining that his services would be appreciated after all. Parker was commissioned a captain and sent to Vicksburg, where Grant was keeping engineers busy around the clock.

Yet Grant saw more than an engineer in

Parker. He knew of Parker's training in law, which had included drafting documents of various sorts, and he made Parker his personal secretary. Parker followed Grant throughout the war, drafting letters, orders and even the final surrender agreement between Grant and Robert E. Lee. Parker afterward recollected a comment by Lee at Appomattox. The Confederate general, recognizing Parker as an Indian, extended his hand to shake Parker's. "I am glad to see one real American here," Lee said. Parker grasped Lee's hand, looked him in the eye and answered, "We are all Americans."

Parker stuck with Grant after the war, becoming a confidant of the most powerful military officer in the land. And as a battle loomed with the Interior Department, Grant tasked Colonel Parker, as he now was, with devising his own solution to the Indian problem in the West. Grant reckoned, and Parker realized, that Parker's heritage would give his solution weight Interior would have difficulty matching.

Parker worked quickly. "In compliance with your request," he wrote to Grant a short while later, "I have the honor to submit the following proposed plan for the establishment of a permanent and perpetual peace and for settling all matters of differences between the United States and the various Indian tribes." Parker's plan had four parts. First, the Indian

Bureau must be moved from the Interior Department to the War Department. The civilian agents of the Indian Bureau were utterly unqualified to deal with the violations of Indian treaty rights by aggressive whites. "As the hardy pioneer and adventurous miner advanced into the inhospitable regions occupied by the Indians in search of the precious metals, they found no rights possessed by the Indians that they were bound to respect," Parker wrote. "The faith of treaties solemnly entered into was totally disregarded and Indian territory wantonly violated. If any tribe remonstrated against the violation of their natural and treaty rights, members of the tribe were inhumanly shot down and the whole treated as mere dogs. Retaliation generally followed and bloody Indian wars have been the consequence, costing many lives and much treasure." The Indian agents did nothing, because they could do nothing. "In all troubles arising in this manner, the civil agents have been totally powerless to avert the consequences." A transfer of the Indian Bureau to the War Department, and the replacing of civilian agents by military officers, would change things dramatically, Parker said. "If, in the beginning, the military had had the supervision of the Indians, their rights would not have been improperly molested, or if disturbed in their quietude by any lawless whites, a prompt and summary check to any further aggressions could have been given."

Second, Congress should grant territorial government to the Indians. Since the days of Thomas Jefferson, the government had acknowledged the wisdom of separating whites and Indians, Parker said. The removal policy of Andrew Jackson had codified this approach. "Lands were set apart for tribes removing into the western wilds, and the faith of a great nation pledged that the homes selected by the Indians should be and remain their homes forever unmolested by the hand of the grasping and avaricious white man, and in some cases the government promised that the Indian homes and lands should never be incorporated within the limits of any new state that might be organized." Parker didn't presume to question the sincerity of the pledges at the time they were given, or the avowal that they were intended to preserve the Indian tribes from extinction. But the pledges had not been kept, and they were currently in tatters. "Today, by reason of the immense augmentation of the American population and the extension of their settlements throughout the entire West, covering both slopes of the Rocky Mountains, the Indian races are more seriously threatened with a speedy extermination than ever before in the history of the country." Parker felt obliged to add, "And however much such a deplorable result might be wished for by some, it seems to me that the honor of a Christian nation and every sentiment of humanity dictate that no pains should be spared to avert such an appalling calamity befalling a portion of the human race."

Parker would have preferred a single Indian territory for all the tribes. But he recognized that this might be difficult to achieve, given the many reservations that already existed, and so he settled for the consolidation of the existing reservations, and any future ones, under a single administrative umbrella. "By the concentration of tribes, although in several and separate districts, government can more readily control them and more economically press and carry out plans for their improvement and civilization, and a better field be offered for philanthropic aid and Christian instruction," he said. Above all, such autonomy as given the tribes must be secure and enduring. "The boundaries of the Indian territory or territories should be well defined by metes and bounds and should remain inviolate from settlement by any except Indians and government employees."

Third, Congress should establish an inspection board to ensure that the Indians received the payments due them. Late or short payments had vexed relations with the Indians for decades; the inspectors would be charged with maintaining schedules and auditing accounts. "The results of their labors might be very important and beneficial not only in supervising and promptly checking the delinquencies of incompetent and dishonest agents, but it would be a most convincing proof to the Indians' mind that the government was disposed to deal honestly and fairly by them," Parker said.

Fourth, Congress should create a permanent Indian commission comprising distinguished whites and some of the best-educated Indians. The commission's task would be to visit all the tribes within the United States, perhaps over a period of several years, and hear the Indians' complaints. The commissioners should also articulate the government's policies clearly and forthrightly, and teach the Indians the inevitable facts of modern life. "They shall hold talks with them setting forth the great benefits that would result to them from a permanent peace with the whites, from their abandonment of their nomadic mode of life, and adopting agricultural and pastoral pursuits, and the habits and modes of civilized communities," Parker explained. "It would be wise to convince the Indians of the great power and number of the whites, that they cover the whole land to the north, south, east and west of them. I believe they could easily understand that although this country was once wholly inhabited by Indians, the tribes, and many of them once powerful, who occupied the countries now constituting the states east of the Mississippi, have one by one been exterminated in their abortive attempts to stem the western march of civilization. They could probably be made to comprehend that the waves of population and civilization are upon every side of them, that it is too strong for them to resist, and that unless they fall in with the current of destiny as it rolls and surges around them, they must succumb and be annihilated by its overwhelming force."

Whites, notably white military officers, had long been telling the Indians this; for the message to come from disinterested whites, and especially Indians, would have greater persuasive effect. The presence of the Indians on the commission would reinforce the assertion that the government was not bent on killing all the Indians. "The commission shall assure the tribes that the white man does not want the Indian exterminated from the face of the earth, but will live with him as a good neighbor, in peace and quiet."

Parker anticipated objections that his plan would be too expensive. "I cannot so regard it," he rejoined. "On the contrary, I believe it to be more economical than any other plan that could be suggested. A whole army of Indian agents, traders, contractors, jobbers and hangers-on would be dispensed with." As a general rule, the costs of peace were almost always less than the costs of war, and so they would be here. "The expense of this entire plan for establishing peace, saving lives, making every route of travel across the continent entirely safe, civilizing and perpetuating the Indian race, and developing immense tracts of country now held by hostile bands of Indians, would be but a mere tithe to the amount now annually paid by the government for these purposes."

15

Congress deferred deciding the fate of the Indian Bureau and the Indian agents; amid a bruising contest with President Andrew Johnson over control of Reconstruction in the South, the most the lawmakers could do was authorize a version of the recommendation common to Bogy's and Parker's proposals: the establishment of a commission to treat with the Indians.

Sherman was a member of the commission, as were two other generals. The four civilian commissioners included Nathaniel Taylor, successor to Bogy as head of the Indian Bureau, and John Henderson, the chairman of the Senate's Committee on Indian Affairs. The group arranged to convene in St. Louis in August 1867, and from there proceed to the frontier and meet with any chiefs willing to talk to them. Gifts were promised to the bands of the chiefs who participated.

The commissioners would also speak with the army officers assigned to deal with the

Indians. Red Cloud's campaign against the Powder River forts had become a regular war; the winter pause after the destruction of Fetterman's column was followed by a summer of assaults on the forts, on pack trains supplying them, and on the soldiers sent out to defend the trains. No engagements ended as decisively as the Fetterman ambush, but the Bozeman road became unusable and whites in a large region around it feared for their lives and property.

Winfield Hancock, in command of the Department of the Missouri, had first responsibility for taking on Red Cloud. Hancock had served in the West before the Civil War, but he won his reputation at Gettysburg, where he commanded the corps that turned back the Confederate charge by George Pickett's division on the last day, securing the Union victory. Hancock performed with conspicuous gallantry, was dangerously wounded, and emerged from the battle a popular hero. He carried his renown to the frontier after the war, and he judged the conflict there decidedly inferior to the great war just ended. He chafed at having to wait for Indian attacks to occur before he could respond; he wanted to take the fight to Red Cloud. He believed his men's lives — and his reputation — were being sacrificed in a contest he wasn't being allowed to win.

Sherman respected Hancock as a soldier,

and he thought his opinion should be heard by the commission. Sherman and Commissioner Samuel Tappan traveled to Fort Leavenworth, Kansas, to speak with him.

"State to this commission your rank and territorial command," Sherman instructed Hancock.

"I am a major-general in the army and commander of the Department of the Missouri, consisting of the states of Missouri and Kansas, the territories of Colorado and New Mexico, and the country known as the Indian Territory south of the Arkansas."

"What tribes of Indians, in general, occupy that district?"

"The Comanches, the most powerful tribe; Kiowas; Cheyennes; Arapahoes; Apaches of the Plains; Apaches of New Mexico; the Utes of Colorado and New Mexico; and the Navahos of New Mexico. And remnants of other tribes not hostile and of but little importance. They are to a great extent on reservations. There are a great many half-civilized Indians in the Indian Territory such as the Cherokees, Choctaws, Chickasaws, Creeks, Seminoles, and along the border."

"Are any of these tribes hostile?" asked Sherman.

"All the Indians of the Plains I consider hostile," said Hancock. "I do not know that the Comanches are actually so, although three of them have been killed in my com-

150

mand while committing depredations. Some bands of the Comanches have captives for whom they demand a ransom which we have refused to give. We have demanded them unconditionally. I have no doubt but that the families of those who are fighting are protected by the Comanches because I do not believe that the Kiowas who are with the Comanches a great deal would dare to go to war unless they had the support of the Comanches behind them. In this war the Kiowas, although hostile, have no immediate grievance. At least they have represented none."

"Have these Indians, as far as your memory goes, been more or less hostile?" asked Sherman.

"I have been stationed on the western frontier about twenty-three years and in the Indian Territory about three. I was stationed with General Harney" — William Harney, a member of the peace commission — "at the most western post at that time. I have seen no time when it was considered absolutely safe for people to cross the Plains. Everybody had to go armed and prepared to fight. It is not always the case that we had to fight every Indian, but we had always to be very guarded."

"Are the Indians more hostile this year than formerly?"

"Yes, sir," said Hancock. "I have never

known any period when the war was so general and conducted with so much spirit and malignity."

"Can you give your opinion of what caused this state of things?" asked Sherman.

Hancock had prepared a statement, which he read to the commission. "I consider the origin of the present war with the Indians of the Plains primarily to be owing to the irresistible pressure of civilization against barbarism, as represented by these Indians; by the crowding in toward the center, from the north, south, east, and west of the whites with their improvements which interfere with the habits of the Indian, thus circumscribing the area of their hunting grounds and reducing the quantity of game upon which they depend in the main for subsistence, clothing, and shelter; and in the reduction in the quantity of furs which they are enabled to produce, owing to this cause, materially lessening their means of purchasing supplies of clothing, luxury, etc., which have become necessities since their contact with the whites; and this without adequate provision having been made in season by the Government to meet these conditions."

Hancock elaborated on the government's failures. "To effect an approach to civilization, it is necessary that the Indians should have homes which they could consider securely theirs and their descendants forever.

The policy of the Government hitherto has been to remove them from place to place, from east to west, from west to east, from north to south, from south to north as they might interfere with the advance of the white settlements, until they have been crowded to the center, made uneasy and unhappy, fearing other demands, fearful of starvation in the future, hearing tales of similar encroachments and like troubles from all of the Indians with whom they are thus forced into contact, until they have come to consider the conflict with the whites as irrepressible."

Many of the Indian leaders had learned to view their loss of land as inevitable, and had consented to treaties. "Yet they have not always been able to control their young men," Hancock said. The young men, besides resenting the encroachment of the whites, wanted to win their reputation as warriors. "They have lately concluded to resist en masse. They have long since and repeatedly warned us of their intentions, without referring them to any special grievance."

Not that they didn't *assert* grievances, Hancock said. "They have frequently complained of not having received their dues from the government, and of their having been cheated by agents in the distribution of goods." Hancock didn't doubt that the grievances were real.

But these didn't get to the heart of the matter, which was the Indians' determination to throw back the white advance. "They have announced their intention to cut off the wagon roads and stop the building of railroads and telegraph lines, to put an end to further encroachments of the whites, and to preserve the hunting grounds left to them as their own in the future," Hancock said. "They have found at last that in union is their only hope of success. And in consequence, now for the first time there is a general war from the extreme north to the extreme south covering that portion of the Great Plains traversed by these roaming Indians."

The Indians' aim left the government no choice. "In this condition of things, until they are subdued and made to feel that they cannot resist the progress of the whites, and their military power is broken, we may expect no permanent peace," Hancock said. The peace commission was wasting its time, he implied. Its establishment was the work of "the philanthropic element of the country which always believes that the Indians are the aggrieved party, forgetting that we are all complacently living on soil wrested from them, as they only acceded from fear of the whites, and tempted by money considerations held out to the tribes through their chiefs to abandon their lands from time to time." The do-gooders looked to eleventh-hour treaties, instead of to the force of American arms. "Thus we are never prepared for war. The Indians at this season are always so prepared." The Indians understood the American mind better than many Americans did. "Whenever Indian hostilities are upon us, and before we can have time to strike a formidable blow, the influence of the government to the ends of peace are brought to bear, and before the Indians are subdued, we demand a parley. We ask them to give us a peace on such conditions as we may have to offer them, tendering them goods, presents, and promises in exchange. Such a peace must be temporary, and it would be ignoring past experience to expect that it could now be otherwise."

Hancock made a prediction of the Indians' strategy toward the commission. "The commission has announced that it will meet the southern Indians in the middle of October," he observed. "We have occasional snows on the prairie at that time, and it is then winter or nearly so, and it is time to look about for peace and quiet until the grass springs up again. An arduous campaign has been gone through, and rest and security for their families are acceptable." Cholera had been reported in the Indian camps, adding to their desire for a respite. "They will probably say, 'If the white man will return us our lodges destroyed, give us abundance of clothing, sugar and coffee, allow us to keep the horses, mules, and other property we have captured, we will make peace."

Yet such a peace could never last; the struggle would resume. "The Indians consider it a war of life and death, which must be renewed at a favorable moment," Hancock said. Unless Americans were willing to abandon the railroad and the other roads, withdraw to the East, and leave the plains, the war must be fought to the finish. "To dictate terms to an enemy it is necessary to establish power. We have often promised to punish them if they made war or committed depredations. We have met them frequently, and they do not yet feel that they have been subjected. If a peace promising permanence can be made now, I favor it. It is better to make peace than to continue a war feebly conducted. The innocent suffer, the distant territories languish, and no permanent result is obtained. The war must be vigorous, or arrangements had better be made for its discontinuance."

Any half-hearted or premature peace would be unconscionable. "A peace made now should be lasting, for a promise or belief to that end will only give encouragement to the whites to increase their numbers on the plains, on the railroads and wagon roads, and to advance their settlements," Hancock said. "The next war will be more bloody and inviting to the Indians than the present, from the new want of preparation and from the ad-

156

ditional number of unprotected subjects for the scalping knife and the greater quantity of booty offered."

Hancock had come under criticism for burning an abandoned village of Cheyennes and Lakotas west of Fort Larned, a measure that had been followed by an escalation of fighting on the southern plains. Hancock subsequently explained his actions to Sherman; Sherman now wanted him to inform the commission, for its records.

"I had invited, previously, the agents of the Cheyennes and Kiowas to accompany me to that camp in order that they and the Indians might see that we were acting in harmony and had no disposition to do anything except what was right and that it might be apparent to the agents," Hancock said. "They accompanied me. After I got to the village I found that the Indians by one process of deceit and another had all left the village with the exception of a rearguard of braves and some of the prominent chiefs. They having promised to meet me in council that evening, I sent an interpreter into their camp who brought back two other chiefs who told me that the women and children, being frightened, had gone away. I told them I did not like the appearance of it. They did not tell me that the Sioux had all gone or that the warriors had all gone."

"What camp was this?" asked Sherman.

"The camp of a village on Pawnee Fork, composed of Cheyennes — the dog soldiers or *chirutus* of that tribe — and Pawnee Killer's and other bands of Sioux." The Dog Soldiers were the bravest and most determined of the Cheyennes. Hancock continued, "Brier Bee or Roundtree finally told me if I would give them some horses they would bring their families back by morning. I told them I would do so and that I would not molest their camp, but keep my soldiers from it. They told me those in camp would remain in it during the night. I sent our interpreter into their camp with orders to report to me in person if they went away. About two hours afterwards, he came to me at a gallop and told me that the Indians had all gone, or were then going, and that on leaving they had threatened his life. The chiefs did not go at first, but followed. The horses I loaned the Indians were returned. The interpreter told me the Indians over there had not gone outside of camp. I was very sorry for that condition of things. I then directed General Custer to surround the camp to ascertain the facts. He reported in a few hours that the camp was deserted. I directed him in the night to follow the trail and to ascertain their movements. He went 140 miles while the Indians went about 45 miles to the same point. He found these Indians — six or eight hundred of them — stripped to the buff.

They had crossed Smoky Hill" — the Smoky Hill River — "the day after I arrived at the camp. They burned the lookout station, killed the drivers there, and, after disemboweling them, burned them. They attacked other stations. In the meantime I had told General Custer that I would stay by the village and guard it until it was ascertained what the Indians did. On the 18th I got a letter from Custer relating the facts I mentioned, and that the outrages were committed by the Indians who had left their camp before I approached it. I had then to punish the Indians in some way or go home. I concluded after such outrages I might as well burn their village, so I fired it. I was very sorry that the necessity existed for so doing."

16

Henry Morton Stanley had a front-row seat for the peace commission's activities. Stanley would become the most celebrated news correspondent in the English-reading world, but in 1867 the young Welshman was cutting his journalistic teeth as a reporter for the *Missouri Democrat* of St. Louis. Events would reveal Stanley — the name he had adopted after emigrating to America — to be a resourceful, determined fellow; he started early with Sherman, persuading the general not to hold his wartime service in the Confederate army against him. Stanley had fought at Shiloh, where, with luck, he might have shot Sherman. But Stanley subsequently changed his mind and his uniform, abandoning the Confederate cause for the Union. In any case, Sherman let Stanley tag along with the commission.

"The Indians and their white captives arrived here last night," Stanley wrote from North Platte, a hamlet at the forks of the

Platte, where the first council meeting took place. The captives, taken in raids, were a sign of the Indians' good faith, but also a bargaining chip. "There were two hundred warriors, fresh from bloody exploits, and with their hands dyed with the blood of the unfortunates at Plum Creek." Stanley was stretching here; the Plum Creek attack, in which a dozen westbound emigrants were killed, had taken place three years earlier. "Foremost among the whites, who stood between the village and the advancing Indians, were Sherman, the hero of many battles, Alfred H. Terry, of Fort Fisher fame" — Terry had led Union forces to victory at Fort Fisher, North Carolina — "and Senator Henderson, ready to greet the red men, and give them welcome by a shake of the hand. In the rear of these were ladies and gentlemen, members of the press, and others, who crowded up and gazed curiously at the meeting." The presence of so many civilians, including women, allayed concern among the Indians that they were being drawn into a trap.

"At noon the council was convened," Stanley continued. "Two large wigwams converted into one were to hold the hostile chiefs of Brules, Ogallallas and Cheyennes, and the Peace Commissioners. On one side sat Spotted Tail, Man Afraid of His Horses, Man That Walks Under the Ground, Pawnee Killer,

Standing Elk, Swift Bear, Black Bear, Turkey Foot, Cut Nose, Whistler, Big Mouth, Cold Face, Crazy Lodge and several other minor chiefs. Facing them were Generals Sherman, Harney, Terry and Sanborn, Commissioner Taylor, Colonels Tappan, Dodge and Wolcott, Senator Henderson and several representatives of the press."

The chiefs gathered into small circles and handed around peace pipes. Then Big Mouth and another chief passed their pipes to the commissioners — "who inhaled with befitting gravity three distinct whiffs from each," Stanley wrote. The interpreter announced that the chiefs were ready to speak.

Standing Bear went first. "My friends and all you chiefs that are here today: whatever you say shall be made known all over the country," he said. "It makes my heart glad to see you here today. We have a mode of making peace different from the whites. When we make peace we pray to the Great Spirit. We have no witness, but keep our treaties faithfully, by praying to the Great Spirit."

Nathaniel Taylor answered for the commissioners. "My friends: Your Great Grandfather, whose heart is right, has heard of the troubles of his red children on the plains, and he has sent us to you to see what is the matter. He has heard that there is war, and that blood has been shed. He is opposed to war, and loves peace, and his heart is sad. He has sent all these great white chiefs to ascertain what is wrong. You see, here is the great war chief of old times." Taylor motioned to General Harney. "There is the great warrior" — Sherman — "who leads all the white soldiers on the plains, and here are other great chiefs. Here is a great peace chief" — Senator Henderson — "who helps make laws at the great council chamber at Washington."

Taylor continued, "If the Great Father did not love you, he would not have sent us to you. We are sent out here to inquire and find out what has been the trouble. We want to hear from your own lips your grievances and complaints. My friends, speak fully, speak freely, and speak the whole truth. If you have been wronged, we wish to have you righted, and if you have done wrong, you will make it right. All that you say, we will have written in a book and will not forget it. We will think it all over, and will then speak our minds to you. War is bad, peace is good. We must choose the good and not the bad. Therefore we are to bury the tomahawk and live in peace like brothers of one family." Taylor paused, then concluded, "I await what you have to say."

The chiefs responded in turn. Pawnee Killer, of the Cheyennes, sounded skeptical. "Who is our Great Father?" he said. "What is he? Is it true that he sent you here to settle our troubles? The cause of our troubles is the

163

Powder River road running north, and the Smoky Hill road on the south. In that little space of country between the Smoky Hill and the Platte River there is game. That is what we have to live upon. By stopping these roads, I know you can get peace." Pawnee Killer didn't mind the railroad so much as the others. "If the Great Father stops the Powder River road, I know that your people can travel this road" — the Union Pacific — "without being molested."

Turkey Foot, of the Cheyennes, seconded this view. "My friends: You that are here, are you chiefs? Is it true that the Great Father sent you here? Will the white people that travel this road" — the Union Pacific — "and the Arkansas road listen to what you say? If so, then listen to me. Tell the Great Father to stop these roads — the one on the Smoky Hill and the Powder River road."

Big Mouth, of the Brulé Lakotas, had a reputation as an orator. "My friends," he said, addressing the commissioners, "and you, my people" — the other chiefs — "open wide your ears and listen. Towards the north there are a great many Ogallalas, south there are Ogallalas, and I with my people stand between. But I am strong and bold. I wish to succeed in establishing peace between my people and the pale-faces." Big Mouth knew William Harney. "This day, you, General Harney, tell me: Did the Great Father send you here? Do you tell the truth? You are a great chief. I am a big chief, also. I hope that the Great Father sent you to us."

Big Mouth turned to the chiefs. "All you that are sitting here in the council, I want to advise you. Be quiet. Behave yourselves. Leave the whites alone. Who and what are you? The whites are numerous as the years. You are few and weak. What do you amount to? If the whites kill one of your number, you weep and feel sorry. But if you kill one of the whites, who is it that weeps for them? I am saying this for your good."

Big Mouth turned back to the commissioners. "Now, you whites, I speak to you," he said. "*Stop* that Powder River road. That is the cause of our troubles. The great evil grows daily. It is just like setting fire to prairie grass. The evil is spreading among all the nations. Red Cloud and Man Afraid of His Horses had a talk with General Sanborn last spring at Laramie. Did you tell the Great Father what we said? Here are the Sioux on one side and the Cheyennes on the other side. I stand between two fires, and you, after talking and talking, and making treaties, and after we have listened to you, go and make the great evil larger. You set the prairie on fire. My Great Father told me through men like you that he would give twenty years' annuities for these two roads — the Powder River road and the Smoky Hill road. Where are those annuities? I stand between the pale-faces and the Indians. My people have come from afar. Give them presents and make their hearts glad."

The speeches filled hours, and the council adjourned until the following day, when Sherman answered the chiefs. "Friends, we have heard your words, and have thought of them all night," he said. "You say that the Smoky Hill and Powder River roads are the principal causes of your troubles. The government supposed that the Cheyennes and Arapahoes agreed to give up that road four years ago, and it has been traveled by the whites ever since. Military posts and mail stations were built along it two years ago, and they were not then considered to be a cause for war. The government thought that to build an iron road would be nothing more to you. To us it was more convenient and rapid, and it was necessary to our people in Colorado and New Mexico. And the road will be built."

Sherman let the determination he expressed sink in. He proceeded: "We are to meet the Cheyennes next month, in October, on the Arkansas, and if we find that the road is damaging to them, we will make them compensation. But the roads will be built, and you must not interfere with them. The Powder River road was built to furnish our men with provisions. No white settlements have been made along the road, nor does travel destroy the buffalo, nor the elk, nor the antelope. The Indians are permitted to hunt the buffalo as usual. The Great Father thought that you consented to give up that road at Laramie last spring; but it seems that some of the Indians were not there, and have gone to war. While the Indians continue to make war upon the road, it will not be given up. But if, on examination at Laramie in November, we find that the road hurts you, we will give it up or pay for it. If you have any claims, present them to us at Laramie."

Others besides Big Mouth had asked for presents; their list included ammunition to hunt the buffalo. Sherman allowed that they would receive some powder and lead. "But we will not give you much till we come to a satisfactory agreement," he said. "Very recently you killed white people, innocent immigrants; some of you attacked a train and killed people who were carrying provisions to whites and Indians." The whites could tell good Indians from bad, Sherman said. "To Spotted Tail, Standing Elk, Two Strike, Swift Bear and their bands, we are willing to give them almost anything they want, because they have remained at peace all spring and summer. But the rest of you must work with your bows and arrows" — hunting — "till you satisfy us you will not kill our people."

Sherman had additional advice. "We know

well that the red and white men were not brought up alike," he said. "You depend upon game for a living, and you get hats and clothes from the whites. All that you see white men wear, they have to work for. But you see they have plenty to eat, that they have fine houses and fine clothes. You can have the same, and we believe the time has come when you should begin to own these things, and we will give you assistance. You can own herds of cattle and horses like the Cherokees and Choctaws. You can have cornfields like the Poncas, Yanktons and Pottawatomies. You see for yourself that the white men are collecting in all directions, in spite of all you can do. The white men are taking all the good land. If you don't choose your homes now, it will be too late next year. This railroad up the Platte and the Smoky Hill railroad will be built, and if you are damaged we must pay you in full, and if your young men will interfere, the Great Father, who, out of love for you, withheld his soldiers, will let loose his young men, and you will be swept away.

"We therefore propose to let the whole Sioux nation select their country up the Missouri River, embracing the White Earth and Cheyenne Rivers, to have their lands, like the white people, forever. And we propose to keep all white men away except such agents and traders as you may choose. We want you to cultivate your land, build houses, and raise cattle. We propose to help you there as long as you need help. We will also teach your children to read and write like the whites. The Cheyennes and all the southern Indians shall have similar homes in the country on the Arkansas, and if the Sioux Indians prefer to go down there, they can enjoy the same privilege."

Sherman acknowledged that he and the commissioners were asking more of the Indians than had been previously asked. "A great many agreements have been made by people gone before us," he said. "We propose to stand by them, but I am afraid they didn't make allowances for the rapid growth of the white race. You can see for yourselves that travel across the country has increased so much that the slow ox wagon will not answer the white man. We build iron roads, and you cannot stop the locomotive any more than you can stop the sun or the moon. You must submit, and do the best you can, and if any of you want to see the wealth and power of the whites, you can do so, and we will pay your expenses."

None knew the scale of modern warfare better than Sherman. "Our people east hardly think of what you call war here," he said. "But if they make up their minds to fight you, they will come out as thick as a herd of buffalo. And if you continue fighting, you will all be killed."

Sherman repeated his advice: "Choose your homes and live like white men, and we will help you all you want." He added, for comparison, "We are doing more for you than we do for white men coming over the sea." Returning to his main point, he said, "This commission is not only a Peace Commission, but it is a War Commission also. We will be kind to you if you keep the peace, but if you won't listen to reason, we are ordered to make war upon you in a different manner from what we have done before."

Sherman knew he was asking much of the chiefs. And so he gave them time to consider their answer. "We shall be here again in November, until which time you can hunt on the Republican River. Then you must meet us here again. Then we shall want to know whether you are willing to go up next spring to the White Earth or down on the Arkansas. We will feed you till spring, on Brady Island." He repeated that it was a big decision. "Think of these things," he said. "We want to hear your reply, but we don't propose to make the final agreement till the first of November."

Sherman's words had a sobering effect on the chiefs. "Perfect silence reigned throughout the council wigwam," Henry Stanley wrote. "The inhaling of the calumet as it passed around was plainly audible. The features of the Indians exhibited no emotion; they were grave and taciturn throughout, though it was evident that the refusal of the Peace Commissioners to accede to their wishes had displeased them."

Standing Bear, of the Poncas, articulated the displeasure. "I was here, and was friendly to the whites," he said. "I thought I brought the red men here to make peace. I told them what you told me. You have made me tell a lie. I understood there were six Peace Commissioners come here to make peace. I made these men lay down their arms, and come to the council to make peace. I told them so. They are here. After doing all this work, I thought you would take pity upon them and give them powder and ball." Standing Bear didn't like the false position the commissioners had placed him in. "My friends, take pity upon me this day. I have been friendly. Give these men some ammunition. They don't want much. We won't kill you; we want powder and ball to kill game as we go to our villages. I am an Indian, but I believe what the pale-face tells me."

Man That Walks Under the Ground acted out his displeasure. He removed his headdress of eagle feathers and hurled it to the ground. "The white man takes off his hat," he said. "I will do also, as I am going to speak. Look at me well. I am an Oglala. I was born and raised on this ground." He had come to the council because he had been promised presents. "I am poor. You are rich. When you come to our villages, we always share with you. Where is the present I am to get? What am I to do? This day I ramble around with nowhere to go. I cannot make powder nor can I make ball." Sherman's withholding of arms and ammunition was dishonest and unfair. "Those people from whom I came have been doing very wrong this summer, but we heard that you were going to make peace," Man That Walks Under the Ground said. "After a battle, when two nations meet and they shake hands, they ought to be at peace." And peace should include presents.

The most meaningful riposte, however, might have been unspoken. Henry Stanley summarized the reaction among the chiefs at Sherman's declaration that there would be no treaty at this council. "The Indian chiefs have humiliated themselves already; they have begged in an abject manner and they feel it," Stanley wrote. "Frowns are seen upon their features, and still the commissioners deliberate." One chief said nothing, but *did* something ominous. "Pawnee Killer creeps away, and disappears under the flap of the wigwam. He hurries to his tent. He comes out, his face painted a fiery red. His faithful horse stands near, the lariat is cut, and with one spring Pawnee Killer is mounted, heading directly for the bluffs of North Platte." The remaining chiefs accepted a provisional peace in exchange for the small supply of ammunition Sherman had offered. Stanley observed, "It is rather dubious whether the Cheyennes will keep the peace, as the head chief absented himself."

17

Shortly after the council adjourned, Sherman received a summons from the president to travel to Washington at once. Sherman suspected political foul play, for Andrew Johnson was on the verge of being impeached by the House of Representatives. Johnson had violated the Tenure of Office Act, a recent measure that limited a president's ability to dismiss officials of the executive branch without Senate approval. The Republicans in Congress sought to prevent the removal of Secretary of War Edwin Stanton, who was more sympathetic to their views on Reconstruction than Johnson was. The contest had already entangled Grant, as the army's commanding general, and Sherman feared it was about to entangle him.

In the event, he avoided the worst of the mess, although it took him months to do so. Meanwhile the Indian commission continued its work, with Christopher Augur substituting for Sherman. A second council was held at

Fort Larned in western Kansas. The tribes of the southern plains were well represented, and the speeches of both the Indian chiefs and the white commissioners echoed the sentiments heard at the council on the Platte. As this second council ended and the commission concluded the fact-finding phase of its work, Henry Stanley detailed the key element in the commission's success in attracting nearly all the important chiefs of the plains. "Over $150,000 worth of provisions have been distributed to the tribes," Stanley recorded. "Also two thousand suits of uniform, two thousand blankets, fifty quarter boxes tobacco, twenty bolts of Indian cloth, three bales of domestics, one bale linsey, twelve dozen squaw axes, one bale of ticking, fifty revolvers (navy size), besides an assortment of beads, butcher knives, thread and needles, brass bells, looking glasses, and sixteen silver medals."

The commissioners retired to Washington to prepare their report, which appeared at the beginning of 1868. Signed by all the commissioners, including Sherman, the report recounted how the attacks on the Bozeman road, including the Fetterman massacre, had prompted the creation of the commission, with its charge to find an end to the plains war. "Of one thing we are satisfied," the commissioners said, "that so long as the war lasts the road is entirely useless to emigrants. It is worse than that; it renders other routes insecure, and endangers territorial settlements." Fortunately, there was an alternative, which became more attractive as the railroad advanced west. "A road to Montana leaving the Pacific railroad further west and passing down the valley west of the Big Horn mountains, is preferable to the present route. The Indians present no objection to such a road, but assure us that we may travel it in peace."

The prospective agreement about the road suggested hope for other agreements. "If it be said that the savages are unreasonable, we answer that, if civilized, they might be reasonable," the commissioners declared. "At least they would not be dependent on the buffalo and the elk; they would no longer want a country exclusively for game, and the presence of the white man would become desirable. If it be said that because they are savages they should be exterminated, we answer that, aside from the inhumanity of the suggestion, it will prove exceedingly difficult, and if money considerations are permitted to weigh, it costs less to civilize than to kill."

The commissioners doubted they could win over all the Indians. "It is now rather late in the day to think of obliterating from the minds of the present generation the remembrance of wrong," they said. And wrong had indeed been done, with the current war the result. "Among civilized men war usually springs from a sense of injustice. The best possible way, then, to avoid war is to do no act of injustice. When we learn that the same rule holds good with Indians, the chief difficulty is removed. But it is said our wars with them have been almost constant. Have we been uniformly unjust? We answer unhesitatingly yes."

The commissioners didn't blame the American people for the injustice done the Indians. "The masses of our people have felt kindly toward them," they said. Rather, the blame lay with Congress. Yet the injustice resulted more from neglect than malice. "The legislation of Congress has always been conceived in the best intentions" — the commissioners felt obliged to flatter Congress, whose members were the principal audience for the report — "but it has been erroneous in fact or perverted in execution. Nobody pays any attention to Indian matters. This is a deplorable fact." Philanthropy did no better. "While our missionary societies and benevolent associations have annually collected thousands of dollars from the charitable to be sent to Asia and Africa for the purposes of civilization, scarcely a dollar is expended or a thought bestowed on the civilization of Indians at our very doors."

The commissioners lamented that whites and Indians had never learned to get along. "If they could have lived together, the Indian by this contact would soon have become civilized and war would have been impossible." What was it that prevented Indians from living with whites? "First, the antipathy of race. Second, the difference of customs and manners arising from their tribal or clannish organizations. Third, the difference in language, which in a great measure barred intercourse and a proper understanding each of the other's motives and intentions." These influences showed little sign of easing. Separation, therefore, was prerequisite to peace.

Separation — Indian removal — had been done badly in the past. "The policy was not designed to perpetuate barbarism, but such has been its effect," the commissioners said. The past could not be changed, but the future might be handled better. "One thing, then, remains to be done with honor to the nation, and that is to select a district or districts of country, as indicated by Congress, on which all the tribes east of the Rocky Mountains may be gathered." This was Ely Parker's suggestion. So too was the next: "For each district let a territorial government be established."

The territorial governor should be appointed by the federal government and paid a salary sufficient to put him beyond temptation. The army might police the territory at first, but in time this function would be assumed by the residents — that is, the Indians.

178

And those Indians should be encouraged to think of themselves as Indians and not as members of rival tribes. "The object of greatest solicitude should be to break down the prejudices of tribe among the Indians; to blot out the boundary lines which divide them into distinct nations, and fuse them into one homogeneous mass." Education in the English language would help, for it would give the Indians a common language. The Indians should be educated in the useful arts, with the goal of self-sufficiency. "Money annuities, here and elsewhere, should be abolished forever. These more than anything else have corrupted the Indian service, and brought into disgrace officials connected with it." Annuities in kind — clothing and foodstuffs — should be phased out over time.

Humanity dictated such an approach. "Aside from extermination, this is the only alternative now left us. We must take the savage as we find him, or rather as we have made him. We have spent 200 years in creating the present state of things. If we can civilize in 25 years, it will be a vast improvement on the operations of the past."

Congress must set the boundaries of the new Indian territory or territories. The commission took Sherman's advice and suggested two: one north of the railroad corridor and one south. By the commission's count, the former would become the home of some

54,000 Indians, mostly Sioux of the various bands and the northern wings of the Cheyennes and the Arapahos. The latter would comprise 86,000 Indians, including Cheyennes, Arapahos, Comanches, Apaches and the tribes living in the existing Indian Territory, much of which the new territory would subsume.

The commission's final recommendation involved supervision of the Indian Bureau. Whether the bureau should answer to the military or to civilians depended on the policy adopted by Congress toward the Indians, the commissioners said. "If we intend to have war with them, the bureau should go to the Secretary of War. If we intend to have peace, it should be in the civil department." For the moment, the commission proposed a compromise: an independent bureau or department, answerable directly to the president.

18

The peace commission's report caught Congress in the act of impeaching Andrew Johnson. And though the president escaped conviction, by a single vote, the trial and the furor that produced it left his administration dead in the water. Washington awaited his successor, who would be elected within months.

Sherman returned to the work of the commission, which hadn't ended on the filing of the report. With fellow commissioner Samuel Tappan he traveled to eastern New Mexico in the spring of 1868 to hear the case of the Navajos. Four years earlier the tribe had been forced off its ancestral lands in the high desert of western New Mexico and confined on the reservation of Bosque Redondo. By all measures the relocation had been a failure, exacting a heavy toll on Navajo lives and steep expense on the U.S. Treasury. The Navajos weren't causing trouble at the moment, but neither Sherman nor most other

American officials expected them to die quietly. They might very well break out of the reservation and resume the raiding that had prompted their removal in the first place.

"The commissioners are here now for the purpose of learning and knowing all about your condition," Sherman told a gathering of the Navajos. "And we wish to hear from you the truth, and nothing but the truth. We have read in our books and learned from our officers that for many years, whether right or wrong, the Navajos have been at war with us, and that General Carleton had removed you here for the purpose of making you agriculturists. With that view, the government of the United States gave you money and built this fort to protect you until you were able to protect yourselves. We find you have done a good deal of work here in making acequias" — irrigation ditches — "but we find you have no farms, no herds, and are now as poor as you were four years ago when the government brought you here. Before we discuss what we are to do with you, we want to know what you have done in the past and what you think about your reservation here."

Sherman waited while his words were translated from English to Spanish, and then from Spanish to Navajo.

Barboncito, the leader of the Navajos present, told the story of his people. "The bringing of us here has caused a great decrease of our numbers," he said. "Many of us have died, also a great number of our animals. Our grandfathers had no idea of living in any other country except our own, and I do not think it right for us to do so, as we were never taught to." The Navajos had never lived anywhere besides the region from which they had been taken. "When the Navajos were first created, four mountains and four rivers were pointed out to us, inside of which we should live. That was to be our country and was given to us by the first woman of the Navajo tribe. It was told to us by our forefathers, that we were never to move east of the Rio Grande or west of the San Juan River. I think that our coming here has been the cause of so much death among us and our animals."

The Navajos were inseparable from their land, Barboncito said. "Our God when we were created — the woman I spoke of — gave us this piece of land and created it specially for us and gave us the whitest of corn and the best of horses and sheep." Without their land, the Navajo would die. Barboncito pointed to the other chiefs. "I think that when the last of them is gone, the world will come to an end."

Barboncito didn't directly blame the whites' government, at least not to Sherman's face. "We have been taken good care of since we have been here," he said. The Navajos had worked hard, and done what was asked of them. "As soon as we were brought here, we started into work making acequias. I myself went to work with my party. We made all the adobes" — houses of sun-dried mud — "you see here. We have always done as we were told to. If told to bring ashes from the hearth" — to strengthen the adobe — "we would do so; carry water and herd stock. We never refused to do anything we were told to do." The problem was the land. "This ground we were brought on, it is not productive. We plant but it does not yield. All the stock we brought here have nearly all died. Because we were brought here, we have done all that we could possibly do, but found it to be labor in vain, and have therefore quit it. For that reason we have not planted or tried to do anything this year. It is true we put seed in the ground, but it would not grow two feet high."

Barboncito had asked himself what the problem was, and identified but one answer. "This ground was never intended for us. We know how to irrigate and farm, and still we cannot raise a crop here. We know how to plant all kinds of seed, also how to raise stock and take care of it." But nothing flourished. "The commissioners can see themselves that we have hardly any sheep or horses. Nearly all that we brought here have died, and that has left us so poor that we have no means wherewith to buy others. There are a great

184

many among us who were once well off; now they have nothing in their houses to sleep on except gunny sacks. True, some of us have a little stock left yet, but not near what we had some years ago in our old country."

Barboncito recalled the former times. "When we had a way of living of our own, we lived happy. We had plenty of stock. Nothing to do but look at our stock, and when we wanted meat, nothing to do but kill it." Again he pointed toward the other chiefs. "They were once rich," he said. Poverty crushed a man's spirit. "I feel sorry at the way I am fixed here. I cannot rest comfortable at night. I am ashamed to go to the commissary for my food. It looks as if somebody was waiting to give it to me."

The land they occupied was not simply barren but deadly. "It seems that whatever we do here causes death. Some work at the acequias, take sick and die. Others die with the hoe in their hands. They go to the river to their waists and suddenly disappear. Others have been struck and torn to pieces by lightning. A rattlesnake bite here kills us. In our own country a rattlesnake, before he bites, gives warning, which enables us to keep out of its way. And if bitten we readily find a cure. Here we can find no cure."

In their new home, the Navajos were beset by new enemies. "I think that all nations around here are against us," Barboncito said.

"I mean Mexicans and Indians." The Comanches were the worst. "The Comanches are against us. I know it for they came here and killed a good many of our men. In our own country we knew nothing about the Comanches."

Barboncito said he had taken hope when he learned that a commission was coming to hear them out. He had expressed his people's plight. Now he conveyed their desire. "I am strong and hearty, and before I am sick or older, I want to go and see the place where I was born," he said. So did all the Navajos. "I am speaking for the whole tribe, for their animals from the horse to the dog, also the unborn. All that you have heard now is the truth and is the opinion of the whole tribe."

He and his people looked to Sherman to relieve their suffering. "It appears to me that the General commands the whole thing as a god," he said. "I hope therefore he will do all he can for the Indian. This hope goes in at my feet and out at my mouth. I am speaking to you, General Sherman, now as if I was speaking to a spirit, and I wish you to tell me when you are going to take us to our own country."

Sherman waited for the double translation to finish. "I have listened to all you have said of your people, and believe you have told us the truth," he replied. "You are right. The world is big enough for all the people it contains, and all should live at peace with their neighbors. All people love the country where they were born and raised." He paused. "But the Navajos are very few indeed compared with all the people in the world. They are not more than seven leaves to all the leaves you have ever seen. Still we want to do to you what is right, right to you, and right to us as a people. If you will live in peace with your neighbors, we will see that your neighbors will be at peace with you. The government will stand between you and other Indians and Mexicans."

Sherman offered an alternative to the Navajos' current reservation. "For many years we have been collecting Indians on the Indian Territory south of the Arkansas, and they are now doing well and have been doing so for many years," he said. "We have heard you were not satisfied with this reservation and we have come here to invite some of your leading men to go and see the Cherokee country, and if they liked it we would give you a reservation there. There we would give you cattle to commence with and corn, it being much cheaper there than here; give you schools to educate your children in English or Spanish, and take care of you until such time as you will be able to protect yourselves."

When Barboncito appeared skeptical, Sherman added, "We do not want you to take our word for it, but send some of your wisest men to see for themselves. If you do not want that, we will discuss the other proposition, of going back to your own country, and if we agree, we will make a boundary line outside of which you must not go, except for the purpose of trading. We must have a clearly defined boundary line and know exactly where you belong. You must live at peace and must not fight with other Indians. If you go to your own country, the Utes will be the nearest Indians to you. You must not trouble the Utes, and the Utes must not trouble you. If, however, the Utes or Apaches come into your country with bows and arrows and guns, you of course can drive them out, but must not follow them beyond the boundary line. You must not permit any of your young men to go to the Ute or Apache country to steal. Neither must they steal from Mexicans. You can come to the Mexican towns to trade. Any Navajo can now settle in this territory and he will get a piece of land not occupied. But he will be subject to the laws of the country."

Sherman summarized the offer: "Our proposition now is to send some of you at the Government expense to the Indian Territory south of Kansas. Or if you want to go to your own country, you will be sent, but not to the whole of it, only a portion which must be well defined."

Barboncito needed no time to consider. "I

hope to God you will not ask me to go to any other country except my own. It might turn out another Bosque Redondo. They told us this was a good place when we came, but it is not."

Sherman insisted that Barboncito discuss things with his people. "Tomorrow at ten o'clock, I want the whole tribe to assemble at the back of the hospital, and for you then to delegate ten of your men to come forward and settle about the boundary line of your own country, which will be reduced to writing and signed by those ten men."

Barboncito knew what the answer would be. "I am very well pleased with what you have said," he told Sherman. "And if we go back to our own country, we are willing to abide by whatever orders are issued to us. We do not want to go to the right or left, but straight back to our own country."

Sherman wrote to his brother John, the senator, a short while later. "I have now been in New Mexico three weeks along with Col. Tappan, peace commissioner, for the purpose of seeing the Navajos, and making some permanent disposition of them," he said. "These Indians seem to have acquired from the old Spanish a pretty good knowledge of farming, rearing sheep, cattle and goats, and of making their own clothing by weaving blankets and cloth. They were formerly a numerous tribe, occupying the vast region between New Mexico and the Colorado of the West, and had among them a class of warriors who made an easy living by stealing of the New Mexicans and occasionally killing." But the tribe had fallen on hard times after being removed to Bosque Redondo. "We found 7200 Indians there, seemingly abject and disheartened," Sherman wrote. "They have been there four years. The first year they were maintained by the army at a cost of about $700,000 and made a small crop. The second year the cost was about $500,000, and the crop was small. Last year the crop was an utter failure, though all the officers say they labored hard and faithfully. This year they would not work because they said it was useless. The cost has been diminished to about 12 cents per head a day, which for 7000 Indians makes over $300,000, and this is as low as possible, being only a pound of corn and a pound of beef with a little salt per day."

These were the grim facts — grim for the Navajos, and grim for the Treasury. "We could see no time in the future when this could be amended," Sherman told John. "The scarcity of wood, the foul character of water, which is salty and full of alkali, and their utter despair, made it certain that we would have to move them or they would scatter and be an utter nuisance. So of course we concluded to move them. After debating all the country at our option, we have chosen a small part of their old country, which is as far out of the whites and of our probable future wants as possible, and have agreed to move them there forthwith, and have made a treaty which will save the heavy cost of their maintenance and give as much probability of their resuming their habits of industry as the case admits of."

In his memoirs, Sherman reflected on his time among the Navajos. "Mr. Tappan and I found it impossible to prevail on the Navajos to remove to the Indian Territory, and had to consent to their return to their former home, restricted to a limited reservation west of Santa Fe," he wrote. "And there they continue unto this day, rich in the possession of herds of sheep and goats, with some cattle and horses; and they have remained at peace ever since."

19

The commission met for the final time in Chicago in October 1868. Indian agents and army officers apprised the members of progress in implementing the treaties that had been signed and sealed, and in gathering additional signatures on treaties left open. General Terry moved that the Indian Bureau be transferred to the War Department; Commissioner Taylor countered with an amendment directing that the bureau become an independent department or bureau. The generals on the commission at this point outnumbered the civilians, and the amendment failed and the motion passed. But the resolution was only recommendatory; Congress would make the final decision. The concluding entry in the minutes read: "General Sherman offered a motion that the Commission, having discharged the duties imposed upon it by law, do now adjourn, sine die. The motion was carried and the Commission adjourned accordingly."

There was one loose end to tie off. The commission's recommendation to abandon the posts on the Bozeman road was put into effect in the summer of 1868, and no sooner had the white troops left than the Lakotas entered and set the forts aflame. Yet Red Cloud still refused to sign the treaty. Not until nearly the start of winter did he appear at Fort Laramie, accompanied by a hundred other chiefs, including many signers and others who appeared to be waiting on him. The post commander, Colonel William Dye, greeted the chief with interest and some trepidation. "Red Cloud affected a great deal of dignity and disinterestedness while other chiefs arose, advanced and shook hands with the officers with apparent cordiality," Dye wrote. "He remained seated and sulkily gave the ends of his fingers to the officers who advanced to shake hands with him." He acted as though signing the treaty was beneath him. "Red Cloud stated that were the Commission here, or any one in high authority, he would talk to them frankly, but there being no one present but officers of the army, the result of the council could not be satisfactory to either party."

Dye told Red Cloud that the commission had disbanded; it had finished talking to the Indians. Yet it had left a copy of the treaty for him to sign, as so many of the other chiefs had done.

Red Cloud grudgingly inquired about the terms of the treaty. These were explained. When the explanation started on the boundaries of the reservation and the farming that would take place there, he motioned for the speaker to stop. "He stated that he had learned from others all he cared to know about that, as they did not wish to leave their present home, abounding in game, to go to a new country," Dye said. "He thought it was wrong to try to induce them to abandon the chase and go to farming on the reservation."

Red Cloud apparently had another reason for not signing. "He feared being involved in the difficulties of the southern Indians," Dye wrote. "His name to the paper would mean peace, and he did not wish to make any promises to the Government which in justice to the red man he could not execute."

Red Cloud stated frankly his reason for coming to the council at all. "He had not come because he had been sent for, but because he wished to hear the news and get some powder, lead, knives, axes, etc. to fight the Crows," Dye said. Dye informed him that he would receive none of these until he signed the treaty and stopped his war with the whites. Red Cloud rejoined that the Crows were getting arms, which they were using against his people. Dye answered that the Crows were not at war with the whites. Dye, concluding that nothing more would happen that day, told Red Cloud to weigh the matter overnight. "We facilitated a favorable result by gladdening, during the day, their bellies with a feast," he added.

The next day Dye reviewed the terms of the treaty again. Red Could remained reluctant. Dye made his pitch once more. "We repeated the anxieties of the whites to be in friendly relations with the red man, and particularly with Red Cloud," he wrote. He said the whites considered Red Cloud the first among the chiefs. "Red Cloud is evidently conscious of his importance," Dye observed in an aside. Another feast was given. Red Cloud was asked to ponder the matter another night. Did he desire peace or war for his people?

He returned the following day. He reiterated his people's need for arms and ammunition. Dye repeated that these would be forthcoming only after Red Cloud signed the treaty. The chief hesitated a bit longer, then gave in. "Red Cloud with a show of reluctance and tremulousness washed his hands with the dust of the floor, then he, with the other chiefs above named, signed it, and required all the whites present to touch the pen."

Red Cloud's demeanor changed at once. "He then shook hands with more cordiality, and stated the great cause of war between the whites and Northern Indians was the

195

establishing of the Powder River Road without their consent; that he was at Laramie in 1866, when a heavy cloud (his talisman) hung in the heavens portending war; and that he left the post saying that he would not return until the new road was closed to emigration, and their country inviolate was restored to them. The great cause of trouble he says is now removed. The cloud which hung in the heavens has cleared away." Indeed, the weather had been clear and pleasant during the council. "He rejoices to again take the white man by the hand, as he and their fathers did years ago, when the country was filled with traders instead of military posts."

Red Cloud looked to a future like the past before the road had been built. "He hoped that the officers now at Laramie would treat them as they were treated in years gone by, and that the old traders would again be allowed to trade with them," Dye wrote. "He says he will live up to the treaty so long as the white man."

Yet honesty compelled Red Cloud to add, "For a time it may be difficult to control all the young braves."

Red Cloud's agreement to the Fort Laramie treaty converted him from a devil in the eyes of most Americans to something approaching a hero. And it led to an 1870 victory tour of the East Coast. Red Cloud and an entourage of some twenty younger chiefs visited Washington to speak to the new Great Father, Ulysses Grant. But first they were introduced to the new head of the Indian Bureau. Ely Parker seemed an obvious choice to Grant, being both an Indian and a military officer. Even as president, Grant hadn't succeeded in moving the bureau out of the Interior Department, but he put that department under the leadership of Jacob Cox, a Union general during the Civil War and subsequently governor of Grant's home state, Ohio. And he appointed Parker to head the Indian Bureau.

Parker greeted Red Cloud and welcomed him to Washington. Perhaps the Lakota chief was surprised to see a Seneca at the head of the white man's Indian office; perhaps he thought it appropriate. In any event, he had other things on his mind when he spoke to Parker and Cox. "Father, I am chief of the Sioux nations and six tribes, and came here to talk plainly with my Great Father," he told Cox. "You have not treated me as I ought to have been treated. When I was a young man I was poor. In a war with other nations I was in eighty-seven fights. There I received my name and was made chief of my nation. But now I am old and am for peace. I want to raise my children just the same as you do yours." The whites had made this difficult. "I have never quarreled or had any trouble with the traders living in my country, but since my Great Father sent troops and put a road through my country, blood has been shed there. It is not my fault, but your fault."

Red Cloud recited some history. "In the treaty of 1851" — the first Fort Laramie treaty, the one securing passage for emigrants across Sioux country — "I was promised fifty-five years of presents. I received part of them for only ten years; afterward they were stolen from me. I lent that road to the government for fifty-five years; if blood has been scattered over the road, it is not my fault." Whites had continued to encroach on Lakota land, building the new road through the Powder River valley and constructing forts filled with soldiers. Red Cloud and his followers had been left with no option but resistance. And they had continued to fight even after the white men called for peace. "After all these promises, I could not put any more faith in my White Father," Red Cloud said. "Therefore, when three years ago General Sherman sent for me to come in, I said, 'I will not come in until you remove the posts.' And after you removed them, I came to Fort Laramie and signed the treaty."

He had hoped to see a fresh start in dealings with the whites. But Indian agents had misbehaved, and promised payments had fallen short. "I have not received anything from you for two years," Red Cloud told

Jacob Cox. "When I leave here I want you to make our hearts glad, so that we may tell our people what you have done for us." The government must provide protection to the Indians. "It is time my father put a line around my country, so that I may know what belongs to me."

Cox replied that the recent Fort Laramie treaty superseded the earlier treaty, and so Red Cloud's complaints about that one were without current foundation. Cox acknowledged occasional malfeasance. "There have been bad white men and bad Indians. We need not count them up and see how many bad ones are on either side. The best way is to be friendly and deal honestly with each other." Regarding Red Cloud's request for a line around Lakota territory, Cox said with some puzzlement that there *was* a line around that territory; it had been specified in the recent treaty. He produced a map to show the land that had been ceded by the Indians and the land that remained to them.

Now Red Cloud expressed consternation. He said he knew nothing about giving away any land. The treaty he had signed was simply for the cessation of hostilities, in exchange for the removal of the forts and the abandonment of the Bozeman road. He had been told nothing about ceding territory.

Cox insisted on the treaty's terms, as written.

"This is the first time I have heard of such a treaty," Red Cloud said. "I have never heard of it and do not mean to follow it."

Bear in the Grass, in the Lakota delegation, seconded Red Cloud's version of events. "The Great Spirit hears me today," he said. "I tell nothing but what is true when I say these words of the treaty were not explained. It was merely said the treaty was for peace and friendship." Bear in the Grass recalled the signing ceremony. "When we took hold of the pen, they said they would take the troops away so we could raise children."

Cox refused to accept Red Cloud's protest. "These things were done by Generals Sherman, Sanborn, Harvey, Tappan, Augur and Terry, who would not tell a lie to save their lives."

"I do not say the commissioners lied, but the interpreters were wrong," Red Cloud said. "When the forts were removed, I came to make peace. You had your war-houses, or forts. When you removed them, I signed a treaty of peace." He had not signed away Lakota land. "We want to straighten things up," he said.

Cox reiterated that a treaty was a treaty. He offered to give Red Cloud a written copy, which his own interpreter could read to him.

Red Cloud would have none of it. "All the promises made in treaties have never been fulfilled," he declared. "The object of the whites was to crush the Indians down to nothing. The Great Spirit will judge these things hereafter." Cox could keep his copy. "I am chief of thirty-nine nations. I will not take the paper with me. It is all lies."

Red Cloud had no better luck with the Great Father himself. After the three forts on the Bozeman road had been abandoned, the army built a new post, Fort Fetterman, farther south and east. It wasn't in the Powder River valley, but on the North Platte, yet it seemed to Red Cloud a deception and an insult. He demanded that the army remove it, to no avail. On his Washington visit he raised the issue in a White House meeting with Grant. The fort was unnecessary, he said, and it was a provocation. Soldiers behaved badly, and the Indians couldn't help responding. This was no way to foster the peace the new treaty was supposed to secure, and it was no way to treat the Lakotas.

Grant responded that the fort would stay where it was. He said it was for the protection of Indians from whites, as much as the opposite. And it could be used as a trading post for the Indians. Grant said he had always desired to live at peace with the Indians, and he still did. As long as peace was in his power, there would be peace.

A friendlier audience awaited Red Cloud in New York. A group of reform-minded New

Yorkers had created an alternative Indian commission, with the goal of doing better by the Indians than the government's own commission was doing. Peter Cooper, who had built the first railroad locomotive in America, grown rich in industry, and then turned to philanthropy, was a prime mover of the shadow Indian commission; he hosted a reception for Red Cloud at the eponymous Cooper Institute.

Red Cloud addressed the group. "My brothers and my friends who are here before me today," he said. "God Almighty has made us all, and He is here to hear what I have to say to you today. The Great Spirit made us both. He gave us lands, and He gave you lands. You came here and we received you as brothers. When the Almighty made you, He made you all white and clothed you. When He made us, He made us with red skins and poor. When you first came, we were many and you were few. Now you are many, and we are few."

Red Cloud was aware that whites often called the Indians savages and barbarians, not to mention robbers and killers. These labels were a slander on his people. "You do not know who appears before you to speak," he said. "He is a representative of the original American race, the first people of this continent. We are good and not bad. The reports which you get about us are all on one side.

You hear of us only as murderers and thieves. We are not so. If we had more lands to give to you, we would give them, but we have no more. We are driven into a very little island."

Red Cloud didn't know how much influence Peter Cooper and the others had in Washington, but he thought it couldn't hurt to ask for their support. "We want you, our dear friends, to help us with the government of the United States." He appealed to the humanity they shared. "You have children. We too have children, and we wish to bring them up well. We ask you to help us do it." He appealed to their common belief in God. "The Great Spirit that made us both wishes peace to be kept; we want to keep peace. Will you help us?" He explained how he and his people had been swindled. "In 1868, men came out and brought papers. We could not read them, and they did not tell us truly what was in them. We thought the treaty was to remove the forts, and that we should then cease from fighting." Only days ago did he discover the deception. "When I reached Washington, the Great Father explained to me what the treaty was, and showed me that the interpreters had deceived me. All I want is right and justice. I have tried to get from the Great Father what is right and just."

Red Cloud blamed the agents and traders the government had sent out recently for many of his people's ills. "I was brought up among the traders, and those who came out there in the early times treated me well, and I had a good time with them. They taught us to wear clothes and to use tobacco and ammunition. But by and by, the Great Father sent out a different kind of men, men who cheated and drank whisky, men who were so bad that the Great Father could not keep them at home and so sent them out there." He hoped his listeners would help in having these bad men removed. "I want to have men sent out to my people whom we know and can trust."

Red Cloud was aware that his talks with Cox and Grant had been reported in the papers, but he didn't know if they had been reported accurately. "I was afraid the words I spoke lately to the Great Father would not reach you, so I came to speak to you myself," he told his New York audience. His time in the East was nearly over. "You belong in the East and I belong in the West, and I am glad I have come here and that we could understand one another," he said. "I go home this afternoon. I hope you will think of what I have said to you."

20

Sherman rarely smiled when pondering the operation of American politics. But he allowed himself a grin when he reflected how Red Cloud got his wish that the corrupt Indian agents be replaced with better men. "The peace, or 'Quaker' policy, of which so much has been said, originated about thus," Sherman wrote a few years later. "By the act of Congress, approved March 3, 1869, the forty-five regiments of infantry were reduced to twenty-five, and provision was made for the 'muster out' of many of the surplus officers, and for retaining others to be absorbed by the usual promotions and casualties." This addressed the problem of too many soldiers left over from the Civil War. But the army was still left with too many officers, whom President Grant, an officer himself, was loath to terminate. So Grant devised a workaround. "On the 7th of May of that year," Sherman continued, "by authority of an act of Congress approved June 30, 1834, nine field-officers and fifty-nine captains and subalterns were detached and ordered to report to the Commissioner of Indian Affairs, to serve as Indian superintendents and agents. Thus by an old law surplus army officers were made to displace the usual civil appointees, undoubtedly a change for the better, but most distasteful to members of Congress, who looked to these appointments as part of their proper patronage. The consequence was the law of July 15, 1870" — approved just weeks after Red Cloud returned to the West — "which vacated the military commission of any officer who accepted or exercised the functions of a civil officer." This prevented the army officers from double-dipping; it also deprived the politicians of their patronage.

The members of Congress were not happy, and they quickly blocked the new plan. "Certain politicians called on President Grant, informing him that this law was chiefly designed to prevent his using army officers for Indian agents — 'civil offices' — which he believed to be both judicious and wise; army officers, as a rule, being better qualified to deal with Indians than the average political appointees," Sherman recorded.

Grant puffed on one of the cigars that were never far from his mouth. "Gentlemen, you have defeated my plan of Indian management," he acknowledged. "But you shall not succeed in your purpose, for I will divide these appointments up among the religious churches, with which you dare not contend."

Sherman completed the story. "The army officers were consequently relieved of their 'civil offices,' and the Indian agencies were apportioned to the several religious churches in about the proportion of their supposed strength — some to the Quakers, some to the Methodists, to the Catholics, Episcopalians, Presbyterians, etc., etc. — and thus it remains to the present time, these religious communities selecting the agents to be appointed by the Secretary of the Interior. The Quakers, being first named, gave name to the policy, and it is called the 'Quaker' policy today."

Sherman's account of the shift in policy was correct in all essentials, and it captured the outcome of the contest over the location of the Indian Bureau. Sherman and Grant would have preferred that the Indian agents be army officers, but they couldn't get around the congressional veto. On its face, this failure was surprising, in that the patronage in play wasn't large. The number of Indian agents was minuscule compared, for example, with the number of postmasters. But Congress in the Gilded Age had elevated the practice of log-rolling to a high art; members supported colleagues on issues they cared little about, in exchange for reciprocal support on issues that *did* matter to them. Moreover, as events would prove before Grant left office, the corruption in the awarding of offices relating to Indian agencies and trade had eaten deep into the government. Any change in the status quo threatened relationships that were very lucrative to those on the inside.

Events would prove something else: that the "Quaker policy" label was more accurate than "peace policy." Grant *sought* peace with the Indians, but he didn't find much of it. The Quaker agents, and the agents of other denominations, inspired fewer complaints from the Indians than their predecessors had, but they couldn't change the underlying dynamics of the struggle for dominance in the West. Whites continued to venture west, and to covet the lands of the Indians. The white population continued to grow relative to the Indian population. Fewer and fewer Indians were able and willing to contest the expanding white presence. But some still fought, and the war for America continued.

Other changes by the new administration affected Sherman more personally. Grant had been general-in-chief before becoming president; that role now fell to Sherman, who assumed it reluctantly. Commanding the entire army was an honor but also a burden. And the burden grew greater when Sherman discovered that his authority was less than it seemed, and less than he had been led to believe it would be. In recent years the chain of command from the president to army officers in the field had been bent and then broken by the controversy that resulted in the impeachment trial of Andrew Johnson. The office of the secretary of war had managed to inject itself into the military chain, until appointments were made and orders were sent without the approval or even the knowledge of the army's commanding general. Grant found this annoying, and he told Sherman it had to be changed. Sherman took this as assurance that it *would* be changed once Grant became president. In this belief, Sherman accepted Grant's old job.

The change, however, was not made. On surveying the Washington horizon from the White House, Grant decided that a battle with the War Department was one he didn't want to fight. The status quo persisted, and it drove Sherman mad. "Members of Congress daily appeal to the Secretary of War for the discharge of some soldier on the application of a mother," Sherman explained. "Or some young officer has to be dry-nursed, withdrawn from his company on the plains to be stationed near home. The Secretary of War, sometimes moved by private reasons, or more likely to oblige the member of Congress, grants the order, of which the commanding general knows nothing till he reads it in the papers. Also, an Indian tribe, goaded by the pressure of white neighbors, breaks out in revolt. The general-in-chief must reinforce the local garrisons not only with men, but horses, wagons, ammunition, and food. All the necessary information is in the staff bureaus in Washington, but the general has no *right* to call for it" — because the staff reported to the war secretary rather than to the general. Sherman found this nearly intolerable, reflecting badly on the army and on himself. "The general in actual command of the army should have a full staff, subject to his own command. If not, he cannot be held responsible for the results."

Refusing to remain a fifth wheel in Washington, Sherman eventually removed his headquarters to St. Louis. The decision wasn't as extreme as it sounded. During the Civil War, the command of the army had been wherever Grant happened to be. Sherman now applied the same principle to his own command. Because his personal staff was small, it could readily go with him. St. Louis was eight hundred miles closer to the front of actual fighting by the army. And it was a city he knew and liked from previous experience.

But most important, the move got Sherman out of Washington. Earlier, on receiving an order from Andrew Johnson to relocate to Washington to command the military division of the Atlantic, Sherman had written a letter of lament to Grant. "I never felt so troubled in my life," Sherman said. "Were it an order to go to Sitka, to the devil, to battle with rebels or Indians, I think you would not hear a whimper from me." But this was far worse. "Like Hamlet's ghost, it curdles my blood." Sherman said he was thinking of resigning from the army.

He managed to dodge that assignment and stay in St. Louis. But his aversion to the politics of Washington only increased, the more after he became general-in-chief, and it drove him back to St. Louis.

21

Ohio would become known for producing presidents, but in the decade after the Civil War it was more famous for grooming generals. Grant and Sherman, the senior and second-ranking officers in the army, were Ohioans. So was Philip Sheridan, the third-ranking officer upon the 1872 retirement of George Meade. Sheridan was a decade younger than Grant and Sherman, but he grew up in the same part of Ohio as Sherman, and the Sheridan family knew the Ewings, Sherman's foster family. Like Grant and Sherman, Sheridan attended West Point.

On graduation he was posted to Texas. America's war against Mexico had ended, but the country's war against the Indians of Texas — a conflict bequeathed from the Spanish empire, independent Mexico, and the republic of Texas — had just begun. Sheridan was assigned to Fort Duncan, on the Rio Grande near Laredo. There he encountered the challenges of existence on the

Texas frontier, and gained a healthy respect for those who had learned to overcome them. From the natives of the region he borrowed techniques for filling out a scanty diet. "Our food was principally the soldier's ration: flour, pickled pork, nasty bacon — cured in the dust of ground charcoal — and fresh beef, of which we had a plentiful supply, supplemented with game of various kinds," he recalled afterward. "The sugar, coffee, and smaller parts of the ration were good, but we had no vegetables, and the few jars of preserves and some few vegetables kept by the sutler were too expensive to be indulged in. So during all the period I lived at Fort Duncan and its sub-camps, nearly sixteen months, fresh vegetables were practically unobtainable. To prevent scurvy we used the juice of the maguey plant, called pulque, and to obtain a supply of this anti-scorbutic I was often detailed to march the company out about forty miles, cut the plant, load up two or three wagons with the stalks, and carry them to camp. Here the juice was extracted by a rude press, and put in bottles until it fermented and became worse in odor than sulphureted hydrogen. At reveille roll-call every morning this fermented liquor was dealt out to the company, and as it was my duty, in my capacity of subaltern, to attend these roll-calls and see that the men took their ration of pulque, I always began the duty by drinking a cup of the repulsive stuff myself. Though hard to swallow, its well-known specific qualities in the prevention and cure of scurvy were familiar to all, so every man in the command gulped down his share notwithstanding its vile taste and odor."

Sheridan experienced the constraints of fighting Indians on the border. A band of Lipan Apaches skirted around the fort on their way to Mexico, but in doing so killed a herder, a former drummer-boy of the post. Sheridan joined the party that set out in pursuit. "We found the body of the boy filled with arrows, and near him the body of a fine looking young Indian, whom the lad had undoubtedly killed before he was himself overpowered," he said. The Apaches made little effort to hide their tracks, and Sheridan's unit closed rapidly. "But as soon as they found we were getting near they headed for the Rio Grande, made the crossing to the opposite bank, and were in Mexico before we could overtake them. When on the other side of the boundary they grew very brave, daring us to come over to fight them, well aware all the time that the international line prevented us from continuing the pursuit."

Sheridan didn't discourage easily, though. "That night, in company with Lieutenant Thomas G. Williams, I crossed over the river to the Mexican village of Piedras Negras, and on going to a house where a large baille, or dance, was going on, we found among those present two of the Indians we had been chasing," he recounted. "As soon as they saw us they strung their bows for a fight, and we drew our six-shooters." But the hosts of the dance closed around the Indians and rushed them out of the house. Sheridan and Williams had to content themselves with enjoying the dance.

From Texas, Sheridan was sent to California, arriving eight years and one war after Sherman had landed there. Sheridan was sent to Fort Reading, located near the town of Redding on the upper Sacramento River. He had no sooner reached the fort than he was ordered to continue north, to catch an expedition scouting railroad routes to Oregon. Some risk attended the chase, as bands of Pit River Indians of the area had been raiding farms and ambushing wagon trains. Sheridan decided to run the risk, and set out with three comrades. They spied the marauding Indians just as the Indians were about to overtake the expedition party. Sheridan discovered why the Indians were marauding. "They were a pitiable lot, almost naked, hungry and cadaverous," he recalled. "In prosperity they mainly subsisted on fish, or game killed with the bow and arrow. When these sources failed they lived on grasshoppers, and at this season the grasshopper was their principal food. In former years salmon were very abundant in the streams of the Sacramento Valley, and every fall they took great quantities of these fish and dried them for winter use, but alluvial mining had of late years defiled the water of the different streams and driven the fish out." The Indians were starving, and they approached the army column not to attack but to beg for food. The commander, a Lieutenant Williamson, listened to their pleas. "When they had made Williamson understand that they were suffering for food, he permitted them to come into camp, and furnished them with a supply, which they greedily swallowed as fast as it was placed at their service, regardless of possible indigestion. When they had eaten all they could hold, their enjoyment was made complete by the soldiers, who gave them a quantity of strong plug tobacco. This they smoked incessantly, inhaling all the smoke, so that none of the effect should be lost. When we abandoned this camp the next day, the miserable wretches remained in it and collected the offal about the cooks' fires to feast still more, piecing out the meal, no doubt, with their staple article of food — grasshoppers."

Other tribes responded more aggressively to the encroachment of whites. Yakima Indians launched a war that disrupted traffic along the Columbia River. Sheridan was dispatched with a column to reopen the river and teach the Yakimas not to try it again. Amid the campaign he met Joseph Meek, a mountain man from the early days of the fur trade and now a farmer in the Tualatin Valley of northwest Oregon. Meek visited Sheridan's camp inquiring after a friend, a Chinook chief named Spencer, who with his family had come up the Columbia from Fort Vancouver to serve as a mediator between the army and the warring tribes. Meek had cautioned Spencer about going, and especially about taking his family. But Spencer relied on the goodwill he had accrued over many years and went ahead. Meek hadn't heard from Spencer for some time, although he had learned that Spencer had decided to send his family back down the river. Meek worried for their safety, and he asked Sheridan if he had seen Spencer or his family.

"In reply to Meek's question, I stated that I had not seen Spencer's family," Sheridan recounted. Meek worried the more. "He remarked, 'Well, I fear that they are gone up,' a phrase used in that country in early days to mean that they had been killed." Given Meek's background, Sheridan didn't take him for the worrying type, and concluded that he must have reason for being fearful. He sent a messenger to find out if Spencer's wife and children had reached Fort Vancouver.

They had not. "Their non-arrival aroused

217

in me suspicions of foul play," Sheridan recorded. He gathered all the men the campaign could spare. "I went in search of the family, deploying the men as skirmishers across the valley, and marching them through the heavy forest where the ground was covered with fallen timber and dense underbrush, in order that no point might escape our attention. The search was continued between the base of the mountain and the river without finding any sign of Spencer's family, until about 3 o'clock in the afternoon, when we discovered them between the upper and lower landing, in a small open space about a mile from the road, all dead — strangled to death with bits of rope. The party consisted of the mother, two youths, three girls, and a baby. They had all been killed by white men, who had probably met the innocent creatures somewhere near the blockhouse and driven them from the road into the timber, where the cruel murders were committed without provocation, and for no other purpose than the gratification of the inordinate hatred of the Indian that has often existed on the frontier, and which on more than one occasion has failed to distinguish friend from foe. The bodies lay in a semicircle, and the bits of rope with which the poor wretches had been strangled to death were still around their necks. Each piece of rope — the unwound strand of a heavier piece — was about two feet long, and encircled the neck of its victim with a single knot, that must have been drawn tight by the murderers pulling at the ends. As there had not been quite enough rope to answer for all, the babe was strangled by means of a red silk handkerchief, taken, doubtless, from the neck of its mother. It was a distressing sight. A most cruel outrage had been committed upon unarmed people — our friends and allies — in a spirit of aimless revenge. The perpetrators were citizens living near the middle blockhouse, whose wives and children had been killed a few days before by the hostiles, but who well knew that these unoffending creatures had had nothing to do with those murders." Thirty years later, the images of the dead mother and children still haunted him. "I have been obliged to look upon many cruel scenes in connection with Indian warfare on the Plains since that day, but the effect of this dastardly and revolting crime has never been effaced from my memory."

The Civil War pulled Sheridan back east, where he came to the attention of William Sherman. Sherman recognized in Sheridan a kindred fighting spirit and recommended him for promotion. The appointment ran afoul of politics, but Sheridan impressed others, including Ulysses Grant, who gave him a division and responsibility for destroying the productive capacity of the Shenandoah Valley, the breadbasket of Lee's Army of Northern Virginia. "Do all the damage to railroads and crops you can," Grant ordered Sheridan in the summer of 1864. "Carry off stock of all descriptions, and negroes, so as to prevent further planting. If the war is to last another year, we want the Shenandoah Valley to remain a barren waste."

Sheridan did all that and more. Even while Sherman was cutting his swath of devastation through Georgia, Sheridan broke the economic back of Virginia. "I have destroyed over 2,000 barns, filled with wheat, hay and farming implements; over 70 mills, filled with flour and wheat; have driven in front of the army over 4,000 head of stock; and have killed and issued to the troops not less than 3,000 sheep," Sheridan reported to Grant. "The destruction embraces the Luray Valley and Little Fort Valley, as well as the main valley. A large number of horses have been obtained, a proper estimate of which I cannot now make." Nor was Sheridan quite finished. "Tomorrow I will continue the destruction of wheat, forage, etc., down to Fisher's Hill. When this is completed, the Valley, from Winchester up to Staunton, ninety-two miles, will have but little in it for man or beast."

Reflecting afterward on what he had wrought, Sheridan explained his philosophy of war. It closely mirrored Sherman's, having been forged in the same crucible of conflict. "I do not hold war to mean simply that lines of men shall engage each other in battle, and material interests be ignored," Sheridan wrote. "This is but a duel, in which one combatant seeks the other's life; war means much more, and is far worse than this. Those who rest at home in peace and plenty see but little of the horrors attending such a duel, and even grow indifferent to them as the struggle goes on, contenting themselves with encouraging all who are able-bodied to enlist in the cause, to fill up the shattered ranks as death thins them. It is another matter, however, when deprivation and suffering are brought to their own doors. Then the case appears much graver, for the loss of property weighs heavy with the most of mankind; heavier often, than the sacrifices made on the field of battle. Death is popularly considered the maximum of punishment in war, but it is not; reduction to poverty brings prayers for peace more surely and more quickly than does the destruction of human life, as the selfishness of man has demonstrated in more than one great conflict."

Sheridan carried this thinking back to the West after the war. He oversaw Reconstruction in Texas, a thankless task in what he came to view as an insufferable place. He might not actually have said, "If I owned hell and Texas, I'd rent out Texas and live in hell," but the widely reported statement didn't endear him to the Texans. And he was more than happy to leave for Fort Leavenworth, to serve under Sherman as commander of the military district encompassing Kansas, Missouri, the Indian Territory and New Mexico.

He took up his new command in the wake of the councils and treaties of the Indian Peace Commission, which were supposed to have settled the affairs of the plains. Sheridan discovered that they had not. While the older chiefs of the tribes in his area had signed a treaty at Medicine Lodge, Kansas, that was a southern counterpart to the Fort Laramie treaty, many of the young warriors refused to accept the treaty's terms or to enter the reservations it specified. Their refusal gave rise to sporadic raids during the early months of 1868; to put a stop to the raiding, Sheridan traveled to the heart of the trouble, the vicinity of Fort Larned and Fort Dodge in western Kansas.

On his arrival he received a request from several chiefs for a council. Like him, they hoped to quell the uprising within their tribes. They hoped to get a new concession from the government. Sheridan refused to see them. "Congress had delegated to the Peace Commission the whole matter of treating with them, and a council might lead only to additional complications," he reasoned.

The tension grew. "Denunciations of the treaty became outspoken, and as the young braves grew more and more insolent every day, it amounted to conviction that, unless by some means the irritation was allayed, hostilities would surely be upon us when the buffalo returned to their summer feeding-grounds between the Arkansas and the Platte," Sheridan wrote.

Without reopening the treaty negotiations, he tried to calm things. He increased rations and sent out scouts to talk with the chiefs. The mood seemed to be easing, when a band of Cheyennes raided a Kaw village and the ranches of several whites. The raid caused the Indian Bureau to suspend the distribution of arms and ammunition pending an investigation. The suspension remained in effect when delegations of Comanches and Kiowas came to Fort Larned for the annuities promised them in the Medicine Lodge treaty, including weapons. When they didn't get their weapons, they departed in anger.

A Sheridan subordinate, Alfred Sully, fearing a broader conflict, appealed to the chiefs, who said they couldn't control their young men without a reversal of the decision on arms. Sully obliged and issued the weapons.

"This issue of arms and ammunition was a fatal mistake," Sheridan wrote later. Far from calming matters, the concession convinced the warriors that the government could be intimidated. A war party of two hundred Cheyennes, with a few Arapahos and Sioux, embarked on a campaign of murder, rape, kidnapping and theft across western Kansas. Comanches and Kiowas, the latter led by a chief named Satanta, soon did the same.

Sheridan considered his options. "At the outbreak of hostilities I had in all, east of New Mexico, a force of regulars numbering about 2,600 men — 1,200 mounted and 1,400 foot troops," he recounted. "With these few troops all the posts along the Smoky Hill and Arkansas had to be garrisoned, emigrant trains escorted, and the settlements and routes of travel and the construction parties on the Kansas-Pacific railway protected. Then, too, this same force had to furnish for the field small movable columns, that were always on the go, so it will be rightly inferred that every available man was kept busy from the middle of August till November; especially as during this period the hostiles attacked over forty widely dispersed places, in nearly all cases stealing horses, burning houses, and killing settlers. It was of course impossible to foresee where these descents would be made, but as soon as an attack was heard of assistance was always promptly rendered, and every now and then we succeeded in killing a few savages. As a general thing, though, the raiders escaped before relief arrived, and when they had a few miles the start, all efforts to catch them were futile."

Sheridan determined to apply what he had learned during the Civil War to the war on the plains. "At the period of which I write, in 1868, the Plains were covered with vast herds of buffalo — the number has been estimated at 3,000,000 head — and with such means of subsistence as this everywhere at hand, the 6,000 hostiles were wholly unhampered by any problem of food-supply," he wrote. "The savages were rich too according to Indian standards, many a lodge owning from twenty to a hundred ponies; and consciousness of wealth and power, aided by former temporizing, had made them not only confident but defiant. Realizing that their thorough subjugation would be a difficult task, I made up my mind to confine operations during the grazing and hunting season to protecting the people of the new settlements and on the overland routes, and then, when winter came, to fall upon the savages relentlessly, for in that season their ponies would be thin, and weak from lack of food, and in the cold and snow, without strong ponies to transport their villages and plunder, their movements would be so much impeded that the troops could overtake them." Just as Sheridan's campaign in the Shenandoah Valley had threatened starvation for Lee's army and compelled its surrender, so his winter campaign on the plains would threaten starvation for the

Cheyennes, Comanches and Kiowas and force *their* capitulation.

Yet a winter campaign would test his own troops almost as much as it taxed the Indians. Sheridan readied his men for six months of fighting. He asked Sherman for additional cavalry, and got some, but not as many as he thought he needed. He appealed to the governor of Kansas for volunteers, and was permitted to recruit. He laid in stores enough to last till spring. Not least, he secured the services of guides, men who knew the country and its inhabitants. William Cody had earned the nickname "Buffalo Bill" as a supplier of meat to the construction crews of the Kansas-Pacific Railroad, but Sheridan was more impressed with his savvy in delivering crucial messages. Employed, at this point, by the army quartermaster at Fort Larned, Cody carried a dispatch from that fort to Sheridan at Fort Hays, sixty-five miles away, across territory controlled by hostile Indians. "The despatch informed me that the Indians near Larned were preparing to decamp, and this intelligence required that certain orders should be carried to Fort Dodge, ninety-five miles south of Hays," Sheridan recalled. "This too being a particularly dangerous route — several couriers having been killed on it — it was impossible to get one of the various 'Petes,' 'Jacks,' or 'Jims' hanging around Hays City to take my communication. Cody, learning of the strait I was in, manfully came to the rescue, and proposed to make the trip to Dodge, though he had just finished his long and perilous ride from Larned." Sheridan accepted the offer. "He mounted a fresh horse and hastened on his journey, halting but once to rest on the way, and then only for an hour, the stop being made at Coon Creek, where he got another mount from a troop of cavalry. At Dodge he took six hours' sleep, and then continued on to his own post — Fort Larned — with more despatches. After resting twelve hours at Larned, he was again in the saddle with tidings for me at Fort Hays, General Hazen sending him, this time, with word that the villages had fled to the south of the Arkansas. Thus, in all, Cody rode about 350 miles in less than sixty hours, and such an exhibition of endurance and courage was more than enough to convince me that his services would be extremely valuable in the campaign." Sheridan made Cody chief of scouts for a regiment of the Fifth Cavalry.

Other veterans of the West tried to persuade Sheridan to cancel his campaign. Jim Bridger was the most famous of the mountain men, having been on some of the first expeditions across the plains as the Rocky Mountain fur trade was beginning. Now deep into his seventh decade, he traveled from St. Louis to warn Sheridan that his soldiers would never survive a winter on the plains. Sheridan thanked him for his trouble in coming, but continued the preparations.

The campaign commenced on November 15, with Sheridan in the lead. "The first night out a blizzard struck us and carried away our tents; and as the gale was so violent that they could not be put up again, the rain and snow drenched us to the skin," Sheridan recalled. "Shivering from wet and cold, I took refuge under a wagon, and there spent such a miserable night that, when at last morning came, the gloomy predictions of old man Bridger and others rose up before me with greatly increased force." But he refused to turn back. On the sixth day Sheridan's column rendezvoused with one led by George Custer, who had served under Sheridan in the Civil War. Sheridan had crossed a fresh trail of Indians; he ordered Custer to follow the trail and strike a blow if he could.

Custer set off in a blizzard, which abated the next day, leaving drifts of snow beneath blue skies that kept in none of the earth's warmth. The snow had covered the tracks of the Indians, but continuing in the direction the trail had headed, Custer guessed that the Indians wouldn't be expecting pursuit and so wouldn't take evasive action. The trail led Custer's scouts — some friendly Osages — to the Washita River, where they spied the

Indians' camp. Custer reconnoitered in person, creeping on foot to the crest of a ridge overlooking the camp. Satisfying himself that the camp could be taken by surprise, he broke his force into four parties and arrayed them for a dawn attack. At first light, Custer's buglers blasted "Garry Owen," an Irish jig adopted by cavalry of the United States and other English-speaking countries, to launch the four-pronged charge.

The surprise was complete, but the Indians — Cheyennes and Arapahos — recovered quickly and mounted a stiff defense, firing on the soldiers from behind trees, rocks and the steep bank of the river. Custer, realizing that mounted men simply made bigger targets, ordered his men off their horses. They returned the Indians' fire and slowly forced them back. By mid-morning Custer had taken the camp, with the death of perhaps a hundred warriors and the capture of some fifty women and children and a large herd of ponies. Following Sheridan's orders, Custer set fire to the camp, destroying tents, blankets, foodstuffs and everything else the Indians hadn't had time to carry off.

Some of the Indians who escaped took the word of Custer's attack to a nearby camp of Comanches and Kiowas. They gathered for a counterattack, putting Custer in a fix. The Indians outnumbered Custer's force, and they were fresh and vengeful. Custer consid-

229

ered striking straight at them nonetheless, but he thought better of it. Instead he started killing the captured ponies while parrying the probes of the augmented Indian force. Under cover of darkness he slipped away, making his escape with his prisoners.

Custer's victory on the Washita got Sheridan's winter campaign off to an encouraging start. Sheridan accounted it a fitting reprisal for the earlier killings and destruction by the hostile bands. But there was one uncertainty that made the victory incomplete. A squadron of soldiers under Major Joel Elliott had galloped off in pursuit of the fleeing Cheyennes and Arapahos and not returned. Custer, assuming they would find their way back to the main camp, and busy with extricating his own force, had not sent relief after them.

Randolph Keim was a journalist who caught up with Sheridan and joined the winter campaign. He was present when Custer rejoined Sheridan's camp, and couldn't account for Elliott and his men. Keim accompanied Sheridan and Custer on the search the next day. They headed first for the destroyed Indian village. "A ride of an hour and a half brought us to the immediate vicinity of the battle-ground," Keim wrote. "At a distance, looking down from a divide, which the column was crossing to avoid a large bend in the river, the scene was one of the most intense solitude. The sunlight glistening upon the heavy frost, which had not yet disappeared from the trees and long grass of the lowlands, lent the only charm to the landscape. The barren hills, the wild and silent valley, the leafless and lifeless vegetation, formed the picture of desolation." The stillness persisted almost until they reached the remains of the Indian camp. "Suddenly lifting from the ground could be seen thousands of ravens and crows, disturbed in their carrion feast. The dense black mass, evidently gorged, rose heavily, and passing overhead, as if to take revenge for the molestation, set up the greatest confusion of noises. The cowardly wolves started from their abundant repast on human flesh, reluctantly left the spot, and while slowly getting out of the reach of danger often stopped to take a wishful look behind."

Sheridan and the others viewed the work of Custer's arsonists. "Entering the space lately occupied by the Indian lodges, on all sides were scattered the remains of Black Elk's village," Keim wrote. "The conflagration started by the troops had done its work effectively. Scarcely anything of a combustible character escaped."

They viewed the killing fields of the ponies. "On the right of the village, at a distance of less than two hundred yards, were strewn the carcasses of the ponies of the village, which had been shot by the troops," Keim said.

231

"The bodies numbered not less than seven hundred, and covered an area of several acres."

They moved on, following the Washita River in the direction taken by Elliott's troop. "We crossed the stream and proceeded down the south bank until we descended a high divide, from which an extensive view could be had of the surrounding country," Keim wrote. "Descending on the other side, the party had not proceeded but a hundred yards when the body of a white man was found, perfectly naked and covered with arrow and bullet holes. The head presented the appearance of having been beaten with a war-club. The top of the skull was broken into a number of pieces, and the brain was lying partly in the skull and partly on the ground."

Sheridan ordered the spot marked, and the group pressed on. "Crossing, with some difficulty, a small ravine, about the center of an extensive plain, at a distance of two hundred yards farther on, objects were seen lying in the grass, and were supposed to be bodies," Keim said. The group galloped to the spot. "A scene was now witnessed sufficient to appall the bravest heart. Within an area of not more than fifteen yards lay sixteen bodies — all that remained of Elliott and his party. The winter air swept across the plain, and its cold blasts had added to the ghastliness of death the additional spectacle of sixteen naked corpses frozen as solidly as stone. There was not a single body that did not exhibit evidences of fearful mutilation. They were all lying with their faces down, and in close proximity to each other. Bullet and arrow wounds covered the backs of each; the throats of a number were cut, and several were beheaded."

As sobering as the deaths of their comrades were, the soldiers were more touched by two other casualties discovered that day. "During the journey to the battlefield, a detachment moving close along the banks of the river, found near the remains of the Kiowa camp the bodies of a white woman and child," Keim wrote. "The bodies were brought into camp and examined. Two bullet holes penetrating the brain" — of the woman — "were found, also the back of the skull was fearfully crushed, as if by a hatchet. There were no marks on the child except a bruise on the cheek. This fact led to the conclusion that the child had been seized by the feet and dashed against a tree. When brought in, the body of the woman was recognized as Mrs. Blynn. This woman was captured by Satanta, chief of the Kiowas, near Fort Lynn, while on her way to her home in the 'States.' At the time of her capture, she was in a wagon in the center of a civilian train. The men with the train, it appears, fled, and left Mrs. Blynn and her child to fall into savage hands. Satanta kept her as his captive until the time of the fight of the Kiowas, when she was ruthlessly murdered. The body was dressed in the ordinary garments of a white woman; on the feet were a pair leather gaiters, comparatively new. Upon the breast was found a piece of corn-cake, and the position of the hands indicated that the woman was eating when she, unexpectedly, received the fatal blow. The body presented the appearance of a woman of more than ordinary beauty, small in figure, and not more than twenty-two years of age."

The loss of Elliott and his men, and the murder of Mrs. Blynn and her baby, stiffened Sheridan's resolve to push the campaign to a conclusion. He led his column farther down the Washita. "But before going far it was found that the many deep ravines and canyons on this trail would delay our train very much, so we moved out of the valley and took the level prairie on the divide," Sheridan recounted. "Here the traveling was good, and a rapid gait was kept up till midday, when, another storm of sleet and snow coming on, it became extremely difficult for the guides to make out the proper course." Afraid that they might get lost and have to spend the night on the open plain, he gave the order to head back toward the river. Yet this was no easy task. "A dense fog just now enveloped us, obscuring all landmarks." They continued in the direction they had been going before the fog descended, and hoped for the best. "We had the good luck to reach the valley before nightfall, though there was a great deal of floundering about, and also much disputing among the guides as to where the river would be found." Their luck included striking the river at a large stand of trees, which promised shelter. The snow kept falling past dark, when the sky cleared and the temperature plunged. The men were tolerably warm in their tents, but come morning they battled frozen fingers in trying to bundle the tents, saddle the horses and otherwise break camp.

They marched for three more days, when the scouts brought intelligence that they were nearing more villages. "Wishing to strike them as soon as possible, we made a very early start next morning," Sheridan wrote. He was readying the order to attack when his hand was stayed by the arrival of an Indian delegation carrying a white flag. They indicated that they had a letter for Sheridan. The letter proved to be from William Hazen, the commander at Fort Cobb. Hazen pronounced that he was in council with the tribes near Fort Cobb, in particular the Kiowas and Comanches, and that so long as he was, those tribes should be treated as friendly. Hazen indicated that Kiowa chiefs Satanta and Lone Wolf would give information about the Cheyennes and Arapahos, who remained out and hostile. "Of course, under such circumstances I was compelled to give up the intended attack," Sheridan recounted. He soon wished he hadn't. "When I informed the Kiowas that I would respect Hazen's letter provided they all came into Fort Cobb and gave themselves up, the two chiefs promised submission, and, as an evidence of good faith, proposed to accompany the column to Fort Cobb with a large body of warriors, while their villages moved to the same point by easy stages, along the opposite bank of the river," Sheridan wrote. The villages had to go slowly because of the women and children and the winter-stressed condition of the ponies. "I had some misgivings as to the sincerity of Satanta and Lone Wolf, but as I wanted to get the Kiowas where their surrender would be complete, so that the Cheyennes and Arapahoes could then be pursued, I agreed to the proposition." The combined column moved on.

Things went well the first day. "But the next it was noticed that the warriors were diminishing, and an investigation showed that a number of them had gone off on various pretexts — the main one being to help along the women and children with the villages," Sheridan wrote. "With this I suspected that they were playing me false, and my suspicions grew into certainty when Satanta himself tried to make his escape by slipping beyond the flank of the column and putting spurs to his pony." Sheridan had warned his troops to be ready for such a maneuver, and several officers gave chase and ran Satanta down. "I then arrested both him and Lone Wolf and held them as hostages, a measure that had the effect of bringing back many of the warriors already beyond our reach," Sheridan said.

He proceeded to Fort Cobb with the prisoners. He waited there while most of the Comanches came in, but saw nothing of the rest of the Kiowas. He gave the laggards another two days. "There were no signs to indicate their coming," he observed. "So I put on the screws at once by issuing an order to hang Satanta and Lone Wolf, if their people did not surrender at Fort Cobb within forty-eight hours. The two chiefs promised prompt compliance, but begged for more time, seeking to explain the non-arrival of the women and children through the weak condition of the ponies; but I was tired of their duplicity, and insisted on my ultimatum."

It worked. "Runners were sent out with messages by the two prisoners, appealing to their people to save the lives of their chiefs, and the result was that the whole tribe came in to the post within the specified time," Sheridan wrote. He was pleased that his tactic had worked, but his satisfaction didn't last. "The two manacled wretches thus saved their necks, but it is to be regretted that the execution did not come off, for some years afterward their devilish propensities led them into Texas, where both engaged in the most horrible butcheries."

With the Kiowas now subdued, Sheridan turned to the Comanches still out. "This party was made up of a lot of very bad Indians, outlaws from the main tribe," he said. "We did not hope to subdue them except by a fight." Sheridan made sure they got it. He sent a column under Andrew Evans toward their camp at the base of the Wichita Mountains; it arrived on Christmas Day. "In the snow and cold his approach was wholly unexpected, and he was thus enabled to deal the band a blow that practically annihilated it," Sheridan said. "Twenty-five warriors were killed outright, most of the women and children captured, and all the property was destroyed." The survivors joined their fellow Comanches at Fort Cobb.

The crushing of the Comanche band alarmed the Cheyennes and Arapahos who remained at large. In years and decades past, winter was when the Indians could rest and recover, while the soldiers stayed in their barracks. Sheridan's winter campaign erased this expectation. Their food supplies were failing, their ponies dead or dying, their tepees and blankets burned. The women were suffering and their children crying. And the soldiers kept them constantly on the move amid the snow and cold.

They told Sheridan they wanted to talk. He consented to meet with Little Robe, chief of the Cheyennes, and Yellow Bear, of the Arapahos, on the condition that they surrender at once and agree to settle on their reservations in the spring. Seeing no alternative but death on the plains, they accepted his terms.

■ ■ ■ ■

PART III
ADOBE WALLS AND
LAVA BEDS

■ ■ ■ ■

22

Sherman's war against the Indians was unlike either of his previous wars in crucial ways. The war against Mexico had been fought almost entirely on foreign soil, against an army trained and operating according to standards conventional in Western Europe and the Europeanized parts of the Americas. The Civil War had commanded the undivided attention and resources of the Union government. By contrast, the Indian war was fought within American borders; it was fought against foes whose tactics and strategy were unconventional by Euro-American standards; and it had to compete with other events and issues for the attention and especially the resources of the government.

This last point compounded another difference for Sherman personally. He had not been in charge of the Mexican war or the Civil War. He *was* in charge of the Indian war. He was the one who had to balance aims against means, stretch insufficient budgets, adjudicate the competing grievances of settlers and Indians, enforce treaty provisions against violations by both settlers and Indians, and explain to Congress why the war dragged on longer than the Mexican war and the Civil War combined.

He often longed for the simpler days of those earlier wars, when all he had to do was fight. But then he picked up his pen and resumed writing orders and reports.

"Left San Antonio with an escort of seventeen men of the 10th Infantry," wrote Randolph Marcy in his journal on May 2, 1871. Marcy was the inspector general of the army; he was accompanying Sherman on a tour of the Texas frontier. Sherman had received complaints of raids by Indians said to be based at the reservation at Fort Sill in the Indian Territory, across the Red River from Texas. The Texans demanded more protection, which would entail greater spending on forts and garrisons. Sherman didn't have the money, which Congress had declined to appropriate. Much of what money Sherman *did* have was still going to support operations in the parts of the South that remained under military governance. Indeed, the military role in certain parts of the South appeared likely to expand. During this same period, President Grant was preparing a martial law proclamation for counties in South Carolina where the

Ku Klux Klan raged out of control. Sherman supposed suppressing the Klan would take priority over battling the Comanches in Texas. And so he hoped to learn that the complaints of the Texans were exaggerated, as complaints of whites on the frontier often were.

Sherman's party traveled thirty miles the first day, over what Marcy described as "an undulating and rather sandy section with sparse and poor settlements." They passed a cold night in the open and resumed the march at dawn the next day. The first community they encountered was Boerne, consisting of a dozen houses built and inhabited by German immigrants. The Germans had started arriving in the days of the Texas republic, and they formed a German-speaking belt that extended a hundred miles north and west of San Antonio. This location put them in the southeastern portion of the Comanchería, the realm the Comanches had carved for themselves during the previous century at the expense of Apaches, Kiowas and other inhabitants of the southern part of the buffalo range. Because the Germans built their homes and farms close together, rather than far apart in the manner of the American settlers, they suffered less at the hands of the Comanches and other tribes than the Americans did. But they were always on the watch.

Sherman and his party reached the Germans' principal town of Fredericksburg, named for Prince Frederick of Prussia. "Quite a thriving place of about one thousand inhabitants," Marcy remarked. "There are several stores, mechanics shops, and private houses here, nearly all of which are built of stone." Sherman's party was neither the first nor last to note that the diligent Germans constructed their homes and businesses to stand for generations, building of stone rather than wood. The habit, acquired in the old country, served them well in the Texas hill country, where limestone, easily shaped for building, was everywhere, and trees readily converted to lumber were rare.

Yet even the Germans couldn't overcome the vagaries of the West Texas climate. "The crops seem to be wanting rain," Marcy noted. They often did. As settlement pushed out onto the Great Plains, the settlers discovered by practical experiment that the 100th meridian of west longitude marked the start of the zone where crops wouldn't grow without irrigation. The Texas Germans were part of that experiment. Fredericksburg lay almost athwart the 99th meridian, which put it in a marginal zone; some years enough rain fell to support the crops, others years it didn't. From what Sherman and the others could see, 1871 was shaping up to be one of those other years.

They proceeded west from Fredericksburg.

"The country traveled today has been arid and the grass short," Marcy noted. This would be the rule: the farther west, the drier the country.

And the drier the country, the more it appealed to the Comanches. The Comanches were a relatively new tribe, a splinter from the Shoshones of the Platte River region of what would become Wyoming. They were even newer to Texas, having arrived a couple of centuries after the Spanish. At some point they laid hands on the Spaniards' great gift to the peoples of the plains: the horse. Most of the tribes of the West and Southwest had been part-time farmers, planting low-maintenance crops like corn, beans and squash before heading out on the hunt. They would return to harvest the crops. Some tribes, including the Apaches, continued that connection to the soil even after acquiring horses. But others, notably the Lakotas and especially the Comanches, placed all their bets on a nomadic, equestrian lifestyle. It was indeed a bet, for while full-time nomadism freed them to roam where they chose, it made them crucially dependent on the buffalo. While the buffalo lasted, the Comanches and Lakotas might thrive, but if the buffalo ever failed, they would be doomed — or at least compelled to return to a more sedentary, more agricultural existence. That, or find another large ungulate to prey upon.

"Met a detachment of Negro infantry at our camp," Marcy wrote on May 4. "They had been scouting the country between Fort McKavett and here." The army had not been known for progressive politics during most of its existence; people who choose to defend their country often equate the country with the status quo. But during the Civil War, the army became an engine of revolution — even as it preserved the status quo of the Union's unbrokenness. The Emancipation Proclamation, besides making freedom for slaves a war aim of the Union, included a clause inviting freed slaves to join America's armed services. They did so in large numbers; by war's end, nearly two hundred thousand had enlisted.

As with the white troops, the great majority of the blacks mustered out after Appomattox. But some of the black soldiers wanted to stay on, judging their prospects better with their emancipators than with their erstwhile enslavers. And the army was willing to let them stay, especially if they agreed to serve at western forts where whites weren't eager to serve. Congress obliged by authorizing several regiments of black troops, both cavalry and infantry. When these troops encountered Indians of the plains, the latter called the former "buffalo soldiers," presumably likening the hair of the soldiers to the tightly curled wool on the head of the bison. The name caught on.

The Sherman party continued its journey. "The country becomes more dry as we go west," Marcy wrote on May 5. The names of the settlements — Cold Spring, Rock Spring — reflected the growing importance of reliable water in the increasingly arid landscape. They struck the San Saba River the next day, on which was located the hamlet of Menardsville. "At our camp we are only about a mile from the old Spanish Fort San Saba, which was quite a large work of solid masonry."

But not solid enough to withstand Comanche attack. The Spanish presence at San Saba had been short-lived. A mission was established there for the benefit of the Apaches, who had expressed interest. But by the time the mission and its presidio — fort — were built, the Apaches had cooled on the idea. It turned out that they were feeling the pressure of the Comanches, then invading Texas, and didn't want to make themselves easy targets by settling down at the mission. The missionaries soon found themselves the targets, when an army of a thousand Comanche and allied warriors descended on the mission and presidio, massacred the priests and the soldiers, drove off the livestock, and burned whatever would combust. The Spanish abandoned the site, falling back to the vicinity of San Antonio.

Whether Sherman and his party, arriving a century later, learned the full story of the fort they saw is uncertain. But the silent ruin made clear that the reign of the Comanches was challenged only at the peril of the challengers.

The next day they heard of the contemporary peril from some who had felt it. "Met three armed men who said three Indians had that morning ran off twenty five of their horses directly before their eyes," Marcy recorded. Perhaps Sherman and the others thought horse theft didn't rise to the degree of culpability reflected in the ruins they had just seen, but even if they did, they couldn't dispute the reasoning of their visitors that violence fed on itself: theft of property today, theft of life tomorrow.

The Sherman party reached Fort McKavett, farther west on the San Saba River. An earlier post on the spot had been abandoned before the Civil War, under the pressure of the Comanches; the current fort had been operating for two years. It was garrisoned, at the time of Sherman's arrival, by four companies of infantry and two of cavalry — "all colored," observed Marcy.

The fort itself occupied a legal limbo resulting from the peculiar history of Texas. Every other western state and territory started as federal land, with the result that the army essentially had its pick of sites for posts. Texas had been an independent country before joining the Union, and so when Texas became a state, its land was all either state-owned or privately held. When the U.S. Army identified a site for a fort, it had to negotiate with the owners. Fort McKavett sat on property leased from a private owner for twenty years, until 1875. Part of Sherman's task on this trip was determining whether the lease should be renewed, the land — a parcel of more than two thousand acres — purchased outright, or the fort abandoned.

On May 10 the group arrived at Fort Concho, whose future was even more uncertain. "The ground upon which the fort is built is owned by several different persons, some of whom are in Europe and some in Texas," Marcy wrote. "And strange as it may appear, no purchase or lease has ever been made of the land for military purposes." Actually, this was less strange than Marcy thought, as his next sentence suggested. "It is said that at least two hundred thousand dollars has been expended here" — on handsome stone structures roomy enough for eight companies of troops. Likely the owners of the post acreage had interests in the enterprises that built and supplied the fort, and profited thereby. Further, the lack of a lease or sale left *them* in control of the situation. They could dictate terms of lease or sale, and if the army didn't like the terms, it could always depart — leaving the buildings and other improvements to the owners.

Sherman saw through the scheme. "General Sherman directed the commanding officer, Major Hatch, to represent the matter to General Reynolds" — Joseph Reynolds, commander of the military Department of Texas — "in order to have some arrangement made to secure this reservation to the government," Marcy recorded.

North and west they went. Rarely did they see people, although they saw evidence of human habitation. By this time the great southern herd of buffalo had been drastically reduced by overhunting. The decline seems to have begun before the arrival of whites themselves, as their guns and their horses made deadlier hunters out of the tribes who had previously tracked the bison on foot and dispatched them with lances and arrows. But the decline grew more rapid the closer whites came, as Indians and then white buffalo hunters supplied the growing demand for buffalo tongues and then buffalo hides.

The demise of the buffalo suited the interests of cattlemen, who drove longhorns from the plains of South Texas to the Llano Estacado — Staked Plain — of West Texas. Where the horse had revolutionized the culture of the Plains tribes, the cow had much less effect. Horses gave Indians something they hadn't had: a form of swift transportation that didn't require the expenditure of their own energy. Cows merely provided a substitute for something they already had: meat on the hoof. And a poor substitute at that, in the culinary judgment of most of the Indians.

But a poor substitute is better than no substitute at all, and when the Comanches, Kiowas and other tribes could no longer find buffalo to kill, they turned to cattle. In doing so they ran afoul of white notions of property rights. No one had owned the buffalo, which could be claimed by whoever first put arrow, spear or bullet through an animal's heart. But cattle carried the brands of their owners, who expected those brands to be honored.

"We passed immense herds of cattle today, which are allowed to run wild upon the prairies, and multiply very rapidly," Marcy observed. "The only attention the owners give to them is to brand the calves and occasionally go out to see where they range." Marcy didn't say so, and neither did Sherman, but they might well have acknowledged that the Indians could be forgiven, at least at first, for seeing little difference between herds of buffalo and herds of cattle.

But it was what the cattle theft led to that was the real problem. The cattlemen took umbrage at the loss of their cattle, and resisted with such force as they could muster. The Indians responded with force of their own — greater force, often, than that of the whites. "The remains of several ranches were observed today, the occupants of which have been either killed or driven off to the more dense settlements by the Indians," Marcy wrote. He had been stationed in Texas before the Civil War, and it now appeared to him that the whites were losing ground to the Comanches. "This rich and beautiful section does not contain today so many white people as it did when I visited it eighteen years ago." The future, he thought, looked even worse than the recent past. "If the Indian marauders are not punished, the whole country seems to be in a fair way of becoming totally depopulated."

Depopulated of whites, that is. Indians would still live there. And yet Marcy — and Sherman and many other whites — took the depopulation argument seriously. They could not see what moral claim the fifteen thousand or so Comanches had to an area large enough to support a hundred thousand whites. God hadn't given the land to the Comanches, unless it was the god of war who favored Comanche arms over those of the Apaches and others they drove off. And if conquest conveyed the right to land — well, that was precisely Sherman's line of work.

Curiously, for all the evidence of past theft and killing, Marcy and Sherman saw few signs of active depredations. While Marcy kept the log of the journey, Sherman wrote letters to Joseph Reynolds, the army's Texas commander. Overseeing Reconstruction in Texas, Reynolds had gotten thoroughly embroiled in the politics of the state, favoring Unionist Republicans over formerly Confederate Democrats, but in a manner that antagonized important segments of the former even as it alienated all of the latter. His troubles left him little time to inspect the Texas frontier; Sherman's letters filled him in on what he had missed.

At first Sherman was inclined to think Reynolds hadn't missed much. The claims of injury by the frontier folk indeed appeared to be exaggerated. "I hear of small parties of Indians stealing horses by night, but up to this point the people manifest no fears or apprehensions, for they expose women and children singly on the road and in cabins far off from the others as though they were in Illinois," Sherman wrote to Reynolds from Fort Concho. "Of course, I have heard other stories, but actions are more significant than words."

Several days on, the evidence of Indian peril remained sketchy. "I have seen not a trace of an Indian thus far," Sherman wrote to Reynolds from Fort Griffin, "and only hear the stories of people which indicate that whatever Indians there be only come to Texas to steal horses and that whilst they approach the frontier in parties of 30 or 40, they invariably scatter to steal and to escape." This was a bother but hardly a crisis. Further, rustling raids didn't lend themselves to a military solution. "As against these, troops are almost useless, and the people within a hundred miles of the frontier ought to take precautions such as all people do against all sorts of thieves." The people could not reasonably ask the army to stand guard on their herds.

Sherman suspected that the problem arose from the continuing separation of responsibility between the army and the Indian Bureau. The latter ran reservations such as the one at Fort Sill, and if Indians were leaving that reservation to raid Texas, it was the bureau's failure, not the army's. Sherman hoped to get to the bottom of the matter. "After I get to Fort Sill, I will endeavor to form some definite opinion whether these thieves come from that quarter or whether they come from the Staked Plains," he told Reynolds. "I have heard nothing or seen nothing as yet which could not be accounted for by a hundred Indians such as we know the Comanches and Kiowas to be." In other words, this was a matter for law enforcement, not the army.

Sherman's thinking hadn't changed three days later. Writing from Fort Richardson, he told Reynolds of the rough and arid country just traversed. "Of course we saw no Indians," he continued, "but heard, especially at Belknap" — Fort Belknap — "of their frequent incursions in small parties to steal horses. We found large numbers of cattle feeding by the road, so I suppose the Indians do not want to steal them. But no horses or mules were seen except in corrals or ridden by men." A small community, Jacksboro, had sprung up beside Fort Richardson. "A delegation of the people are coming to see me this afternoon to complain of the frequent incursions of the Indians and to accuse the Reservation Indians at Fort Sill. I do not doubt that some of the Kiowas and Comanches from the Reservation do come down to Texas to steal horses, and they never object to killing and scalping when tempted, but these Indians are in the custody of the Indian Bureau, and the Army has no more control over it than the Post Office Department has."

Sherman allowed that non-reservation Indians might be responsible for some of the raiding. "The Comanches that still belong properly to Texas are enough in numbers to account for all the horse stealing we hear of," he wrote. "They probably use most of the horses so stolen in hunting, but some are doubtless sold to New Mexico and some up in Kansas." He expected to know more soon. "If the Indians in the Fort Sill Reservation have many Texas horses with brands on, I will find it out at Fort Sill and will labor to have the thing stopped through the Commissioner of Indian Affairs." He added, "Of course it is a great outrage if Indians who

receive annuities from the United States
make a refuge for stolen stock, and when the
truth is ascertained, some means can be
devised to stop it."

23

The very next day, Sherman discovered that the Indian problem in West Texas involved more than thievery. Randolph Marcy's diary recounted the news brought to Sherman at Fort Richardson: "This morning, five teamsters who, with seven others, had been with a mule wagon train en route to Fort Griffin with corn for the post, were attacked on the open prairie about ten miles east of Salt Creek by one hundred Indians, and seven of the teamsters killed and one wounded." Sherman reacted at once. "General Sherman immediately ordered Colonel Mackenzie to take a force of about one hundred and fifty cavalry, with thirty days' rations on pack mules, and pursue and chastise the murderers."

The pursuit party galloped to the site of the attack. Ranald Mackenzie sent back a report confirming the story of the surviving teamsters. "Five mules lie dead among the wagons," he wrote. The rest of the animals had been stolen. "The sergeant in charge of the detail sent out in advance found five of the men about the wagons, their heads split open and otherwise mutilated. One was found chained to a wagon wheel and burnt in many places to a crisp."

While the pursuit proceeded, Sherman continued to Fort Sill. "Passed today several large herds of cattle en route for Kansas," Marcy recorded. The herds were going to Kansas because Kansas held the nearest railroad. The railroad would take the cattle to Chicago, where they would be slaughtered and the beef shipped in refrigerated cars to the cities of the East. The whole process encapsulated the difference between the Indians' traditional method of harvesting meat from the plains and the whites' industrial approach. In the Indian model, the humans did the moving, going to where the meat was. In the whites' version, the meat was moved to where the humans were. The Indian model limited the number of humans who could feed on the buffalo; only so many hunters and families could or would take up the chase. The whites' model met no such limits. The technology of railroads and refrigeration allowed the long-distance transport of cattle and beef. The principal limit on the white model was the grass that fed the cattle. Much of the struggle for the plains was the result of whites' efforts to lift this limit by removing the buffalo, thereby freeing up grass for cattle. The demise or displacement of the Indians who depended on the buffalo was a side effect.

"Crossed Red River at Red River Station and encamped on the north side," wrote Marcy. "This is the great crossing for the herds of cattle going from Texas to Kansas. The stock raisers in Texas keep an agent here who registers the cattle of different brands that cross the river into the Indian country. Each drover is required by law to keep a record of the number, brand, name of the vendor, and date of purchase of all the cattle he drives, the whole signed and acknowledged by the vendors. When the drover arrives at Red River, he exhibits his purchase list to the agent, who verifies it by count and examination, and notes the result upon his tally register. This prevents drovers from taking off cattle that may have mixed with their herds and not been paid for."

The private initiative responsible for the cattle registry was what Sherman had hoped would solve the problem of horse theft. But the killings at Salt Creek made him think the calls for the army to take charge might become irresistible. It was to deflect such calls that he had acted so quickly in sending out Colonel Mackenzie with sufficient soldiers to overwhelm the perpetrators.

As usual, the first problem would be to find them. Sherman expected a long chase. In the meantime he continued his inspection. His party reached Fort Sill, where the agent to the Comanches and Kiowas on the reservation there paid him a call. Marcy described the man, Lawrie Tatum, as "a most benevolent and conscientious Quaker gentleman." Yet Tatum was at his wits' end. "The first remark he made was that he had been able to accomplish nothing in civilizing his Indians, that they paid no attention to his injunctions and continued going to Texas where they committed murders and lawless depredations upon the whites of that section, while at the same time they were being fed from week to week by the United States." Tatum wasn't entirely surprised at the resistance among the adults, but he had experienced no better luck with the youngsters. "A school had been established for these Indians, but he had been unable to persuade them to send a single child to it. One Comanche boy had been in the school for a few days, but his entire family camped near the school house all the time, and they soon took him away, for fear probably that he would be bewitched or contaminated by contact with our people."

Tatum felt his Quaker convictions weakening. "The agent does not presume to go to the camp of these savages without a strong guard, and he begins to realize the necessity of a more vigorous policy towards them," Marcy recorded. "They must, he thinks, be made to feel the strong arm of the government, and be punished when they perpetrate atrocities. It is considered unsafe to go five miles from the fort without an escort. Last summer, these merciless miscreants murdered four men in one day within three miles of the fort."

Sherman toured the fort and interviewed its commander. He climbed a peak in the nearby Wichita Mountains on which had been constructed a heliostat signaling station. The rain that day prevented a demonstration of its capacity to flash messages, via the reflected rays of the sun, over many miles at the speed of light.

He extended his visit awaiting news from the pursuit party. A week after the Salt Creek attack, he had heard nothing. He wasn't surprised. Nor was he concerned. Colonel Mackenzie still had another three weeks of provisions.

He *was* surprised the next day when he learned that the leaders of the attack were in fact at Fort Sill. Agent Tatum was distributing rations to the Indians when several Kiowa chiefs, including Satanta, Satank, Kicking Bird and Lone Wolf, came for theirs. Tatum asked the chiefs to come into his office, where he told of the killings in Texas and asked them if they knew which Indians were responsible.

"Yes," said Satanta, according to Tatum's later account. "I led in that raid. I have repeatedly asked for arms and ammunition, which have not been furnished. I have made many other requests which have not been granted. You do not listen to my talk. The white people are preparing to build a railroad through our country, which will not be permitted. Some years ago they took us by the hair and pulled us here close to Texas where we have to fight them. More recently I was arrested by the soldiers and kept in confinement several days. But that is played out now. There are never to be any more Kiowa Indians arrested. I want you to remember that."

Satanta continued: "On account of these grievances, a short time ago I took about one hundred of my warriors, whom I wished to teach how to fight, to Texas. I also took the chiefs Satank, Eagle Heart, Big Tree, Big Bow and Fast Bear. We found a mule train, which we captured, and killed seven of the men. Three of our men got killed, but we are willing to call it even. It is all over now, and it is not necessary to say much more about it. We don't expect to do any raiding around here this summer, but we expect to raid in Texas. If any other Indian claims the honor of leading that party, he will be lying to you. I led it myself."

Tatum retold the story to Sherman and

insisted that he arrest the criminals. Sherman didn't have to be persuaded, yet he did consider just how to handle the matter. In hot pursuit he wouldn't have hesitated to send troops onto the reservation, but knew the Indian Bureau would object and complain to the bureau's patrons in Congress. He decided to test whether Satanta was sufficiently proud of his exploit to tell it to the commanding general of the U.S. Army. He sent an invitation to Satanta and the other leaders to come speak with him.

Satanta didn't need the invitation. He had heard that a big general was at the fort, and he wanted to be sure the general got the story from his own mouth. He repeated what he had told Tatum.

Sherman listened, and informed Satanta that he and the others were going to be arrested and held in the Fort Sill jail until they could be transported to Texas for trial.

The Indians were taken aback. Their leader began to change his story. "Satanta, seeing that he was likely to get into trouble, replied that although he was present at the fight, yet he did not kill anybody himself," Marcy wrote. "That his young men wanted to have a little fight and to take a few white scalps, and he was prevailed upon to go with them merely to show them how to make war, but that he stood back during the engagement and merely gave directions. He added that some time ago, the whites had killed three of his people and wounded four more, so that this little affair made the account square, and he was now ready to commence anew."

Sherman would have none of it. "The General told him it was a very cowardly thing for one hundred warriors to attack twelve poor teamsters, who did not pretend to know how to fight. That if he desired to have a battle, the soldiers were ready to meet him at any time." Sherman reiterated that Satanta and the others were going to Texas for trial.

"Seeing no escape, Satanta remarked that rather than be sent to Texas, he preferred being shot on the spot," Marcy wrote.

Another Kiowa chief, Kicking Bird, had not come in with Satanta, but having learned of the meeting with Sherman, he appeared at this time. Kicking Bird had been described by agent Tatum as one of the most influential chiefs and one who generally behaved well. He presented himself to Sherman. "He arose and said that he, as General Grierson" — the Fort Sill commandant — "and the agent well know, had done everything in his power to prevent the young warriors from leaving the reservation and going to Texas for marauding purposes," Marcy recorded. "That he had invariably endeavored to keep his followers in the right path, and for the sake of the good he had done he now asked the general to release his friends from arrest, and he would return the captured mules."

Sherman heard Kicking Bird out. He replied that he appreciated the good things the chief had done. He hoped the chief would continue to do good, and he promised that Kicking Bird would be treated kindly so long as he did. But Satanta and the other bad chiefs were going to Texas.

At this point some twenty soldiers entered the piazza where Sherman and the rest were meeting. The soldiers were fully armed and apparently had been sent by the commandant. Their arrival caused a stir. "The Indians seemed quite excited, nearly every one of them having a Spencer carbine or Colt's revolver," Marcy wrote. Perhaps they thought Sherman was going to grant Satanta's request after all, and have them shot there.

Kicking Bird continued to plead the case of Satanta and the others. He said he was friendly to the whites and would feel sorry if war broke out as a result of this misunderstanding. But if it did, he would have no choice. He would side with his own people.

Another chief, Lone Wolf, now rode up on a handsome horse. He dismounted and laid two Spencer carbines and a bow and a quiver of arrows on the ground. He tied his horse to a fence rail. Then he removed the blanket from around his shoulders and fastened it about his waist. He picked up the carbines in one hand and the bow and arrows in the other — "and with the most deliberate and defiant air, strode up to the piazza," wrote Marcy. "Then, giving one of his carbines to an Indian who had no arms, and the bow and arrows to another, who at once strung the bow and pulled out a handful of arrows, he seated himself and cocked his carbine. At which the soldiers all brought their carbines to an aim upon the crowd — whereupon Satanta and some of the other Indians held up their hands and cried out 'No! No! No!' "

Sherman told the soldiers not to fire.

"But just at this moment we heard shots fired outside the fort," Marcy wrote. The tension increased again. What had happened was that the sentries at the gate of the fort had been ordered to let no Indians leave until Sherman gave the signal. Some of the Indians inside, disliking how the meeting was going, tried to get past the guards. The guards told them to stop, and one of the Indians fired an arrow, wounding a guard. The arrow was answered by rifle fire, and the Indian was killed.

Getting this explanation took some time, during which the tension in the piazza continued high. But it gradually subsided, with no shots fired in the piazza.

Sherman reverted to what Kicking Bird had said about the mules. They must be returned, Sherman said.

Kicking Bird, taking this as a good sign,

268

said he would get the mules at once. He rode off to the camp. It wasn't far, and everyone awaited his return. When he reached the camp, he discovered that the commotion in the fort had frightened the women in the camp, and they had departed, taking most of the mules with them. Only eight remained. These he gathered and took back to the fort.

Sherman accepted the mules but refused to reconsider the detention of the leaders of the Texas attack. They were placed in irons and sent to the fort's jail, under close guard. The rest of the Indians were allowed to leave.

24

The guard on the prisoners was partly for their own protection. Sherman supposed the Texans in the vicinity of the killings might be tempted to take justice into their own hands with Satanta and the others. "They must not be mobbed or lynched, but tried regularly for murder and as many other crimes as the attorney can prove," he wrote to the commander at Fort Richardson, who would receive the prisoners. At the same time, every effort should be made to prevent escape. "The military authorities should see that these prisoners never escape alive, for they are the very impersonation of murder, robbery, arson and all the capital crimes of the statute book." Sherman added a postscript: "Let the Jacksboro people know of this."

Sherman expected positive results from the prosecution of Satanta and the others. "It will, I *know,* do the Kiowas a heap of good," he wrote. And he directed the Fort Sill commandant to arrange lessons. "If you and

MacKenzie can lay a trap to catch some party of horse thieves in Texas, near the line, and hang every one of them, it will stop this raiding," Sherman said. "And tell Kicking Bird, when he comes in, which he will sooner or later, that if another raiding party goes from the reservation to Texas, we will have to search his camps for stolen stock, and if that will not do, we must abrogate the treaty, declare them outlaws, and open their reservation to settlement."

Satanta, Satank and Big Tree were loaded into wagons for return to Texas. Satank resisted his restraints and made sufficient fuss that he was moved to a different wagon from the other two, with his own guard. A Caddo Indian happened by Satank's wagon as the party was leaving the fort. "I wish to send a message by you to my people," Satank called out to him. "Tell them that I am dead. I died the first day out, and my bones will be lying on the side of the road. I wish my people to gather them up and take them home."

As the party marched out, Satank complained loudly, in Kiowa, to Satanta and Big Tree in the other wagon, that he was a warrior and a chief, too old to be treated like a child. He pointed to a tree ahead on the road. "I shall never go beyond that tree," he said. He began singing the Kiowa death song: "Oh Sun, you remain forever, but we Kaitsenko must die! Oh Earth, you remain forever, but we Kaitsenko must die!"

When he finished his song, he pulled out a knife he had managed to conceal, and attacked his guard. Other guards saw what was happening and shot Satank dead. His body was left beside the road, where his people, having been alerted by the Caddo, retrieved it.

Satanta and Big Tree reached Jacksboro without further incident. The trial drew wide attention, for bringing to the bar of justice the confessed murderers of the Texas teamsters, but also for being the first time Indian chiefs had been tried in a civil court. The people of the town and countryside started arriving hours before the proceedings commenced; when Judge Charles Soward declared the trial begun, the courtroom was crammed to the full. The adults in the audience knew more or less what to expect; the many children, towed in by their parents, simply gathered that it was important, or they wouldn't have been there.

The prosecuting attorney was hardly more than a child himself. Samuel Lanham had celebrated his twenty-fifth birthday the day before the trial, but he seemed destined for greater things, and in fact would become governor of Texas. His most conspicuous talent was a way with words, which poured from his lips in a powerful stream. "This is a novel

272

and important trial and has, perhaps, no precedent in the history of American criminal jurisprudence," he declared. "The remarkable character of the prisoners, who are leading representatives of their race; their crude and barbarous appearance; the gravity of the charge; the number of victims; the horrid brutality and inhuman butchery inflicted upon the bodies of the dead; the dreadful and terrific spectacle of seven men, who were husbands, fathers, brothers, sons and lovers, on the morning of the dark and bloody day of this atrocious deed, and rose from their rude tents bright with hope, in the prime and pride of manhood — found, at a later hour, beyond recognition in every condition of horrid disfiguration, unutterable mutilation and death, lying 'stark and stiff, under the hoofs of vaunting enemies!' "

Lanham addressed the audience in the courtroom even as he described them: "This vast collection of our border people; this sea of faces, including distinguished gentlemen, civic and military, who have come hither to witness the triumph of law and justice over barbarity and assassination; the matron and the maiden, the gray-haired sire and the immature lad, who have been attracted to this tribunal by this unusual occasion, all conspire to surround this case with thrilling and extraordinary interest."

He characterized the defendants as they

wished to be seen by the world: "Satanta, the veteran council chief of the Kiowas, the orator, diplomat, the counselor of his tribe, the pulse of his race; Big Tree, the young war chief, who leads in the thickest of the fight, and follows no one in the chase, the mighty warrior athlete, with the speed of the deer and the eye of the eagle."

But in the courtroom their true character emerged, Lanham said. "We recognize in Satanta the arch fiend of treachery and blood, the cunning Cataline, the promoter of strife, the breaker of treaties signed by his own hand, the inciter of his fellows to rapine and murder, the artful dealer in bravado while in the power and the most abject coward in the field, as well as the most canting and double-tongued hypocrite when detected and overcome! In Big-Tree we perceive the tiger-demon, who has tasted blood and loves it as his food, who stops at no crime how black soever, who is swift at every species of ferocity and pities not at any sight of agony or death; he can scalp, burn, torture, mangle and deface his victims with all the superlatives of cruelty, and have no feeling of sympathy or remorse."

Lanham said more in like vein about Satanta and Big Tree before turning his baleful gaze upon the Indian Bureau for treating such monsters as ordinary men and suitable wards of the United States. The tender souls at the bureau were complicit in the killing of the teamsters, he said. "Mistaken sympathy for these vile creatures has kindled the flames around the cabin of the pioneer and despoiled him of his hard earnings, murdered and scalped our people, and carried off our women into captivity worse than death. For many years, predatory and numerous bands of these pets of the government have waged the most relentless and heart-rending warfare upon our frontier, stealing our property and killing our citizens. We have cried aloud for help; as segments of the grand aggregate of the country we have begged for relief; deaf ears have been turned to our cries, and the story of our wrongs has been discredited."

But fate — or dumb luck, perhaps — had intervened. "Had it not been for General W. T. Sherman and his most opportune journey through this section, his personal observation of the debris of this scene of slaughter, the ensanguined corpses of the murdered teamsters, and the entire evidence of this dire tragedy, it may well be doubted whether these brutes in human shape would ever have been brought to trial." Some in the courtroom might have known that Lanham was stretching here. Sherman's party had indeed passed the site of the slaughter, but before it happened. Some were surmising that Satanta's war party, lying in wait, had watched Sherman's party yet let it pass, as too well armed and not rich enough in booty. Sherman had not gone back or seen the corpses.

One in the courtroom, Ranald Mackenzie, who had led the pursuit of Satanta and the others, and had transported the prisoners from Fort Sill, did know this, but he chose not to dispute Lanham, especially after the prosecuting attorney singled him out for praise. "We are greatly indebted to the military arm of the government for kindly offices and cooperation in procuring the arrest and transference of the defendants," Lanham said. "If the entire management of the Indian question were submitted to that gallant and distinguished army officer who graces this occasion with his dignified presence" — Lanham nodded toward Mackenzie — "our frontier would soon enjoy immunity from these marauders."

Lanham turned to the evil deed itself. By this time all in the courtroom knew the gory details, yet the prosecutor repeated them. All knew of Satanta's confession; Lanham recounted this too. The circumstantial evidence was compelling; it received thorough treatment.

The conclusion was inescapable, Lanham told the jury. "All the elements of murder in the first degree are found in the case," he said. "The jurisdiction of the court is complete, and the State of Texas expects from you a verdict and judgment in accordance with the law and the evidence."

The verdict probably was inevitable, but the judge made certain the defense did its part. The two attorneys appointed by the court for Satanta and Big Tree pressed the prosecution at all points. And they put Satanta on the stand to speak for himself. He had a reputation as an orator, but he labored here under the double difficulty of being in handcuffs, which limited his gestures, and of speaking in Comanche, there being no Kiowa translator present. "I cannot speak with these things on my wrists," Satanta said, holding up the cuffs. "I am a squaw." He looked around the courtroom. "I have never been near so many Tehannas" — Texans — "before. I look around me and see your braves, squaws and papooses, and I have said in my heart, if I ever get back to my people I will never make war upon you. I have always been the friend of the white man since I was so high" — he gestured at the height of his waist. "My tribe have taunted me and called me a squaw because I have been the friend of the Tehannas." This statement corroborated something agent Tatum had conjectured to Sherman: that Satanta's fear of losing face had contributed not simply to his launching the raid into Texas but to his boasting of having led it.

"I am suffering now for the crimes of bad Indians — of Satank and Lone Wolf and

277

Kicking Bird and Big Bow and Fast Bear and Eagle Heart," Satanta continued. "And if you will let me go, I will kill the three latter with my own hand." The jury and the audience doubtless wondered at this: whether Satanta meant it, and whether he could accomplish it. He assured them he could. "I am a big chief among my people, and have great influence among the warriors of my tribe. They know my voice and will hear my word." He would use his power for good, or for ill. "If you will let me go back to my people, I will withdraw my warriors from Tehanna. I will take them all across the Red River, and that shall be the line between us and the pale faces. I will wash out the spots of blood and make it a white land, and there shall be peace, and the Tehannas may plow and drive their oxen to the banks of the river. But if you kill me, it will be like a spark in the prairie and make a big fire."

The verdict came quickly. The jury found Satanta and Big Tree guilty of first-degree murder. The sentence was death.

The courtroom audience erupted in cheers. Finally, it seemed, the government was acting with suitable rigor against those who had been murdering Texans and stealing their property. Many present hoped to return to Jacksboro for the hangings, scheduled for September 1.

But efforts were already under way to commute the sentences. After delivering Satanta and the other chiefs into Sherman's hands, Tatum had second thoughts. "Permit me to urge, independent of my conscientious views against capital punishment, as a matter of policy it would be best, for the inhabitants of Texas, that they be not executed for some time, and probably not at all," he wrote to Sherman. "If they are kept as prisoners, the Indians will hope to have them released and thus have a restraining influence in their actions. But if they are executed, the Indians will be very likely to seek revenge in the wholesale murder of white people."

Tatum made the same appeal to the trial judge, who concurred in the reasoning. Yet Judge Soward, having witnessed the reaction in the courtroom, didn't want to take on public opinion himself. Instead he put the burden on Texas governor Edmund J. Davis. "I would have petitioned your Excellency to commute their punishment to imprisonment for life, were it not that I know a great majority of the people on their frontier demand their execution," Soward wrote. "Your Excellency, however, acting for the weal of the State at large, and free from the passions of the masses, may see fit to commute their punishment. If so, I say, Amen!"

Edmund Davis had never much cared for public opinion. He flouted the secessionist majority in Texas during the Civil War and fought on the side of the Union. He owed his 1869 election to the presence of Union troops commanded by Phil Sheridan. By the summer of 1871, the days of Reconstruction in the state were numbered, and with them Davis's political future. Concluding he had little left to lose on the popular front, and presumably moved by Tatum's argument, he accepted the agent's recommendation and commuted the death sentence to life in prison. Satanta and Big Tree were transported to the state penitentiary in the East Texas town of Huntsville.

Sherman followed the trial via the newspapers. He was satisfied with the verdict of the court, believing the death penalty fully warranted by the murder of the teamsters. He was pleased, moreover, that the civil judiciary had proven capable of dealing with crimes committed by Indians. He hoped that the precedent would be accepted broadly, and that the army could get out of the business of law enforcement.

He must have been surprised by Tatum's plea for clemency, after the agent's insistence on rigorous treatment of malefactors in their interview at Fort Sill. And he was exasperated by Governor Davis's decision to commute the death sentences, which undid much of the good that had been accomplished by the trial.

But mostly he was concerned that the new sentences of life imprisonment would never stick. The do-gooders in the Indian Bureau would use Satanta and Big Tree as bargaining chips with the Kiowas, offering the chiefs' parole in exchange for another Kiowa promise to be good. By this time Sherman tried to have as little to do with the bureau or the Interior Department as possible, but when a bargain along the lines he had feared came into view, he gave the interior secretary, Columbus Delano, a piece of his mind. "Knowing as I do how Satanta and the Kiowas have on former occasions broken every promise they had ever made, I mistrust absolutely their present promises of good behavior. Indeed, my idea is that the Indian by nature can't help it. He should no more be tempted by a horse or a convenient scalp than a child should be with candy." Sherman cited a recent example of lying by some Cheyennes in support of his theory. "But I will say no more," he concluded, "leaving the case to take its official and natural course, and feel my conscience relieved by having represented the case pretty strongly."

In fact, Sherman did say more. He added a postscript: "I hope when Satanta is released, and when he is actually killed at the head of a raiding party off his reservation (as certain as next year comes), you will simply decree that the Kiowas are outlawed, their property confiscated, and their most valuable reservation restored to the public domain. Such an example will be worth the experiment."

The bargain did go through; the experiment was made. In granting parole, Governor Davis suggested that Sherman could have averted much trouble by dealing summarily with Satanta and Big Tree at Fort Sill.

Sherman hadn't liked Davis when he had to deal with him on matters of Reconstruction; he liked him even less now. "You are in error in supposing that I had any authority whatever to execute them at Fort Sill, or to order their trial by a military court or commission," Sherman wrote to Davis. "I had authority to do exactly what I did, viz.: with the assent and approval of the agent, Tatum, on the spot, to send them to the jurisdiction of the court having authority to try and punish. Once there they passed under a Texas court, and under your authority as governor of the state. Without the interposition of your authority, these murderers would have been hung as a matter of course, but you remitted them to the penitentiary, and then afterwards set them free."

Sherman reminded Davis of the circumstances of his journey across Texas. "In making the tour of your frontier, with a small escort, I ran the risk of my life," he said. "I will not again voluntarily assume that risk in the interest of your frontier." He concluded with a grim prediction and a scathing preference: "I believe that Satanta and Big Tree will have their revenge, if they have not already had it, and that if they are to have scalps, that yours is the first that should be taken."

25

Billy Dixon wasn't born to be an Indian fighter. By 1850, the year of his birth, the war for Virginia between the English tribe and the Indian tribes had long since ended, with the defeat by death and dispersal of the natives. Another war, between the white tribes, was about to start, but Billy was too young to fight. His mother died when he was ten and his father when he was twelve, and amid the Civil War he and his younger sister were packed off from their Virginia home to live with an uncle in Missouri. Billy didn't have anything against his uncle, but neither did he like being dependent, and after his sister succumbed to typhoid fever, he lit out for the territories, like another lad from Missouri at about the same time.

But where Sam Clemens got as far as Nevada, crossing the Great Plains and Rocky Mountains in stagecoach style, Billy Dixon only made Kansas, and that afoot. He and a friend fell in with a pack train taking supplies for the army to Fort Leavenworth. Billy, fifteen at this point, found the bull-whackers a fascinating crew, snapping their great whips over the heads of the plodding beasts. He learned a bit about getting along. "Between Lawrence and Leavenworth the country was well settled, and every farm-yard was filled with chickens, turkeys, ducks and geese, many of which disappeared about the time we passed that way," he recounted years later. "Of course I would not be willing to admit that I helped steal any of them, but it would be useless for me to say that I did not help eat from many a well-filled pot." He was introduced to an important institution of western life, the saloon. "Like all frontier towns, Leavenworth City was well supplied with saloons. It is not surprising that in the West most men drank, as the saloon was the main starting place for an outfit like ours, and a man who did not take at least one drink was considered unfriendly. I wish to empha-size this last word, for my statement is liter-ally true. Inviting a man to drink was about the only way civility could be shown, and to refuse an invitation bordered upon an insult."

Billy Dixon's train delivered its supplies to Fort Leavenworth, and the twenty-five wag-ons and three hundred oxen were sold. At first he thought he was out of a job, but the buyer needed drivers, and Billy by this time counted as a veteran. With his pay from the first train he purchased a proper outfit for the trail: a sombrero, a Colt's revolver and gun belt, a Bowie knife and a bull whip.

The train's new owner had contracted to deliver goods to Fort Collins, Colorado Territory, at the foot of the Rockies on the far side of the plains. Billy Dixon eagerly looked for Indians and buffalo, having heard of the fierceness of the former and the multitude of the latter. He and the other drivers did see signs of where Indians had *been:* burned farmhouses and crossroads stores, graves with planks in lieu of headstones. But no live Indians, nor any buffalo. Dixon learned that the double absence was not an accident: the buffalo hadn't yet migrated north from the southern plains that season, and neither had the Indians, who followed the buffalo.

On the return trip from Fort Collins, Dixon found his next job, with a government mule train. The train was waiting out the worst of the winter near Leavenworth, and during those months the muleskinners were expected to top off the larder with game they killed. Dixon displayed a knack with a rifle, and was promoted to chief provisioner of the camp. "I always attributed my skill with the rifle to my natural love for the sport, to steady nerves, and to constant, unremitting practice," he said. "Where other men found pleasure in cards, horse-racing and other similar amusements, I was happiest when ranging the open country with my gun on my shoulder and a dog at my heels, far out among the wild birds and the wild animals." Dixon was being modest: in fact he was a virtuoso with the long barrel. Shortly he would be accounted the marksman par excellence of the plains.

It was this skill that carried him into buffalo hunting. Bull-whackers and muleskinners were hired hands, their advance limited by the difficulty of amassing capital to purchase animals and wagons of their own. But hunters could be free lances, and the best could write their own tickets with hunting outfits, or strike out independently. As Billy Dixon's gift with a gun became generally known, he attracted offers he found more appealing than coaxing oxen and mules through muddy stretches of road and across treacherous streams.

"I was now eighteen years old, in perfect health, strong and muscular, with keen eyesight, a natural aptitude for outdoor life, an excellent shot, and had a burning desire to experience every phase of adventure to be found on the Plains," he recalled. His timing couldn't have been better. As the Kansas Pacific Railroad pushed out onto the plains, it created markets where markets hadn't existed before. Hunters heretofore had killed buffalo for their tongues, but tongues didn't travel well, and the market was limited. The construction of the railroad coincided with the development of new techniques for tanning buffalo hides, which yielded leather suitable for belts to link steam engines to looms, lathes and other tools in the burgeoning American factory system. Demand for buffalo hides soared, with the limiting factor being the speed at which hunters could kill the animals and skinners strip the hides from the carcasses.

"The hunting of buffaloes for their hides began in the spring of 1870," Dixon recalled. "As I remember, the hunting was started by a firm of eastern hide-buyers whose agents came to Hays City" — in western Kansas — "and other towns near the buffalo range and offered prices that made hide-hunting a profitable occupation. We were in the very heart of the best buffalo country between the Dominion of Canada and the Rio Grande." The money was more than Dixon had been earning. "The first offers were $1 each for cowhides" — the hides of female buffalos — "and $2 each for bull hides, which enabled us to make money rapidly."

Dixon roamed along the Republican River in western Kansas. "Generally, there were three or four men in an outfit, each having contributed his share for necessary expenses," Dixon said. "They went where the range was best, and buffaloes most plentiful. A dugout was built and occupied as permanent headquarters camp, the hunters ranging for miles through the surrounding country. The only kind of dugout worth having was one with a big, open fire-place, near the edge of a stream of good water, with plenty of wood along its banks." The hunters would occupy the dugout for a month or two. "Then, as the buffaloes grew less plentiful, we shifted our camp and built a new dugout, which was easily and quickly done. From where the buffaloes were killed in the range, we hauled the hides to camp, where we dried them and hauled them to market."

Dixon was good at what he did, and proud of it. "There were very few men who could excel me in marksmanship," he said.

He became the head of his own small firm. "I always did my own killing, and generally had two experienced men to do the skinning," he recounted. "A capable man could skin fifty buffaloes a day, and usually was paid $50 a month. I have paid as much as twenty-five cents a hide to a good skinner."

The herd was large, but with Dixon killing a hundred buffalo a day, the numbers diminished. Dixon had to find a new range. He moved his operation south of the railroad, into land still claimed by the Comanches, Kiowas and Cheyennes. He understood the risk, but weighed against the profits to be made, it seemed a risk worth taking. "We hunted along the Saline and Solomon, frequently encountering small bands of Indians," he said. "Generally, they were going north or south, and though they were supposed to be friendly, we watched them closely. Occasionally, we heard of a hunter being killed, but this did not bother us, so long as we were not molested. Sometimes, Indians came into our camp. They were always hungry. We always fed them. They love sugar and coffee, and for either were willing to trade anything they had. The Kiowas were especially fond of sugar."

The spring of 1874 found him where southwestern Kansas abuts the Oklahoma panhandle, the thirty-four-mile-wide strip above the panhandle of Texas. The growing scarcity of buffalo drew him south, ever deeper into Indian territory. "At intervals we struck small bands of bulls," Dixon recalled. "Buffaloes were surprisingly scarce. Sometimes we killed them, and at other times did not molest them. Generally, there were from four to ten in a bunch. The scarcity of buffaloes rather discouraged us, and we redoubled our efforts to locate a big herd." In May he and his crew camped near the Canadian River. "The season was delightful. The air was fresh and invigorating, the grass was green, flowers were blooming, the sky was clear, the sunshine pleasant, and a feeling of joy and happiness everywhere. Those were splendid nights, out there under the stars. The mornings came with dazzling splendor. At this season sunrise on the Plains presented a scene of magnificence. I always had the feeling that it came with a thunderous sound."

While they waited for the buffalo herd to come north, they visited Adobe Walls, a trading post first built decades earlier but subsequently abandoned. The crumbling walls of the original buildings had long been a landmark for travelers in the neighborhood, and the growing trade in buffalo hides prompted a reclamation of the site. Dixon and other hunters reprovisioned at the stores there, relaxed at the saloon, and had their guns repaired at the blacksmith's shop. A trail sufficient for pack wagons ran a hundred and fifty miles from Adobe Walls to Dodge City, Kansas, and the railroad there.

The visitors to Adobe Walls shared intelligence about the movement of the herd. "All of us hunters acquainted with the habits of the buffalo knew that the herds would soon be coming north from the Staked Plains region where they had spent the winter," Dixon said. The spring was late, which slowed the migration. There was nothing to do but wait. "We could lie around camp or vary the monotony by going to Adobe Walls and joining in the fun that was rampant at that place. Our amusements were mostly card-playing, running horse-races, drinking whisky and shooting at targets, the latter to improve our marksmanship."

Dixon chafed to be shooting buffalo and making money. He crossed the Canadian River and ventured out onto the high plains. "Here I found an ideal camping place, with plenty of wood, grass and water. I decided to build our permanent camp, and was soon industriously at work. I knew by the signs that buffaloes had been through here, and it was certain that they would soon be coming back." His partners were one "Frenchy," of presumably Gallic background, and Charley Armitage, of demonstrably English descent.

They made ready for what was certain to come. "Getting up one morning earlier than my companions, I chunked the fire for breakfast, and stood waiting for it to begin blazing," Dixon said. "Then a familiar sound come rolling toward me from the Plains — a sound deep and moving, not unlike the rumbling of a distant train passing over a bridge. In an instant I knew what was at hand. I had often heard it. I had been listening for it for days, even weeks. Walking out on a high point near camp, I gazed eagerly toward the horizon. I could see nothing save the vast undulating landscape. My ears, however, had revealed to me what my eyes could not see. The buffaloes were coming!"

He hurried back to camp and told Frenchy and Armitage. They finished making breakfast — coffee, fried meat, toasted bread — while he saddled his horse. He ate quickly and galloped south. "After I had ridden about five miles, I began striking small bunches of buffalo bulls, all headed north and all moving," Dixon said. He rode another eight miles onto the plains until he saw what he was looking for. "As far as the eye could reach, south, east and west of me there was a solid mass of buffaloes — thousands upon thousands of them — slowly moving toward the north. The noise I had heard at early daybreak was the bellowing of the bulls. At this time of year — the breeding season — the bellowing of the countless bulls was continuous, a deep, steady roar, that seemed to reach to the clouds. It was kept up night and day, but seemed to be deepest and plainest at early morning."

The herd was moving toward Dixon's camp. He rode back and told Frenchy and Armitage to get ready to work. Before long the herd approached the camp, proving Dixon an apt student of buffalo behavior. "In sight of it I shot thirty-five or forty, all bulls," he said. "The boys were soon busily at work with their skinning knives. By night buffaloes were passing within gunshot of our camp."

During winter the hunters lived off previous earnings or took on debt; in the spring they had to make it up. Even while firing away, Dixon planned to expand. "Where buffaloes were as plentiful as they were here, I could easily kill enough in a day to keep ten skinners busily at work," he reckoned. "I killed enough next day to keep Frenchy and Armitage employed for several days, and went down to Adobe Walls in a light wagon, to see if I could hire more skinners. I found one man who would go with me, but for only a few days, until his partner should return with a load of hides." It was the best Dixon could do. "All the other hunters had heard the good news, and had pulled out for the buffalo range. Adobe Walls was deserted, save for the merchants and their clerks. By offering this man twenty-five cents a hide for skinning, I induced him to go with me for a week or ten days."

They rode back to camp. "No mercy was shown the buffaloes," Dixon said. "I killed as many as my three men could handle, working them as hard as they were willing to work. This was deadly business, without sentiment; it was dollars against tenderheartedness, and dollars won."

Dixon had agreed to drive the new man back to Adobe Walls when his time was up. The day came and they set out. Rain had swollen the Canadian River, making the regular crossing too dangerous. Dixon drove the wagon along the bank to a spot where a creek entered the river and created a shoal. He tested the depth by wading into the stream, and convinced himself that a crossing was feasible, without the wagon. He would unhitch the mules and swim them over, and he and the skinner would ride on to Adobe Walls. Dixon would pick up the wagon on the way back.

But just then two men from Adobe Walls rode up from the other side. Crossing, they said that two buffalo hunters had been killed by Indians some twenty-five miles down the river. They were hurrying back to their camp to warn the men there. Dixon decided he couldn't leave his wagon. The Indians would burn it if they happened by. He determined to get it over the river. "Choosing a point on the opposite side of the river where we wished to land, we drove in, hoping for the best," he recounted. "In a moment the swift current caught us, and both mules were swimming. In water a mule has less sense than a horse, and the ginger is soon knocked out of him if he gets his ears full of water. Having smaller feet, the mule cannot equal a horse in traversing quicksand." Dixon reacted quickly. "I sprang into the water to help the frightened animals, getting on their upper side and seizing the mule nearest me by his bridle. In this way I was able to keep his head above water. The other mule, terrified by its surroundings, alternately rose and sank." The current got under the wagon, which started rolling over. "We saw that if the wagon kept turning over, the team might get drowned, so we cut the harness, and after the greatest exertion got the mules ashore." The wagon drifted away. "The near mule lay down on the sand and died without a struggle," Dixon said. "It seemed ridiculous that the mule should succumb after being taken from the water, yet there he lay." The other mule was saved. The wagon, having tumbled several more times, came to rest downstream. It was recovered, but not the belongings that had fallen out and sunk to the bottom. "Our greatest misfortune was the loss of our guns," Dixon observed.

He still felt the loss decades later. "When we lined up on the north side of the river we were a sorry lot — two bedraggled, unarmed men and a water-logged mule three miles from Adobe Walls, in danger of attack by Indians at any moment. Ordinarily, I was not easily discouraged. This, however, was a jolt from the shoulder. I stood in greatest need of my gun, a big 50" — a .50-caliber rifle specially designed for shooting buffalo. "We could dig out the wagon, but not the guns, and somewhere in the depths of the Canadian they are rusting this very day."

Dixon and the other man straggled into Adobe Walls, which they found aflutter with talk of Indian attacks. At first they were taken for survivors of an attack, so unkempt and forlorn did they look. They learned the details of the killing they'd been apprised of on the riverbank. Three hunters had been working from a camp on Chicken Creek. One had ridden into Adobe Walls for supplies, and on his return had discovered the other two, dead. "Through the breast of one had been driven a heavy wooden stake, pinning him to the ground," Dixon recounted. "Both were scalped, and otherwise mutilated in a shocking manner."

Dixon thought of Frenchy and Armitage. "I was impatient to return to my own camp as quickly as possible," he said. But he had to replace the mule that had died, and his gun. He finally found a horse its owner was willing to part with. The best he could do for a weapon was an inferior model of Sharps rifle. He was about to leave when a hunter rode in, with news of another killing, of two men on the Salt Fork of the Red River. Their camp had been destroyed and their stock stolen.

Dixon made double haste getting back to his camp. He was relieved to find Frenchy and Armitage safe; in fact they were unaware of any cause for alarm.

He told them what had happened. "All of us agreed that a blind man could see that it was entirely too risky to stay in camp with Indians all around us, so we lost no time in loading our outfit and pulling into Adobe Walls, arriving there by noon the next day." The place was filling up. "The story of the

Indian depredations had spread to all the hunting camps, and by the time we reached the Walls a large crowd had gathered in from the surrounding country." They remained for a week.

The Indian attacks formed the principal subject of conversation. But there was something odd about the attacks. "None of the hunters had seen an Indian nor a sign of one," Dixon recalled. "The Indians evidently had carefully picked their time, watching closely and waiting until only two or three men were in camp, whereupon they attacked and then slipped stealthily away. All of us felt that these murders had been perpetrated as a warning to the buffalo-hunters to leave the country."

Dixon wasn't going to be scared off. Nor were the others. "Every man of us was dead set against abandoning the buffalo range," he said. "The herds were now at hand, and we were in a fair way to make a pile of money. Furthermore, the buffaloes were becoming scarcer and scarcer each year, and it was expedient that we make hay while the sun shone, for soon the sun would be no longer be shining in the buffalo business. Its night was close at hand. We decided that the best and safest plan would be for three or four outfits to throw in together and all occupy the same camp. After all, it was not unusual to hear of two or three buffalo-hunters being

298

killed and scalped every year, and perhaps there would be no further outbreaks by the Indians. It was agreed, however, that everybody should be very careful and take every precaution against surprise and attack."

Most of the hunters moved north and west, away from where the Indians were thought to be. But Dixon liked the camp he had set up, southwest of the Walls. "I resolved to take the risk and establish myself at that point, and went there with three skinners I had hired."

The first thing they did was carry back to Adobe Walls the hides Dixon and Frenchy and Armitage had already acquired and processed. This took several days. Dixon recalled feeling uneasy the whole time. "Something seemed to be wrong. There was Indian in the air, and I could not shake myself loose from thinking about the possible danger." He grudgingly decided to move the camp, to the north side of the Canadian River. He and the new men rode once more to Adobe Walls, to buy provisions enough for the season.

While there, Dixon was approached by James Hanrahan, who owned the saloon, as well as a buffalo hunting outfit. Hanrahan asked Dixon if he would team up with him. "He said he had been having trouble in getting a man who could hunt fast enough to keep his skinners busy," Dixon recalled. Hanrahan had seven skinners; with Dixon's there would be ten. "I told him that nothing would please me more than to go into partnership with him, and that I could easily kill enough buffaloes to keep twenty skinners hard at work every day." Dixon liked the proposed terms. "Hanrahan offered to give me half of all the profits, which was as liberal as any man could wish for."

They shook on the deal, bought everything they'd need, and loaded the wagons for departure the next day. Dixon made a final transaction. "I had been unable to replace my big 50, lost in the Canadian, with a gun that suited me in every way, but it was highly important that I should be well-armed if I expected to fulfill my promises to Hanrahan," he said. "The only gun at the Walls that was not in use was a new 44 Sharp's, which was next best to a 50. This gun had been spoken for by a hunter who was still out in camp; he was to pay $80 for it, buying it from Langton who was in charge of Rath & Wright's store. Langton told me that if necessary he would let me have the gun, as he had ordered a case of guns and was expecting them to arrive any day on the freight train from Dodge City, and he probably would have them in stock before the owner of the gun came in from the buffalo range." As it happened, just hours before Dixon and his new crew were to depart, Langton learned that the freight wagons were almost to Adobe Walls. He found Dixon and told him the gun was his.

Dixon took the gun and purchased a case of ammunition. But, afoot, he left the ammunition with Langdon, for pickup on the way out of town.

He gathered with other hunters for a send-off. Thoughts of hunting and making money pushed discussions of Indians to the back of their minds. "The night was sultry" — this was late June — "and we sat with open doors. In all that vast wilderness, ours were the only lights save the stars that glittered above us. There was just a handful of us out there on the Plains, each bound to the other by the common tie of standing together in the face of any danger that threatened us. It was a simple code, but about the best I know of. Outside could be heard at intervals the muffled sounds of the stock moving and stumbling around, or a picketed horse shaking himself as he paused in his hunt for the young grass. In the timber along Adobe Walls Creek to the east, owls were hooting. We paid no attention to these things, however, and in our fancied security against all foes frolicked and had a general good time. Hanrahan did a thriving trade."

Dixon eventually turned in for the night. Adobe Walls had few beds; hunters like Dixon slept on the ground. "I spread my blankets near the blacksmith's shop, close to my wagon," he remembered. "I placed my gun by my side between my blankets, as usual, to protect it from dew and rain." A man's gun and his horse were his most valued possessions at that place and time, for on them his life could depend. Dixon had picketed his horse on a long rope near the wagon. "Every door was left wide open, such a thing as locking a door being unheard of at the Walls. One by one the lights were turned out, the tired buffalo-hunters fell asleep, and the Walls were soon wrapped in the stillness of night."

The small community — that night there were twenty-eight men and one woman, the wife of the owner of the restaurant, in Adobe Walls — fell asleep. But a few hours before dawn, two men sleeping in the saloon were awakened by a loud cracking sound. At first they thought it was gunfire, but the absence of any more such sounds prompted an investigation of the building, and they discovered that a cottonwood log that held up the roof of the saloon had cracked. The roof of the building, like the roof and walls of the other buildings, was made of compacted dirt, and was quite heavy. If the ridge beam broke entirely, the roof would cave in and the building become useless. A small crew, including Dixon, was gathered to lighten the roof by scraping off dirt, and to prop up the beam with another timber. The commotion awoke most of the population of the hamlet.

The eastern sky was starting to redden with dawn by the time the job was finished. Dixon decided to gather his skinners and make an early start. He rolled his blankets and tossed them into the wagon. He picked up his gun and headed toward his horse. He could see it near the other horses. He suddenly stopped. "Something else caught my eye," he said. "Just beyond the horses, at the edge of some timber, was a large body of objects advancing vaguely in the dusky dawn toward our stock and in the direction of Adobe Walls. Though keen of vision, I could not make out what the objects were, even by straining my eyes."

He looked away, then looked back again, in case that helped. It did. "I was thunder-struck," he said. "The black body of moving objects suddenly spread out like a fan, and from it went up one single, solid yell — a war whoop that seemed to shake the very air of the early morning. Then came the thudding roar of running horses, and the hideous cries of the individual warriors, each embarked in the onslaught. I could see that hundreds of Indians were coming."

Dixon assumed the Indians were trying to run off the stock. He dashed for his horse. "The first mighty war whoop had frightened my horse until he was frantic," he recalled. "He was running and lunging on his rope so violently that in one more run he would have pulled up the stake pin and gone to the land of stampeded horses." Dixon succeeded in grabbing the rope and tying it to the wagon.

He ran back for his gun. Still assuming the Indians were rushing the horses and would wheel away, he wanted to get in a few shots before they were out of range.

In seconds he realized his mistake. Far from turning away, the Indians were tearing straight at the buildings of Adobe Walls, shouting louder and whipping their horses more vigorously the closer they came.

From decades later, Dixon could still see the charge. "There was never a more splendidly barbaric sight," he said. "Hundreds of warriors, the flower of the fighting men of the southwestern Plains tribes, mounted upon their finest horses, armed with guns and lances, and carrying heavy shields of thick buffalo hide, were coming like the wind. Over all was splashed the rich colors of red, vermillion and ochre, on the bodies of the men, on the bodies of the running horses. Scalps dangled from bridles, gorgeous war-bonnets fluttered their plumes, bright feathers dangled from the tails and manes of the horses, and the bronzed, half-naked bodies of the riders glittered with ornaments of silver and brass. Behind this head-long charging host stretched the Plains, on whose horizon the rising sun was lifting its morning fires. The warriors seemed to emerge from this glowing background."

The older Dixon granted that he appreciated the sight the better for having survived it. At the moment, it was terrifying. "War-whooping had a very appreciable effect upon the roots of a man's hair," he said. He fired a single shot, then turned and ran for the saloon. Others had beaten him there, and the door was closed and barred. He pounded to be let in, while the Indians drew ever closer. "Bullets were whistling and knocking up the dust all around me." After the longest few seconds of his life, the door opened and he ducked inside.

As Dixon and others later reconstructed the events of that day, the attacking force consisted of some seven hundred Comanches, Cheyennes and Kiowas. Their leaders were Quanah Parker and Isa-tai. Quanah was the son of a Comanche chief named Peta Nocona and Cynthia Ann Parker, a white woman who had been captured as a girl and taken into the tribe. Isa-tai was a Comanche medicine man and prophet who preached a Comanche revival and united the several Comanche bands in the struggle against the whites. Quanah had organized the alliance with the Cheyennes and Kiowas.

Arrayed against the attackers were the handful of residents of Adobe Walls and the twenty-odd hunters who happened to be there that morning. The defenders were divided into three groups, according to which building — the two stores and one saloon — they happened to be closest to when they heard the war whoops.

The Indians had the advantage of surprise, but not as much advantage as they had hoped for. The accident of the cracking of the saloon's roof timber meant that most of those who would have been asleep were awake and able to respond more quickly than the Indians expected. Still, the attackers surged forward undaunted. They rode right up to the buildings, blazing away and even beating on the doors with their rifle butts.

But they couldn't get in, and the hunters, having gathered their wits and their rifles, fired back with increasing effect. "The Indians stood up against this for a while, but gradually began falling back, as we were emptying buckskin saddles entirely too fast for Indian safety," Dixon said. "Our guns had longer range than theirs." The Indians killed two hunters, brothers who had been sleeping in their wagon and didn't reach the safety of one of the buildings. Both men were scalped. So was the brothers' dog, a Newfoundland the attackers shot. The Indians hacked a piece of fur and skin from the dog's side.

Spontaneously or on the order of Quanah, many of the Indians leaped off their horses to fight as foot soldiers. But they soon thought better of this. On foot they made easier targets for the sharpshooters in the buildings.

The Indians remounted and retreated.

Further charges ensued. Yet these had less luck than the first. The earthen walls of the buildings protected the defenders, who could fire out with little danger to themselves. The charges became less frequent.

Early in the battle, the hunters were surprised to hear the sounds of a bugle. Several, including Dixon, had been in or around the army, and they recognized the various calls. When it blew the rally, the warriors rallied to their leaders. When the bugle blew the charge, the Indians charged. The use of the bugle made the Indian attack better coordinated than any the hunters had ever seen. But it also eased the task of the defenders, for they intercepted the attackers' signals as soon as the signals were given.

No one knew, or ever found out, who the bugler was. Some of Dixon's comrades supposed it was a deserter from the Tenth Cavalry, one of the buffalo soldiers who got fed up with barracks life. Dixon didn't think so. He had heard of a captured Mexican living among the Kiowas and Comanches who somewhere had learned to play the bugle; Dixon thought he was the one at Adobe Walls. But he admitted he couldn't be sure.

The fighting devolved into a static exchange of rifle fire. The Indians hoped to draw the hunters out far enough that they could be killed or wounded. Knowing that they greatly outnumbered the hunters, they knew that an even trade of casualty for casualty would win the battle for them.

But the hunters refused to be drawn. *Their* calculation was that the Indians would tire of getting picked off by shooters they couldn't even see. Indian warriors, even in the larger tribes, were always risk averse. The existential problem of every tribe was declining numbers, and when losses in a battle began to mount, they typically broke off and departed, hoping for better luck the next time.

Yet it was tempting for this group of Indians to besiege the defenders. The nearest relief for Adobe Walls was in Dodge City, and it would take days for anyone there to hear of the attack.

Ammunition wasn't a problem. Adobe Walls was, after all, a staging point for professional hunters. Dixon *did* run short momentarily, until he remembered the case of ammunition he had left in the store. Dixon and James Hanrahan decided to make a run for it. They checked outside to see if any Indians could get a clean shot at them. "The coast looked clear, so we crawled out of a window and hit the ground running, running like jackrabbits," Dixon said. "The Indians saw us, however, before the boys could open the door" — of the store — "and opened at long range. The door framed a good target. I have no idea how many guns were cracking away at us, but I do know that bullets rattled round us like hail. Providence seemed to be looking after the boys at Adobe Walls that day, and we got inside without a scratch, though badly winded."

The fighting kept up till early afternoon, when the Indians withdrew beyond range of the hunters' rifles. The hunters valued the respite, but couldn't tell what it meant. "Since early morning, we had been able to hold the enemy at bay," Dixon remarked. "We were confident that we could continue to do so as long as we had ammunition. We thanked our stars that we were behind thick adobe walls, instead of thin pine boards. We could not have saved ourselves had the buildings been frame, such as were commonly built in frontier towns in those days. Still, there was no telling how desperate the Indians might become, rather than abandon the fight; it was easily possible for them to overwhelm us with the brute force of superior numbers by pressing the attack until they had broken down the doors, and which probably would have been attempted, however great the individual sacrifice, had the enemy been white men. Luckily, it was impossible to set the adobes on fire, or else we should have been burned alive."

Dixon and the others understood the Indians' strategy. "They had planned to put every man of us afoot, thereby leaving us without means of escape and powerless to send for aid save as some messenger might steal away in the darkness, to traverse on foot the weary distance and the dangerous and inhospitable region that lay between us and Dodge City," he said. "By holding us constantly at bay and keeping fresh detachments of warriors rallying to the attack they probably thought it possible to exhaust our strength, and then overwhelm us." The odds were in the Indians' favor. "Adobe Walls was scarcely more than a lone island in the vast sea of the Plains, a solitary refuge uncharted and practically unknown. For the time we were at the end of the world, our desperate extremity pressing heavily upon us, and our friends and comrades to the north ignorant of what was taking place."

The Indians had largely succeeded in stranding the hunters. The horses they hadn't stampeded in the initial assault they had mostly killed with gunshots or arrows. "We counted fifty-six dead horses scattered in the immediate vicinity of the buildings," Dixon said. Twenty-eight oxen were killed similarly.

Night fell without further attack. Sleep came slowly and troubled inside Adobe Walls. "What we had experienced ate into a man's nerves," Dixon said. "Somewhere out there in the darkness our enemies were watching to see that nobody escaped from the beleaguered adobe buildings. Inasmuch as Indians

310

rarely, if ever, attack at night, preferring the shadows of early morning when sleep is soundest, and when there is less chance of their being ambushed, we felt reasonably certain of not being attacked before daybreak. As for myself I dreamed all night, the bloody scenes of the day passing in endless procession through my mind — I could see the Indians charging across the valley, hear the roar of the guns and the blood-curdling war-whoops, until everything was a bewildering swirl of fantastic colors and movements."

The night indeed brought no attack, but the next morning afforded little reason for hope. "With every horse dead or captured, we felt pretty sore all round," Dixon said. "The Indians were somewhere close at hand, watching our every movement. We were depressed with the melancholy feeling that probably all the hunters out in the camps had been killed."

The afternoon of the second day yielded a glimmer. The Indians hadn't entirely encircled Adobe Walls, and a German immigrant named George Bellfield drove a wagon and team into the post without realizing it had been under attack. Bellfield let one of the hunters, Henry Lease, use one of his horses to try to reach Dodge City. He waited until dark to take his leave. "He carefully examined his pistols and his big '50,' filled his belts with plenty of ammunition, shook hands with us and rode away in the night," Dixon said. "I doubt if there was a man who believed that Lease would get through alive. It was a certainty, however, that there would be a pile of dead Indians where he fell, if he were given a fighting chance for his life."

That same night, two more hunters slipped out to warn other hunters in the district that the Indians were at war, and to bring back those still alive who were willing to defend Adobe Walls.

The third day produced no attack, but the Indians were still in sight, on a bluff three-quarters of a mile away. Dixon had acquired a Sharps 50 and was known as the best shot in the area. One of the hunters asked him if he could hit the Indians on the bluff. "A number of exaggerated accounts have been written about this incident," Dixon observed modestly. "I took careful aim and pulled the trigger. We saw an Indian fall from his horse. The others dashed out of sight behind a clump of timber." Dixon didn't want to claim too much. "I was admittedly a good marksman, yet this was what might be called a 'scratch' shot" — one hard to repeat.

Perhaps the Indians decided they didn't want to tangle any longer with hunters who could shoot like Billy Dixon. Perhaps they had already concluded they'd made clear that the southern plains would not be safe for the buffalo hunters. This was the purpose of the attack. Quanah Parker and the other Indians didn't have to kill all the hunters; they merely had to disrupt the hide trade before the hunters killed all the buffalo. Dixon and the other hunters were in the business to make money, not to become heroes. Simply by raising the cost of securing and delivering hides — by requiring the hunters, for example, to post guards around their camps, or compelling the pack trains carting the hides to Dodge City to enlist armed escorts — Quanah might make the hide trade unprofitable and thereby force the hunters to abandon it.

In the event, Billy Dixon's long shot — which soon became legendary — marked the end of the siege. The hunters didn't immediately realize that the battle was over; they fortified the buildings against further attack, and they welcomed reinforcements in the persons of outlying hunters who came to Adobe Walls for their own safety, thereby contributing to *its* safety. By the fifth day the greatest danger to those at the post was from themselves: one of the lookouts accidentally shot himself in the head and died.

26

Nelson Miles was the nephew by marriage of William Sherman, having wed the daughter of Sherman's brother Charles. Mary Sherman had visited the West with her father, who was a commissioner of the Union Pacific Railroad, but when Miles, a Civil War volunteer from Massachusetts who rose to the rank of major general, was posted to Kansas in 1869, it was his first trip beyond the Missouri. "At Fort Hays, the headquarters of the Fifth Infantry" — Miles's new unit — "I found a splendid regiment composed of very intelligent, efficient officers and strong, brave soldiers," he wrote. "A few miles away, in a beautiful valley, was the camp of the Seventh United States Cavalry, commanded by Gen. George A. Custer." Miles had served honorably in the Civil War, but Custer had become a hero. "He was one of the most enterprising, fearless cavalry leaders the great war produced," Miles reflected. "He was most ambitious and enterprising and soon rose to command of a regiment and brigade, and later commanded, with great success, one of the active cavalry divisions." Miles and Custer were nearly the same age; both turned thirty in 1869. In the shrunken postwar army, they were, as Miles conceded, "rivals in the military profession."

He added, less convincingly, that they were "the best of friends." He had no choice, for his wife's sake if not his own. Mary Miles and Elizabeth Custer shared the fate of army wives in the West, following their husbands from post to post, dependent for company, if any, on the wives of other officers. Rank among wives wasn't so strictly enforced as among the officers themselves, but it mattered, and the wife of a commandant had almost no one in whom she could really confide. Because Custer and Miles were peers, their wives could be too, even if the competition between the men sometimes made the relationship between the women tense. Yet Miles wasn't one to betray secrets, even in his memoirs. "Mrs. Custer and Mrs. Miles became lifelong friends," he said. "We all enjoyed the splendid exercise of riding over the plains."

Like Custer — and Sherman and Phil Sheridan and nearly every other army officer — Miles had spent more time on the frustrating task of Reconstruction than he cared to. He treated his transfer to the West as an escape. "It was a pleasure to be relieved of the anxieties and responsibilities of civil affairs, to hear nothing of the controversies incident to race prejudice, and to be once more engaged in strictly military duties," he wrote. In the West, soldiers could do what they were trained to do: employ force, even lethal force, to accomplish their mission. In the South, force was typically disallowed. Soldiers there were glorified policemen. No wonder Miles — and Sherman and Sheridan and Custer — liked the West better.

The West held another appeal. Commanding officers were largely unsupervised. "When an officer marched over the Divide" — the line where the arid plains began — "with a command, great or small, he was immediately thrown upon his own resources," Miles said. "He had to think, plan and act for himself and for the welfare and safety of his command." Commanders were occasionally chastised for insufficient use of force, but almost never for excessive use. Put simply, peace policy or no peace, the part of the West where the soldiers were stationed was a war zone, and the rules of war applied.

Miles found much to admire in the Indians of the plains. "They were the most democratic people of the world," he said. "Their government was dictated by council, where reason and logic held sway. The power of argument developed the best natural orators. Their illustrations were usually drawn from nature, and most impressive. Our government often sent members of the Cabinet, Senate, and House of Representatives, and other prominent citizens to meet them in council, and these were usually met by native talent of equal force and eloquence."

They were masterful hunters, knowing how to blend almost perfectly with their surroundings. "I have seen hunting or war parties in the summer or spring time, when the fields and trees were covered with rich verdure, with their horses and parts of their bodies painted green, and wearing green blankets, leggings and moccasins. Later in the season, when the leaves were turning and the grass was dead, they would be mounted on dun or roan ponies and clad in covering of different colors. In winter they would have snow-white ponies, white blankets, caps, leggings, moccasins — everything about them as white as the driven snow."

They were matchless as mounted warriors — "the most expert horsemen in the world," Miles said. They required nothing they couldn't take from the land or from the people who lived on it. This gave them a mobility the white soldiers could never match. "Their young men went on expeditions from their villages, sometimes being absent for twelve months at a time." The army struggled to mount expeditions that lasted even a month.

Miles decried the double standard whites typically employed against Indians. "The art of war among the white race is called strategy, or tactics; when practiced by the Indians it is called treachery," he wrote. Miles never met more honest people than Indians. They stole from their enemies, but they never stole from one another, or from those to whom they had pledged their trust. Miles related a story of a bishop who had come west to speak to a council of the Sioux. The bishop had a fur coat he valued. Before addressing the council, the bishop asked the principal chief if he might leave his coat to the side while he spoke. "The stalwart warrior, straightening himself up to his full height with dignity, said that he could leave it there with perfect safety, 'as there was not a white man within a day's march of the place,' " Miles wrote.

And yet the Indians were doomed. Or, rather, their wild manner of life was doomed. "The wave of civilization was moving over the western horizon," Miles said. "Its onward march was irresistible. No human hand could stay that rolling tide of progress. The pale faces moved over every divide; they cordelled" — hauled by rope — "or pushed their boats up every river. They entered every valley and swarmed over every plain. They traveled in wagons and prairie-schooners, on foot or horseback. Herding their little bands and flocks of domestic stock, they built their homes on every spot of ground that could be made productive."

And now the whites had come to the southern plains. The first wave consisted of the buffalo hunters, the daring entrepreneurs who risked life and limb ravaging the great herd to keep the factories humming in the East. Miles saw as well as the Indians themselves that the destruction of the buffalo would mean the end of the Indians' independence. This was why they had attacked the hunters at Adobe Walls.

And their attack was why he had to go to war against them. The respect with which he spoke of the Indians suggested he might have wished, in another life, to have been one of them, in the days before the whites appeared. "They believe that the Great Spirit has given them this beautiful country with all its natural resources, advantages, and blessings for their home," he wrote. "With deep emotion and profound reverence they speak of the sun as their father and the earth as their mother. Nature they worshiped, upon it they depended, with it they communed, and cherished it with deepest affection." They scorned and pitied the whites for the drudgery of white life. "They had no respect for those who lived by digging the ground, or by trading, as the traders were ever seeking to take

319

advantage of the Indians. As for the miner who went down into a hole in the ground in the morning and remained until night, his life to them was like that of the gopher." Miles had difficulty disagreeing. The Indians had things far better. "Their life on the plains was independent and most enjoyable. In whatever direction they moved they were sure to find in a day's march beautiful camping grounds, plenty of timber and grass, pure water, and an abundance of food. Besides the flesh of animals they also had Indian corn, wild vegetables, berries, fruits, and nuts that were easily obtainable."

But Miles was not an Indian; he was a white soldier. And because the Indians had taken white lives and stood athwart the advance of white civilization, he had to fight them. Besides, the Indian idyll was a thing of the past, its end decreed the moment the first Europeans set foot in America. Miles understood why the Indians so hated giving up their wild ways; in their place, who wouldn't? Yet he was compelled to agree with most American officers at least since Andrew Jackson, that the Indians had two alternatives: bending before the tide of white advance, or perishing beneath it.

He organized his response in the weeks after the Adobe Walls fight. He would lead one column south from Kansas into the region along the Red River in Oklahoma and

Texas. Three other columns would approach from the other points of the compass. The Indians would likely scatter before the troops, since they could never stand up to them.

To his men, Miles insisted on certain principles for the campaign: "Never, by day or night, to commit my command to be surprised; to hold it in such condition at all times, whether marching or camping, that it could be ever ready to encounter the enemy; to keep the divisions in communication and supporting distance of each other whenever possible, and always ready to act on the offensive."

The column marched the first hundred miles, out of Kansas and into the Indian Territory, without incident. The country, always dry, had been parched by drought for many months; under the August sun it seemed scorched. The soldiers saw Indians in small groups at a distance; occasionally they skirmished. At other times the soldiers saw nothing but barren prairie. Miles kept his men alert by repeating the saw learned by generations of travelers in Indian country: "When you see Indians about, be careful; when you do not see them, be more careful."

Some of the skirmishes, while not large, were intense. Miles offered Billy Dixon a job as a scout, impressed by his knowledge of the country and his prowess with a rifle. Dixon,

321

reckoning that the Indian outbreak had fairly ruined the season for hunting, accepted. Miles dispatched Dixon and another scout with messages for Fort Supply, a post in the Indian Territory established by Phil Sheridan for his winter campaign against the Kiowas, Cheyennes and Comanches. Miles offered as many troops as Dixon wanted for an escort; Dixon, preferring to move quickly and unobtrusively, chose just four.

"Leaving camp, we traveled mostly at night, resting in secluded places during the day," Dixon recalled. "War parties were moving in every direction, and there was danger of attack at every turn." The first day brought no problems, but the second day delivered all the excitement Dixon thought he could handle. "We were nearing a divide between the Washita River and Gageby Creek," he said. "Riding to the top of a little knoll, we found ourselves almost face to face with a large band of Kiowa and Comanche warriors. The Indians saw us at the same instant and, circling quickly, surrounded us. We were in a trap. We knew that the best thing to do was to make a stand and fight for our lives, as there would be great danger of our becoming separated in the excitement of a running fight, after which the Indians could the more easily kill us one by one." They also realized they could defend themselves better on foot than on horseback, so they dismounted, giving the reins of all the horses to one of the soldiers, George Smith, at whom the Indians now directed their fire. "In a moment or two poor Smith was shot down, and the horses stampeded," Dixon said. He and the others thought Smith had been killed, and in their concern for their own lives, they forgot about him.

"I realized at once that I was in closer quarters than I had ever been in my life," Dixon said. The Indians, too, understood the fix they had put the white men in. "The Indians seemed to feel absolutely sure of getting us, so sure, in fact, that they delayed riding us down and killing us at once, which they could easily have done, and prolonged the early stages of the fight merely to satisfy their desire to toy with an enemy at bay, as a cat would play with a mouse before taking its life."

Dixon and the four others didn't like their chances on the open hillside where the Indians had caught them. A quarter-mile away was a mesquite grove; they resolved to make their stand there. Before they could move, another man, Amos Chapman, was shot, and fell to the ground. "Our situation was growing more desperate every minute," Dixon said. "I knew that something had to be done, and quickly, or else all of us in a short while would be dead or in the hands of the Indians."

Dixon, accustomed to spotting signs of buffalo, noticed a low place where the animals wallowed after rains. "I ran for it at top speed," he said. "It seemed as if a bullet whizzed past me at every jump, but I got through unharmed. The wallow was about ten feet in diameter. I found that its depth, though slight, afforded some protection. I shouted to my comrades to try to come to me, which all of them save Smith and Chapman, commenced trying to do. As each man reached the wallow, he drew his butcher knife and began digging desperately with knife and hands to throw up the dirt round the sides. The land happened to be sandy, and we made good headway, though constantly interrupted by the necessity of firing at the Indians as they dashed within range."

So long as they were busy digging their shallow fortification, Dixon and the others could push aside thoughts of what might befall them. But when they would pause to catch their breath, their grim fate loomed large. "Many times that terrible day did I think that my last moment was at hand," Dixon said. "Once, when the Indians were crowding us awfully hard, one of the boys raised up and yelled, 'No use, boys, no use; we might as well give it up.' We answered by shouting to him to lie down. At that moment a bullet struck in the soft bank near him and completely filled his mouth with dirt. I was so amused that I laughed, though in a rather sickly way, for none of us felt much like laughing."

Fatigue calmed their nerves. "We were keenly aware that the only thing to do was to sell our lives as dearly as possible," Dixon said. "We fired deliberately, taking good aim, and were picking off an Indian at almost every round." Their fire kept the Indians guessing at their condition. "Had they known so many of us were wounded" — only Dixon and one other man hadn't been hit — "undoubtedly they would have rode in and finished us."

The charges came nonetheless. "The Indians would ride toward us at headlong speed with lances uplifted and poised, undoubtedly bent upon spearing us," Dixon said. "Such moments made a man brace himself and grip his gun." Each time, though, Dixon or one of the others would put a bullet into the leader of the charge, and the others would peel away. The charges gradually grew less frequent.

But the Indians' activity didn't stop. "All that long, hot September day the Indians circled round us or dashed past, yelling and cutting all kinds of capers," Dixon said. The men's canteens had been lost with the horses; since the start of the fight they had been without water. The wounded men suffered especially. Dixon's tongue and lips felt like a whetstone.

They fought on, with the courage of desperation. "We knew what would befall us if we should be captured alive," Dixon said. "We had seen too many naked and mangled bodies of white men who had been spread-eagled and tortured with steel and fire to forget what our own fate would be. So we were determined to fight to the end, not unmindful of the fact that every once in a while there was another dead or wounded Indian."

September afternoons on the southern plains often bring thunderstorms. "About 3 o'clock a black cloud came up in the west," Dixon recalled. "And in a short time the sky shook and blazed with thunder and lightning. Rain fell in blinding sheets, drenching us to the skin. Water gathered quickly in the buffalo wallow, and our wounded men eagerly bent forward and drank from the muddy pool. It was more than muddy — that water was red with their own blood that had flowed from their wounds and lay clotting and dry in the hot September sun."

Dixon had hoped for more from the rain than a relieving of thirst. And he got it. "The wind had shifted to the north and was now drearily chilling us to the bone," Dixon said. "An Indian dislikes rain, especially a cold rain, and these Kiowas and Comanches were no exception to the rule. We could see them in groups out of rifle range sitting on their horses with their blankets drawn tightly around them. The Plains country beats the world for quick changes in weather, and in less than an hour after the rain had fallen, the wind was bitterly cold. Not a man in our crowd had a coat, and our thin shirts were scant protection. Our coats were tied behind our saddles when our horses stampeded, and were lost beyond recovery. I was heart-sick over the loss of my coat, for in the inside pocket was my dearest treasure, my mother's picture, which my father had given me shortly before his death. I was never able to recover it."

The rain meant they weren't going to be killed at once. But it left them as surrounded as ever. And their ammunition was running low. If they couldn't shoot, the Indians could walk right up and slaughter them. "Late in the afternoon, somebody suggested that we go out and get Smith's belt and six-shooter, as he had been shot early in the fight and his belt undoubtedly was loaded with cartridges," Dixon recalled. Peter Rath, one of the soldiers, offered to go. Dixon didn't argue with him. Rath went and soon returned with Smith's ammunition — and with the news that Smith was not dead but alive. Dixon, like Rath, was mortified; the code of the plains, no less than that of the army, was to never leave a comrade on the field.

The two retrieved Smith and brought him to the wallow. They could tell they were too late. "There was no chance for him," Dixon said. And, for what it was worth, they could see there never had been a chance. "He was shot through the left lung and when he breathed, the wind sobbed out of his back under the shoulder blade." They stuffed a handkerchief in the hole in Smith's back and tried to make him comfortable, but expected him to expire at any moment.

"Night was approaching, and it looked blacker to me than any night I had ever seen," Dixon said. "Ours was a forlorn and disheartening situation. The Indians were still all around us. The nearest relief was seventy-five miles away. Of the six men in the wallow, four were badly wounded, and without anything to relieve their suffering. We were cold and hungry, with nothing to eat, and without a blanket, coat or hat to protect us from the rain and the biting wind. It was impossible to rest or sleep in the two inches of water in wallow."

Dixon and Rath decided they had to get the wounded men off the ground. They would have gathered grass for bedding, but the drought had burned it all away. Instead they found some tumbleweed, wiry tangles that rolled across the prairie before the wind. These lacked the softness of grass, but, smashed down, they served their elevating purpose.

In the night, Dixon and Rath concluded that one of them needed to go for help. It would be dangerous, but it was imperative. "I insisted that I should go, as I knew the country, and felt confident that I could find the trail that led to Camp Supply," Dixon said. "I was sure that we were not far from this trail."

He discovered that the wounded men weren't sleeping. They at once protested. "They were willing that Rath should go, but would not listen to my leaving them." Nobody shot like Billy Dixon, and they wanted his rifle by their sides.

Rath concurred, and Dixon bade him good luck. Rath disappeared into the night. To the disappointment of all, he returned within two hours. He had not been able to find the trail.

By now Smith was in grave pain. He begged Dixon or Rath to put him out of his misery. They couldn't bring themselves to do so. Neither would they give him a gun that he might do the deed. Another part of the code was that as long as life lasted, so did hope. "Poor Smith endured his agony like a brave soldier," Dixon said. "Our hearts ached but we could do nothing to relieve his pain. About 10 o'clock that night he fell asleep and we were glad of it, for in sleep he could forget his sufferings. Later in the night one of the boys felt of him, to see how he was getting along. He was cold in death. Men commonly think of death as something to be shunned. There are times, however, when its hand falls as tenderly as the touch of a mother's hand, and when its coming is welcomed by those to whom hopeless suffering has brought the last bitter dregs of life. We lifted the body of our dead comrade and gently laid it outside the buffalo wallow on the mesquite grass, covering the white face with a silk handkerchief."

There was one exception to the ban on suicide. Dixon had been considering it, after a less drastic measure. "When the fight was at its worst, with the Indians closing in on all sides, and when it seemed that every minute would be our last, I was strongly tempted to take my butcher knife, which I kept at razor edge, and cut off my hair," he said. "In those days my hair was black and heavy and brushed my shoulders. As a matter of fact, I was rather proud of my hair. Its luxuriance would have tempted any Indian to scalp me at the first opportunity." As for the suicide exception: "I had a further and final plan — to save my last bullet for self-destruction."

The thoughts, and others like them, came back as he watched Smith die. "That night is indelibly stamped in my memory," Dixon said. "Many a time have its perils filled my dreams, until I awoke startled and thrilled by a feeling of imminent danger. Every night the same stars are shining way out there in the

Panhandle, the winds sigh as mournfully as they did then, and I often wonder if a single settler who passes the lonely spot knows how desperately six men once battled for their lives where now may be plowed fields, and safety and the comforts of civilization."

In the morning the survivors agreed that Dixon should go for help. Moving by day was far more dangerous than going by night, for on the open plains he would be visible to sharp-eyed Indians for miles. But there was no other choice.

He took off, constantly looking all around for Indians. He saw none, and evidently none saw him. He'd traversed less than a mile when he hit the trail to Camp Supply. He walked more quickly than before, still keeping a lookout in every direction. He spied a dark mass on the plains a couple of miles off. At first he couldn't make it out. Then it moved, and he concluded it was Indians or soldiers. Carefully he approached. When he saw that the riders were moving abreast, he concluded that they were soldiers, for Indians always rode in file.

"I never felt happier in my life," Dixon recalled. "I whanged loose with my old .50 to attract the attention of the soldiers, and saw the whole command come to a halt." They didn't know if the shot was fired in anger or supplication. "I fired my gun a second time, which brought two soldiers to me. I told them of our condition, and they rode rapidly back to the command and reported."

The commanding office was a Major Price; his troop was accompanying a supply train from Fort Supply to Nelson Miles's field headquarters. Price explained, upon hearing Dixon's account, that the same band of Indians that had attacked Dixon's group had previously besieged the supply train. Price and his troop had happened on the siege and driven off the Indians. They had just abandoned the siege when they encountered Dixon's crew.

Price agreed to send his surgeon and two men to see to the wounded in the wallow. Dixon started to join them, but Price wanted to hear more about the attackers. Dixon gave directions and the surgeon started off. While talking to Price, Dixon watched the surgeon, who appeared to be wandering off course. He fired his rifle to get the surgeon's attention, then waved the gun in the correct direction. The surgeon and the two soldiers adjusted accordingly.

Minutes later, another shot rang out across the plain, from the direction of the wallow. The horse of one of the surgeon's soldiers collapsed, tumbling the trooper to the ground. "I ran forward as rapidly as possible, not knowing what the men would do next," Dixon recalled. "They were soon able to recognize me, and lowered their guns. When we got to them the men said that they had heard shooting — the shots I had fired to attract the attention of the troops — and supposed that the Indians had killed me and were coming for them. They were determined to take no chances, and shot at the surgeon and the two soldiers the moment they got within range."

The surgeon did little for the wounded men, judging that they weren't about to die. The soldiers gave them some hardtack and dried beef they had behind their saddles. Then they and the surgeon rejoined Price, who — to the astonishment of Dixon and the others at the wallow — ordered his troop to move on. "Major Price refused to leave any men with us," Dixon recalled, still angry years later. "For this he was afterwards severely censured, and justly." Nor did he provide them firearms or ammunition. He left them as helpless as he had found them, if slightly less hungry.

Yet Dixon took comfort from knowing that Miles would learn of their plight once Price reached him, as he seemed intent on doing. "We were sure that help would come the moment General Miles heard the news," Dixon said.

It did come, but not until midnight on the second day after Price's troop had departed. "A long way off in the dark we heard the faint sound of a bugle," Dixon said. "It made us swallow a big lump in our throats and bite our lips. Nearer and clearer came the bugle notes. Our nerves were getting jumpy, so strong was our emotion. We fired our guns, to let them know where we were, and soon the soldiers came riding out of the darkness." The wounded men received treatment; they all were given food. They buried Smith in the wallow, covering the body with the dirt they had scratched aside for their breastworks.

When Nelson Miles heard the story of the fight at the buffalo wallow from Dixon and the other survivors, he commended their performance to the War Department. In due course they were voted the Medal of Honor by Congress. "He was delighted when the medals came from Washington," Dixon said of Miles. "With his own hands he pinned mine on my coat when we were in camp on Carson Creek, five or six miles west of the ruins of the original Adobe Walls."

The broader Red River War, as the conflict on the southern plains was styled, continued into the autumn. Miles pursued the Comanches and Kiowas onto the Llano Estacado, which daunted the soldiers even as it amazed them. "The only country I have ever seen like it is the steppes of Russian Siberia," Miles wrote. "It is a high plateau or tableland of some four hundred miles north and south, and in places nearly two hundred miles wide, covered with short buffalo grass and level as a billiard-table, without a tree or shrub to be seen as far as the eye can reach. We marched over it sometimes for days, and it seemed like being in mid-ocean in a dead calm." The Indians knew it better than the soldiers did, and they found refuge in the broken canyons at the eastern edge of the Llano. But Miles pursued them, and his column and that of Ranald Mackenzie, guided by Tonkawa scouts, cornered the Indians in Palo Duro Canyon. A running battle ensued, ending with the scattering of the Indians, the destruction of their camps, and the capture of hundreds of their ponies.

Yet it was the weather that broke the back of the resistance. "The approach of winter was our best ally," Miles wrote. He had prepared for the winter, furnishing his troops with warm clothing and ample food. They harassed the Indians relentlessly, keeping them constantly on the move. The Indian women and children suffered from hunger and exposure, until their chiefs had no alternative but to surrender. Small parties and then larger laid down their arms and agreed to go onto the reservation. The last one to yield was Quanah Parker, whose Quahadi Comanches held out until the spring of 1875.

27

The fighting on the southern plains was so bitter not least because the Indians and the buffalo hunters were competing for the same resource. What one side gained, the other lost; buffalo killed by the hunters were denied to the Indians. Friction between whites and Indians elsewhere showed less symmetry, at least at the start. The first whites who settled in the mountains and high desert of southwestern Oregon and northern California were looking for gold, which meant nothing to the Klamaths, Modocs and other tribes of the region. The gold hunters didn't find enough of the yellow metal to trigger a rush on the scale of that to California in 1849, and so the trouble between whites and Indians remained sporadic for two decades.

But by the early 1870s, farmers and ranchers had followed the miners, and their growing numbers triggered regular fights with the Indians, who responded in ways that caused the whites to demand protection from the army and the removal of the Indians to reservations. As elsewhere, some of the Indians resigned themselves to the new order, which in this case entailed a reservation near Klamath Lake in southern Oregon. Again as elsewhere, other Indians disdained reservation life and clung to their inherited lands and inherited habits.

A Modoc chief called Captain Jack tried reservation life for a time. But he discovered that the Indian agents were unable to protect his band against the larger tribes there, who were traditional enemies of the Modocs. So Jack led his people off the reservation to their old home on the Lost River, straddling the Oregon-California border. They clashed with the whites who now occupied the valley, killing several and stealing livestock, and the army was summoned to force them back to the reservation.

William Sherman considered the Modoc problem a modest one. Captain Jack led perhaps a hundred warriors, and his whole band, with women and children, comprised no more than three hundred. John Schofield commanded the army's Division of the Pacific, based in San Francisco, and Edward Canby the Department of the Columbia, in Portland. "Both are fully competent to act," Sherman wrote to William Belknap, the secretary of war. Sherman conceded that the Modocs possessed an advantage in local

337

knowledge and perhaps motivation, but he said they couldn't withstand the numbers and firepower Canby and Schofield would bring to bear.

Canby, in particular, appreciated the vote of confidence, for he had a delicate job. The governor of Oregon was urging the most stringent measures against Captain Jack. "Use your authority and influence to have all peaceable Indians not implicated in hostilities placed on reservation," La Fayette Grover telegraphed to Canby, "but Captain Jack's band, and all implicated in hostilities with him, are to be captured and crushed out, and all the murderers are to be turned over to the civil authorities for trial and punishment."

Canby couldn't object to the central thrust of Grover's message: that the killers should be punished and the peaceable Indians simply put on the reservation. But Grover's presumption in ordering Canby to do anything was off-putting; any officer in the army — let alone a general — took orders from his military superiors, not from a state governor. Grover's insistence that state courts try the offenses was equally presumptuous. This was a question that would be decided in Washington, but the governor was trying to force Canby's hand, knowing that once state officials got hold of Jack and the others, the federals wouldn't be able to pry them loose before ropes snapped the Indians' necks.

Other civilians were even less circumspect than Grover. The Modoc depredations, like similar offenses elsewhere on the frontier, triggered calls for extermination and offers of help in doing so. The helpers expected to be put on the federal payroll, thereby serving self-interest and, as they argued, the interest of the community. Canby was bombarded with demands to wipe out the whole tribe of Modocs.

He pushed back against this indiscriminate animus. "Aside from the abstract injustice of making the Indians referred to in these dispatches responsible for the sins of others," he wrote to Grover, "the only result that will attend the threatened attack upon them will be to increase the difficulties, and probably add to the deplorable loss of life that has already been incurred, by making active enemies of those, also, who have been and are still disposed to be friendly."

Canby moved deliberately. Time, and winter, were on his side, he judged. "I do not think that the operations will be protracted," he wrote to Schofield, his immediate superior. "The snow will drive the Indians out of the mountains, and they cannot move without leaving trails that can be followed. It will involve some hardship upon the troops, but they are better provided and can endure it better than the Indians."

Canby's caution irked the Oregon governor,

339

whose complaints echoed to Washington. Sherman's confidence in Canby was questioned. But Sherman stuck with him. "At this distance it is impossible to judge of the steps necessary to maintain the peace of the frontier," he wrote to Belknap. "But Gen. E. R. S. Canby is in actual command of all the troops and resources of the country, and will doubtless bring this matter to a satisfactory end."

It wouldn't be easy, though. Three days later Sherman received a telegram from Canby. "Colonel Wheaton attacked the Modoc stronghold on the 17th instant" — January 17, 1873 — "with a force of four hundred men, and failed to dislodge them after a fight lasting from 8 o'clock in the morning until dark," Canby wrote. The Modoc stronghold was a position in a convoluted landscape of cooled lava on the California side of the border. The Modocs knew it well, and turned that knowledge to their benefit. Canby went on to say he had ordered troops from elsewhere in Oregon to the Modoc region. "This leaves some parts of the country inadequately guarded, if other Indians should take part with the Modocs or be disposed to make war on their own account." For this reason he had decided to accept the offers of volunteers, not simply from Oregon but from northern California as well.

Fuller reports followed Canby's summary.

Lieutenant Colonel Frank Wheaton's account of the battle made clear what the soldiers were up against in the lava beds. "We attacked the Modocs on the 17th with about four hundred good men," Wheaton wrote. "We fought the Indians through the lava-beds to their stronghold, which is in the center of miles of rocky fissures, caves, crevices, gorges and ravines, some of them one hundred feet deep. In the opinion of any experienced officer of regulars or volunteers, one thousand men would be required to dislodge them from their almost impregnable position, and it must be done deliberately, with a free use of mortar batteries. The Modocs were scarcely exposed at all to our persistent attacks; they left one ledge to gain another equally secure. One of our men was wounded twice during the day, but he did not see an Indian at all, though we were under fire from 8 a.m. until dark." Wheaton added, "I have been twenty-three years in the service of the Government, and have been employed a greater portion of that time on our remote frontier, and generally engaged in operating against hostile Indians. In this service I have never before encountered an enemy, civilized or savage, occupying a position of such great natural strength as the Modoc stronghold, or have I seen troops engage a better-armed or more skillful foe."

■ ■ ■ ■

Sherman didn't have a thousand troops to send to fight the Modocs. Nor did he want to raise anywhere close to that number of volunteers. Captain Jack couldn't cause much trouble cooped up in his lava-bed stronghold. Sherman took the matter to Grant, who agreed that sitting tight made the most sense for the moment. "It is the desire of the President to use the troops to protect the inhabitants as against the Modoc Indians, but if possible to avoid war," Sherman relayed to Canby.

The pause coincided with, and was partly motivated by, a push from the Indian Bureau to resolve the Modoc question peacefully. Sherman was as skeptical as ever of the motives and efficacy of Indian agents and their superiors, but they had the president's ear. "Let all defensive measures proceed," he ordered Canby. "But order no attack on the Indians till the former orders are modified or changed by the President, who seems disposed to allow the peace men to try their hands on Captain Jack."

The peace men proposed a commission to meet with Captain Jack and try to talk him onto the reservation. Canby thought the time was ripe, especially after he got in a few last licks. "In late operations, eight Modocs have been killed and many wounded, and nearly all their ponies captured," he reported to Sherman in early February. "They seem disposed to make peace, and have sent messages to that effect."

Predictably, the Oregon authorities were *in*disposed toward peace. Governor Grover filed a protest against the peace commission, declaring that it would reward murder and encourage repetition. Grover suggested that the people of Oregon might act on their own against the Modocs.

Grover's threat caused the secretary of the interior, the boss of the Indian Bureau, to issue a threat of his own. "If the authority of the United States is defied and resisted by state authorities, the United States will not be responsible for results, even if the state should be left to take care of Indians without assistance from the United States," Columbus Delano wrote. Sherman couldn't have put it better himself.

Sherman directed Canby to cooperate with the commissioners but keep his powder dry. "All parties here have absolute faith in you but mistrust the commissioners," he said. "If that Modoc affair can be terminated peacefully by you, it will be accepted by the Secretary of the Interior as well as the President. Answer me immediately and advise the names of one or two good men with whom you can act, and they will receive the

343

necessary authority; or if you can effect the surrender to you of the hostile Modocs, do it, and remove them under guard to some safe place, assured that the Government will deal by them liberally and fairly."

Canby did as directed. "I sent word to Captain Jack yesterday that I would send out wagons to bring in his sick and wounded," he replied to Sherman. He had moved from his headquarters in Portland to a spot a bit south of the Oregon-California line, to facilitate peace talks. "The messenger has just returned with information that they would come in day after tomorrow." Canby was hopeful. "If nothing untoward happens to stampede them, I think they will come in," he said. "If they do, I propose to send them to Angel Island" — in San Francisco Bay — "to be kept there until their final destination is determined upon. If they do not, I will at once advise you."

In fact they did not. "The Modocs failed yesterday at the time and place appointed by themselves," Canby informed Sherman. They needed a nudge. "Some movement of troops will be necessary to keep them under closer observation, but nothing more until authorized by you."

Sherman told him to hold steady. "It is manifestly desired that by all in authority that this Modoc affair should be settled amicably," he wrote to Canby. "For that reason I advise you to exercise considerable patience." Canby should cooperate with the commissioners to the extent possible. The government was willing to entertain suggestions for a new reservation for the Modocs; Canby should support this initiative. But patience had limits, Sherman said. "Should these peaceful measures fail, and should the Modocs presume too far on the forbearance of the Government, and again resort to deceit and treachery, I trust you will make such use of the military force that no other Indian tribe will imitate their example, and that no other reservation for them will be necessary except graves among their chosen lava-beds."

Canby assured Sherman they were thinking along the same lines. "The utmost patience and forbearance toward the Modocs has been exercised, and still it will be," he telegraphed. Yet he was preparing for action should events warrant it. "The troops will be so posted as to watch the places of egress, and keep them more closely under observation than they have been pending the negotiations of the commission. Apprehending that their last action was only a trick to gain time and make their escape, I directed a reconnaissance to be made around the lava-beds, which was completed last night." The reconnaissance found the Modocs still in their camp. And it sent the Modocs a message. "I wish them to see that we are fully prepared for anything they may attempt, and this may incline them to keep their promises in the future."

Sherman informed Canby that his combination of patience and resolve had the full support of the administration. Interior Secretary Delano had told Belknap that the "wisdom and discretion" of General Canby offered the best hope of averting a war and bringing the Modoc affair to a peaceful resolution. Sherman stressed the crucial role Canby was playing. "The whole question now rests with you," he said.

Canby sent spies — friendly Modocs — into Captain Jack's camp to discover what he and the other warriors were thinking. One returned with useful intelligence regarding the missed meeting. "The last moment, their hearts failed them, and they could not bring themselves to the point of abandoning their old homes and going to a distant country," Canby related to Sherman, paraphrasing the spy's report. "They are evidently not now in a disposition favorable to any arrangement, although they profess a willingness to have another talk." This was just as well, for the commission wasn't yet ready to commence negotiations. Canby said he would employ the time. "The troops will be put in positions that cover, as far as possible, all points of egress from the lava-beds. I think that a system of gradual compression, with an exhibition of the force that can be used against them if the commission should again fail, will satisfy them of the hopelessness of any further resistance, and give the peace party sufficient strength to enable it to control the whole band." Yet the moment wouldn't last forever. "Time is becoming of the greatest importance, as the melting of the snow will soon enable them to live in the mountains. This will greatly increase the difficulties we have to contend with, as they will then break up into small parties and can more readily make their escape than from their present location." Canby determined to move things along. "I propose to open communication with them again in the course of two or three days," he told Sherman.

Canby's approach won him Washington's carte blanche to deal with the Modocs. Secretary Delano had become his strongest supporter. "He is so impressed with your wisdom and desire to fulfill the peaceful policy of the Government that he authorizes you to remove from the present commission any members you think unfit, to appoint others to their places, and to report through us" — Sherman's office — "to him such changes." Sherman told him, "This actually devolves on you the entire management of the Modoc question."

Canby accepted the responsibility and moved ahead. He took one other officer, Colonel Alvan Gillem, and approached the

Modoc camp. "Had an unsatisfactory meeting with Captain Jack in the neighborhood of his camp," he telegraphed to Sherman. "The result confirmed the impression previously reported, that the war faction is still predominant. Captain Jack's demeanor was that of a man under duress and afraid to exhibit his real feelings. Important questions were evaded or not answered at all; the substance of all that could be elicited from him was that he did not want to fight, that the lava bed was a bad place, and that he wanted to go to his home on Lost River. He wanted all of the soldiers moved out of the country; if anybody wanted to talk to him they must come to his camp, and if anything was to be done for him, it must be done there."

Canby explained that the meeting had been partly accidental. "I had not intended to communicate with Captain Jack until the troops were in their new positions, but the conference was invited by the Indians," Canby told Sherman. Jack had proposed that he and another leader, John Schonchin, meet with Canby at a spot near the Modoc camp. But something changed between the invitation and the meeting itself. "When we reached the place, we found that the war faction had substituted their leader for Schonchin, no doubt for the purpose of watching Captain Jack and seeing that he did not commit himself, to their prejudice."

The meeting let Canby know of the strains within the Modoc camp, and it told Jack and his minder that Canby was standing pat. It also bought time for Canby to strengthen his hand. "The troops are now moving into their positions," he told Sherman. There would be no more talks until the movement was complete. "Then communications may again be opened with the Modocs with hope of better results."

Four days later, the troops had almost reached their new positions. Two Modocs accosted Colonel Gillem, who was inspecting the deployment. Gillem spoke to them briefly. "He is of the opinion that they are more subdued in tone and more amenable to reasoning than at the last previous interview," Canby wrote to Sherman. "I think that when the avenues of escape are closed, and their supplies cut off or abridged, they will come in."

Jeff Riddle was the son of Frank Riddle and Winema, a Modoc woman. Frank Riddle, a Kentuckian by birth, had ventured west to win his fortune, and reached northern California with the gold hunters. There he met and married Winema, whom the whites called Tobey. She learned English and became an interpreter between the whites and her people. Their son Jeff was ten years old at the time of the Modoc war, and he accompanied his mother to meetings between the whites and the Indians. Jeff grew up to write a history of the Modoc war, drawn from his own recollections, the testimony of his mother and other relatives, and public records.

Jeff Riddle recounted a conversation between his mother and Captain Jack during the period when the peace commissioners were headed to the Modoc country. She accompanied two white men from Yreka, the closest California town. Jack wasn't eager to talk, but Winema explained that they came to talk peace. They wouldn't be put off. "We intend to stay all night," she said.

A Modoc called Scar-Face Charley answered derisively, "Yes, you folks might stay here longer than you want to." To Winema specifically he said, "You know we have been fighting the white people; we have not quit yet."

"Charley, we know all what you say," Winema responded. "But listen, these men here are your friends, and I am a Modoc. That is the reason we come here among you. We know you will not harm us. We are here to help you people, not to destroy you."

"All right," said Charley. "We will see."

Captain Jack listened to the words of the whites, and of Winema and her husband, Frank Riddle, all urging him to talk with General Canby and the commissioners. Finally he agreed. "Go back and tell those great men that I am willing to hear them in council and see what they have got to offer me and my people. Tell them to come and see me at any time, or send for me. I will go and see them if they will protect me from my enemies while I am holding these peace councils. Tell them that I am willing to hear anything they have to offer, if it is reasonable."

Arranging the parley took time, but finally Captain Jack and four other Modocs met with Canby and commissioners Alfred Meacham and Eleazar Thomas. Meacham and Thomas were ministers; Meacham was also superintendent of Indian affairs for Oregon. Canby laid the ground rules. "We on our side will not commit any act of war as long as these peace councils are going, if you do not commit any act of war on your side," he said.

Captain Jack agreed. He added, "My word is good and solid as a big rock. I will live up to my compact with you."

Having accomplished its introductory purposes, and established the goodwill of both sides, the meeting adjourned shortly. Two weeks were required for the principals to regather. This time Captain Jack came prepared to negotiate. "We can make peace quick if you will meet me even half way," he told Canby. "If you will only agree to half of what I and my people want, why, we can get along fine."

Canby replied that Jack must have been misinformed. Canby was not going to compromise, and he was not going to let Jack dictate the course of the talks. "You are not to dictate to me," he said. "I am to make peace with you, nothing else."

"General, I hardly think *you* ought to dictate to *me,*" Jack said. "I think you ought to be aware of the fact that I am not your prisoner or slave, not today, anyway. All I ask of you is to give me a reservation near Hot Creek or Fairchild's ranch." Hot Creek was close to the lava beds and got its name from the geothermal structures that had spewed the lava; Fairchild's ranch was in the same vicinity.

"Jack, you know I cannot do that," said Canby. Actually, he probably could have, given the leeway Washington had granted him. But he wasn't going to accept Jack's opening demand.

"Then give me these lava beds for my home. No white man will ever want to make homes here."

Alfred Meacham broke in. "Jack, the general or any of us can't promise you any place until we make peace," he said.

"If that is the way you explain it to me, how will we make peace?" said Jack. The white men wanted him to give in before they offered anything. That was no way to make peace. "I will not agree on anything you men may offer until *you* agree to give me a home in my native country." Jack had heard that the whites often sent Indians far from their homelands.

Eleazar Thomas interjected, "Captain Jack, you never could get along with the white people in this country because there has been blood spilt here by your people."

John Schonchin, who had accompanied Jack, objected that they had been told past events were not going to be held against them in the peace talks.

Thomas responded that he was simply being realistic. The white people of the region hadn't agreed to forget the past.

Captain Jack indicated his displeasure. "If that is the case," he said, "then we never will make peace."

Canby maintained his firm position. "Listen to me," he told Jack and the others, "you Indians have got to come under the white man's laws. The white man's law is strong and straight."

Jack wouldn't budge. "All I want is your promise that you will give us a home in this country," he said.

"We cannot make that promise," Meacham reiterated. "You never could get along."

Canby brought the talk back to the simple matter of peace. "I tell you, Jack, get all your people together and come out under a flag of truce. A white flag means peace. No one will hurt you under the white flag."

Jack knew better, from his own experience. "Look here, Canby, when I was a boy a man named Ben Wright called forty-five of my people under the flag of truce," he said. "How many do you think got away with their lives?" He held up one hand, indicating its five fingers. With two of his fingers he pointed to the lava beds. "Two of them are there, alive today. You ask me to come out under a flag of truce. I will not do it. I cannot do it."

Canby shook his head. "That was wrong," he said.

"Your white people at Yreka didn't say it was wrong," Jack answered. "They gave him a big dinner and dance at night, called him the hero."

Meacham said, "Jack, we are different men. We are not like Wright. We want to help you people so you can live in peace."

"If you want to help us, give me and my people a home here in our own country," Jack said. "We will harm no one."

Canby shook his head again. "We have told you and Schonchin that we are unable to give or even promise you a home in this country, so do not say or ask anything that is not in our power to grant," he said.

Captain Jack said that Canby was the representative of the Great Father in Washington; he could grant a home if he wanted.

Eleazar Thomas appealed to a greater

father. "Brother Jack, let me talk next," he said. "God sent me here to make peace with you, brother. We are going to do it. I know it. God says so. All we have to do is trust God. Everything will come around right. God sees and hears everything."

Captain Jack scoffed. "Brother Thomas, I may trust God," he said. "But what good will that do me? I am sorry to say I cannot trust these men that wear blue cloth and brass buttons."

Canby responded angrily, "What have these blue cloths and brass buttons done to you? Tell me!"

"They shot our women and little babies," said Jack, getting angry himself.

"Did not your men kill settlers, and them innocent?" retorted Canby.

"The men killed were not innocent," said Jack. "They were the first to fire on my people on the north banks of Lost River."

Winema, the interpreter, interrupted. "Mr. Canby, do not get mad," she said. "You cannot make peace this way." To Captain Jack she said, "You, too, Jack, be a man. Hold your temper."

Meacham added his voice. "It is getting late," he said. "I think we had better quit for the day. Maybe in our next council we will be able to come to terms."

Canby and the commissioners retired to wait,

Captain Jack and the Modocs to argue. Opinions were split among the Modocs, as they had been among nearly every tribe from the moment of first contact with whites. To resist, or to accommodate? — that was the question, and always had been. The older men in a tribe, with nothing to prove, often preached accommodation, while the younger men, with reputations as warriors still to win, demanded resistance. In the case of the Modocs, near the end of their tether, the positions were reversed. John Schonchin, on returning to camp after the meeting with Canby and the others, stood up in council and said, "My people, I am old. I have been trapped and fooled by the white people many times. I do not intend to be fooled again. You all see the aim of these so-called Peace Commissioners; they are just leading us Indians on to make time to get more soldiers here. When they think there are enough men here, they will jump on us and kill the last soul of us. I know it."

A Schonchin ally, called Black Jim, mounted a large rock so that all could see and hear him. "Schonchin, you see things right," he said. "I for one am not going to be decoyed and shot like a dog by the soldiers. I am going to kill my man before they get me. I make a motion that we kill those peacemakers the next time we meet them in council. We might just as well die a few days from now as to die a few weeks from now." Black Jim asked that all who agreed step forward. A dozen men did so.

One who did not was Weuim, called William Faithful. "I am a Modoc; I am one of you," he said. "I object to the way you decide. Schonchin is not head chief. Captain Jack is our head chief. I have not seen him tonight." In fact Captain Jack had not arrived. "Let us hear Captain Jack's opinion," Weuim said.

Black Jim and Schonchin agreed, and Black Jim went to find Captain Jack. In a few minutes Jack stood before the rest.

Weium framed the question. "You have been holding peace councils with the peacemakers," he said. "You are our head man. Now I want you to tell these people here tonight what you think of these councils. What is your intention? Tell us. You ought to know by this time. Do not be hasty. Weigh your words, Jack, for you know I for one depend on you and will stand by your judgment."

All eyes looked to Captain Jack. He in turn searched the faces in the firelight. He had sensed the dissatisfaction with his meetings with Canby, Meacham and Thomas. But he apparently didn't know that Schonchin and Black Jim had just demanded the white men's murder. "Weium, I do not know how to commence," Jack said. "But I will say I have a hard fight ahead of me in the coming councils

357

to save my men that killed the settlers, and to win my point to secure a piece of land in this country for our future home. But I am going to do it without any trouble. All I have to do is to hold the councils and stick to my point. I shall win. At least I think I will." He looked around the gathering. "All I ask you people to do is to behave yourselves and wait. I do not want to do anything rash. That will not do. We may go to Yainax, where our other Modoc people are." Yainax was in southern Oregon, near the Klamath reservation. "They live in peace; why can't we?"

Schonchin objected. "I have a brother at Yainax," he said. "I know he enjoys life there with his people. But he nor any of his Yainax people killed whites, but we have. We never could get along there, even with our own people, let alone the whites."

"Oh, yes, we could," said Jack. "I will work it so no whites will bother us. They will protect us in time. The way I intend to do it is this, with the peace-makers: I will hold out for a reservation at Hot Creek or right here in the lava beds, as I have been doing. When they see I insist on either one of these places, they will offer us Yainax. Then I will accept with the understanding that I will take all my people, and none will be tried for murder." Jack looked again around the gathering. "My people, depend on me. I will pull you through all right."

Black Jim felt the mood shifting toward Captain Jack. He got back up on his rock to stop it. "Jack, you will never save your people," he said. "You can't do it. Are you blind, my chief? Can't you see soldiers arriving every two or three days? Don't you know that the last soldiers that came brought big guns with them that shoot bullets as big as your head? You say you are going to win your point — never! The commissioners intend to make peace with you by blowing your head off with one of those big guns. You mind what I tell you, Jack. The only way we can get an even start with the peace-makers is to kill them next council. Then all we can do is fight until we die. If I had my way, those peace shammers would have been killed long ago, before so many soldiers got here. They are going to force us to leave our country or fight, and I am going to fight, and soon, too. I will not be trapped like our fathers were."

Where in other cases the old warriors who called for peace had nothing left to prove, Black Jim spoke as one with nothing left to *lose*. Captain Jack couldn't take that view. Black Jim and Schonchin might go down fighting, but Jack had to think of the women and children who would suffer for the warriors' last gasp. Jack heard Black Jim out, and he continued to listen while others followed Jim in the same vein.

Then he spoke. "My men, your talk looks

reasonable," he said. "But does not my talk look reasonable and safer for all of us?"

He had waited too long. Or perhaps he had lost the group before the council started. The irreconcilables clamored around him, shouting him down. "Your talk is not good," they said. "Let us take the advice of Black Jim. We are doomed. Let us fight so we die sooner. We have to die anyway."

Captain Jack pushed them back. "I cannot agree with you tonight," he said. He tried to walk away.

Black Jim confronted him. "You are head chief; promise us that you will kill Canby the next time you meet him," he demanded.

"I cannot do it and I will not do it," Jack said.

Another of the irreconcilables, Hooker Jim, challenged Jack. "You will kill Canby or be killed yourself," he said. "You are not safe any place. You will kill, or be killed by your own men."

Jack looked around for support. He saw none. "This is not fair, my men," he said. "Why do you want me to do a coward's act?"

The insurgents shouted him down again. "It is not a coward's act we ask you to do," they said. "It will be brave to kill Canby in the presence of all these soldiers. You show them you dare to do anything when the time comes."

Jack still resisted. "My men, I will not

360

promise just now."

One of the insurgents came forward and said, "You will!" as he put a woman's hat on Jack's head. Another threw a woman's shawl over Jack's shoulders. One tripped Jack and several pushed him to the ground. "You coward! You squaw!" they taunted. "You are not a Modoc. We disown you. Lie there, you woman, you fish-hearted woman!"

Jack couldn't stand the humiliation. He fought his way to his feet. He tore off the hat and shawl. "I will do it," he promised. "I will kill Canby, although I know it will cost me my life and all the lives of my people. But I will do it. Still, I know it is a coward's work. But I will do it."

Jeff Riddle remembered going with his mother to the Modoc camp a few days after the confrontation between Captain Jack and the insurgents. Winema carried a message that Canby and the commissioners wanted to meet again. Jack accepted the invitation, for the next day.

Jeff Riddle remembered that he and his mother had started back toward the soldiers' camp when Weium, the Modoc who had opposed Schonchin and Black Jack, stepped out from behind a rock. Weium was Winema's cousin, and he had a warning. "Tell the peace-makers not to meet these Indians in council any more," he said. "They will be killed."

He had scarcely finished speaking when another Modoc appeared. Knowing Weium's view, he questioned him suspiciously. "What are you telling Winema?" he demanded.

Weium thought quickly. "I just told cousin here that in case we go to war, I want her to care for my little girl over at Yainax," he said.

Satisfied, the other Modoc let Winema and Jeff go. As they departed, Winema looked back at Weium. "I will do as you say," she said.

They rode to the soldiers' camp. Just before they got there, Winema turned to Jeff. "My son," she said, "in case I and your father get killed, stay with Mr. Fairchilds" — a friend. "He will care for you till my brother comes after you." Jeff Riddle remembered her words, and those that followed: "But if I can prevent it, the peace commissioners shall not meet Captain Jack and his men in council any more." Only by this means could the war be averted.

Winema wept as she said this. "Her heart was broke," her son wrote later.

She said more. "My boy, you heard the word that Weium said. I believe him. I know he tells the truth. Now it lays with me and you to save the commissioners, and if it is in my power to do it, I will, God knows. We must save them."

When they got to camp, Winema told her husband, Frank Riddle, what they had heard. She said they must warn the commissioners. The three went to see Alfred Meacham. Jeff Riddle recalled Meacham joking with him, saying, "Well, Jeff, I hope you and your mother brought Captain Jack to terms today."

Winema told Jeff to tell Meacham what they had learned. Jeff recounted Weium's warning that the commissioners were to be killed at the next meeting.

Meacham was stunned. "Is that the fact?" he asked Winema.

She said it was.

Frank Riddle now spoke. "Mr. Meacham, I have known you for many years. That is the reason we took you into our confidence. My wife's life is in danger. I know you will keep what you have been told by my boy and wife as a secret."

Meacham assured Riddle the secret was safe with him.

Riddle said he would need a similar pledge from Canby and Thomas before they were told. They were summoned, and gave the required pledge.

Winema spoke. "My friends, I depend on you," she said. "I was told this evening by my cousin Weium on this side of the Modoc camp that the next time you meet Jack and his men in council you would all be shot to death." She said she believed Weium, who was a friend of the white men. "If he had not been your true friend, he never would have told me. What I tell you is the truth. Take my warning. Do not meet those people in council any more. If you do, you will be carried to this camp dead, from the peace tent."

Jeff Riddle remembered Canby smiling as he heard this. "I believe you are telling us just what was said by your cousin," Canby said. "I will not tell on you or your cousin, but I'll say this: The little handful of Modocs dare not do that — kill us in the presence of a thousand men. They cannot do it."

Eleazar Thomas looked for protection elsewhere. "God will not let them do such a thing," he said. "I trust in God to protect us."

Frank Riddle echoed his wife's warning. "Gentlemen, I have known these Modocs for a long time. If they have decided to kill you commissioners, they will do it. I know it. If you men go tomorrow to meet those Modocs, you will never see the sun rise again in this world."

Canby and Thomas remained skeptical and determined to meet. Meacham took the warning to heart but didn't think he could back out. He sat down and wrote a letter. "My dear wife," he said. "You may be a widow tonight; you shall not be a coward's wife. I go to save my honor."

■ ■ ■

The next morning, before the scheduled meeting, two of the Modocs, called Bogus Charley and Boston Charley, rode into the soldiers' camp. Eleazar Thomas saw them and strode right up. "Good morning, Bogus Charley," he said. "Good morning, Boston." He put a hand on the shoulder of each man and said, "Why do you Indians want to kill us? Don't you know we are your friends?"

"Who said we wanted to kill you?" demanded Bogus Charley.

"Riddle's squaw, Tobey," Thomas replied, referring to Winema.

Bogus Charlcy said she lied if she said that.

"I thought she lied, Charley," said Thomas. "That's why I ask you."

Bogus Charley remained with Thomas, but Boston Charley remounted. "Boston Charley turned back right from the spot for Captain Jack's stronghold, to tell the chief that Tobey had betrayed them," her son Jeff remembered bitterly.

Bogus Charley walked with Thomas to Alfred Meacham's tent. Canby joined them there. Bogus Charley exuded friendliness. "We want to make peace right away," he said. By this time Tobey had arrived, to interpret. Hooker Jim showed up about the same time. He told Tobey that Captain Jack wanted to talk to her. She said she would get her horse and ride to the Modoc camp.

Meacham asked what Jack wanted with Tobey. Hooker Jim said, "He wants Tobey to tell him why she lied."

"Who said she lied? And about what?" demanded Meacham.

"You know, old man Meacham," Hooker Jim said. "She told you we were going to kill you the next time we met in council."

"Who said she told us that?" asked Meacham.

"That old man you call God's man, Thomas," Jim said.

Meacham quickly found Tobey, about to depart. "Come to my tent," he said. She followed him, with Frank Riddle.

"It is dangerous for you to answer Jack's summons," Meacham said. "If Jack wants to see you, we will ask him to come here. I don't want you to go."

"I'm not afraid to go, Meacham," said Tobey. She said she'd risk anything to end the fighting. "I'm going."

Meacham handed her a small pistol. "Take this," he said. "You may need it." He reiterated, "I'd rather for you not to go."

Thomas walked in suddenly. He acted as though nothing had happened. "Hello, friends — getting ready for council?" he said jovially.

Frank Riddle glared at Thomas. "You lied

like a yellow dog last night when you promised my wife that you would not say anything about what she was to tell," Riddle said. "Jack has sent for her. You are the cause of it. I tell you this, Reverend, if my wife ain't back here by sundown, I'll take my gun and shoot you in the right eye, you black-hearted son of a dog."

Thomas seemed shocked, at the language as much as the substance. "Brother Riddle, get down on your knees and pray to almighty God for forgiveness," he said.

Riddle grew hotter. "You living yellow dog," he said. "You could get down and pray the caps off your knees, and even then God would not forgive *you.*"

Tobey left her husband murderously angry at the minister, and rode to the Modoc camp. A crowd awaited her. She dismounted but kept a firm hand on the horse's halter rope. "I am here," she said to Captain Jack. "What can I do for you?"

"I understand you told the peace-makers we were going to kill them the next time we met," Jack said. "Did you?"

"Yes, I warned them against you," Tobey answered. "You know I told them the truth, don't you?" She went on, "You do intend to kill them. My husband too."

"Tobey, tell me who told you about it," Jack demanded.

Tobey didn't want to betray her cousin.

"The spirits told me," she said. "I believe in spirits. They never lie."

"Tobey, do not play with me," said Jack. "I am desperate today, so the quicker you tell me who told you, the better."

Tobey turned it back on Jack. "You deny, then, that you intended to kill the commissioners?"

"I will say, whoever said I was going to kill the peace-makers, lies," Jack said. "If I find out who started the lie on me, I will make him or her suffer." He demanded again, "Who told you?"

Tobey jumped up on a rock and unbuttoned her coat. "I am a Modoc," she declared. "Every drop of blood in my veins is Modoc blood." She looked at the faces turned toward hers. "I told the commissioners of your plot and cowardly intention to kill them. I did not dream it. The spirits did not tell me of it, either. But one of your men told me that he knows all about it. He is right here now among you. I see him right now, but I will never tell you who he is."

She took the pistol from her pocket and brandished it over her head. She struck herself on the breast with her other hand. "Shoot me right here if you dare," she said to Jack. "Shoot me if you dare, Jack." She let her words sink in. "You are not brave enough to shoot me when I tell the truth," she continued. "I have a loving husband and a dear son, but I am not afraid to die while I am doing my duty. Shoot me, I say again, if you dare! The soldiers will avenge my death. You will never be able to fight the white man."

Several guns were leveled at Tobey, to do what Captain Jack appeared loath to do. Jack waved his arm and told the wielders to put their weapons down. They did so.

Eight men, including Weium, stepped to Tobey's side. "We die with this noble, brave woman," they vowed.

Captain Jack joined them. "I do too," he said. He offered his hand to Tobey. She took it. He said, "No one shall hurt you in my presence. They will have to step over my dead body first. You are a true Modoc today. You have proved it."

Jack went on, "Someone told you a mistake. We are not going to kill anyone if everything goes right. You tell the peace-makers that we will be at the tent early tomorrow, six of us, unarmed. Nothing will happen if they talk sense to me." He told Tobey she could leave. "Go back to your husband and boy," he said. He offered to send as an escort the eight men who took her side.

She said she didn't need an escort.

Jack insisted. "Some of my men have evil hearts," he said.

Jeff Riddle and his father were waiting when she reached the soldiers' camp. The three found Canby and Meacham. Tobey told them

369

what had happened, and what Captain Jack had said.

"I congratulate you on your safe return," Canby said. "We shall see what Captain Jack will do tomorrow at our council."

Tobey didn't trust Captain Jack, and said so. "Canby, take my word. Do not go. You will be killed."

Meacham seconded her warning. "We don't have to meet Jack tomorrow," he said. "Tobey is giving us good advice."

Canby thanked Tobey for her concern. But he couldn't accept her advice. "Where my duty calls me, I go, as a soldier," he said. To Meacham, Canby said, laughing, "Tobey has got you scared. Do not show the white feather. If you don't go, I'll meet them alone tomorrow." He asked Meacham to listen to reason. "These Modocs are not fools. They won't try to harm us, only half a mile from our army in plain view."

The next day the commissioners and Tobey and Frank Riddle rode to the peace site. They arranged themselves to meet the Modocs. Canby and Eleazar Thomas were to the left of Tobey Riddle, who once again would interpret. Meacham and then Frank Riddle, who was also interpreting, were to her right. Leroy Dyar, Indian agent on the Klamath reservation, who had just joined the commissioners, was beside Frank Riddle.

370

The Modocs arrived and entered. Captain Jack faced Canby; Schonchin faced Meacham; Boston Charley was opposite Thomas. Bogus Charley and Black Jim fronted Tobey Riddle and Frank Riddle, respectively. Hooker Jim faced Dyar. A seventh Modoc, Slolux, stood behind the others.

Canby opened. "My Modoc friends, my heart feels good today," he said. "I feel good because you are my friends. I know you are my friends. We will do good work today. I know you people better every time I meet you. I know I will be able to make you see things right today. You will see as I see. I am willing and ready to help you."

Canby spoke directly to Captain Jack. "Jack, I know you are a smart man. That is the reason I want you to come to my terms and make peace. It is bad to fight. Be a man, and live like one. As long as you live in these rocks, you won't be living like a man." Canby said that the Great Father at Washington wanted the Modocs to have a home, but not in the lava beds. He wanted them to have a home where they would not have trouble. Jack must listen to the Great Father. "He has many, many, many soldiers. He will make you go. He sent me, Dr. Thomas and Meacham here to see you and talk good to you and make peace." It was no good to fight anymore. "If you kill all these soldiers, the Great Father will send more soldiers. Next time you cannot kill all of them." Canby promised to protect Captain Jack and the other Modocs. "I won't let the soldiers hurt you," he said. "The white man's law is straight and strong. What I say is law, that is if you and I agree on anything."

Captain Jack grew agitated on listening to Canby. He could hold still no longer. "Canby, your law is as crooked as this," he said, holding up a sagebrush stick. "The agreements you make are as crooked as this" — he drew a jagged line in the dirt. Jack said Canby had agreed to suspend military action during the peace talks, but he had violated that agreement.

"What have I done?" said Canby. "Tell me."

"You all moved right under my nose, more soldiers arriving every three or four days, bringing big guns that shoot balls as big as your head," Jack said. "Does that look like peace? No! Many times no!" He became angrier. "Do you think that I can't see what's going on? How can you expect me to believe you now? I have learned that you are not a man of your word; if a man goes back on one thing, he will go back on another. Take away your soldiers; take away your big guns. Then we can talk peace. Either do that or give me a home at Hot Creek. Do not tell me of your beautiful country away off. Hot Creek is good enough for me."

Captain Jack waited for the interpretation.

372

He continued, "I want to tell you, Canby, we cannot make peace as long as these soldiers are crowding me. If you promise me a home somewhere in this country, promise me today; although your word is not much good, I am willing to take you at your promise. Thomas and Meacham will make it stronger if they promise with you. *Now,* Canby, promise me! I want nothing else. *Now* is your chance."

Perhaps Canby heard the desperation in Captain Jack's voice. Perhaps not. Hooker Jim apparently did. He and Schonchin didn't want an agreement. Hooker Jim created a distraction. He walked over to Meacham's horse. He took Meacham's overcoat from the back of the saddle and put it on himself — slowly, never taking his eyes off Meacham. Then suddenly he straightened, slapped himself on the chest and said, "Me Meacham now!"

Meacham humored him. He took off his hat and handed it to Hooker Jim. "Here, Jim, take my hat and put it on. Then you will be Meacham."

Captain Jack didn't appreciate the sideshow. "Canby, do you agree to what I ask of you, or not?" he demanded. "Tell me. I am tired of waiting for you to speak."

Meacham turned to Canby. "General, for heaven's sake, promise him!" he said.

Now Captain Jack moved. He walked behind Meacham's horse. While he did, Schonchin spoke for the first time. "Give us Hot Creek!" he said in a loud voice. "Give us Hot Creek, I say!"

Jack had come around from behind Meacham's horse. He stood directly in front of Canby. He said sharply to the other Modocs, in their own tongue, "Let's do it!" As he spoke he pulled out a pistol and leveled it at Canby's face. He squeezed the trigger, but the gun misfired. He quickly drew back the hammer and squeezed again. The bullet hit Canby under the right eye. Canby stood up and tried to run from the tent. Bogus Charley tripped him, and when he fell, Charley produced a knife and slit his throat.

Boston Charley meanwhile drew a pistol and shot Eleazar Thomas in the chest. Thomas fell backward but caught himself on his left elbow. Boston Charley stood over him and said, "You believe the squaw now, I guess."

"I believe her," Thomas said. "She told the truth."

Boston Charley shoved Thomas onto the ground. He taunted the preacher, asking him if his God would save him.

Thomas, whispering words of prayer, died.

Amid all this, Schonchin shot Meacham. Meacham had brought a derringer, and tried to defend himself, but his gun failed to fire. Schonchin's shot might have been fatal but

374

Tobey struck Schonchin's arm just as he fired. The bullet hit Meacham in the left shoulder. Schonchin kept firing, even as Tobey kept trying to stop him. Meacham received several wounds.

Schonchin angrily turned on Tobey. "Beware, woman," he said. "I may forget that you are a woman."

Tobey dared him to fire. "Kill me if you want to, you coward."

Schonchin didn't shoot. But another Modoc, who rushed up amid the melee, knocked her down while stealing her horse. "You white man's sister, I'll leave you among your dead brothers if you bother me again," he said.

He turned to mount the horse. Tobey regained her feet, picked up a rock, and struck him with it from behind. "You coward, you cannot fight your equal," she said. "You will not take my animal. Kill me first."

He proposed to do just that. He drew his gun and was about to shoot her when Captain Jack aimed a pistol at his head. "If it was not for the good you will do in our war against the whites, I would blow your head off and leave you right here to rot, you coward," he said. "What do you mean by striking that woman? If you say another word to her, I will kill you now."

Jack then turned to Tobey. "I have thrown myself and my life away today," he said. "I did something today that I thought I would never do, but I have done it. I killed an unarmed man. I know I will be killed, but when I fall there will be soldiers under me."

Boston Charley took out his knife to scalp Meacham. Tobey pleaded with him not to. He ignored her pleas and started in. Tobey, realizing she couldn't stop him, leaped back and shouted that the soldiers were coming. The Modocs dashed to escape, without noticing that there were no soldiers in sight.

Tobey's ruse saved the life of Meacham, whose several wounds hadn't quite killed him. She could do nothing for Canby and Thomas, who were already gone.

Civil War hero William Sherman received the dubious honor of command of the campaign against Indian resistance in the West.

Apache leader Geronimo proved to be Sherman's most resourceful and determined foe.

Andrew Jackson set the framework of American policy by persuading Congress to approve the Indian Removal Act.

Ulysses Grant discovered that the power of presidents was limited—by Congress, by headstrong officers, by pushy settlers and by unyielding Indians.

George Custer was one of those headstrong officers; his rashness resulted in his death and the deaths of hundreds of his men.

Philip Sheridan was less impetuous than Custer and far more successful.

Ely Parker (second from right, while on Grant's staff during the Civil War), was a Seneca Indian who embodied one Indian strategy for dealing with the whites: assimilation. He became head of the Indian Bureau in Grant's presidency.

Lakota chief Red Cloud conducted a spirited defense of the Powder River Valley before accepting the Treaty of Fort Laramie and leading his followers onto the Sioux reservation.

Sitting Bull was one of the last Lakota holdouts, taking refuge in Canada before resigning himself to life on the reservation.

The inspirational leadership of Joseph of the Nez Perce won him support and sympathy among many in the American East.

The Modoc resistance under Captain Jack took advantage of the convoluted topography of the lava beds of northern California.

Kiowa chief Satanta ran
afoul of Sherman on the
southern plains.

Quanah Parker was the
last great war chief of the
Comanches, and the first
great success of his people
in post-surrender life.

George Crook chased Geronimo across the deserts and mountains of Arizona and Mexico, bringing him to the point of surrender— only to lose him at the crucial moment.

Nelson Miles finished what Crook started, and much more.

By the time of surrender, Geronimo's band had dwindled to a hardy few.

Fort Sill became Geronimo's final home.

Geronimo, defeated but undaunted.

Sherman, victorious but ambivalent.

28

Sherman received news of the murder of Canby and Thomas when a special courier brought a message to his Washington home at midnight. He consulted Grant the next day; they agreed that peace was off the table until the Modoc resistance had been crushed. He directed John Schofield to employ unre- mitting force to that end. "I hope to hear that they have met the doom they so richly earned by their insolence and perfidy," Sherman said. "You may be sure that any measure of severity will be sustained." To the field com- mander, Colonel Gillem, Sherman wrote directly and more forcefully. "Your dispatch announcing the terrible loss to the country of Gen. Canby by the perfidy of the Modoc band of Indians has been shown to the President, who authorizes me to instruct you to make the attack so strong and persistent that their fate may be commensurate with their crime," Sherman said. "You will be fully justified in their utter extermination."

The sentiment wasn't simply Sherman's, or Sherman's and Grant's. Interior Secretary Delano, typically determined to take the Indians' part against the army, delivered his own condemnation. "The Indians have murdered their best friend," he said, referring to Canby. "I hope they shall be punished severely, and shall ask for no mercy for them."

Yet the solid front of the administration didn't prevent Sherman, as the spokesman of the army, from coming under harsh criticism. A person more attuned to political gamesmanship — Grant, for example — would have known not to employ the word "extermination" in an order that was certain to be leaked to the public, as Sherman's directive to Gillem immediately was. But Sherman took pride in speaking his mind, and upon learning of the treacherous killing of his fellow officer — for whose safety Sherman as commanding general took responsibility — his anger was what surfaced first.

When his anger cooled — as it always did, usually soon — Sherman could express himself in ways that revealed the complexities of his mind and the problem before him. Within the week he wrote a long letter answering a critic who charged the army with pursuing an unconscionably brutal policy toward the suffering Indians. "The army has no 'policy' about Indians or anything else," Sherman said. "It has no voice in Congress, but accepts the laws as enacted and the interpretations thereof by the proper officials, and executes them with as much intelligence, fidelity and humanity as any other body of citizens." This critic, like most of Sherman's critics, complained that Indian policy should be under the direction of civilians, not soldiers. Sherman supplied background: "From the organization of the Government up to about 1850, the Indians and Indian Bureau were under the War Department, so that nearly all the civilization and Christianization of the Indians thus far accomplished occurred under army supervision," he wrote. "And today, in case an Indian suffers a wrong, I believe he will be more likely to appeal to the commanding officer of the nearest military post than to his own agent, for in the one he sees with his eyes the evidence of a force to compel obedience, whereas in the other nothing of the kind." Similar considerations applied to the government payments the Indians received, or did not receive. "I believe the annuities to treaty Indians would reach the parties in interest quite as surely through army officers as through civilians." And the annuities would be a more effective tool of policy if administered by army officers. "When Indians have committed depredations — as is very common — and the annuities are chargeable with the amount of damages, such stoppages could more safely be made by a commanding officer, having soldiers at his back, than by an agent afraid of his life, as too many of them are and have reason to be." Sherman had nothing against the agents personally. "The present Indian agents as a class are very good men," he said. "But they lack force, the one power which savages alone respect."

Sherman summarized the current state of affairs. "The existing policy, usually called the peace policy, is to gradually assemble the wandering nomadic tribes on reservations with boundaries clearly defined, and then through civilians to instruct them in agriculture and the ruder arts, and to educate them so far as possible," he said. None of the army officers objected to this policy, Sherman said. He continued, "When the Indians leave their reservations to steal, murder and plunder, they fall under the jurisdiction of the army. This is the theoretical condition of things, but it would require ten times our present army to make a cordon around the reservations, so that murders are done, the stealing of cattle, horses, etc. perpetrated, and the Indians quickly escape to their reservations, where the troops cannot follow. So that in fact these reservations help them in their lucrative business."

Sherman cited experience and reliable reports in declaring, "Half the horses and mules now owned by the Kiowas, Comanches, Arapahoes, Cheyennes, Sioux, etc. — all treaty Indians, all at peace, with agencies and annuities — have been stolen from the United States or from citizens. I have myself seen at the Kiowa and Comanche agencies, and at several of the Sioux agencies, horses and mules branded 'U.S.' led up to be packed with annuity goods, and I have never heard of an agent demanding the restitution of one for that reason. And though murders are of frequent occurrence, I do not hear of the murderers being surrendered as is required by all treaties. Again, though the Sioux and Cheyennes are at peace, the army has to send escorts with all trains and parties of surveyors who go rightfully to work within the borders of such states as Kansas and Nebraska, as though actual war existed." In fact, it was worse than being at war. "The army has a much more difficult task now than if we were actually at war, and could anticipate depredations and follow the perpetrators to their very camps, as I did in the case of the Kiowas two years ago."

Sherman elaborated on the Kiowa case. "Then the Texas people were constantly complaining that the treaty Indians were depredating on their property, killing their people, and taking refuge on their reservations," he said. "I could not believe it till I went in person, and was actually nearby when Satanta killed seven poor teamsters in Texas, one of whom was found burned, tied at the wagon wheel. And a few days after, he" — Satanta — "came to the agency at Fort Sill, boasting of the deed. With the approval of the agent Mr. Tatum, I arrested him and two others and sent them to Texas for trial." Sherman had recently learned of Satanta's prospective release from prison. "I am told that Satanta is to be turned loose again, although I believe he has committed fifty murders, and has notoriously violated every promise hitherto made."

Sherman acknowledged that Indian policy was a complicated matter. "No general rule will answer for the government of every tribe," he said. "Each must be treated according to their conduct." Army officers, as a rule, were better than the civilian Indian agents at making sound judgments — "though I am by no means anxious that the disagreeable duty should be imposed on us," Sherman said. "If the Christian agents can better control the wild savages, I wish them all success; but surely the white people who venture into the wilderness to labor and toil are entitled to the protection of their lives and property, and it is natural that they should feel the greatest interest."

Easterners often looked down on the men and women who had settled the West, Sherman said. "Many good people residing east of the Alleghenies mistake the character of the immigrant population who have of late years brought millions of acres under cultivation, and produced 50 or 60 millions of dollars of gold and silver, where twenty years ago a white man dared not venture. These people are of the same kind as settled Ohio, Indiana and Iowa; they are as good as we are, and were we in their state, we would act just as they do. I know it, because I have been one of them." Sherman was speaking here of his decade in California. "They now pay their full share of taxes and contribute to our national wealth and power." The westerners, and some others, objected to the idea that the Indians might be on the government dole forever. "If Indians are willing to work as they used to do in the gold mines of California, nobody will prevent them," Sherman said. "Today if the Cheyennes, Arapahoes and Kiowas will utilize the beautiful pastoral land assigned them, in raising stock, they will soon become the richest people in the Southwest. But this they have not done, and it looks as though they never will."

Friction between whites and Indians was older than the republic. "The pressure of white settlements on the borders of Indian reservations is nothing new," Sherman said. "It has gone on for two hundred years and must go on; and the Indian must conform. In some instances they will do it without resistance; in others they will resist. And in some cases injustice will be done. But surely our government can never admit to practice the principle that one wrong justifies another and a greater; that because the soldiers in New Mexico chase and kill a few Cheyennes near Fort Bascom who are more than a hundred miles off their reservation to steal horses, they can go and kill the surveyors near Camp Supply, engaged in a lawful survey."

Sherman turned to the Modoc question. "The affair with the Modocs is not regarded as an exceptional case nor has it any connection whatever with the affairs of the Apaches, Sioux, Cheyennes, Arapahoes, and Kiowa, that wander over a region of country four or five times as great as the whole state of California," he said. "The Modocs are a small remnant of what used to be called the Pit River Indians or Rogue River Indians, with whom there have been several wars. They're familiar with the habits and customs of the whites, have seen gold dug from the canyons of their mountains, and have participated in it; have seen the wild valleys where they used to hunt and fish converted into prosperous farms and ranches; but in this they seem not to have imitated their white neighbors. Whether they have sustained wrongs or not is not in question. But they have taken refuge in a natural fortress, have defied the civil and military agents, and lastly under a flag of truce killed General Canby, who was their best friend; and this was not an isolated fact, for about the same time they decoyed Lieutenant Sherwood within reach of their rifles at another and distant part, and also stealthily attacked Colonel Mason's camp on the opposite side from that where General Canby and the peace commissioners were shot. All the Modocs are involved, and do not pretend that the murder of General Canby was the individual act of Captain Jack. Therefore the order for attack is against the whole, and if all be swept from the face of the earth, they themselves have invited it."

Sherman didn't relish the killing of noncombatants. But the Modocs, by taking women and children into their stronghold, in the heart of the battlefield, made such killing inevitable. "The place is like a fortress and during an assault the soldiers cannot pause to distinguish between male and female, or even discriminate as to age," Sherman said. The soldiers would do their best to minimize unnecessary deaths. "As long as resistance is made, death must be meted out, but the moment all resistance ceases, the firing will stop, and survivors be turned over to the proper Indian agent." But the deed must be done, and done thoroughly. "There is not much danger of too much harm being done. To be effective and exemplary the blow must involve the terrible, enough to impress the kindred tribes of Klamaths and Paiutes." Sherman didn't think this view was peculiar to officers of the army. "I believe the civilians and soldiers wish the same end, and in fact do not much differ as to the process. All Indians must be made to know that when the government commands, they must obey, and until that state of mind is reached through persuasion or force, we cannot hope for peace."

The blow Sherman ordered against the Modocs did fall, and produced nothing like annihilation. The troops surrounding Captain Jack's stronghold were reinforced until the soldiers outnumbered the Modoc warriors twenty to one. The big guns Jack complained about to Canby bombarded the stronghold until it became uninhabitable. Despite the cordon of soldiers, Jack and the other Modocs slipped through in the dark of night. But once beyond the lava beds they were easily pursued, overtaken and compelled to surrender. Not even Jack fought to the bitter end. He surrendered with the rest.

Sherman recommended that the murderers of Canby and Thomas be tried in a military court. Other Modocs who had killed settlers could be tried in the civil courts of Oregon and California, but decisions of civil courts might be overturned by political pressure, as had occurred with Satanta. Moreover, the killing of Canby and Thomas took place under a flag of military truce and therefore violated military law. The rest of the Modocs should be transported far away and dispersed among other tribes. "Thus the tribe of Modocs would disappear," Sherman explained to the secretary of war, "and the example would be salutary in dealing with other Indians similarly disposed and similarly situated."

Sherman received a dispatch from Jefferson C. Davis, who had succeeded Canby. Davis said the prisoners were well guarded. He added, "I had already made arrangements to execute eight or ten of the ringleaders; scaffold and ropes were prepared." Sherman's order caused him to halt, reluctantly. "I have no doubt of the propriety and the necessity of executing them on the spot at once," he said. "I had no doubt of my authority as department commander in the field to thus execute a band of outlaws, robbers, and murderers like these, under the circumstances. Your dispatch indicates a long delay of the cases of these red devils, which I regret. Delay will destroy the moral effect which their prompt execution would have had upon other tribes, and also the inspiring effect upon the troops." But he would do as directed, and hold the prisoners for military and civilian trial.

Davis appended a plea for clemency in the cases of several of the prisoners who, after surrendering, offered to help in the hunt for

Captain Jack and the remaining fugitives. These included Hooker Jim, Bogus Charley and a man called Steamboat Frank. "Their daring exploits and usefulness in capturing Jack has won the admiration of all," Davis said. "Without their services, we might not have succeeded yet in capturing Jack and his band." Davis said he had promised them nothing, and he supposed the sight of the noose had influenced their decision to co-operate. Yet they had done good work, whatever the motive. "It was my intention to exempt them from the death penalty, at least," he said. "Honor on my part requires me to urge their exemption to this extent, although two of them, Hooker Jim and Frank, have been among the worst of the band."

Sherman wished he hadn't spoken so soon. "It is to be regretted that General Davis was interrupted in his proposed dealing with the Modoc criminals," he remarked. But the matter had gone to the president and the attorney general, and there was nothing to be done.

The attorney general agreed with Sherman, and Grant approved. A military commission was established to try the killers of Canby and Thomas. Six men, including Captain Jack, John Schonchin and Boston Charley, but not the Modocs who became scouts for Davis, were charged with murder in violation of the laws of war. The six were convicted and sentenced to death. The sentences of two of the convicted men were commuted to life imprisonment. Captain Jack, Schonchin, Boston Charley and Black Jim were hanged at Fort Klamath in October 1873.

The rest of the Modocs, numbering 153, were sent as prisoners of war to Fort McPherson in Nebraska. From there they were relocated to the Indian Territory for permanent residence.

■ ■ ■ ■

PART IV
BEYOND THE
GREASY GRASS

■ ■ ■ ■

29

Struggles like that among the Modocs which led Captain Jack to murder Edward Canby were played out in every tribe. By the 1870s it was clear that the tide of white settlement was irresistible and that even the remotest tribes would not be able to defend the whole of the territory they once had claimed. The question for each tribe's leaders and members was how much of a loss they were willing to accept. The government promised them land they could have for their own. The land was never as much as they wanted, and the government's record of honoring past promises was checkered, to say the least. But what was the alternative? Fighting to the death?

To some of the warriors, that *was* the alternative, and the one they preferred. Better to die gloriously in battle than to grow old on a reservation. But the chiefs had to think beyond the warriors. Glory didn't await the women and children in a continued campaign — only cold, hunger, wasting and slow death. The children were the future of the tribe; the tribe couldn't survive if its leaders didn't protect them.

"What do you know of the Black Hills?"

Sherman's question to Phil Sheridan was prompted by recent events in the mountainous district of southwestern Dakota Territory, which had been the source of speculation and excitement since the early 1870s. Sheridan commanded the military district that included the Black Hills, and Sherman wanted to learn what he knew.

Sheridan responded with an intriguing story that was meant to be reassuring. "My first knowledge of the Black Hills was derived from an interview with the late Father De Smet, a noted Catholic missionary, whom I met many years ago on the Columbia River in Oregon," Sheridan said. De Smet was a great storyteller, and he spun a tale for Sheridan. "I heard an Indian romance of a mountain of gold in the Black Hills, and his explanation of that extraordinary and elusive story of the Indians, frontiersmen and explorers of the Black Hills country."

Sheridan paused to explain that the Black Hills were so called on account of "the black scrubby character of the timber which grows on the sides and tops of the mountains and hills." He might have added the forests weren't really black but seemed so by comparison with the bright, open plains from which they rose like a shadowed island in a sea of sunlight. The Lakota Sioux, in their conquest of the northern plains, had reached the Black Hills in the second half of the eighteenth century and given them that name, He Sapa, which echoed names employed by the tribes they displaced.

"Father De Smet's story," Sheridan continued in his letter to Sherman, "was that while living with the Sioux Indians, he was shown by them nuggets of gold, which they informed had been obtained at different points in the Black Hills, supposed to be from the beds of the Bighorn, Rosebud and Powder rivers, and from the branches of the Tongue River. And on his representing that such yellow metal was a great value, they told him that they knew where a mountain of it was to be found."

De Smet was a Jesuit priest, pledged to poverty. But even he couldn't resist the allure of a "mountain of gold." He investigated, only to discover that the Indians misconceived what they spoke of. "The Indian mountain of gold was nothing more than a formation of yellow mica, such as may be found in a number of places in the above described country," Sheridan said.

Yet the story didn't die. "I had scarcely given the story a thought after this until about three years ago, when I happened to be in

New York, and it was there brought to my recollection by a prominent gentleman, who asked me where Father De Smet was to be found, and insisted that someone should be sent at once to get from him the secret of the gold mountain, which would pay the national debt. After I informed him that it was an old and exploded story, his ardor cooled and the excitement about the mountain of gold again subsided."

But not for long. The lust for gold never disappeared, and the severe depression that followed the financial panic of 1873 put millions out of work, with time to chase down rumors of the next big strike in western gold. Prospectors infiltrated the Black Hills, despite its being reserved to the Lakotas. The Grant administration declared that trespassers would be removed and prosecuted; when this failed to stem the excitement, Grant ordered an expedition to the Black Hills to refute the rumors of gold there.

The expedition succeeded scientifically but failed politically. George Custer's crew found gold, but not more than could be found in any number of places around the West, and not enough to pay the expense of finding and collecting it. Yet the boosters of business in Dakota, desperate for revenue after the Northern Pacific Railroad suspended construction on its line through the region, took any glint as ground to proclaim a boom. "All

Bismarck is ready and anxious to start immediately for the new El Dorado, which bids fair to rival the gold fields of California in their palmiest days," shouted a scribe in the territorial capital. "Only the rudest kind of prospecting by the use of the mining pan was done, yet the results obtained were truly wonderful. Using the amount of fine gold collected from one pan of earth as a basis of calculation, and making a liberal allowance for exaggeration, the most valuable diggings found, in Custer's Gulch, will yield $20 a day per man, worked with a pan; the ordinary method of sluice mining would give a return of over $100 per day, while the profits of a systematic course of hydraulic mining would be something enormous. Where so much surface gold exists there must necessarily be extensive quartz ledges" — underground veins — "which being of a more permanent character than placer mining" — surface mining — "will open a large field for the investment of Eastern capital."

Sheridan dismissed the El Dorado talk for the flackery it was. "Although I have the utmost confidence in the statements of General Custer and General Forsyth of my staff, that gold has been found near Harney's Peak," he told Sherman, "I may safely say that there has not been any fair test yet made to determine its existence in large quantities. There is not a territory in the West where gold does not exist, but in many of them the quantity is limited to the color, which is as much as has yet been obtained near Harney's Peak. The geological specimens brought back by the Custer expedition are not favorable indications of the existence of gold in great quantities."

Sheridan allowed that Custer might have looked in the wrong place. "To go back to Father De Smet's information, there's not much doubt of the correctness of his statement that gold exists in the Black Hills, but much further west than the Black Hills of the Cheyenne" — where Custer had looked. "I have seen nuggets from the Big Horn and Tongue rivers, and many specimens from near Fort Stambaugh, in the upper Wind River country, where the mining has failed for want of water for alluvial washing and from the hostility of the Indians; and I have good reason to believe — in fact it is quite certain — that gold exists in the Owl Creek Mountains on the lower Wind River, and on the headwaters of the Powder River and the Rosebud."

Sherman worried that Sheridan might be right about gold elsewhere in the Black Hills, but for public consumption he emphasized the scantiness of the findings to date. "It is very thin," he told a reporter who had asked about Custer's gold. "Why, these fellows can't make any money there. In the first place, they will be so far from markets that food will cost them a dollar a pound. It will be just as it was in the earlier mining days" — in California. "A man might dig $16 a day, but his meals cost him $3 a piece, or $9 a day, and everything else in proportion, so he never made a cent. It will be just so again, and though there may be, as I have no doubt there is, gold in those hills, it is comparatively inaccessible from the expense attendant upon digging it out."

Sherman didn't deny that people would try to find gold in the Black Hills, despite the best efforts of the army to keep them out. In fact, he acknowledged that the very efforts to keep them out might be contributing to their desire to get in. "It's the same old story, the story of Adam and Eve and the forbidden fruit," he said. "These people know they have no right there; they know the government prohibits any trenching on that ground, and so they have made up their minds to go there."

Sherman reiterated Grant's warning that the army would use force to prevent trespass, yet he conceded that he lacked the troops to cordon off the Black Hills completely. He expected trouble with the Lakotas when the gold hunters broke through. "Of course, there will be a great deal of scalping done by the Indians," Sherman said. The gold hunters would have only themselves to blame. "We can't help it if we don't see it, nor can we avenge it. If these men go there, they stand in the position of so many burglars, forcibly entering another man's property. This reserve has been given to the Indians by the government in payment for almost limitless tracts of other land, and the United States will certainly not attack those Indians for protecting the property they have thus purchased, against marauders. Of course the army will protect the miners against death so far as it can, for life is worth more than property at any time; but after the miner is killed, the government will not seek to avenge his death."

Few if any Lakotas read the issue of the *St. Louis Globe* that carried Sherman's interview. Any who did might not have credited his ability to withstand political pressure to punish Indians who killed white miners. On the other hand, they might not have cared much one way or the other. The invasion of the Black Hills, which proceeded despite the army's efforts, was one cause of renewed war between the Lakotas and the army, but it wasn't the only one. Sitting Bull and Crazy Horse, the leaders of the Lakota campaign, resented the whole white presence in country the Lakotas had won for themselves at no little cost. The two leaders had refused to sign the Fort Laramie treaty of 1868 or to recognize the Sioux reservation it established. They opposed the penetration of the Northern Pacific into the Lakota hunting grounds along the Yellowstone River. The invasion of the gold hunters was simply the last straw, the one that provoked them to regular war against the whites.

They were accompanied by northern Cheyennes. The Lakotas didn't normally require allies; most neighboring tribes, in particular the Crows, were their enemies. But Sitting Bull concluded that in what he hoped would be the climactic struggle against the whites, the Lakotas could use help. He joined the Cheyennes for a sun dance in the summer of 1875, laying the groundwork for a military alliance the following summer.

By then the government had formally ordered all Lakotas onto the Sioux reservation. Those that stayed out would be subject to attack by army forces. Sitting Bull and Crazy Horse ignored this order as they had ignored the other decrees of the whites, and the number of warriors on their side was increased not simply by the Cheyennes but by Lakotas who wintered on the reservation yet summered on the old lands, roaming and raiding as their fathers had done. More than a few of the summer warriors likely guessed that this would be their last chance.

"I was born seventy-seven winters ago, near

Grand River, South Dakota," remembered She Walks With Her Shawl at the one-third mark of the twentieth century. "My father, Slohan, was the bravest man among our people. Fifty-five years ago we packed our tents and went with other Indians to Pejislawakpa." The Lakota term translated to Greasy Grass River; the whites called it the Little Bighorn. "We were then living on the Standing Rock reservation. I belonged to Sitting Bull's band. They were great fighters. We called ourselves Hunkpapa. This means confederated bands." Hunkpapa was alternatively translated as "head of the circle." The Hunkpapa were one of the seven bands of the Lakota Sioux. They didn't cooperate as closely as the Six Nations of the Iroquois, for example, not least since their nomadic ways made such cooperation nearly impossible. But Sitting Bull and Crazy Horse had managed to bring parts of each band together for their campaign against the whites.

She Walks With Her Shawl had been on campaign before. "When I was still a young girl, about seventeen, I accompanied a Sioux war party which made war against the Crow Indians in Montana," she said. Slohan was a veteran of many campaigns. "My father went to war seventy times. He was wounded nearly a dozen times."

The battle she remembered best was the one on the Greasy Grass against the soldiers led by Custer. She was twenty-three that summer. "Several of us Indian girls were digging wild turnips," she said. "The morning was hot and sultry." They were some distance from the Hunkpapa camp when they saw a cloud of dust rising behind a ridge to their east. "We girls looked toward the camp and saw a warrior ride swiftly, shouting that the soldiers were only a few miles away and that the women and children and old men should run for the hills in the opposite direction."

She Walks With Her Shawl dropped her digging stick and ran toward her tepee. "I saw my father running toward the horses," she said. "When I got to my tent, my mother told me that news was brought to her that her brother had been killed by the soldiers. My brother had gone early that morning in search for a horse that strayed from our herd. In a few moments, we saw soldiers on horseback on a bluff just across the Greasy Grass River. I knew that there would be a battle because I saw warriors getting their horses and tomahawks."

The battle began almost at once. "I heard Hawkman shout, 'Ho-ka-he!' " she remembered. This was the call to charge. "The soldiers began firing into our camp." Then came a pause she couldn't account for. "They ceased firing." The current of the battle veered in another direction.

She Walks With Her Shawl did her part. "I

sang a death song for my brother who had been killed. My heart was bad. Revenge, revenge for my brother's death!" At the time, she didn't think revenge was a bad thing; that would come later. "I ran to a nearby thicket and got my black horse. I painted my face with crimson and unbraided my black hair. I was mourning. I was a woman, but I was not afraid."

"By this time the soldiers" — a company under Major Marcus Reno — "were forming a battle line in the bottom about a half mile away," she said. "In another moment I heard a terrific volley of carbines. The bullets shattered the tepee poles. Women and children were running away from the gunfire. In the tumult, I heard old men and women singing death songs for their warriors who were now ready to attack the soldiers. The chanting of death songs made me brave, although I was a woman."

The fighting was all around them. "I saw a warrior adjusting his quiver and grasping his tomahawk," She Walks With Her Shawl said. "He started running toward his horse when he suddenly recoiled and dropped dead. He was killed near his tepee. Warriors were given orders by Hawkman to mount their horses and follow the fringe of a forest and wait until commands were given to charge. The soldiers kept on firing. Some women were also killed. Horses and dogs too."

Confusion reigned. "The camp was in great commotion," she said. "Father led my black horse up to me and I mounted. We galloped toward the soldiers. Other warriors joined in with us. When we were nearing the fringe of the woods, the order was given by Hawkman, 'Ho-ka-he! Ho-ka-he!' The warriors were now near the soldiers. The troopers were all on foot. They shot straight, because I saw our leader killed as he rode with his warriors."

The Indian charge forced the soldiers back. "The soldiers ran to their horses and, mounting them, rode swiftly toward the river. The Greasy Grass River was very deep. Their horses had to swim to get across. Some of the warriors rode into the water to tomahawk the soldiers. In the charge the Indians rode among the troopers and with tomahawks unhorsed several of them. The soldiers were very excited. Some of them shot into the air. The Indians chased the soldiers across the river and up over a bluff."

The Indians drew back to the valley where the fighting had started. "The warriors rode in a column of fives. They sang the victory song." But the battle wasn't over. "We heard a commotion far down the valley," She Walks With Her Shawl remembered. "Someone said that another body of soldiers were attacking the lower end of the village. I heard afterwards the soldiers were under the command of Long Hair" — Custer. "With my father and other warriors I rode in that direction. We crossed the Greasy Grass below a beaver dam — the water is not so deep there — and came upon many horses. One soldier was holding the reins of eight or ten horses. An Indian waved his blanket and scared all the horses. They got away from the men" — the soldiers.

"On the ridge just north of us, I saw blue-clad men running up a ravine firing as they ran," she said. She couldn't see much more. "The dust created from the stampeding horses and powder smoke made everything dark and black. Flashes from carbines could be seen. The valley was dense with powder smoke. I never heard such whooping and shouting." She understood what the Lakotas were saying. One, Red Horse, shouted, "There never was a better day to die!" She couldn't understand the cries from the troopers, as she didn't know English.

The shape of the battle became clearer. "Long Hair's troopers were trapped in an enclosure. There were Indians everywhere. The Cheyennes attacked the soldiers from the north, and Crow King from the south. The Sioux Indians encircled the troopers. Not one got away. The Sioux used tomahawks."

She Walks With Her Shawl took care to explain that the soldiers weren't massacred. The fight was a battle to the end. "Very few soldiers were mutilated, as often has been said by the whites. Not a single soldier was burned at the stake. Sioux Indians do not torture their victims after the battle."

But they did claim the spoils of victory. "The Indians took all the equipment and horses belonging to the soldiers. The brave men who came to punish us that morning were defeated." She Walks With Her Shawl toured the battlefield. "We saw the body of Long Hair. Of course we did not know who the soldiers were until an interpreter told us that the men came from Fort Lincoln. On the saddle blankets were the crossed-saber insignia and the number seven" — the emblem of the Seventh Cavalry.

The battle was a Lakota triumph but a costly one. "The victorious warriors returned to the camp, as did the women and children who could see the battle from where they took refuge. Over sixty Indians were killed, and they were also brought back to the camp for scaffold burial. The Indians did not stage a victory dance that night. They were mourning for their dead."

The battle looked different to the warriors. One Bull was an adopted son of Sitting Bull and in the prime of life for fighting. "I was a strong young man, twenty-two years old," he remembered. "On the day of the fight, I was sitting in my tepee combing my hair." One

Bull was as proud of his hair as Billy Dixon was of *his* locks. One Bull had just returned from gathering his horses. "I saw a man named Fat Bear come running into camp, and he said soldiers were coming on the other side of the river." One Bull wanted to see for himself. "I came out of my tepee and saw soldiers running their horses toward our camp on the same side of the river. We could hear lots of shooting."

One Bull spied his chance. "I went to the tepee of my uncle Sitting Bull, and said I was going to take part in the battle. He said, 'Go ahead. They have already fired.' I had a rifle and plenty of shells, but I took that off and gave it to Sitting Bull, and he gave me a shield. Then I took the shield and my tomahawk and got on my horse and rode up to where the soldiers were attacking us."

The battle was fierce. "They were firing pretty heavy," One Bull said of the soldiers. "They were all down near the river in the timber. Lakotas were riding around fast and shooting at them. I rode up to some Lakota and said, 'Let's all charge at once.' I raised my tomahawk and said, 'Wakan Tanka, help me, so I do not sin but fight my battle!' " He was calling on the Great Spirit.

"I started to charge. There were five Lakotas riding behind me. We charged for some soldiers that were still fighting, and they ran to where their horses were in the timber.

Then the soldiers all started for the river. I turned my horse and started that way too, and there was a man named Mato Washte" — Pretty Bear — "right behind me, and he and his horse were shot down. I followed the soldiers. They were running for the river. I killed two with my tomahawk. Then the soldiers got across the river. I came back to where Pretty Bear was and got him up on my horse. He was wounded and covered with blood."

One Bull carried Pretty Bear to safety, then resumed the fight. "I went across the river after the soldiers," he said. "I killed one more of them with my tomahawk. Then I saw four soldiers ahead of me running up the hill. I was just about to charge them when someone rode along beside me and said, 'You better not go any farther. You are wounded.'" The speaker was Sitting Bull. "I was not wounded, but I was all covered with blood that got on me when I had Pretty Bear on my horse," One Bull recalled. Yet he followed orders. "I did what Sitting Bull told me."

Not for long, though. "Sitting Bull rode back but I went on," he said. Another warrior joined him in the chase after the four soldiers. "He had a rifle and shot one of them off his horse. One of the soldiers kept shooting back but without hitting us. The man that was with me was Lakota, but I did not know who he was. Now the soldiers were getting together up on the hill and we could see other soldiers coming with the pack mules a long way off." One Bull and his comrade were outnumbered, and they decided not to press the matter.

"I went back across the river and rode down it away," he said. "Then I rode with the man who was shooting at the four soldiers and we crossed the river again just east of Sitting Bull's camp. We saw a bunch of horsemen up on a hill to the north and they were Lakotas. We rode up to them and I told them I had killed a lot of soldiers and showed them my tomahawk. Then I said I was going up and help kill Custer's soldiers."

Once more he was ordered to stand down. "Sitting Bull told me not to go," One Bull said. There were plenty of warriors to deal with Custer; Sitting Bull wanted to hold some in reserve. "So I didn't go, but we rode up where we could see the Lakotas and Cheyennes killing Custer's men. They had been shooting heavy, but the Indians charged them straight from the west and then some rode around them shooting, and the Indians were knocking them off their horses and killing them with tomahawks and clubs. They were all killed."

They fought hard before they died. "There were a lot of Sioux killed," One Bull remembered. "The others were picking them up on their horses and taking them back to camp."

But the victory was worth celebrating. "We had a war dance all night."

They learned the next morning that the battle wasn't over. "We heard that the soldiers with the pack mules were up on the hill," One Bull said. This was Reno's command. "I went with Sitting Bull and volunteered to go help kill these soldiers but Sitting Bull said no. So we watched the fight from a hill. I didn't have my rifle with me then, just my tomahawk. The Sioux surrounded them, and they fought that way all day. The soldiers had ditches dug around the hill. Then along toward sundown the Sioux broke camp and went south to the mountains. The Sioux did not take any prisoners that I know of. I didn't see any."

The battle gave One Bull a glimpse of Sitting Bull's thinking and style of leadership. "I was with Sitting Bull all the time we were in camp on the Little Bighorn, and I saw him during the battle," he said. "He was telling his men what to do." Sitting Bull was pleased with the victory but didn't want to test his luck. "Before we broke camp that night, we saw the walking soldiers" — the infantry — "coming from down the river, but my uncle said, 'We won't fight them. We have killed enough. We will go.' "

30

Sherman learned the details of the battle from a report by Marcus Reno. The senior surviving officer of the Seventh Cavalry described how the regiment, under Custer's command, had left camp on the Yellowstone River on the afternoon of June 22 and ascended the Rosebud River twelve miles before halting for the night. The next day they made thirty-three miles up the Rosebud, passing several old Indian camps and following the trail of a large body of Indians, which was days or weeks old. On June 24 they continued up the Rosebud, apparently closing on the Indians to judge by the freshening of the trail. After twenty-eight miles they camped, awaiting intelligence from scouts Custer had sent ahead. "At 9:25 p.m. Custer called the officers together and informed us that beyond a doubt the village was in the valley of the Little Big Horn, and in order to reach it, it was necessary to cross the divide between the Rosebud and the Little Big

Horn, and it would be impossible to do so in the day-time without discovering our march to the Indians," Reno wrote. The regiment embarked an hour before midnight, angling away from the Rosebud up the ridge that separated that river from the Little Bighorn. At two on the morning of June 25, Custer's scouts told him that at the rate the march was going, they wouldn't cross the divide before daylight. Having lost the element of surprise he had hoped for, Custer called a halt to let the men and horses rest.

They resumed the march at dawn and at eight were in the valley of the Little Bighorn. "By this time Indians had been seen and it was certain that we could not surprise them," Reno wrote. "It was determined to move at once to the attack." Reno's account reached a point that would provoke controversy. "Previous to this, no division of the regiment had been made since the order had been issued on the Yellowstone annulling wing and battalion organizations, but Custer informed me that he would assign commands on the march" — that is, he would divide the regiment. Reno was assigned three companies and Captain Frederick Benteen another three, while Custer kept five companies. A final company remained with the pack train.

"I assumed command of the companies assigned to me, and, without any definite orders, moved forward with the rest of the column, and well to its left," Reno continued. This lack of orders would become controversial as well. "I saw Benteen moving farther to the left, and, as they passed, he told me he had orders to move well to the left, and sweep everything before him. I did not see him again until about 2:30 p.m. The command moved down to the creek toward the Little Big Horn Valley, Custer with five companies on the right bank, myself and three companies on the left bank, and Benteen farther to the left, and out of sight."

Around eleven they entered a deserted village. "Custer motioned me to cross to him, which I did, and moved nearer to his column," Reno wrote. The two columns continued moving forward. At half past noon, one of Custer's aides approached. "Lieutenant Cook, adjutant, came to me and said the village was only two miles above, and running away; to move forward at as rapid a gait as prudent, and to charge afterward, and that the whole outfit would support me. I think those were his exact words."

Reno ordered his men to a fast trot. After two miles they reached a ford in the river. "I crossed immediately, and halted about ten minutes or less to gather the battalion, sending word to Custer that I had everything in front of me, and that they were strong," Reno wrote. "I deployed, and, with the Ree" — also called Arikara — "scouts on my left, charged down the valley, driving the Indians with great ease for about two and a half miles. I, however, soon saw that I was being drawn into some trap, as they would certainly fight harder, and especially as we were nearing their village, which was still standing; besides, I could not see Custer or any other support, and at the same time the very earth seemed to grow Indians, and they were running toward me in swarms, and from all directions."

Reno had to change plans on the fly. "I saw I must defend myself and give up the attack mounted. This I did. Taking possession of a front of woods, and which furnished, near its edge, a shelter for the horses, we dismounted and fought them on foot, making headway through the woods. I soon found myself in the near vicinity of the village, saw that I was fighting odds of at least five to one, and that my only hope was to get out of the woods, where I would soon have been surrounded, and gain some high ground. I accomplished this by mounting and charging the Indians between me and the bluffs on the opposite side of the river."

They got to the top, but at the cost of thirty-two officers and men killed and seven wounded. On cresting the bluff they saw Benteen's force approaching, and the two forces linked up. Shortly the pack train joined them. This gave Reno command of seven companies, comprising nearly four hundred officers and men. He had no idea where Custer and the other five companies were.

He discerned their location only after resuming, along the top of the bluff, his approach toward the village. "We had heard firing in that direction and knew it could only be Custer," Reno wrote. "I moved to the summit of the highest bluff, but seeing and hearing nothing, sent Captain Weir with his company to open communication with him. He soon sent word by Lieutenant Hare that he could go no farther, and that the Indians were getting around him. At this time he was keeping up a heavy fire from his skirmish line."

Reno reconsidered again. "I at once turned everything back to the first position I had taken on the bluffs, and which seemed to me the best," he said. "I dismounted the men and had the horses and mules of the pack-train driven together in a depression, put the men on the crests of the hills making the depression, and had hardly done so when I was furiously attacked. This was about 6 p.m. We held our ground, with the loss of eighteen enlisted men killed and forty-six wounded, until the attack ceased, about 9 p.m."

Reno realized his force was on its own against the Indians. "As I knew by this time their overwhelming numbers, and had given up any support from that portion of the regiment with Custer, I had the men dig rifle pits, barricaded with dead horses and mules and boxes of hard bread the opening of the depression toward the Indians in which the animals were herded, and made every exertion to be ready for what I saw would be a terrific assault the next day." While the men were busy digging in, the Indians held a scalp dance within earshot.

The assault began at first light. "I heard the crack of two rifles," Reno wrote. "This was the signal for the beginning of a fire that I have never equaled. Every rifle was handled by an expert and skilled marksman, and with a range that exceeded our carbines, and it was simply impossible to show any part of the body before it was struck." The prospect grew worse before their eyes. "We could see, as the daylight brightened, countless hordes of them passing up the valley from the village and scampering over the high points toward the places designated for them by their chiefs, and which entirely surrounded our position. They had sufficient numbers to completely encircle us, and men were struck on opposite sides of the lines from where the shots were fired." Reno had never seen so many Indians. "I think we were fighting all the Sioux Nation, and also all the desperadoes, renegades, half-breeds, and squaw-men between the Missouri and the Arkansas and east of the Rocky Mountains, and they must have numbered at least 2,500 warriors."

Yet Reno's men held on. And with the pack train, they didn't have to ration their fire. The attack persisted for hours, slackening only in late morning, when the Indians regrouped for a charge, which came soon enough. Apparently the Indians were running low on ammunition, for they employed bows and arrows for the charge. Reno's troops turned them back, but only after desperate fighting.

A new problem arose. "We now had many wounded, and the question of water was vital, as from 6 p.m. the previous evening until now, 10 a.m., about sixteen hours, we had been without," Reno said. He ordered a skirmish line to cover men who ventured down to the river with canteens. Several of the men were wounded, but the water they brought back eased the thirst of the men most in need.

Something unexpected added to their hopes of survival. "To our astonishment the Indians were seen going in parties toward the village," Reno wrote. He and his men wondered what this meant. Perhaps the Indians were going for more ammunition or for something to eat. Or perhaps Custer was coming. Reno ordered his men to take advantage of the lull by fetching more water. Soon they had kettles full.

"But they" — the Indians — "continued to withdraw, and all firing ceased save occasional shots from sharp-shooters sent to annoy us about the water," Reno wrote. "About 2 p.m. the grass in the bottom was set on fire and followed up by Indians who encouraged its burning, and it was evident to me it was done for a purpose, and which purpose I discovered later on to be the creation of a dense cloud of smoke behind which they were packing and preparing to move their village. It was between 6 and 7 p.m. that the village came out from behind the dense clouds of smoke and dust. We had a close and good view of them as they filed away in the direction of the Big Horn Mountains, moving in almost perfect military order. The length of the column was full equal to that of a large division of the cavalry corps of the Army of the Potomac, as I have seen it in its march."

Reno realized that he and his surviving troops wouldn't die that day. And now they had time to wonder what had become of Custer. Reno and the other officers concluded that the Indians had driven Custer down the Little Bighorn toward the Yellowstone. Reno assumed that the departure of the Indians would allow Custer to re-ascend the valley and reconnect with the rest of the regiment. Toward this end, Reno had his men gather still more water, in case Custer's force was short.

The night passed with no sign of Custer.

419

"Early on the morning of the 27th, and while we were on the *qui vive* for Indians, I saw with my glass a dust some distance down the valley," Reno wrote. "There was no certainty for some time what they were, but finally I satisfied myself they were cavalry, and, if so, could only be Custer, as it was ahead of the time that I understood that General Terry could be expected." Alfred Terry was known to be coming with reinforcements. Reno dispatched three men to determine the cause of the dust. "The men started, and were told to go as near as it was safe to determine whether the approaching column was white men, and to return at once in case they found it so, but if they were Indians to push on to General Terry." They returned in short order, with word that Terry himself was making the dust. He had received a message from a Crow scout that Custer had been badly beaten, but he hadn't believed it.

Terry and Reno dispatched Benteen to find out the truth. The news was worse than any of them had imagined. The ground where Custer and his men had fought was littered with their bodies. "I proceeded with the regiment to the battleground of Custer and buried 204 bodies," Reno wrote. He pieced together the grim course of events. "After traveling over his trail, it was evident to me that Custer intended to support me by moving farther down the stream and attacking the village in flank; that he found the distance greater to ford than he anticipated; that he did charge, but his march had taken so long, although his trail shows that he had moved rapidly, that they" — the Indians — "were ready for him; that Companies C and I, and perhaps part of E, crossed to the village or attempted it at the charge, were met by a staggering fire, and that they fell back to find a position from which to defend themselves, but were followed too closely by the Indians to permit him to form any kind of a line."

Reno allowed himself to second-guess Custer. "I think had the regiment gone in as a body, and from the woods from which I fought advanced upon the village, its destruction" — the village's destruction — "was certain," Reno wrote. "But General Custer was fully confident they were running away, or he would not have turned from me. I think (after the great number of Indians there were in the village) that the following reasons obtain for the misfortune: His rapid marching for two days and one night before the fight; attacking in the day-time at 12 m., and when they were on the *qui vive,* instead of early morning; and lastly, his unfortunate division of the regiment into three commands."

Reno said he could only estimate the number of Indians killed. He himself had seen the bodies of eighteen, and his scouts had observed many graves along the Indians' line of march away from the battlefield. "It is simply impossible that numbers of them should not be hit in the several charges they made so close to my lines. They made their approaches through the deep gulches that led from the hill-top to the river, and, when the jealous care with which the Indian guards the bodies of killed and wounded is considered, it is not astonishing that their bodies were not found. It is probable that the stores left by them and destroyed the next two days was to make room for many of these on their travois."

Reno hoped one lesson at least could come from the tragedy. With other officers, he deeply resented having to fight Indians armed and provisioned by the same government that armed and provisioned his own men. "The harrowing sight of the dead bodies crowning the height on which Custer fell, and which will remain vividly in my memory until death, is too recent for me not to ask the good people of this country whether a policy that sets opposing parties in the field, armed, clothed, and equipped by one and the same Government should not be abolished," he said.

The news of the debacle on the Little Bighorn reached the American East just after the hundredth anniversary of the Declaration of

422

Independence. The centennial celebration, including a world's fair in Philadelphia, had raised American spirits dealt a blow by the continuing economic depression; the Custer catastrophe beat those spirits down again. The initial reports included lurid tales of grisly treatment of the corpses by the victorious Indians; one version told that Custer's heart had been cut out and paraded on a pole.

Editors weighed in on what should be done. "It is time to quit the Sunday-school policy and let Sheridan recruit regiments of Western pioneer hunters and scouts, and exterminate every Indian who will not remain upon the reservations," the *Chicago Tribune* declared. "The best use to make of an Indian who will not stay upon a reservation is to kill him."

The *New York Times* noted variety in reactions to the Custer defeat. "All through the West there is manifested a wild desire for vengeance against the so-called murderers of our soldiers," the paper said. "The press echoes with more or less shamelessness the frontier theory that the only use to which an Indian can be put is to kill him." Sober voices in the East didn't go that far. But an excitable populace often did. "Public opinion, not only in the West but to some extent in the East, has apparently decided that the Indians have exhausted the forbearance of heaven and earth, and must now be exterminated as though they were so many dogs." While hold-

423

ing itself above such passion, the *Times* joined the call for sterner policies. "We are now at war, and there is nothing left but to prosecute the struggle with the utmost rigor. Peace can be obtained only by the most thorough defeat of the enemy, and for the moment any peace policy must necessarily be suspended."

The *New York Herald* carried a piece aimed directly at Sherman. Wendell Phillips had won renown as an abolitionist, railing against the mistreatment of African Americans. After the Civil War he broadened his humanitarian agenda to include the aboriginal Americans. And in the wake of the news from the Little Bighorn, he lectured Sherman on Indian policy. Describing himself as "an American citizen entitled and bound to inquire whether the officers of the Republic are men or something below humanity," Phillips demanded, in an open letter to Sherman, "Are the journals correct when they represent you as advising the extermination of the Indians?" He continued, "This charge has been made several times during the last three years. If it be false, I beg you, for the honor of the nation and of the service to deny it. While you neglect to do so, the press uses your supposed example to commend that infamous course and to create a public opinion which shall approve and demand it."

Phillips recited the litany of wrongs done

the Indians, by the government but also by the settlers. He questioned Sherman once more: "Can it be possible, then, that with such knowledge and such experience, you, sir, the head of the army, and bound to show at least outward respect to civilization, have no counsel to give except extermination — the extermination of these plundered victims of a greedy, unscrupulous and cruel people? Can you advise a professedly Christian people steeped in guilt, not to reform, but to consummate its wickedness by such hideous barbarism as only the most inhuman tyrants have ever attempted? The worst possible of infidels, do you affirm that a wise and power- ful nation is safe only when it sinks below the level of savage life to clutch a coward's peace by sweeping every man, woman and child of this insignificant race in blood from our path?"

Sherman grew livid on reading the piece. Had Phillips been much closer than Boston, he might have confronted him face to face. Instead he wrote a letter to Samuel Tappan, his associate from the peace commission and a known friend of Phillips. "Several days ago there appeared in the *New York Herald* a let- ter from Wendell Phillips of Boston, ad- dressed to General W. T. Sherman, in which Mr. Phillips attributes to me certain absurd declarations about exterminating all the

Indians, which he then proceeded to assail," Sherman wrote to Tappan. "He did not quote from me or even indicate the newspaper in which he had seen me charged as in favor of exterminating the Indians, but simply assumed all his facts. I have never met Mr. Phillips in my life. Nor have I ever received a letter from him, nor can I admit his right to address me through the newspapers. He might, I should think, ventilate his peculiar thoughts and feelings on the complicated problem of Indian management without dragging my name into the papers."

Sherman explained why he was writing to Tappan. "I don't intend to answer his published letter, because it was not written *to* me, but *at* me," he said. "You know that I have never advocated the killing of anybody, white or Indian, except as punishment for crime, or to save the lives and property of our own. You and I were members of the same commission in 1867–8, and you know that it was composed of seven members, four civilians and three army officers; that I was simply a member and not the head of the commission, as asserted by Phillips; that we all differed in opinion as honest men do and should; but that we all agreed to sign the final report, which was as usual a compromise, written by Senator Henderson."

Sherman mentioned the journey he and Tappan had taken to New Mexico. "You and

426

I removed the Navajo Indians without killing a single one, and these Indians live now in comparative peace where we placed them," he wrote. "The Kiowas, Comanches, Arapahoes and Cheyennes, who used to roam from the Platte to the Rio Grande, now live on the reservation assigned them by our commission, in the Indian Territory west of Arkansas." Sherman remarked that he had had everyday charge of the entire region of the plains during the late 1860s. "During all this time I did not 'exterminate' an Indian or think of such a thing." Nor did he do so later. "When I inspected the frontier of Texas in 1871, I caught Satanta, Satank, and Big Tree, fresh from the murder of seven teamsters in Texas on a frequently traveled road over which I had passed the same day, and instead of exterminating them, I turned them over to a civil court for trial, just as I would have done with white murders."

Sherman noted that he had frequently been examined by committees of Congress; never had he advocated extermination. Nor had he done so in orders to subordinates or recommendations to superiors. "Therefore I assert that my opinions on this Indian question are a matter of official publication in my own chosen words, and I ask, What right has Mr. Phillips to assert the contrary and what I believe he knows to be false, in order to preach me a sermon full of malice and presumption?"

Sherman urged Tappan to correct his friend on the subject. "Tell him, once for all, that his assault on me in the *New York Herald* is simply infamous and unwarranted; that I answer daily hundreds of letters in the utmost sincerity and frankness, and would have answered him, had he written me before he published his letter. . . . Had he been even honest, he would have written me a simple letter of enquiry, instead of asserting that he had seen me charged in newspapers with the absurd declaration that I favored universal extermination. I challenge him to produce the newspapers, because I have not seen them, and I don't believe they exist. But even if such a statement as he alludes to did appear in one or more of the 10,000 newspapers, still as a professed gentleman and scholar, he was bound to enquire of you or of some responsible person on whom reliance could be placed."

Sherman stated his and the army's policy succinctly: "Peaceful Indians have by me, and by all the army, always been treated with the utmost kindness; but the hostile savages like Sitting Bull and his band of outlaw Sioux, and like some that we dealt with in 1868, must feel the superior power of the government, before they can realize that they must not kill, must not steal, and must not continue to carry into practice their savage instincts and customs."

Phillips, speaking for many in the East, had decried as vicious and provocative the actions of the settlers of the West. Sherman himself had often blamed settlers for stirring up trouble, but in this letter he defended the group as a whole. "It is folly for Mr. Phillips to charge all the immigrants that are today laboring to build up civil communities in Kansas, Nebraska, Colorado, and Montana as a set of thieves and robbers, giving a shadow of excuse for these Indian barbarians. They are of the same blood and race as those who settled New England, Pennsylvania, Ohio, and Iowa, and they will resent the doctrine of Mr. Phillips's fraudulent letter to me. In the Declaration of Independence, with which Mr. Phillips ought to be familiar, our forefathers made this very matter one of the alleged causes of grievance against England's sovereign. 'He has excited domestic insurrection among us and has endeavored to bring on the inhabitants of our frontiers the merciless Indian savages, whose known rule of warfare is an undistinguished destruction of all ages, sexes and conditions.' Sitting Bull and the hostile Sioux are the same now as in 1776: our western frontiersmen have the same feelings today as the inhabitants of New England and New York had in 1776, and should Mr. Phillips's doctrine prevail they would resent it in the same language, if not

429

by the same acts of resistance."

Sherman admitted that he had belabored Phillips's letter longer than he had meant to. But he felt obliged to defend the reputation of the army, if not his own. "I don't want publication or controversy, nor do I want the good people of New England to be led into a belief that our present army is in any ways different from what it always has been, as humane as it is brave. But it will always do its duty, and execute the will of the nation as defined by statute law."

Sherman protested too much. While he had never advocated the extermination of Indians in general, he *had* used the word in regard to Red Cloud's Lakotas after the Fetterman killings and to Captain Jack's Modocs following the murder of Edward Canby.

Sherman was a keen thinker and an able writer; he should have known that "extermination" doesn't lend itself to qualification. In neither of those cases was Sherman implying the extermination of all Indians, and in both cases the concept was conditioned on those particular Indians' insistence on fighting to the death. When they did not insist, Sherman was the first to welcome their surrender, alive. The execution of Captain Jack and the three other Modocs was for murder, not for being Indians.

Sherman's response to Phillips had no apparent effect. Whether Tappan passed it along, Sherman never found out. He let the matter drop.

But one aspect of the criticism had to be addressed, if only because Congress called Sherman to testify about it. The House committee on military affairs wanted to know about the needs of the army. Could it handle the new situation in the West? Shouldn't Sherman accept the offers of volunteers that were coming from the western states and territories?

Sherman shook his head. "I have not a particle of doubt that if the Indians will stick together, Crook" — General George Crook, commander of the Department of the Platte — "alone can whip them, or Terry alone can whip them," he said. "Jointly, there is no doubt of it. But the Indians may scatter, and probably will scatter, and the mountainous character of the country will facilitate their concealing themselves. They will divide up into small parties, and that will probably necessitate an increase of force over that which would be necessary to whip them in the aggregate. If the Indian scatters, then we'll have to divide up into detachments, and each detachment is liable to encounter the whole of these Indians if they should assemble again."

The committee members might have wondered where Sherman was going with this.

He enlightened them, saying that volunteers weren't up to demands likely to be placed on soldiers in the campaign he envisioned. "With old sergeants and about thirty standard men in each company, you can engraft upon that company any kind of men, and in six months the new men are very good soldiers," he said. "But in the case of volunteers, officers and non-commissioned officers are popular men, not men who have seen service. They are men who do not know how to cook their provisions or provide for themselves or their men. It takes about a year to make a good infantry soldier, and about three years to make a good cavalry soldier." The army didn't have the luxury of that much time.

But what about the volunteer organizations that had already offered their services? Certainly they could do *some* good, could they not?

"No, sir," Sherman replied. "Most of them are from cities like New York, Philadelphia, Pittsburgh, Memphis, and New Orleans, and though they are brave men and men of individual capacity, they would be like children in that Yellowstone country."

He took time from his official duties to write a private letter of condolence to Custer's widow. "I have waited until the telegraph has given me assurance of your arrival at Monroe, Michigan" — her family home — "to convey to you my heartfelt sympathy in the awful calamity which has overwhelmed you, and draped in mourning our whole country," Sherman wrote. "All of us, from long habit, had grown to believe that Custer at the head of the Seventh Cavalry could sweep as a whirlwind through any number of savages, and this confidence has led to his untimely and heroic death, surrounded by the men he loved and who looked to him as their natural leader in camp, on the march and in battle."

Sherman tried to calm Libbie Custer's mind about the circumstances of her husband's demise. He dismissed the rumors of torture and mutilation. "I believe he met his death near the river bank when he was endeavoring to cross over," Sherman wrote, on the basis of no evidence; "that he was thence carried, probably by his own brother" — Thomas Custer, his aide — "to the hill where his body was found; and round about him fell all that devoted and heroic band, with none left to tell the tale."

Sherman reflected on the life of the soldier. "How mysterious are the ways of Providence!" he declared. "Custer, who for years seemed to court death" — during the Civil War — "when heavy columns of cavalry gave to war a glorious aspect, was doomed to fall and sleep on the far off hills of the Bighorn. Yet he was engaged in a war as necessary as any which history delights to record, a war between civilization and barbarism, a war between the peaceful agriculturalist and the savage hunter."

George Custer would be remembered, Sherman told his widow. "When, in years soon to come, the Yellowstone becomes the highway of travel between the East and West, when peaceful farmers and grazers occupy the valleys of the Rosebud and Bighorn, people will point to the spot where Custer and his brave companions fell that they and their children might live in peace in a land soon to be rescued from the possession of the bloody Sioux. I know that one such life as Custer's is worth those of the whole Sioux nation combined, but we all hold our lives by the same feeble tenure which the leaden messenger promptly cuts, whether it come from the musket of the infantry, the carbine of the cavalry, or the chance weapon of the savage. In either event the soldier dies in the cause of his country, and his name becomes enrolled in the catalogue of heroes."

31

Nelson Miles had scarcely finished giving a patriotic speech to the inhabitants of Leavenworth, Kansas, congratulating them and their country on its hundredth birthday, when he got the news of the calamity on the Little Bighorn. "On the top of the first page of the morning papers of July 5, 1876, in large black letters, was the one word, 'Horrible,' " he wrote later. Almost the next thing he read was an order sending him to Montana to join the pursuit of Sitting Bull and Crazy Horse.

The outbreak of the Sioux war hadn't surprised him, for the grievances of the Lakotas were undeniable. "It was distinctly understood that the government would keep white people from occupying or trespassing upon the lands granted to the Indians," he said of the treaty with the Sioux. "In the main, the Indians adhered to the conditions of the treaty, but unfortunately the government could not, or did not, comply with its portion of the compact." The gold hunters invaded, provoking the Indians. Many of the Sioux, led by Spotted Tail and Red Cloud, still clung to the treaty as their people's best hope of survival. But others, following Crazy Horse and Sitting Bull, had determined to go down fighting.

Miles had deep respect for the martial ability of the Lakotas. "Crazy Horse was the incarnation of ferocity — a fierce, restless warrior, who had made a great reputation as a successful leader of raids and war parties, and had become, at the age of twenty-six, the recognized leader of the Ogalallas, the most warlike tribe of the Sioux Nation." Sitting Bull was a different sort, but no less formidable. "He was the embodiment of everything hostile to civilization, a perfect type of the savage Indian, a natural born leader of men, cunning and courageous. He always advocated war upon the white race." Sitting Bull's leadership had created the alliance that made the current outbreak so dangerous. "He had the power of drawing, molding, and wielding large bodies of his race and inspiring their hearts' emotions until they were prepared to act and move as one," Miles said. His accomplishment was unprecedented. "He became the natural and able leader of the largest, strongest, and best armed confederation of Indians ever created on this continent." And now, following their crushing defeat of Custer's Seventh Cavalry, the Indian alliance was more threatening than ever.

Miles commanded the Fifth Regiment of infantry, and he and his men headed north by train from Leavenworth to Yankton, on the Missouri River in Dakota Territory. By steamer they proceeded up that river to Bismarck and on to the mouth of the Yellowstone. "As we passed some of the military stations and small settlements along the Missouri, we found a condition of gloom existing as the result of the news of the Custer disaster," Miles recalled. But the gloom didn't infect his men. "The spirits of our troops were in marked contrast."

At Fort Buford, near the confluence of the Yellowstone and the Missouri, Miles and the others heard stories of Sitting Bull. "At times he would come in to barter and trade, and he was very peaceable," Miles wrote. "At other times he was a terror, attacking the post, capturing the herd and killing all the white people that he found outside of a defensive position. A favorite amusement of these Indians at such times was to seize the sawmill and beat their tom-toms on the circular saw." One story told of a trader who held his own. "Sitting Bull jumped over the counter at the store, took possession, assumed the position of post trader, and with savage glee and mock authority bartered the merchandise for the buffalo robes and furs of his companions," Miles recounted. "The brave trader, expecting to be scalped and possibly tortured, resorted to a strange device to save his life and property. Lighting his pipe of tobacco, he took his place near an open keg of powder, and then informed them that he would blow the whole establishment into the air and the Indians into eternity unless order was restored." The hijinks ceased.

Miles discovered that the shadow of Custer's defeat had spread over Fort Buford. "The officers and soldiers of the small garrison came to the steamer to greet us, but the stillness of the place was appalling," he wrote. "No salute nor cheers, but the same condition of gloom that had marked the atmosphere of the other places we had passed on the river below."

Miles was pleased that his own men maintained their spirits, but he wasn't surprised. He had noted that the economic depression in the East had caused a different group of men to enlist in the army than had been the norm. They were fitter, better educated, and more ambitious than their predecessors. At Fort Leavenworth, Miles had added to their fitness by requiring calisthenics and athletic conditioning as part of their daily routine, along with shooting practice. "The result was that I had a body of men who were trained athletes and skilled marksmen," he wrote, with obvious pride. "They had had experience in Indian campaigning and fighting" —

against the Comanches and Kiowas — "so that they knew how to take care of themselves, were ever watchful, could not be surprised, and were not afraid to meet the Indians under any circumstances or conditions." Miles hadn't heard Sherman's testimony to Congress, but he would have agreed that these were the men to do battle against the forces of Sitting Bull and Crazy Horse, not untrained volunteers. As Miles put it, "With such a command I had no hesitation in going into any hostile country."

Their steamer carried them up the Yellowstone. They saw herds of buffalo so thick that boats on the river had to stop while the animals crossed the stream. The progress against the current was slow; the men had plenty of time to take in the country. Finally they reached the mouth of the Rosebud, where Miles reported his command to General Alfred Terry. By now the season was too far advanced for serious fighting, Terry judged, and after some reconnaissance marches he prepared for winter. He ordered Miles to have his men construct a cantonment.

Miles obeyed the order. "I intended, however, to do more than hibernate," he said. "To build a cantonment or comfortable shelter for the troops and simply occupy it until spring seemed to me quite unsatisfactory." He and his men had come north to fight, and so they would fight. "I believed that a winter campaign could be successfully made against those northern Indians, even in that extreme cold climate. I told General Terry that if he would give me supplies and a reasonable command, I would clear a zone of that country of hostiles before spring."

Terry was skeptical. He cited an earlier attempt at a winter campaign that had failed miserably and filled the hospital with frostbitten soldiers.

Miles countered that the soldiers hadn't been hardened to the cold, and had been insufficiently equipped. They had gone from warm quarters into the dead of winter, without the necessary gear.

He received permission to try. "I was confident of success and equipped my command as if they were going to the arctic regions," Miles wrote. The men had campaigned in the Southwest when winter temperatures were in the single digits; to campaign where the thermometer plunged to twenty or thirty below zero was another matter, and required the greatest care. Miles outfitted the men with thick wool and fur coats, and masks for their faces. Meanwhile, he kept them out of doors as winter came on, so they grew accustomed to the cold.

He sent out scouts to find out where the Indians were. He called this system "espionage," and it may indeed have gone beyond merely reconnoitering, for he learned not only where the hostile Lakotas were, but where they were going. Perhaps his spies went onto the Sioux reservation. Many of the warriors in Sitting Bull's army had returned to the reservation for the winter, and they might have told Miles's informants what Sitting Bull's plans were.

They said that the allied army of Indians had broken up. Sitting Bull had gone north of the Yellowstone to the valley of the Big Dry River, near the Missouri. Crazy Horse had gone south, to the headwaters of the Rosebud and the Tongue. Each commanded about half the Indians who remained in the field.

Miles decided to find Sitting Bull. But before he could get close, Sitting Bull found him, and attacked. The Lakotas charged his camp, trying to run off his horses and mules. They didn't succeed, but they fired shots into Miles's own tent, just missing him. On another occasion, Sitting Bull led an attack on Miles's supply train, surrounding it until reinforcements arrived and drove the attackers off.

In mid-October, Miles, with four hundred riflemen and one artillery piece, approached Sitting Bull's camp. Suddenly they were confronted by a thousand warriors. "Every Indian was armed with a rifle and had plenty of ammunition," Miles recalled. "They were

441

gorgeously decorated with feathers, beadwork and war paint, were well supplied with fur robes and splendidly mounted on their fleet, hardy war ponies."

Miles expected an attack and deployed his own troops for battle. But Sitting Bull sent a flag of truce and asked for a meeting. Miles assumed Sitting Bull wanted to gauge the strength and determination of this new force and its commander; Miles wanted to do the same with Sitting Bull. Miles agreed to talk, meanwhile instructing his men to keep an eye on any Indians who came too close to where the meeting would take place, halfway between the two armies.

Sitting Bull rode forward with six others; Miles brought six of his own. Sitting Bull spread a robe on the ground and began to speak. "He was a man of powerful physique, with a large, broad head, strong features, and few words, which were uttered with great deliberation — a man evidently of decision and positive convictions," Miles recounted.

Miles had convictions, too. "I explained to them that all Indian wars had resulted in the Indians becoming loyal to our government; that it was useless for the Indians to contend against the government or the power and numbers of the white race," he wrote. "If they would discontinue their warlike attitude and depredations and go upon a reservation, I could assure them of the good will of the government and my earnest effort on their behalf."

Sitting Bull sneered at Miles's presumption. The white soldiers might have defeated other Indians, but they had not defeated the Sioux, he said. No Indian tribe had ever defeated the Sioux, and neither would the white tribe. "Sitting Bull said that Almighty God had made him an Indian, but not an *Agency* Indian, and he did not intend to become one," Miles wrote. "He said there never was a white man who did not hate the Indian, and there never was an Indian who did not hate the white man."

Miles listened, then told Sitting Bull that he knew his winter plans. As he provided details, Sitting Bull grew angry. "Every feature showed intense excitement and the deep emotions of his fierce nature," Miles said. "His strong jaws were firmly set, and his eyes were like balls of fire."

While they were talking, some Indians had been sidling closer to the meeting ground. Miles saw out the corner of his eye that his men were watching them carefully. He told Sitting Bull that unless those Indians moved away, the meeting would come to an abrupt end.

Sitting Bull had been watching the soldiers watch his own men, and he waved the Indians back.

Miles didn't want to press his luck. He told

Sitting Bull to think overnight about what he had said. He gathered his escort and they rode back to his lines. He withdrew his troops three miles and camped for the night.

The next morning Miles led his column back toward the Lakota camp, approaching closer than the previous day. Again Sitting Bull sent a truce flag. Again they met. Miles repeated that resistance was useless. He would take Sitting Bull's people back to the reservation, peacefully if possible but by force if necessary. Sitting Bull responded with the same scorn he had shown the day before.

Miles sprang an ultimatum on Sitting Bull. The chief had fifteen minutes to surrender. Otherwise the two armies would fight.

Without saying a word, Sitting Bull left. Riding back toward his camp, he called out to his chiefs and warriors to prepare for battle.

"Immediately the prairie was alive with Indians dashing in every direction," Miles recounted. "They assembled or deployed, took position *en masse* on the prairie or behind mounds and hills, wild with excitement and anxious for the combat." Miles ordered his men to form a large open square, which proceeded deliberately toward the village.

The Indians set fire to the prairie grass, which burned toward the troops while the Indians completed their encirclement. All this required less than the fifteen minutes Miles had given Sitting Bull. The Indians began shooting.

The soldiers shot back. Their rifles kept the Indians from closing, and their artillery piece created havoc in the Indians' rear. The grass fire failing to spread, the soldiers advanced inexorably upon the village. The soldiers' discipline appeared to unnerve the Indians, who gave up the village, leaving goods and some ponies behind.

Miles ordered a pursuit. The soldiers followed the Indians for two days. Every so often the Indians made a stand, and Miles closed, hoping for a decisive battle. But each time the Indians broke off and retreated the more.

Miles's stubbornness finally got to them. On the third day they sent a new flag of truce, which led to talks that produced an agreement to return to the reservation. Crucially, though, this group no longer included Sitting Bull, who had split off with a large band and kept going.

Miles returned to the cantonment that served as his base and readied another command to go after Sitting Bull. This round of the pursuit presented new challenges. "At that time the country was entirely unknown," Miles said. "The steamers had passed up and down the Yellowstone and Missouri rivers, but the Indians had held the country so tenaciously that it had never been surveyed and was a blank on the official maps."

Autumn gave way to winter. "We would find indications of Indians and strike their trail, but the blinding snowstorms of November and December obliterated all traces, and often we were obliged to march slowly by the compass." They sometimes seemed to go in circles. "We crossed and recrossed the Missouri River with artillery and loaded trains on the solid ice, the cold being intense." The snow piled deep over their path. "The soldiers were obliged to march single file, taking turns in the advance to break down the snow."

Nights were the worst. "Usually at night we would camp in the valleys, where dry fuel could be obtained, but at other times, in crossing the high divides, we could not obtain fuel and the soldiers were obliged to lie down at night on the snow without fires." At such moments, the advance planning saved lives. "They were so well equipped that though they suffered from the extreme cold, it caused no permanent injury."

He divided his command into three columns, the better to search a wide area. One column found Sitting Bull on the Big Dry, where Miles's spies had said to look. Unprepared for a winter fight, the Lakotas were compelled to retreat, leaving behind horses, food and blankets. Miles assumed the Indians wouldn't last long in the cold.

Leaving Sitting Bull to freeze, Miles organized another thrust, against Crazy Horse. He led more than four hundred riflemen and two artillery pieces up the Tongue River. "The artillery I concealed in my wagon train by covering the guns and gun carriages with wagon bows and canvas, intending to give the Indians a surprise," he said. Deep snow slowed the marching, but frozen creeks hastened it by easing their crossing.

Skirmishing commenced as they neared Crazy Horse's camp. In one clash, an advance guard captured four women and three children, besides one warrior. This got the attention of Crazy Horse, who sent three hundred warriors to free the captives. Miles prepared for battle. In the cold and open country, he realized how isolated his command was. "We were then three hundred miles from the nearest settlement on the west, and four hundred miles from the terminus of the Northern Pacific on the east. In the impending engagement with this powerful body of Indians, defeat would mean disaster and annihilation, and it would have been weeks before our fate would have been known."

Miles moved his men into a defensible position and camped for the night. At dawn his scouts reported the Indians advancing in large numbers. "From a high bluff with a field glass, I watched them come out of the canyon

447

and move down the valley, and I thought the last one would never appear," he recalled. "There were at least a thousand or twelve hundred well armed and well mounted warriors." Their war cries taunted the soldiers, predicting their imminent doom.

Miles held his soldiers' fire until the Indians were within range. Then they opened up. At the same time, he had his artillerymen uncover the field guns and commence firing. He assumed this caught them by surprise, for they paused in their advance, as if deciding whether to continue. His soldiers held their ground, though hemmed in on all sides.

Miles surveyed the situation. "The key of the Indians' position was a high bluff in front of the left of our line," he wrote. "To charge and take this strategic point was a difficult undertaking for a part of our troops, while the rest were engaged." Yet Miles gave the order, and the charge commenced.

The Indians, directed here by a chief named Big Crow, opened a heavy fire. Big Crow had promised his warriors that his medicine would protect them from the white men's bullets; he showed the courage of his conviction by galloping conspicuously in front of the soldiers. "His strong voice could be heard up and down the valley whenever there was a lull in the fighting," Miles said. "He was unharmed for a time, as it is not easy to hit a man when he is in quick action."

But his medicine ran out. "Some cool-headed soldier fired more deliberately and dropped him dead."

At the same moment, the troops reached the top of the bluff. This, and the failure of Big Crow's medicine, dispirited the Indians, and they quickly fell back. Their retreat became a flight, rendered all the more confusing by a swirling blizzard that set in just then.

Miles ordered the Indians pursued far enough to ensure that they weren't regrouping to counterattack. He then had his men seize such of the Indians' stores as were useful, and destroy the rest. They returned to the cantonment.

Miles still held the captives. He made sure they were well fed and courteously treated. After a month he sent three of the captives to the Indian camp with a message renewing his call for them to surrender. During that month the Indians had been shivering and starving, and the healthy condition of the captives made a distinct impression. "The result was that a strong delegation of nineteen chiefs and warriors came down to the cantonment to learn fully what terms of surrender would be granted to them," Miles recalled. They were told they must give up their ponies and their rifles. The horses would be sold, and the proceeds used to purchase stock for them on the reservation.

The meeting of this delegation with the rest

of the captives sealed the bargain. The women didn't hide their emotions. "They shed tears of joy at seeing again those nearest and dearest to them," Miles observed. The warriors tried to be more stoic, but their emotions were evident, too. "One was observed to take up a little child in his arms with the utmost tenderness."

Not every emotion was joyful. One of the hostages was a young woman, hardly more than a girl. She expected to see her lover, a young warrior, with the peace delegation. When she didn't, she asked the other warriors about him, and something they said made her think her lover didn't care for her anymore. Her state of mind came to the attention of Miles only in the tragic denouement. When the delegation had gone back to the Indian camp with his offer, she and the other captives remained. At first light a day or two later, the report of a pistol rang through the cantonment. The young woman, having hid a small handgun against abuse by her captors, had killed herself. The tale grew only more poignant when news arrived that her lover had not abandoned her, but simply had not known of the delegation going to the cantonment.

Miles's offer met the reluctant approval of the Indians at the camp. Some three thousand moved over the divide and into the valley of the Tongue, on their way to the cantonment and surrender. But a hitch developed when a runner from the Spotted Tail Agency of the Sioux reservation brought a message urging them to go there to surrender. They would receive better terms, the message said, and they would be closer to their friends.

The slow march to the cantonment halted. A new delegation, of a hundred chiefs and warriors, approached Miles and asked if he could improve his terms.

Miles replied that his terms were unchanged. Yet if they wanted to surrender at the agency, that was their choice. But surrender they must, or continue fighting. If they surrendered, he would be their best friend; if they fought, their worst enemy.

"At the close of my remarks, absolute silence prevailed for at least five minutes," Miles recalled. "Those were five anxious moments of my life. Peace or war was then to be determined." The silence was broken first by a movement. Little Chief, a famous warrior and orator, came forward and threw the buffalo robe from his shoulders, then stripped off his shirt to reveal his scars. "His manner, movements and gestures were the perfection of dignity and grace," Miles said. "With eloquence and deep feeling he recited the history and misfortunes of his race, their devotion to their country, and their efforts to defend and retain it. Finally he said, 'Your terms are cruel and harsh, but we are going to accept them.' "

32

When Sherman wasn't being branded an exterminator by the likes of Wendell Phillips, he was being touted for president by leaders of the Republican party. Sherman's distaste for politics was notorious, but that simply made him more attractive to the many voters who professed to share it. The voters had twice elected Grant, whose aversion to politics almost equaled Sherman's. Yet Grant was more susceptible to the argument that if he didn't run for president, the office would go to an unscrupulous Democrat, who would squander what had been won at such cost in the Civil War. Grant's dealings with Andrew Johnson — a Democrat, despite being Lincoln's vice president — convinced him that the threat was real. He accepted the nomination of the Republicans and was swept to victory in 1868 on the votes of millions of admiring veterans of the war. A few bumps with scandal didn't prevent his reelection in 1872. The Republicans would have been happy to nominate him a third time if not for the de facto ban on third terms established by George Washington.

That left Sherman as the heir apparent. Sherman was the Union's second favorite general, and although Sherman seemed the devil incarnate to most Southerners, the Republicans still didn't have to win any Southern states to carry the election. The Republicans would wring votes out of the Civil War — "wave the bloody shirt," in the parlance of the day — as long as they could. And who better to help in the wringing than the man who had bloodied the South more ruthlessly than any other?

Sherman would have none of it. Since the Civil War he had answered every question about his political ambitions in the same negative way. Yet the questions still arose. In the spring of 1876, while Republican politicos were pondering who should succeed Grant, he was asked again. The reporter paraphrased the response: "General Sherman, in speaking of the mention of his name in connection with the presidency, said that he had been behind the Harrison, Taylor, Lincoln, Johnson, and Grant administrations, and that he had learned enough to be entirely satisfied with his present position. He does not think the chief magistrate's seat, exalted and revered as it is, is a place to be envied. As for himself, he wishes to do his duty as a soldier,

454

bring up his family properly, and to be a useful citizen. Political honors have no temptation, he says, for him."

Certain aspects of politics couldn't be dodged. One of the more serious scandals of the Grant administration ensnared William Belknap, the war secretary, who was caught taking bribes for awarding trading concessions at army posts. A reporter buttonholed Sherman as the scandal was surfacing. Was Sherman surprised to hear that Belknap had engaged in such behavior?

"I certainly was," said Sherman. "I did not believe that General Belknap would be guilty of such conduct."

Was Sherman aware that some of the post traders were not of the highest character?

"Certainly," he replied. "I have received numerous complaints that the post traders were not what they should be, and that they charged extortionate prices. Whenever officers complained to me, however, I deprecated any talk or trouble, telling them that this matter was beyond their province, and their best course, where a trader did not give satisfaction, was to withdraw their patronage from him. You see, soldiers are not bound to make purchases of traders, as all supplies that are absolutely necessary are furnished them by the government. But soldiers are generally improvident and reckless with their earnings, and they will invest considerable amounts each month in tobacco, etc., no matter how extortionate the prices." This said, the unfolding scandal went beyond anything Sherman had imagined. "I had never suspected that Belknap was actuated by corrupt motives in making his appointments, but thought that he selected parties through considerations of friendship, possibly without regard to their fitness," he said. "This is the most grievous and disgraceful affair. I think it is the first case I ever heard of where a man so high in office was guilty of selling positions."

Belknap dodged prison but not disgrace, and the nomination Sherman refused went to Rutherford Hayes. An Ohioan like Sherman, Hayes had fought in the Civil War, but he lacked the distinction of Grant or Sherman and lost the popular vote to Democrat Samuel Tilden. The electoral contest was close and controversial, with the outcome hinging on disputed results from a handful of states. Congress tried and failed to resolve the dispute, then handed it off to a special commission, which argued the matter almost until inauguration day. The deadlock finally broke when the Democrats agreed to give Hayes the presidency in exchange for a tacit pledge to pull the army out of Southern politics once and for all.

No one was happier than Sherman with the latter part of the bargain. He had considered the army's role in the politics of the former

Confederate states an utterly thankless perversion of what soldiers were supposed to do. The job of soldiers was to fight the country's enemies, not to police elections, quell riots, and make enemies of American citizens. Now, in the spring of 1877, that sad chapter in the army's history came to an end. It was time to get back to fighting.

But there wasn't much fighting to do. Nearly all the Lakotas who had survived the winter at large found their way to the reservation during the spring of 1877. Crazy Horse surrendered in May. Sitting Bull was the lone important holdout among the Sioux. Hating the whites as much as ever, he led a small band to Canada.

And of the noteworthy hostiles of other tribes, the one most in the news was impossible to make a villain of. Indeed, Young Joseph of the Nez Perce might have been the most admired Indian in American history. He certainly was America's favorite Indian in the 1870s, with as many whites rooting for him against the army, as for the army against him. It didn't hurt that he was handsome, at a time when photography was finding a place in journalism. Or that he understood how to pluck the heartstrings of Americans who cherished the idea of the noble savage. "My friends, I have been asked to show you my heart," Joseph declared in an article published in the *North American Review.* "I am glad I have a chance to do so. I want the white people to understand my people."

Whites held many misconceptions about Indians, Joseph said. "Some of you think an Indian is like a wild animal. This is a great mistake. I will tell you all about our people, and then you can judge whether an Indian is a man or not. I believe much trouble and blood would be saved if we opened our hearts more. I will tell you in my way how the Indian sees things. The white man has more words to tell you how they look to him, but it does not require many words to speak the truth. What I have to say will come from my heart. I will speak with a straight tongue. Ah-cum-kin-i-ma-me-hut" — the Great Spirit — "is looking at me, and will hear me."

In fact, not many readers of the *North American Review* were inclined to think of Indians as wild animals. The Boston journal attracted reformist types more apt to deem William Sherman and Phil Sheridan blood-thirsty barbarians than most Indians. Wendell Phillips was a regular contributor.

Consequently, Joseph could expect a sympathetic audience as he told his story and that of his people. "We did not know there were other people besides the Indian until about one hundred winters ago, when some men with white faces came to our country," he said. "They brought many things with them to trade for furs and skins. They brought tobacco, which was new to us. They brought guns with flint stones on them, which frightened our women and children. Our people could not talk with these white-faced men, but they used signs which all people understand. These men were Frenchmen, and they called our people 'Nez Percés,' because they wore rings in their noses for ornaments. Although very few of our people wear them now, we are still called by the same name."

The first Americans the Nez Perce met were Lewis and Clark, the explorers. "They talked straight, and our people gave them a great feast, as a proof that their hearts were friendly," Joseph said. "These men were very kind. They made presents to our chiefs, and our people made presents to them. We had a great many horses, of which we gave them what they needed, and they gave us guns and tobacco in return. All the Nez Perce made friends with Lewis and Clark, and agreed to let them pass through their country, and never to make war on white men. This promise the Nez Perce have never broken. No white man can accuse them of bad faith, and speak with a straight tongue. It has always been the pride of the Nez Perce that they were the friends of the white men."

The missionaries followed Lewis and Clark by three decades. The Nez Perce befriended them too. But they weren't honest with the

Indians, for they didn't mention the white people who would come and settle in the Nez Perce country. "At first our people made no complaint," said Joseph. "They thought there was room enough for all to live in peace, and they were learning many things from the white men that seemed to be good. But we soon found that the white men were growing rich very fast, and were greedy to possess everything the Indian had."

Joseph's father had been a chief then. His name was Joseph, too. "My father was the first to see through the schemes of the white man, and he warned his tribe to be careful about trading with them," Young Joseph said. "He had a suspicion of men who seemed so anxious to make money. I was a boy then, but I remember well my father's caution. He had sharper eyes than the rest of our people."

The governor of the white people had traveled to the Nez Perce country. He told them that many more white people would be coming, and he wanted to protect the Indians, to give them land where the whites couldn't go. One of the missionaries urged Joseph's father to sign the treaty that would give the Nez Perce their reservation; he took the hand of Joseph's father and guided it to the treaty. Joseph's father pushed him away. "Why do you ask me to sign away my country?" he said. "It is your business to talk to us about spirit matters, and not to talk to us about parting with our land."

The governor tried to convince Joseph's father. Joseph's father resisted the more. "I will not sign your paper," he said. "You go where you please; so do I. You are not a child; I am no child. I can think for myself. No man can think for me. I have no other home than this. I will not give it up to any man. My people would have no home. Take away your paper. I will not touch it with my hand."

Some of the chiefs of the other bands of the Nez Perce people signed the treaty, and they tried to change Joseph's father's mind. But he was adamant. He warned them against taking presents from the whites. "After a while, they will claim that you have accepted pay for your country," he said.

Joseph's father's refusal created a rift among the Nez Perce. The signers of the treaty accused the non-treaty Nez Perce of causing trouble for them. But not even the taunts of his people could change Joseph's father's mind. And he warned his son against dealing with the white people. "When you go into council with the white man, always remember your country," he said. "Do not give it away. The white man will cheat you out of your home. I have taken no pay from the United States. I have never sold our land."

Joseph's father was particularly attached to the Wallowa Valley of northeastern Oregon. The name meant "winding water," and it was beautiful country, rich with resources for people and stock. He planted poles around the valley, demarking its boundaries. "Inside is the home of my people," he said. "The white man may take the land outside. Inside this boundary all our people were born. It circles around the graves of our fathers, and we will never give up these graves to any man."

The government removed his poles. They told him that he and his followers must come live on the reservation. A majority of the Nez Perce had accepted the treaty, and so must the others. If Joseph's father brought his people to the reservation, all would be well. If he did not, the government's soldiers would force them to move.

A council was called to hear Joseph's father's decision. He was old and feeble by this time, and he sent his son in his place. Young Joseph made his first speech to the white men. "I did not want to come to this council," he said, "but I came hoping that we could save blood. The white man has no right to come here and take our country. We have never accepted any presents from the government. Neither Lawyer" — the leader of the treaty Nez Perce — "nor any other chief had authority to sell this land. It has always belonged to my people. It came unclouded to them from our fathers, and we will defend this land as long as a drop of Indian blood warms the hearts of our men."

The Indian agent at the council said he had orders from the Great Chief at Washington. The non-treaty Nez Perce must move to the reservation. If they did so, the government would help them in many ways.

"I do not need your help," said Young Joseph. "We have plenty, and we are contented and happy if the white man will leave us alone. The reservation is too small for so many people, with all their stock. You can keep your presents; we can go to your towns and pay for all we need. We have plenty of horses and cattle for sale." Again Joseph rejected white help, and the demands that would follow. "We are free now; we can go where we please. Our fathers were born here. Here they lived; here they died; here are their graves. We will never leave them."

The agent went away, and for a time Joseph thought he had won the argument. But his father remained suspicious. The older man grew weaker. As he was dying, he called Joseph to his side. "My son, my body is returning to my mother earth, and my spirit is going very soon to see the Great Spirit Chief. When I am gone, think of your country. You are the chief of these people. They look to you to guide them. Always remember that your father never sold his country. You must stop your ears whenever you are asked to sign a treaty selling your home. A few years more, and white men will be all around you. They have their eyes on this land. My son, never forget my dying words. This country holds your father's body. Never sell the bones of your father and your mother."

Joseph did not forget his father's words. But holding his country became harder and harder. Joseph didn't want war with the whites, for he knew many of his people would die, and they would probably lose in the end.

He defended his land with arguments. "If we ever owned the land, we own it still, for we never sold it," he said. "In the treaty councils, the commissioners have claimed that our country have been sold to the government." That might have been true of the treaty Nez Perce, but not of Joseph's people. "Suppose a white man should come to me and say, 'Joseph, I like your horses, and I want to buy them.' I say to him, 'No, my horses suit me I will not sell them.' Then he goes to my neighbor and says to him, 'Joseph has some good horses. I want to buy them, but he refuses to sell.' My neighbor answers, 'Pay me the money and I will sell you Joseph's horses.' The white man returns to me, and he says, 'Joseph, I have bought your horses, and you must let me have them.' If we sold our lands to the government, this is the way they were bought."

His arguments failed. The pressure from

the whites increased. Every year the agent arrived from the reservation and said Joseph and his people must come in. Every year Joseph refused. "We always replied that we were satisfied to live in Wallowa. We were careful to refuse the presents or annuities which he offered."

The pressure became almost irresistible. "I have carried a heavy load on my back ever since I was a boy," Joseph recollected. "I learned then that we were but few, while the white men were many, and that we could not hold our own with them. We were like deer. They were like grizzly bears."

Every year war was threatened against them, but no war came, until General Oliver Howard took charge of the District of the Columbia, which included the Nez Perce lands. He would give the Nez Perce no rest. "I have a great many soldiers at my back," Howard told Joseph. "I am going to bring them up here and then I will talk to you again. I will not let white men laugh at me the next time I come. The country belongs to the government, and I intend to make you go upon the reservation."

Howard called a council at the Nez Perce reservation at Lapwai in western Idaho Territory. Joseph traveled to Lapwai, and said he was ready to hear what Howard had to say. Howard said this day was for introductions; he would talk the next day.

"I am ready to talk today," said Joseph. "I have been in a great many councils, but I am no wiser." Howard needed to know what the Nez Perce thought. "We are all sprung from a woman, although we are unlike in many things," said Joseph. "We cannot be made over again. You are as you were made, and as you were made you can remain. We are just as we were made by the Great Spirit, and you cannot change us. Then why should children of one mother and one father quarrel? Why should one try to cheat the other? I do not believe that the Great Spirit Chief gave one kind of men the right to tell another kind of men what they must do."

"You deny my authority, do you?" demanded Howard. "You want to dictate to me, do you?"

A Nez Perce with Joseph, Too-hool-hool-suit, stood up. "The Great Spirit Chief made the world as it is, and as he wanted it, and he made a part of it for us to live upon. I do not see where you get authority to say that we shall not live where he placed us."

"I don't want to hear any more of such talk," Howard said angrily. "The law says you shall go upon the reservation to live, and I want you to do so, but you persist in disobeying the law. If you do not move, I will take the matter into my own hand and make you suffer for your disobedience."

"Who are you, that you asked us to talk,

and then tell me I can't talk?" said Too-hool-hool-suit. "Are you the Great Spirit? Did you make the world? Did you make the sun? Did you make the rivers to run for us to drink? Did you make the grass to grow? Did you make all these things, that you talked to us as though we were boys? If you did, then you have the right to talk to us as you do."

"You are an impudent fellow, and I will put you in the guard house," said Howard. He ordered a soldier to arrest Too-hool-hool-suit.

Too-hool-hool-suit made no resistance. "Is that your order?" he said. "I don't care. I have expressed my heart to you. I have nothing to take back. I've spoken for my country. You can arrest me, but you cannot change me or make me take back what I have said."

The soldiers seized Too-hool-hool-suit and took him to the guard house.

Joseph recalled the distress among his Nez Perce companions. "My men whispered among themselves whether they should let this thing be done. I counseled them to submit. I knew if we resisted that all the white men present, including General Howard, would be killed in a moment, and we would be blamed."

Howard delivered an ultimatum. He gave Joseph and his people thirty days to go to their homes, collect their stock and move onto the reservation. "If you are not here in that time, I shall consider that you want to fight, and will send my soldiers to drive you on."

"I want no war," said Joseph. "My people have always been friends of the white man." Besides, what was the hurry? "I cannot get ready to move in thirty days. Our stock is scattered, and the Snake River is very high. Let us wait until fall, then the river will be low. We want time to hunt up our stock and gather supplies for winter."

Howard refused to relent. "If you let the time run over one day, the soldiers will be there to drive you onto the reservation, and all your cattle and horses outside of the reservation at that time will fall into the hands of the white men," he said.

Joseph concluded that Howard was bent on war. If his goal was really to get Joseph's people to the reservation, he would have given them more time. Recalling the moment, Joseph remarked, "I am sure that he began to prepare for war at once."

Joseph returned to his people and called a council. It lasted ten days, and all had a chance to speak. Joseph warned of the destruction war would bring. As hard as it was for him even to think of it, they must consider accepting Howard's terms.

Joseph's caution was hotly challenged. One young warrior, whose father had been killed by a white man several years earlier, demanded revenge. He welcomed war against the whites, he said. When the council did not immediately agree, he stalked off and rode away.

And he contrived to make war unavoidable. He rallied several other young men, who helped him have his vengeance by killing four white men. He rode back to the council and shouted in Joseph's face, "Why do you sit here like women? The war has begun already."

Joseph learned that the young men had secretly been buying ammunition, and that Too-hool-hool-suit, released from custody, had agreed to lead them. "I saw that the war could not then be prevented," he remembered.

Charles Erskine Scott wood would win fame as a civil liberties advocate and legal defender of radicals and revolutionaries. His circle would encompass Emma Goldman, John Reed, Lincoln Steffens, Clarence Darrow and Langston Hughes. In 1877 he was adjutant to Oliver Howard, part of the seven-hundred-man army Howard summoned to enforce his ultimatum against Joseph and the non-treaty Nez Perce.

Wood and Howard's army arrived in the wake of an initial clash between soldiers and Nez Perce. Joseph's band was grazing its horses in White Bird Canyon, just across the border in Idaho, when a company of soldiers, led by scouts from the treaty Nez Perce, came to punish them for the recent murders and take them to the reservation. Joseph's band resisted, and killed more than thirty soldiers.

At the approach of Howard's army, Joseph took up a position on the Clearwater River. "It was a test case — all the hostiles under Joseph against all the soldiers under General Howard," recalled Charles Wood. "The Indians, naturally a brave tribe, now flushed by success and rendered desperate by their lot, seemed not unwilling to try the issue. Leaving their picturesque camp and cone-like tepees protected by the broad mountain stream, they crossed over to meet us, and, swarming out of the river bottom, occupied the rocks and fir-crowned heights of the ravines transverse to the main valley, leaving the troops only the alternative to deploy as skirmishers, and throw themselves flat on the sunburned grass of the open." Joseph tried to work around the soldiers' flanks and get to their rear. But the soldiers, sensing his aim, kept in his front.

Yet the Indians fought on, undaunted. "Nothing could be bolder or more aggressive than the conduct of these Indians," wrote Wood. "Twice this day they massed under shelter, and, leaving their war horses in the timber, charged our line so savagely that they were only repelled by as fierce a counter charge, the two lines advancing rapidly till they almost met; and when the Indians turned, they did so only to regain cover. Their fire was deadly, the proportion of wounded to killed being but two to one." The soldiers were pinned down. "All day long, under the hot July sun, without water and without food, our men crawled about in the parched grass, shooting and being shot. The wounded were carried back to an awning where the surgeons were at work; the dead were left where they fell. All day long the Indians fought hard for the mastery. Among the rocks and scrubby pines their brown naked bodies were seeing flying from shelter to shelter. Their yells were incessant as they cheered each other on or signaled a successful shot."

Two other chiefs, Too-hool-hool-suit and White Bird, seemed to join Joseph in command. But one of the Nez Perce later told Wood that after this fight, Joseph was the one they called the "war chief." Wood saw why. "He was everywhere along the line; running from point to point, he directed the flanking movements and the charges. It was his long, fierce calls which sometimes we heard loudly in front of us, and sometimes faintly resounding from the distant rocks."

The fighting continued till dark. As the soldiers remained watchful, they heard the activity among the Nez Perce. "All through the night, from the vast Indian camp in the river bottom, rose the wail of the death song and the dull drumming of the *tooats*. The

471

dirge of the widows drifted to us through the summer night — now plaintive and faint, now suddenly bursting into shrieks, as if their very heartstrings had snapped." Another strain sent a chill through the soldiers. "Mingling with these unpleasant sounds came the rapid movement of the scalp chant, *hum-hum-hum,* hurrying to the climax of fierce war whoops."

The battle resumed the next day. It raged through the morning and into the early afternoon. And then the Indians suddenly retreated. The soldiers advanced to where the Indians had just been. "Much of their camp was taken standing, the packs and robes lying about, and the meat cooking at the fire," recalled Wood. "Evidently the enemy had not anticipated defeat."

Howard's army followed the Indians for a time, before receiving a flag of truce from Joseph. Some of his band surrendered, but most did not. Wood later reconstructed the thinking in the Indian camp. "The writer" — Wood — "was told long afterward by an Indian of that region that Joseph wished to surrender rather than leave the country or bring further misery on his people, but that, in council, he was overruled by the older chiefs Looking Glass, White Bird and Too-hool-hool-suit; and Joseph would not desert the common cause. According to this informant, Joseph's last appeal was to call a council in the dale, and passionately condemn the proposed retreat from Idaho. 'What are we fighting for?' he asked. 'Is it for our lives? No. It is for this land where the bones of our fathers are buried. I do not want to take my women among strangers. I do not want to die in a strange land. Some of you tried to say, once, that I was afraid of the whites. Stay here with me now, and you shall have plenty of fighting. We will put our women behind us in these mountains, and die on our own land fighting for them. I would rather do that than run I know not where.' "

Joseph lost the argument, and the retreat commenced, along the forbiddingly difficult Lolo Trail. Howard's army pursued. "For ten days we toiled along this pathway," Wood wrote. "The marching hour was sunrise, the camping hour sunset. Often the hillsides were so steep that we could not sleep comfortably without digging out a bed. Each cavalryman had been required to start with ten pounds of grain for his horse, but several times horses and patient pack mules were tied up at night without a mouthful of any kind of fodder."

Howard had a crucial advantage over Joseph: reinforcements from other directions. General John Gibbon had left Fort Shaw in Montana to intercept the Nez Perce. On the Big Hole River in southwestern Montana he fell upon the Indians and engaged them in a sharp battle. The losses were comparable on the two sides, but because the Indians had no reserves to call on, the inconclusive result was one they couldn't stand many more of. They set off once again.

In Montana the Nez Perce arranged something most unusual in the history of America's Indian wars: a truce with white civilians even as they were fighting white soldiers. Perhaps the settlers were happy for the sales of the produce they furnished the Indians, at prices that took advantage of the Indians' distress. Perhaps some recalled the peaceful record of the Nez Perce. But whatever the cause, the settlers helped the Nez Perce survive at a critical moment of the retreat.

The Indians turned toward the Yellowstone national park, which had been proclaimed by Congress five years earlier yet languished for appropriations. Howard's army came close to catching Joseph's rear guard on the way there but missed by a few hours. "This was a great disappointment," recalled Charles Wood, "as we had every reason to believe this time we would intercept him." Howard still hoped to cut Joseph off. The soldiers camped in a meadow of cottonwood trees and camas plants, whose roots supplied a staple food to the Indians. "That night, just before dawn, our sleeping camp was startled into half-bewildered consciousness by a rattling fire of rifles, accompanied by the *zee-zip* of bullets through the air and through tent canvas, accompanied by unearthly war whoops." The

Nez Perce scouts had learned of Howard's approach, prompting the warriors to double back. "Our men, still half-stupid with sleep, groped about for shoes and cartridge-belts and swore at the mislaid articles," said Wood. "But each one knew his drill, and as fast as he equipped himself he crawled away from the dangerous white tents, formed on the line, and began replying to the enemy."

The Indians had infiltrated the soldiers' mule herd and were in the process of driving it off. They were shaking bells they had cut from the necks of the lead animals, and were yelling to frighten the animals. The horses of the cavalrymen, likewise frightened, fought being saddled and mounted, slowing the pursuit. "The dawn showed the mule herd far away over the prairie, disappearing toward the hills," Wood wrote. The cavalrymen were closing, though, and began to round up the mules.

Then the trap was sprung. The Nez Perce warriors were waiting, and the cavalrymen had to fight for their own lives. A column of infantry was sent in support, and general fighting ensued. It went on for hours, until the Indians broke off and resumed their flight. Most of the mules ended up in Joseph's herd.

The loss of the pack animals, combined with sickness among the men, caused Howard to halt for three days. Joseph proceeded into the Yellowstone park, where his warriors encountered a party of tourists. The Indians shot the whites before the chiefs could stop them. One tourist was badly wounded and left for dead, but somehow survived and was nursed to health when the soldiers found him. Another man was shot but escaped and likewise was found by the soldiers and mended. Two women in the party were captured and held until White Bird put them on a horse, escorted them out of the Indian camp, and told them to ride for their lives to where the soldiers were.

Another escapee was a miner named Snively, captured separately. Snively found the soldiers and told Howard that Joseph had used him as a guide, since none of the Nez Perce knew the country.

Without Snively, Joseph wandered, allowing Howard to catch up. Meanwhile a third army column was approaching from the east. Samuel Sturgis commanded the Seventh Cavalry, reconstituted after the Little Bighorn disaster. Howard's direction of the campaign against the Nez Perce should have ceased when he crossed the Continental Divide and left the District of the Columbia, but William Sherman made an exception to army rules and temporarily expanded Howard's jurisdiction. Howard sent messengers to tell Sturgis where to intercept Joseph when the Indians came down from the Yellowstone park, but the messengers didn't get through. "The bodies were found of every courier sent out, of every miner or white man caught in the mountains, for at this juncture the Indians spared nobody," wrote Charles Wood.

Sturgis dispatched his own scouts, who fell for a feint the Nez Perce made before slipping around him, crossing the Yellowstone River and heading for the Missouri. Sturgis gave chase and, with fresh cavalry troops sent by Howard, engaged the Indians in a running battle, in which the chiefs and warriors covered the escape of the women and children.

Nelson Miles had read about Howard's pursuit of the Nez Perce while closing out his own war against the Sioux. It was Miles who, as Sturgis's commanding officer, sent him and the Seventh Cavalry to assist Howard. Miles expected word that Sturgis had stymied the Indians, and that they had surrendered either to him or to Howard. But no word came for weeks. Only later did Miles realize that the messengers had been killed. Finally a courier got through to Miles, bringing a directive from Howard to move at once against the Nez Perce, who appeared to be heading for the Canadian border.

Miles and his men set off on a two-hundred-mile dash, to beat Joseph and the fleeing Indians to the border. Miles commandeered a Missouri River steamboat to ferry his men across that river, and proceeded toward the Bear Paw Mountains. His scouts ranged far in advance, seeking any sign of the Nez Perce, while Miles and the others did all in their power to avoid detection by the Nez Perce scouts. The soldiers marched through great herds of antelope, elk and buffalo, but Miles refused permission for his men to shoot them, lest the noise of a gun or the disturbance of the animals alert the enemy.

At the end of September, one of Miles's scouts reported sighting the Nez Perce camp. Miles at once gave the order to attack. The cavalry galloped to the camp and through it, scattering the horses and mules and forcing the Indians to take cover.

Joseph later admitted to being surprised. "We had no knowledge of General Miles's army until a short time before he made a charge upon us, cutting our camp in two and capturing nearly all of our horses," Joseph said. "About seventy men, myself among them, were cut off. My little daughter, twelve years of age, was with me. I gave her a rope, and told her to catch a horse and join the others who were cut off from the camp. I have not seen her since" — Joseph was writing over a year later — "but I have learned that she is alive and well."

The Indians fought back as best they could. "It seemed to me that there were guns on

478

every side, before and behind me," Joseph said. "My clothes were cut to pieces and my horse was wounded, but I was not hurt. As I reached the door of my lodge, my wife handed me my rifle, saying, 'Here's your gun: fight!' "

Joseph and the others fought. But it wasn't easy. "The soldiers kept up a continuous fire," Joseph said. "Six of my men were killed in one spot near me. Ten or twelve soldiers charged into our camp and got possession of two lodges, killing three Nez Perces and losing three of their men, who fell inside our lines. I called my men to drive them back. We fought at close range, not more than twenty steps apart, and drove the soldiers back upon their main line, leaving their dead in our hands." The fighting continued all day and into the night. By the next morning the struggle had evolved into a siege.

Howard arrived as the siege persisted. Charles Wood came with him, as did two elderly Nez Perce men, treaty Indians who had daughters in Joseph's camp. "The two old Nez Perces, 'George' and 'Captain John,' rode into Joseph's camp next day," Wood recalled. "They told him General Howard was there, with promises of good treatment; that his whole command was only two or three days behind him. With tears in their eyes they begged Joseph to surrender. Joseph asked if he would be allowed to return to

Idaho. He was told that he would, unless higher authority ordered otherwise."

Joseph had a different recollection. He described the debate within the Nez Perce camp. "My people were divided about surrendering," he said. "We could have escaped from Bear Paw Mountain if we had left our wounded, old women, and children behind. We were unwilling to do this. We had never heard of a wounded Indian recovering while in the hands of white men." Yet some of the chiefs wanted to attempt an escape anyway. Looking Glass had been advocating a push to the country of the Crows, whom he considered friends of the Nez Perce. But when he learned that the Crows had thrown in with the whites against the Sioux, he argued for heading to Canada and there joining Sitting Bull's band. In fact he hoped that Sitting Bull, hearing of the approach of the Nez Perce, would come to their aid. That hadn't happened, yet Looking Glass still thought a connection with Sitting Bull was the best course. In the council on Bear Paw Mountain, White Bird agreed with Looking Glass.

Joseph didn't like the idea of permanent exile. He supposed the Wallowa Valley would be off limits to the Nez Perce, but the reservation at Lapwai in Idaho would be better than the bleak prairies of Canada.

Joseph wanted to know if the reservation was an option. Miles assured him it was.

"General Miles said to me in plain words, 'If you will come out and give up your arms, I will spare your lives and send you to your reservation,' " Joseph said. He remembered his thinking on hearing these words. "I could not bear to see my wounded men and women suffer any longer; we had lost enough already," he said. "General Miles had promised that we might return to our own country with what stock we had left. I thought we could start again. I believed General Miles, *or I never would have surrendered.*"

Based on his understanding of Miles's offer, Joseph agreed to surrender. Looking Glass and White Bird still dissented. They tried to break out of the siege. Looking Glass was killed in the attempt, but White Bird and some followers made it to Canada.

Charles Wood transcribed Joseph's surrender speech, as interpreted by a friend of Joseph. "Tell General Howard I know his heart," Joseph said. "What he told me before, I have it in my heart. I am tired of fighting. Our chiefs are killed. Looking Glass is dead. The old men are all dead. It is the young men who say yes or no. He Who Led On the Young Men" — Joseph's brother — "is dead. It is cold and we have no blankets. The little children are freezing to death. My people, some of them, have run away to the hills and have no blankets, no food. No one knows where they are — perhaps freezing to death.

I want to have time to look for my children and see how many of them I can find. Maybe I shall find them among the dead. Hear me, my chiefs; I am tired. My heart is sick and sad. From where the sun now stands, I will fight no more forever."

■ ■ ■ ■

PART V
THE TRAIL TO
SKELETON CANYON

■ ■ ■ ■

33

The surrender of Crazy Horse and Joseph marked the end of organized fighting in the northern tier of the West. Sitting Bull eventually returned from Canada, but only to surrender. The Lakotas, the Nez Perce and the other tribes of the region generally accepted the futility of further armed resistance and settled into life on their reservations.

This left the Southwest as the sole theater of active conflict. And it was active only intermittently, which was to say, when Geronimo decided he'd had enough of reservation life and led his band of Apaches into the wild once more.

"It was a cold and cheerless day — March 10, 1870 — when our little troop, 'F' of the Third Cavalry, than which a better never bore guidon, marched down the vertical-walled canyon of the Santa Catalina, crossed the insignificant sand-bed of the San Pedro, and came front into line on the parade ground of

Old Camp Grant, at the mouth of the Aravaipa," John Bourke recalled. Bourke and his cavalry troop had been ordered to Camp Grant, fifty miles north of Tucson, to fight the Apaches. "The sun was shining brightly, and where there was shelter to be found in the foliage of mesquite or cottonwood, there was the merry chatter of birds; but in the open spaces the fierce breath of the norther, laden with dust and discomfort, made the newcomers imagine that an old-fashioned home winter had pursued them into foreign latitudes. A few military formalities hastily concluded, a few words of kindly greeting between ourselves and the members of the First Cavalry whom we met there, and ranks were broken, horses led to stables, and men filed off to quarters. We had become part and parcel of the garrison of Old Camp Grant, the memory of which is still fragrant as that of the most forlorn parody upon a military garrison in that most woebegone of military departments, Arizona."

Bourke looked more closely at his new home. "Beauty of situation or of construction it had none," he wrote. "Its site was the supposed junction of the sand-bed of the Aravaipa with the sand-bed of the San Pedro, which complacently figured on the topographical charts of the time as creek and river respectively, but generally were dry as a limeburner's hat excepting during the rainy season. Let the reader figure to himself a rectangle whose four sides were the row of officers' quarters; the adjutant's office, post bakery, and guard house; the commissary and quartermaster's storehouses; and the men's quarters and sutler's store, and the plan, if there was any plan, can be at once understood. Back of the quartermaster's and commissary storehouses, some little distance, were the blacksmith's forge, the butcher's corral, and the cavalry stables, while in the rear of the men's quarters, on the banks of the San Pedro, and not far from the traces of the ruins of a prehistoric village or pueblo of stone, was the loose, sandy spot on which the bucking bronco horses were broken to the saddle."

The men's quarters were not all the same. "There were three kinds of quarters at Old Camp Grant," wrote Bourke. "And he who was reckless enough to make a choice of one passed the rest of his existence while at the post in growling at the better luck of the comrades who had selected either one of the others. There was the adobe house, built originally for the kitchens of the post at the date of its first establishment, some time in 1857. There were the 'jacal' sheds, built of upright logs, chinked with mud and roofed with smaller branches and more mud. And the tents, long since condemned and forgotten by the quartermaster to whom they had originally been invoiced."

Each style had its merits. "The occupants of the ragged tentage found solace in the pure air which merrily tossed the flaps and flies, even if it brought with it rather more than a fair share of heat and alkali dust from the deserts of Sonora. Furthermore, there were few insects to bother, a pleasing contrast to the fate of those living in the houses, which were veritable museums of entomology, with the choicest specimens of centipedes, scorpions — 'vinagrones' — and, occasionally, tarantulas, which the Southwest could produce. On the other hand, the denizens of the adobe and the jacal outfits became inured to insect pests and felicitated themselves as best they could upon being free from the merciless glare of the sun and wind, which latter, with its hot breath, seemed to take delight in peeling the skin from the necks and faces of all upon whom it could exert its nefarious powers."

Bourke was assigned to one of the rooms in the adobe. It was nine feet wide and fourteen feet long; its ceiling was seven and a half feet above the earthen floor. "There was not enough furniture to occasion any anxiety in case of fire," he wrote, "nothing but a single cot, one rocking chair — visitors, when they came, generally sat on the side of the cot — a trunk, a shelf of books, a small pine washstand, over which hung a mirror of greenish hue, sold to me by the post trader with the assurance that it was French plate." The trader turned out to be a liar. "There were two window-curtains, both of chintz; one concealed the dust and fly-specks on the only window, and the other covered the row of pegs upon which hung sabre, forage cap and uniform." The room had a fireplace, which was small, on account of the short, moderate winters, and situated American-style in one wall of the room, rather than in a corner, per Mexican practice.

The life of the soldiers was dull, except when engaged in "scouts" — armed reconnaissance missions — against the Apaches, which was one reason they didn't much object to them. Occasionally Apaches showed up at the fort. "The first I remember is a squaw whose nose had been cut off by a brutal and jealous husband," Bourke recalled. "The woman was not at all bad looking, and there was not a man at the post who did not feel sorry for the unfortunate who, for some dereliction, real or imagined, had been so savagely disfigured." Bourke would discover that this practice was not uncommon.

Other visitors followed. "There came an old withered crone, leading a woman somewhat younger but still shriveled with the life of care and drudgery which falls to the lot of the Apache matron, and a third member of this interesting party, a boy ten or twelve years old, who was suffering from the bite of a rattlesnake, which had caused his right leg to shrink and decay." Bourke learned that an Apache medicine man had tried to help the boy, but to no avail. And so his mother and grandmother had come to the fort hoping the white man's medicine might succeed where the red man's had failed. It did not, coming so late.

An old Apache man arrived at the fort. He said he was beyond his fighting days and sought respite from violence. "Battles were for young men only" was how Bourke paraphrased his message. "As people grew older they got more sense, and all should live as brothers. This world was large enough for everybody, and there should be enough to eat for the Indians and the white men too. There were men whose hearts were hard and who would not listen to reason. They wished to fight, but as for himself, his legs could not climb the mountains any longer, and the thorns were bad when they scratched his skin. His heart was good, and so long as this stone which he placed on the ground lasted, he wanted to let the Great Father know that he meant to be his friend. Had his brother, the post commander, any tobacco?"

Bourke befriended the old man, who showed him how to make arrowheads out of shards of beer bottles. The man cadged matches even more persistently than tobacco, which Bourke thought odd, in that he could start a fire in seconds by rubbing two sticks together. Apparently he had decided that he'd rubbed enough sticks together for one lifetime. "Matches were his greatest treasure, and he was never tired of begging for them, and as soon as obtained, he would wrap them up carefully in a piece of buckskin to screen them from the weather."

These Apaches became residents of the fort — not exactly by choice but neither over their protest. "These members of the tribe were all kept as prisoners, more to prevent communication with the enemy than from any suspected intention of attempting an escape," Bourke explained. "They were perfectly contented, were well fed, had no more to do than was absolutely good for them in the way of exercise, and except that they had to sleep under the eyes of the sentinels at night, were as free as anyone else in the garrison."

The garrison itself sallied out after the warrior kin of the prisoner-guests. Bourke discovered why the old man had grown tired of campaigning. "There was the usual amount of rough mountain climbing, wearing out shoes and patience and nerve strength all at one and the same time," he recounted. "There was the usual deprivation of water to be expected in the arid wastes of southern Arizona, where springs are few and far between. There were the usual tricks for getting along without much to drink, such as putting a pebble or twig in the mouth to induce a more copious flow of saliva. And when camp was made and the water was found to be not all that it might be, there were other tricks for cleaning it, or, at least, causing a deposition of the earthy matter held in suspension, by cutting up a few plates of the nopal and letting them remain in the kettle for a short time, until their mucilaginous juice had precipitated everything. But a still better plan was to improve the good springs, which was a labor of love with officers and men, and many a fine water hole in Arizona has been the scene of much hard work in digging out, building up with cracker boxes or something to hold the water and keep it from soaking into the earth."

The heat of Arizona was like nothing Bourke or the other soldiers in the posts there had ever experienced. "The heat in most of them became simply unendurable, although here the great dryness of the atmosphere proved a benefit. Had the air been humid, very few of our garrison would now be alive to tell of temperatures of one hundred and twenty and over, and of days during the whole twenty-four hours of which the thermometer did not register below the one hundred notch." The extreme conditions inspired tall tales among the survivors. "There was a story current that the heat had one time become so excessive that two thermometers had to be strapped together to let the mercury have room to climb," Bourke said. He added, "That was before my arrival, and is something for which I do not care to vouch." Yet he couldn't resist repeating another chestnut, about a sinful soldier who, having died and gone to his reward below, returned to Fort Yuma for his blanket, as hell was too cold for him.

Bourke came to admire the war-fighting skills of the Apaches. These were ideally suited to their homeland and their numbers, he said. He told of an Apache who lay in wait outside the fort for hours, hidden behind a clump of palmella, for a Mexican who was visiting to leave the post. He fell upon him with a lance and pierced him through several times. He left the body in its own blood and disappeared. "To attempt pursuit was worse than useless," Bourke said. "And all we could do was to bury the victim."

Bourke continued, "It was this peculiarity of the Apaches that made them such a terror to all who came into contact with them, and had compelled the King of Spain to maintain a force of four thousand dragoons to keep in check a tribe of naked savages, who scorned to wear any protection against the bullets of the Castilians, who would not fight when pursued, but scattered like their own crested mountain quail, and then hovered on the flanks of the whites, and were far more formidable when dispersed than when they were moving in compact bodies. This was simply the best military policy for the Apaches to adopt — wear out the enemy by vexatious tactics, and by having the pursuit degenerate into a will-o'-th'-wisp chase. The Apaches could find food on every hillside, and the water-holes, springs and flowing streams far up in the mountains were perfectly well known to them. The Caucasian troops, of whatever nationality, would wander about, half-crazed with thirst and maddened by the heat of the day or chilled by the cold winds of night in the mountains, and unable to tell which plants were of value as food and which were not."

Some of Bourke's comrades scorned the Apaches precisely for refusing to stand and fight. Bourke did not. "The Apache was in no sense a coward," he said. "He knew his business, and played his cards to suit himself. He never lost a shot, and never lost a warrior in a fight where a brisk run across the nearest ridge would save his life and exhaust the heavily clad soldier who endeavored to catch him." The Apaches could disappear before a white man's very eyes. "They knew how to disguise themselves so thoroughly that one might almost step upon a warrior thus occupied before he could detect his presence. Stripped naked, with head and shoulders wrapped up in a bundle of yucca shoots or sacaton grass, and with body rubbed over with the clay or sand along which it wriggled as sinuously and venomously as the rattler itself, the Apache could and did approach to within ear-shot of the whites, and even entered the enclosures of the military camps." Bourke had seen Indian footprints inside Camp Grant and other posts, when no one had been aware of the Apaches' proximity.

The Apache struck as quietly as he lurked. "On such occasions he preferred to employ his lance or bow, because these made no sound, and half or even a whole day might elapse before the stiffened and bloody corpse of the herder or wagoner would be found, and the presence of Indians in the vicinity become known. At least twenty such examples could be given from my own knowledge," Bourke said. Nor were the soldiers any safer. He recalled visiting the cemetery at Fort Bowie, in the Chiricahua Mountains, and seeing the inscriptions on the stones: "Killed by the Apaches"; "Met his death at the hands of the Apaches"; "Died of wounds inflicted by the Apaches"; "Tortured and killed by the Apaches." He reflected, "One visit to that cemetery was warranted to furnish the most callous with nightmares for a month."

34

In early 1871 a small group of Apache women appeared at Camp Grant. They said they were searching for a lost boy. Perhaps they were, but perhaps they were sizing up the new commander, Lieutenant Royal Whitman, who said he knew nothing about the boy yet treated the women respectfully. The women left, only to return a week later to trade. Once more Whitman greeted them in friendly fashion. He said he would welcome visits by others of their band.

The women conveyed the message, and in due course a delegation of two dozen warriors appeared at the fort, led by a chief named Eskiminzin. They said they were weary of the violence between their people and the whites. They wanted to make peace. Whitman said he lacked the authority to conclude a treaty, but if they cared to camp near the fort they would have his protection. He would feed them, as well, for the time being. They accepted the offer and pitched their tents on Aravaipa Creek, just above the fort. Meanwhile Whitman wrote to his superior, General George Stoneman, commander of the Department of Arizona, for instructions.

Word got out of the Apaches settling peaceably at Camp Grant. Other Apaches, likewise weary of war, joined them. The numbers grew almost daily, until by the middle of March some three hundred had formed a village, or rancheria. They required more rations than Whitman had on hand, and he had to scramble to keep them fed. He anxiously awaited a response from General Stoneman authorizing expenditure for food and for making permanent arrangements for peace with this sizable segment of the Apaches. Whitman supposed congratulations would come with the authorization.

No authorization arrived. A terse response from Stoneman's headquarters said Whitman's letter had been improperly submitted. In Whitman's haste he had neglected to attach a required summary of the contents of the letter; the general insisted that he follow protocol and resend.

There was more to the rebuff than red tape, though. Stoneman was sensing opposition among whites in Arizona to the idea of putting Apaches on the government dole. In Tucson and elsewhere, the Grant administration's peace policy had drawn indignant protest. The whites complained that the

Apaches hadn't accepted the peace policy. At least, not all of them had: raids, thefts and murders continued. Until they did, Stoneman and the army needed to treat the Apaches as enemies. They most definitely should not be fed and protected by the army, at the expense of the white people of America. An army was for fighting, not for playing nursemaid.

The pressure on Stoneman increased as the territorial press raised the hue and cry over every depredation ascribable to the Apaches. Doubtless the editors and other whites understood the fragmented nature of Apache authority, but it served their purpose to blur the issue and blame all Apaches for the violent actions of any. After a group of Apaches attacked a baggage train and killed a soldier and a civilian and stole the mules, and a separate attack killed a rancher and kidnapped a woman, the *Arizona Citizen* of Tucson harangued Stoneman: "Will the Department Commander longer permit the murderers to be fed by supplies purchased with the people's money?"

Angry residents of Tucson called a meeting to address the outrages. "A great amount of resoluting and speechifying was indulged in, and it was determined to raise a military company at once for which a paper was drawn up and signers called for, to which eighty-two Americans signed their names,"

William Oury, a leading townsman, wrote later. "The writer" — Oury — "was elected captain, and all hands pledged to eat up every Apache in the land upon the recurrence of a new outrage."

The committee sent Oury and two others to talk to Stoneman, who happened to be touring his department and was on the Gila River in the western part of the territory. "The result of the conference with the august personage, General Stoneman, was that he had but few troops and could give us no aid — that Tucson had the largest population in the Territory, and gave us to understand that we must protect ourselves," Oury recalled. "With this cold comfort after a trip of one hundred and fifty miles, and the loss of a valuable mule, we returned to our constituents, and although no public demonstration was made, at a quiet assemblage of some of our ablest and most substantial citizens it was resolved that the recommendation of General Stoneman should be adopted, and that we should, to the best of our ability, endeavor to protect ourselves."

Only days later, news arrived of another Apache attack, on a ranch at San Xavier. The Tucson alarm drum was beaten, and a sign was carried through the town announcing another meeting. But the turnout this time was disappointing. Oury blamed the failure of previous meetings to produce any action of substance. Meanwhile a band of residents galloped in the direction the Indian marauders were said to have gone. They met a party of pursuers from San Xavier itself, and the joint posse managed to catch and kill a single Apache, driving the last of the stolen stock.

A member of the Tucson party, Jesus Elias, identified the dead Indian as one of the Camp Grant Apaches. "Don Guillermo," he addressed Oury after returning to town, "I have always been satisfied and have repeatedly told you that the Camp Grant Indians were the ones destroying us. I have now positive proof. The Indian we have just killed, I will swear, and others will swear, is a Camp Grant Indian. I have frequently seen him there, and know him well by his having his front teeth out. And, as a further proof, when we overtook the Indians, they were making a direct course for Camp Grant."

Elias went on to say, according to Oury's later testimony, that it was Oury's responsibility, as one of the oldest American residents of Tucson, to take the lead in punishing the Apaches. If the Americans could supply arms and ammunition, Elias promised, he would furnish Mexicans to fight. He additionally suggested that he and Oury approach a nearby band of Papago Indians and solicit their cooperation in an assault on the Apaches, their historic enemies.

"We both went to work with all our hearts,

he with his countrymen, the Mexicans, I with mine, the Americans, and both together with our auxiliaries, the Papagoes," Oury explained. He laid his plan before the territorial adjutant general, who supplied the weapons Elias requested. The day for the attack was set: April 28. The forces rendezvoused, and Oury was embarrassed by the low turnout of Americans. The force comprised 92 Papagos, 48 Mexicans, and but 6 Americans. "Don Guillermo, your countrymen are grand on resoluting and speechifying," Jesus Elias said, "but when it comes to action they show up exceedingly slim." "Which," Oury admitted afterward, "in view of the fact that 82 Americans had solemnly pledged themselves to be ready at any moment for the campaign, and only six finally showed up, was, to say the least, rather humiliating."

Elias was elected commander of the operation, and the company saddled up. Oury, worried that word of their coming would precede them to Camp Grant, arranged for a guard to be placed at a pass between Tucson and the post, and that no one from Tucson be permitted through before seven the next morning. He didn't want the bleeding-heart lieutenant at Camp Grant to keep them from doing what he refused to do.

The company marched through the night, splitting into two wings — the Papagos in one, the Mexicans and Americans in the other — before arriving at the rancheria at sunrise. Oury remembered with pride the speed and thoroughness of the attack on the Apaches. "They were completely surprised and sleeping in absolute security in the wicki-ups, with only a buck and a squaw on the lookout on a bluff above the rancheria, who were playing cards by a small fire, and both were clubbed to death before they could give the alarm," he said. "The Papagoes attacked them in the wickiups with guns and clubs, and all who escaped them took to the bluffs and were received and dispatched by the other wing, which occupied a position above them. The attack was so swift and fierce that within half an hour the whole work was ended, and not an adult Indian left to tell the tale. Some 28 or 30 small papooses were spared and brought to Tucson as captives. Not a single man of our company was hurt to mar the full measure of our triumph, and at 8 o'clock on the bright morning of April 30, 1871, our tired troops were resting and breakfasting on the San Pedro, a few miles above the post, in full satisfaction of a work well done."

Lieutenant Whitman at Camp Grant had somehow gathered that there was evil afoot. He dispatched two riders to the rancheria to give warning and tell the inhabitants to come to the fort for protection. The messengers returned within the hour saying there was no one to give the warning to. Dozens were dead, mostly women and children. Any survivors had taken to the hills. The wickiups were burned or burning.

Whitman sent a surgeon with a medical wagon to tend to the wounded and bring them back to the fort. He was too late. "On my arrival I found that I should have but little use for wagon or medicine," the surgeon recalled. "The work had been too thoroughly done. The camp had been fired, and the dead bodies of some twenty-one women and children were lying scattered over the ground. Those who had been wounded in the first instance had their brains beaten out with stones. Two of the best-looking of the squaws were lying in such a position, and from the appearance of the genital organs, and of their wounds, there can be no doubt that they were first ravished, and then shot dead. Nearly all of the dead were mutilated. One infant, of some ten months, was shot twice, and one leg hacked nearly off."

Whitman himself toured the killing ground shortly thereafter. The doleful evidence told the gruesome tale. "So sudden and unexpected was it," he reported of the attack, "that no one was awake to give the alarm, and I found quite a number of women shot while asleep beside their bundles of hay which they had collected to bring in that morning." Whitman had arranged for the Apaches in the village to harvest hay in exchange for their provisions. "The wounded who were unable to get away had their brains beaten out with clubs or stones, while some were shot full of arrows after having been mortally wounded by gunshot. The bodies were all stripped. Of the whole number buried, one was an old man and one was a well-grown boy — all the rest women and children. Of the whole number killed and missing, about one hundred and twenty-five, eight only were men."

Whitman took pains to tell the Apaches who had escaped the killing that he had nothing to do with the massacre. Gradually some chose to believe him and returned to Camp Grant. It was from them that he was able to arrive at the number of dead and missing. The missing included dozens of children carried off by the Papagos or the Mexicans.

The testimony of the returnees revealed their distress and their confirmed distrust of the whites. One of the chiefs told Whitman, "I no longer want to live. My women and children have been killed before my face, and I have been unable to defend them." Whitman reported a collective sentiment among the survivors: "We know there are a great many white men and Mexicans who do not wish us to live at peace. We know that the Papagos would not have come out after us at this time unless they had been persuaded to do so." In his own words, Whitman added,

"What they do not understand is, while they are at peace and are conscious of no wrong intent, that they should be murdered by government arms in the hands of Papagos and Mexicans."

Ulysses Grant couldn't understand it either, and he demanded answers. The massacre made a mockery of his peace policy, and the fact that it occurred at an army post named for *him* made the mockery personal. The president ordered an investigation of the massacre, with the goal of prosecuting those responsible.

While the federal attorney for Arizona Territory was building his case, competing narratives were put forward. Oury, Elias and the other leaders of the attack didn't conceal their role in the affair, but they contended that it was rendered necessary by the failure of the army to protect them and their property from the Apaches. And they claimed that some of the Apache raids had been committed by Camp Grant Indians. Whitman countered with statements denying that the Indians under his protection had anything to do with the raids.

In time a hundred men, Americans and Mexicans, were indicted. The trial took place in Tucson and lasted six days. Despite the undeniable evidence of the massacre, and the undenied participation of those on trial, the

Tucson jury took less than twenty minutes to return a collective verdict of not guilty. From some combination of agreement with the justifiable-homicide argument of Oury and the others, and fear for their own safety if they disagreed, the jurors let the perpetrators all go.

The killers were treated as local heroes. One of the Americans, Sidney DeLong, was elected mayor of Tucson; William Oury dined out on his role in the affair for years, regaling newcomers to Arizona with the story of "that glorious and memorable morning of April 30, 1871, when swift punishment was dealt out to those red-handed butchers, and they were wiped from the face of the earth."

35

Into this atmosphere of Apache distrust and white impunity rode George Crook, who replaced George Stoneman as commander of the army Department of Arizona. Crook was another son of Ohio, having been born not far from William Sherman's birthplace; he attended West Point several classes behind Sherman, and arrived in California as an infantry officer as Sherman was preparing to leave the army and become a San Francisco banker. Like Sherman, Crook cut his military teeth fighting Indians, in his case the tribes who were running afoul of settlers in Oregon and northern California. He returned east for the Civil War, rising to the rank of brevet major general. In the postwar reduction of the army he was reverted to lieutenant colonel and sent back to the West, where he fought Snake, Paiute and Modoc Indians and employed the approach of waging winter campaigns. His success inspired Sherman to send him to Arizona in 1871.

Yet had the matter been up to Sherman alone, he would *not* have sent Crook to Arizona — nor would he have sent any other American soldiers. Responsible for defending the whole West, Sherman had concluded that Arizona was a losing proposition. "The occupation of Arizona by the whites, I am satisfied, was premature, and the cost of maintaining troops there is all out of proportion to the results," he argued to Grant in 1870. "The best advice I can offer is to notify the settlers to withdraw, and then to withdraw the troops and leave the country to the aboriginal inhabitants. It seems to me a great waste of good material to banish soldiers to that desert, where it costs so much to maintain them."

But the settlers — and the railroad and mining interests behind them — branded Sherman as defeatist and demanded he shut up and do his job. Grant, his hands full at this point with the Ku Klux Klan and other problems of Reconstruction, declined to take on the Arizona lobby, and told Sherman to send his best Indian fighter. Sherman chose Crook.

"When General Crook received orders to go out to Arizona and assume command of that savage-infested department, he at once obeyed the order, and reached his new post without baggage and without fuss," John Bourke related. "All the baggage he had would not make as much compass as a Remington typewriter. The only thing with him which could in any sense be classed as superfluous was a shotgun, but without this or a rifle he never traveled anywhere."

Crook got down to business at once. "He arrived in the morning, went up to the residence of his old friend, Governor Safford" — Anson Safford, governor of Arizona Territory — "with whom he lunched, and before sundown every officer within the limits of what was then called the southern district of Arizona was under summons to report to him," Bourke recounted. "From each he soon extracted all he knew about the country, the lines of travel, the trails across the various mountains, the fords where any were required for the streams, the nature of the soil, especially its products, such as grasses, character of the climate, the condition of the pack-mules and all pertaining to them, and every other item of interest a commander could possibly want to have determined."

To not a one, however, did Crook reveal what he intended to do with the information. "He never consulted with anyone; made his own plans after the most studious deliberation, and kept them to himself with a taciturnity which at times must have been exasperating to his subordinates," Bourke said. He was speaking of himself, too, at first. But in time Crook grew on him, not least because Crook led by example. "No officer could claim that he was ever ordered to do a duty when the departmental commander was present, which the latter would not in person lead." Nor was Crook overbearing. "No officer of the same rank, at least in our service, issued so few orders. According to his creed, officers did not need to be deviled with orders and instructions and memoranda; all that they required was to obtain an insight into what was desired of them, and there was no better way to inculcate this than by personal example."

Crook's style was understated in the extreme. "Whenever there was a trouble of any magnitude under Crook's jurisdiction, he started at once to the point nearest the skirmish line and stayed there so long as the danger existed," Bourke said. "But he did it all so quietly and with so little parade that half the time no one would suspect that there was any hostility threatened until after the whole matter had blown over or been stamped out, and the General back at his quarters."

Crook never wore his uniform when he could avoid doing so. He refused to let his orderly trail him around the post. His one passion, aside from his work, was hunting, which in fact proved a honing tool for his methods of dealing with the Apaches. "His senses became highly educated," Bourke said.

"His keen, blue-gray eyes would detect in a second and at a wonderful distance the slightest movement across the horizon. The slightest sound aroused his curiosity; the faintest odor awakened his suspicions. He noted the smallest depression in the sand, the least deflection in the twigs or branches. No stone could be moved from its position in the trail without appealing at once to his perceptions. He became skilled in the language of signs and trails, and so perfectly conversant with all that is concealed in the great book of Nature that, in the mountains at least, he might readily take rank as being fully as much an Indian as the Indian himself."

Crook put his troops in the field at once. "How it all came about, I never knew," wrote Bourke. "No one ever knew. There were no railroads and no telegraphs in those days, and there were no messages flashed across the country telling just what was going to be done and when and how. But be all that as it may, before any officer or man knew what had happened, and while the good people in Tucson were still asking each other whether the new commander had a 'policy' — he had not, but that's neither here nor there — we were out on the road, five full companies of cavalry, and a command of scouts and trailers gathered from the best available sources, and the campaign had begun."

The column set off from Tucson at six in the morning on July 11, 1871. Long before noon the thermometer topped 110 in the shade. Crook's initial destination was Camp Bowie, a hundred miles to the east. From there they would turn north into the mountains, heading to Fort Apache. Then west all the way to Prescott, before returning to Tucson. Only gradually did the soldiers realize this was a shakedown tour, allowing Crook to test the mettle of the men and their officers. "In all, some six hundred and seventy-five miles were traveled, and most of it being in the presence of a tireless enemy" — the Apaches — "made it the best kind of a school of instruction." With the best kind of teacher, one who taught by example. "The first man up in the morning, the first to be saddled, the first ready for the road, was our indefatigable commander, who, in a suit of canvas, and seated upon a good strong mule, with his rifle carried across the pommel of his saddle, led the way."

Central to Crook's strategy were his Indian scouts. Rarely since colonial days had white Americans gone to war against Indians without Indian allies. Sometimes whole tribes, often historic enemies of the Americans' enemies, joined the fight. Sometimes the allies were parts of the same tribe the Americans were warring against, following a split within the tribe. Sometimes the allies were individuals, as in the case of Crook's Indian scouts. These persons had their own reasons, which varied from the political to the mercenary. They might have concluded that the whites were irresistible and that the sooner the resisters were defeated, the better for the tribe as a whole. Or they might simply have needed the pay the army offered, convertible to consumer necessaries and desirables.

"The detachment of scouts made a curious ethnographic collection," observed Bourke. "There were Navajoes, Apaches, Opatas, Yaquis, Pueblos, Mexicans, Americans and half-breeds of any tribe one could imagine. It was an *omnium gatherum,* the best that could be summoned together at the time; some were good, and others were good for nothing." Typically the scouts just scouted, tracking and locating the Apaches and leaving the fighting to the white soldiers. Sometimes they fought, if they had a score to settle or if the Apaches, understandably accounting them enemies, ambushed or otherwise attacked them.

Manuel Duran was a venerable Apache who had scouted for the Americans before. He had also experienced the revolutionary upheavals in Mexico that surrounded the installation of the Austrian Maximilian as emperor of Mexico by the French in the early 1860s. He confessed to Bourke, whom he had come to know well, that he couldn't make out what General Crook was up to. "He had never seen so many troops together before without something being in the wind," Bourke wrote. One morning, before the column commenced its march, Manuel Duran summoned Bourke to the side of the road, where they conversed on horseback.

"You are a friend of the new Comandante," he said. "And I am a friend of yours. You must tell me *all.*"

Bourke replied that he didn't understand what Duran was asking.

"Ah, mi teniente, you cannot fool me. I am too old; I know all about such things."

Bourke remained mystified. "Manuel's right eyelid dropped just a trifle, just enough to be called a wink, and he pointed with his thumb at General Crook in advance. His voice sank to a whisper, but it was still perfectly clear and plain, as he asked, 'When is the Comandante going to pronounce?' "

Pronunciamentos were declarations of revolt; Manuel had encountered them on several occasions in Mexico. In fact, as Bourke reasoned to himself, Manuel had never seen so many troops on the march when their commander did *not* throw down the gauntlet against the existing regime. Bourke had some difficulty convincing Manuel that Crook was not challenging the American government, which had many,

514

many more troops than Crook had. But by the time he did, Manuel Duran was more confident than ever that aiding the Americans, rather than resisting them, was the only viable course for the Apaches.

In due course the column reached Fort Apache, in a valley where two branches of the Sierra Blanca River came together. The site, with its steady supply of water, had appealed to the Apaches before the Americans arrived, and some Apaches had a village nearby, where they lived at peace with the soldiers. They planted and tended corn in their fields, and hunted game in the surrounding area.

Crook requested a meeting with the village elders. He was respectful but straightforward. "He had not come to make war, but to avoid it if possible," Bourke recorded. "Peace was the best condition in which to live, and he hoped that those who were around him would see that peace was not only preferable but essential, and not for themselves alone but for the rest of their people as well. The white people were crowding in all over the Western country, and soon it would be impossible for anyone to live upon game; it would be driven away or killed off. Far better for everyone to make up his mind to plant and to raise horses, cows and sheep, and make his living in that way; his animals would thrive and increase while he slept, and in less than no time the Apache would be wealthier than the Mexican. So long as the Apache behaved himself, he would receive the fullest protection from the troops, and no white man should be allowed to do him harm. But so long as any fragment of the tribe kept out on the war path, it would be impossible to afford all the protection to the well-disposed that they were entitled to receive, as bad men would say it was not easy to discriminate between those who were good and those who were bad."

Crook waited for this to be interpreted and understood. He continued in the same vein. "He wished to ascertain for himself just who were disposed to remain at peace permanently and who preferred to continue in hostility. He had no desire to punish any man or woman for any acts of the past. He would blot them all out and begin over again. It was no use to try to explain how the war with the whites had begun. All he cared to say was that it must end, and end at once. He would send out to all the bands still in the mountains and tell them just the same thing. He did not intend to tell one story to one band and another to another, but to all the same words, and it would be well for all to listen with both ears. If every one came in without necessitating a resort to bloodshed he should be very glad; but if any refused, then he should expect the good men to aid him in running down the bad ones."

Again a pause. Crook reiterated his promise of candor. "He should never say anything to them which was not true," Bourke recorded. "And he hoped that as they became better acquainted, they would always feel that his word could be relied on. He would do all in his power for them, but he would never make them a promise he could not carry out." He would be as fair as he could be. "He wanted to treat the Apache just the same as he would treat any other man — as a man. He did not believe in one kind of treatment for the white and another for the Indian. All should fare alike. But so long as the Indian remained ignorant of our laws and language, it was for his own good that the troops remained with him, and he must keep within the limits of the reservations set apart for him. He hoped the time would soon come when the children of the Apaches would be going to school, learning all the white men had to teach their own children, and all of them, young or old, free to travel as they pleased all over the country, able to work anywhere, and not in fear of the white men or the white men of them."

A final pause, and the conclusion: "He repeated his urgent request that every effort should be made to spread these views among all the others who might still be out in the mountains, and to convince them that the safest and best course for all to adopt was that of peace with all mankind. After a reasonable time had been given for all to come in, he intended to start out in person and see to it that the last man returned to the reservations or died in the mountains."

Crook's audience at Fort Apache listened attentively; when he finished, many indicated assent. This was not surprising, in that their residence near the fort reflected their acceptance of Crook's position. The test of the ultimatum was the response of the Apaches in the mountains.

An early sign came a short while later. From Fort Apache the column headed west, along the rim of the Mogollon Plateau, home of the Tonto band of Apaches. The high country was pleasant, even in summer. "We were riding along in a very lovely stretch of pine forest one sunny afternoon, admiring the wealth of timber which would one day be made tributary to the world's commerce, looking down upon the ever-varying colors of the wildflowers which spangled the ground for leagues," Bourke recalled. The bells of the mules of the pack train tinkled through the trees as the afternoon waned. "All were delighted to be able to go into camp in such a romantic spot — when 'whiz! whiz!' sounded the arrows of a small party of Tontos who had been watching our advance and determined to try the effects of a brisk attack."

The arrows, fired from the cover of the trees, missed their targets but impressed Bourke and the others all the same. "The arrows were discharged with such force that one of them entered a pine tree as far as the feathers, and another not quite so far but still too far to allow of its extraction," he wrote.

The bowmen were part of a small party of Tontos; Bourke guessed fifteen or twenty. They knew they were outnumbered and quickly scattered. Still, the white soldiers gave chase and trapped two at the rim of the plateau. "There they stood, almost entirely concealed behind great boulders on the very edge of the precipice, their bows drawn to a semicircle," he recalled. They gave no thought of surrender, their code of war neither giving quarter nor asking it. "They seemed to know their doom, but not to fear it in the slightest degree."

The white soldiers moved closer. "The Apaches, realizing it was useless to delay further, fired their arrows more in bravado than with the hope of inflicting injury, as our men were all well covered by the trees, and then over the precipice they went, as we supposed to certain death," Bourke said. The action left the soldiers nonplussed. "We were all so horrified at the sight that for a moment it did not occur to anyone to look over the crest, but when we did it was seen that the two savages were rapidly following down the merest thread of a trail outlined in the vertical face of the basalt, and jumping from rock to rock like mountain sheep."

Bourke's commander was the first to react. "General Crook drew bead, aimed quickly and fired; the arm of one of the fugitives hung limp by his side, and the red stream gushing out showed that he had been badly hurt. But he did not relax his speed a particle, but kept up with his comrade in a headlong dash down the precipice and escaped into the scrub oak on the lower flanks."

36

The town of Prescott existed to serve the mines in the region south of the Grand Canyon. Its architecture reflected its recent origins; visitors remarked that, in contrast to the Indian and Spanish appearance of most of Arizona's other towns, Prescott might have been dropped in from New England or Pennsylvania. Its upright buildings and painted picket fences made the Americans who constituted its majority population feel as though they had never left the East. Prescott had served as the territorial capital until Tucson usurped that role; Prescott would reclaim the title for a decade until Phoenix landed the honor permanently.

The commandant of Fort Whipple, the post that protected Prescott, was an Irishman named Tommy Byrne. In a military district short of funds, Fort Whipple fell below the modest median; soldiers there feared the wooden walls of the post would topple in a stiff breeze. Byrne supplemented meager physical resources with Irish charm and eloquence that won over skeptical and even hostile Indians. These included the Hualapai people who inhabited the Grand Canyon and its vicinity. After some white provocation triggered a violent Hualapai response, the newspapers of Prescott and other Arizona towns demanded that the army undertake a major campaign to suppress the savages. Byrne had heard the demands before, knew they would lead to no good, and concluded there was but one way to head them off. He leaped on his horse and, unarmed and unaccompanied, rode straight from the fort to the camp of the Hualapais.

Some of the Indians wanted to kill him, but others insisted on hearing him out. He in turn asked to know what their grievance was. They explained that the Indian agent had been cheating them. They had complained, to no avail. Their only recourse was violence.

Byrne listened. He told them that if they came back to the fort with him, he would make sure they received fair treatment. Some of the Hualapais suspected a trick, having assumed Byrne was in on the scheme. But others, who had known him longer, decided to give him a chance. They trailed him to the fort. They watched as he discovered the manner in which the agent had rigged the scales used to weigh cattle and other goods, in gross favor of the agent. He learned how provisions intended by the government for the Hualapais had been diverted to the mining camps, with the agent pocketing the profit they generated there.

The agent realized his game was up and departed for California. Those among the whites who had wanted a campaign against the Hualapais blamed Byrnes for taking the Indians' side against his own people. John Bourke, observing the aftermath of the affair, wrote, "A great hubbub was raised about the matter, but nothing came of it, and a bitter war was averted by the prompt, decisive action of a plain, unlettered officer who had no ideas about managing savages beyond treating them with kindness and justice."

Sometimes, however, war came despite the efforts of peaceable souls among both the whites and the Indians. Wickenburg was a small settlement southwest of Prescott, in a region frequented by raiding parties of Apaches and neighboring tribes. In the autumn of 1871 a stagecoach bound for California was ambushed and five passengers and the driver were killed. Among the passengers was Frederick Loring, a young correspondent for *Appleton's Journal,* an aspiring magazine of literature and science, which understandably informed its readers of the tragic demise of the promising journalist. The attention paid the "Loring massacre" compelled the government to make capture of the killers a priority.

Circumstantial evidence convinced George Crook that a faction of Apache irreconcilables associated with the Date Creek Indian agency had done the fell deed. Crook demanded that the Date Creek band turn over the culprits. The leaders of the band refused. When Crook insisted, they conspired to murder him during his next visit to the agency. Crook got wind of the plot, but rode into the conspirators' lair as boldly as though he suspected nothing. He sat down for a council with the Apache leaders, and spoke most agreeably about various inconsequential topics. Only when one of the Indians asked for a tobacco smoke — the signal for the surprise attack — did another Apache aim his rifle at Crook and squeeze the trigger. Crook's life was spared by quick reflexes of his lieutenant, who struck the barrel just as the gun was firing. In the melee that followed, several Apaches were killed or wounded while they tried to flee the scene. The ones that got away scattered before regathering at an agreed-upon spot in the mountains.

Crook gave them time to think they had got away. Then, with the aid of Hualapai scouts, he tracked them to their rendezvous point. "There the troops and the scouts attacked suddenly and with spirit, and in less than no time, everything was in our hands, and the enemy had to record a loss of more than forty," John Bourke wrote. "It was a terrible blow, struck at the beginning of winter and upon a band which had causelessly slaughtered a stageful of our best people, not as an act of war, which would have been excusable, but as an act of highway robbery, by sneaking off the reservation where the Government was allowing them rations and clothing in quantity sufficient to eke out their own supplies of wild food."

Crook shortly commenced a winter sweep of the Apache lands. The campaign was hard on his men, who weren't accustomed to living outdoors in the mountains during the cold season, but it was harder on the Apaches, whose resources were typically strained even in peaceful winters. Crook's first target was the Tonto Basin of central Arizona, home to some of the most successful and vexing Apache raiders. Crook arranged for several columns of troops to converge on the basin, trapping the hostiles between them. His orders were straightforwardly stern. "The Indians should be induced to surrender in all cases where possible," Bourke transcribed. "Where they preferred to fight, they were to get all the fighting they wanted, and in one good dose instead of a number of petty engagements, but in either case were to be hunted down until the last one in hostility had been killed or captured." There was more: "Every effort should be made to avoid the killing of women and children. Prisoners of either sex should be guarded from ill-treatment of any kind. When prisoners could be induced to enlist as scouts, they should be so enlisted, because the wilder the Apache was, the more he was likely to know of the wiles and stratagems of those still out in the mountains, their hiding places and intentions." Crook insisted that the campaign yield results. "No excuse was to be accepted for leaving a trail. If horses played out, the enemy must be followed on foot. And no sacrifice should be left untried to make the campaign short, sharp and decisive."

The peculiar topography of the region made the marching a test of endurance. Where possible the troops would camp in canyons or valleys sheltered from the wind and the worst of the cold, but during days they would ascend the heights, often through snow. The snow and rain of winter soaked potential firewood, leaving the men chilled and wet for days on end.

Their scouts found the trail of a band of Apache raiders, which led into a deep, nearly inaccessible canyon. Bourke's company commander ordered him to investigate with a small squadron. "There was no trouble at all in getting down that canyon," Bourke remembered. "The difficulty was to hold onto the trail. Had any man lost his footing, he would not have stopped until he had struck the current of the Salado, hundreds of feet below." They proceeded with the greatest care. The trail suddenly turned around a corner in the cliff face. "We saw the condition of affairs most completely. The precipice forming that side of the canyon was hundreds of feet in height, but at a point some four or five hundred feet below, the crest had fallen back in a shelf upon which was a cave of no great depth. In front of the cave great blocks of stone furnished a natural rampart behind which the garrison" — of Apaches — "could bid defiance to the assaults of almost any enemy."

Bourke waited for the rest of the company to arrive. When it did, its Major Brown called for the Apaches in the cave to surrender. They were trapped and could not fight their way out. "The only answer was a shriek of hatred and defiance, threats of what we had to expect, yells of exultation at the thought that not one of us should ever see the light of another day but should furnish a banquet for the crows and buzzards, and some scattering shots fired in pure bravado," Bourke wrote. Major Brown called on the Apaches to let the women and children come out; they would be protected. "To this the answer was the same as before, the jeers and taunts of the garrison assuring our people that they were in dead earnest in saying that they intended to fight till they died."

A standoff of some minutes ensued. Bourke's company couldn't approach the cave without being exposed to the Apaches' deadly fire of arrows and bullets. Nor could the Apaches escape or even effectively fire on the soldiers without exposing themselves.

Brown decided to employ his advantage in ammunition. He directed his men simply to fire into the mouth of the cave, hoping the bullets would ricochet off the roof and walls and hit the Apaches. He understood that the deflected bullets wouldn't distinguish between warriors and noncombatants, but he had offered safe passage to the latter.

Bourke and several others fired into the cave, then paused. "A wail from a squaw, and the feeble cry of a little babe, were proof that the missiles of death were not seeking men alone," Bourke said. Major Brown again shouted an offering to let the women and children come out.

No answer, nor sound of any kind, came from the cave for several minutes. Then Bourke and the others heard what sounded like a song. "It was a weird chant, one not at all easy to describe — half wail and half exultation, the frenzy of despair and the wild cry for revenge."

The chanting stopped. Nothing for several seconds. Then a flurry of movement. "Over the rampart, guided by one impulse, moving as if they were all part of the one body, jumped and ran twenty of the warriors — superb-looking fellows all of them," Bourke wrote. "Each carried upon his back a quiver filled with the long reed arrows of the tribe; each held in his hand a bow and a rifle, the latter at full cock. Half of the party stood upon the rampart, which gave them some chance to sight our men behind the smaller rocks in front, and blazed away for all they were worth. They were trying to make a demonstration to engage our attention, while the other part suddenly slipped down and around our right flank."

But the soldiers, catching on, moved to cut off escape. "Our men rushed to the attack like furies," Bourke wrote. "Six or seven of the enemy were killed in a space not twenty-five feet square, and the rest driven back into the cave, more or less wounded."

Yet one got away, making it around the flank to the rear of Bourke and the others. He leaped atop a large boulder and commenced a war whoop, as encouragement to his comrades. "His chant was never finished," Bourke reported. "It was at once his song of glory and his death song." The warrior didn't realize there were soldiers behind the line Bourke was in. "Twenty carbines were gleaming in the sunlight just flushing the cliffs; forty eyes were sighting along the barrels." Almost as one the carbines blasted away at the exposed Apache. "He was really a handsome warrior — tall, well-proportioned, finely muscled, and with a bold, manly countenance," Bourke recalled. But he didn't make a pretty corpse. "I have never seen a man more thoroughly shot to pieces than was this one. Every bullet seemed to have struck, and not less than eight or ten had inflicted mortal wounds."

The Apaches in the cave showed no sign of being daunted. Their chant resumed, sung louder and more defiantly than ever. Major Brown decided to press the issue. He gathered his men into one line and ordered them to fire. "The din and tumult increased twenty-fold beyond the last time," Bourke wrote. "Lead poured in by the bucketful."

Amid the barrage an Apache child, a boy three or four years old, wandered from the mouth of the cave. He stared in curiosity at the guns of the soldiers, even as they continued to fire. "He was not in much danger, because all the carbines were aiming upward at the roof," Bourke remarked. Even so, a glancing bullet skinned the boy's scalp and left him crying and bleeding. One of the soldiers' Indian scouts ran out and grabbed the child, yanking him back to safety while the soldiers ceased their fire.

The fighting resumed. "It was exactly like fighting with wild animals in a trap," Bourke said. "The Apaches had made up their minds to die if relief did not reach them from some of the other rancherias supposed to be close by." Such relief never had a chance. Reinforcements arrived first for the soldiers, in the persons of a troop drawn to the brink of the canyon by the sound of the shooting. The captain of the troop lowered two of his men over the brink by suspenders borrowed from their comrades, and they reported that the Apaches had been forced from the cave by the fire of the soldiers below, and were taking refuge at the base of the cliff. The captain first had the dangling men fire down upon the Indians, but their swinging aim was poor. Another idea occurred to him. He had the rest of his troop push boulders over the crest of the canyon down upon the Apaches. "The noise was frightful, the destruction sickening," Bourke said. "The air was filled with the bounding, plunging fragments of stone, breaking into thousands of pieces, with other thousands behind, crashing down with the momentum gained in a descent of hundreds of feet. No human voice could be heard in such a cyclone of wrath; the volume of dust was so dense that no eye could pierce it."

Eventually Major Brown gave the order to cease fire, and signaled to the boulder-rollers to stop. Not a sound came from the cave or the ledge below it. Cautiously Brown ordered his men to advance. "I hope that my readers will be satisfied with the meagerest description of the awful sight that met our eyes," Bourke wrote. "There were men and women dead or writhing in the agonies of death, and with them several babies, killed by our glancing bullets or by the storm of rocks and stones that had descended from above. While one portion of the command worked at extricating the bodies from beneath the pile of debris, another stood guard with cocked revolvers or carbines, ready to blow out the brains of the first wounded savage who might in his desperation attempt to kill one of our people. But this precaution was entirely useless. All idea of resistance had been completely knocked out of the heads of the survivors, of whom, to our astonishment, there were over thirty."

The winter campaign continued, albeit less dramatically. Apache attacks continued as well, but Crook distributed his troops to be able to react almost instantaneously to an Apache strike. A band of the Indians hit a group of ranchos near Wickenburg, where they surprised a party of recent arrivals. "All in the party fell victims to the merciless aim of the assailants, who tied two of them to cactus and proceeded deliberately to fill them with arrows," Bourke recounted. "One of the poor wretches rolled and writhed in agony, breaking off the feathered ends of the arrows, but each time he turned his body, exposing a space not yet wounded, the Apaches shot in another barb." The raiders then robbed the ranchos, stole or killed all the stock and fled toward the Tonto Basin. But within twenty-four hours Crook had his troops on their trail, and the soldiers caught up with the raiders after they had reached the summit of the aptly named Turret Butte. The soldiers ascended the mountain in the dead of night, crawling on hands and feet to avoid dislodging stones and making noise. They lay on the ground until daybreak, when they stormed the Apache camp. So complete was the surprise that several of the Indians leaped over the edge of the turret and fell to their death. The rest were killed by gunfire or taken prisoner.

This fairly shattered the Apache resistance. A delegation from the hostile bands came to Crook's headquarters to indicate a desire for peace. He told them to fetch their chiefs; he would deal only with the headmen. Cha-lipun was the first to arrive, with three hundred of his followers. He said he spoke for all of the Apaches. He said they had never been afraid of the Americans, Bourke recorded. "But now that their own people were fighting against them, they did not know what to do. They could not go to sleep at night, because they feared to be surrounded before daybreak. They could not hunt; the noise of their guns would attract the troops. They could not cook mescal or anything else, because the flame and smoke would draw down the soldiers. They could not live in the valleys; there were too many soldiers. They had retreated to the mountaintops, thinking to hide until the soldiers went home, but the scouts found them out and the soldiers followed them." They had no choice but to surrender. "They wanted to make peace and to be at terms of good will with the whites."

Crook gave the chief his entire attention. When Cha-lipun had finished speaking, Crook grasped his hand. The general said that if the chief would promise to live at peace and stop killing people, he would find Crook to be the best friend he ever had. "Not one of the Apaches had been killed except through his own folly," Crook said, in Bourke's phrasing. "They had refused to listen to the messengers sent out asking them to come in, and consequently there had been nothing else to do but to go out and kill them until they changed their minds. It was of no use to talk about who began this war; there were bad men among all peoples. There were bad Mexicans, as there were bad Americans and bad Apaches. Our duty was to end wars and establish peace, and not to talk about what was past and gone."

Crook spelled out what peace must mean. "The Apaches must make this peace not for a day or a week, but for all time; not with the

Americans alone but with the Mexicans as well; and not alone with the Americans and Mexicans, but with all the other Indian tribes. They must not take upon themselves the redress of grievances, but report to the military officer upon their reservations, who would see that their wrongs were righted. They should remain upon the reservation and not leave without written passes."

Crook explained his government's obligations to the Indians. "They should not be told anything that was not exactly true. They should be fully protected in all respects while on the reservation. They should be treated exactly as white men were treated. There should be no unjust punishments."

Yet if the Indians were to be treated like white men, they had to act like white men. "They must work like white men; a market would be found for all they could raise, and the money should be paid to themselves and not to middlemen. They should begin work immediately; idleness was the source of all evils, and work was the only cure. They should preserve order among themselves; for this purpose a number would be enlisted as scouts and made to do duty in keeping the peace. They should arrest and confine all drunkards, thieves and other offenders." And they must treat their women better. "They should not cut off the noses of their wives when they became jealous."

37

Jason Betzinez observed the actions of Crook and the soldiers from the Apache side of things. Betzinez was a much younger cousin of Geronimo, and a member of the Warm Springs band. He recalled a moment that etched itself into the memory of his people. "While I was still a small boy, Cochise and his band were living in and around what is known as Apache Pass, a canyon just west of old Fort Bowie, which was then probably only a temporary camp," he wrote later. Cochise was the principal chief of the Chiricahua Apaches. Betzinez continued, "An officer of the post, acting, perhaps, under instructions from one of the Indian agents, was attempting to secure the return of some half-breed boy captured by San Carlos Indians. This officer, Lieutenant Bascom, sent an invitation to Cochise to meet with him in a conference in the pass. Not expecting any trouble and not being conscious of having committed any offense against the government, Cochise and his subchiefs prepared to go to the meeting. They had their women give them a good scrubbing, comb their hair, paint their faces, and otherwise make them presentable for such an honored occasion."

The meeting started on a rough note. "The officer in command of the troop detachment accused the Indians of having in captivity a small white boy," Betzinez related. "Cochise replied that he had never heard of this case, which was quite true. The officer didn't believe him." Yet the moment passed, and the tension seemed to ease. "The officer told the chiefs to go into a tent where a fine dinner had been prepared for them." Cochise and the others did so.

They soon realized their mistake. "When they were all inside, the soldiers surrounded the tent and attacked. All the Indians except three were captured. One of those who escaped was Cochise. Evidently he reacted more quickly than the others for he sprang to the side of the tent, slashed it open with his knife, and with two others dashed out into the brush, making good his escape."

Cochise proceeded to waylay traffic on the road to Fort Apache and seize captives. He sent a messenger to Bascom offering to trade his captives for the Apaches Bascom had seized. Bascom refused. "A day or so afterwards Cochise and his men found these Indians hanging from trees where the soldiers had executed them," Betzinez recalled. "The Indians sadly took down the bodies of their friends and buried them. Then they hung all their white captives to the same trees." He added, "This affair changed a prominent, highly-thought-of chief and his band from Indians who had been friendly and co-operative with the government to a bitterly hostile group."

The conflict that followed lasted eleven years; it ended in 1872 with an agreement by Cochise and his band to move to a reservation near Fort Bowie. They remained there until 1876, when the government consolidated several Apache bands on the San Carlos reservation. The Warm Springs band of Jason Betzinez was one of those moved to San Carlos — through no fault of their own, he explained. "East of our Warm Springs reservation, across the Rio Grande, lay the reservation of our kinsfolk the Mescalero Apaches. Whenever these Indians had trouble among themselves or with the Mexicans or white people they would drift into our reservation for refuge. Sometimes they drove in stolen stock. When this was identified by the owners or the authorities we frequently got the blame."

And so they were swept up in the 1876 removal to San Carlos. "Early in the spring of that year we were living contentedly at Warm Springs, the agency being garrisoned by a troop of Negro cavalry with whom we were on friendly terms," Betzinez recalled. "One day another colored troop accompanied by Indian scouts from San Carlos arrived at our agency. We felt that something unpleasant was about to happen but we didn't know what or why. Still, we remained quiet and gave no trouble." A few days later they got the word. "Messengers came to all our camps ordering us to assemble at the agency. Having gathered there we were lined up and searched for weapons by the scouts. No one was overlooked — not a man, woman, or child. Everything was taken from us, even our butcher knives. We opened our eyes in great surprise. What had we done to be treated in such a rude manner? No explanation was made then or later."

The Chiricahua leaders were treated more harshly. "Victorio, Loco, Nanay, Geronimo, and practically all of the able-bodied men were directed to report to the agency blacksmith shop, where iron chains were put on their wrists and ankles," Betzinez said. "In a day or two, they were loaded in wagons and started off under military guard for some unknown destination."

Two days later the rest were ordered out. "Word was passed for us to pack up our belongings. We were formed into a column and started off toward the west," Betzinez remembered. "The column pulled out sorrowfully, some of us on foot, a few on horses or mules, these being mostly women or old people too feeble to walk. Ahead of us marched the Negro troopers, in rear were the Indian scouts. The latter, proud of their status, acted as if they were a guard of honor, which failed, however, to improve our spirits." Those spirits fell the more as the travelers saw what they were heading into. "The land looked parched, barren and unproductive, quite different from our beautiful Warm Springs reservation. After a sweaty, dusty march we came to Fort Thomas, a few miles west of which stood an old house which was to be our sub-agency." The main agency was San Carlos, twenty miles to the west, at the confluence of the San Carlos and Gila Rivers. "We were completely downcast over the prospect of having to live in this hot, desolate country."

Nor would they be living there alone — a fact that made their predicament all the worse. "Many other bands of Apaches had been driven in to this reservation, including the Chiricahuas and Juh's group of outlaws from Mexico. Even had all these bands been on good terms with one another, which they were not, we still would have been unhappy over the inhospitable attitude of the San Carlos Indians. Each of our bands would much have preferred to settle on a separate reservation. I well remember our feeling of indignation and helplessness over this ill turn in our fortunes."

Yet things got still worse. Smallpox broke out among the new arrivals. "Our people were terrified, for that affliction had always proved deadly to the Indians," Betzinez said. "Many Apaches were seriously sick, some died." Despair seized the survivors, who sought escape from what seemed an outdoor prison. Some headed into the mountains north of the reservation, hoping the higher elevation would slow the disease.

Others considered bolder measures. "The younger men began to talk of going on the warpath," Betzinez said. Some began stealing guns and ammunition to make ready for the day. The leaders of this group were Geronimo and Juh. Betzinez observed Geronimo closely, for on Geronimo's decision the fate of Betzinez and his mother and sister might rest. Betzinez saw a personal element in Geronimo's choice. "That summer Geronimo and his family had been camping in the mountains north of Fort Thomas in order to escape the terrific heat of the Gila Valley. One day just about the time of the outbreak Geronimo was scolding his nephew, for no reason at all. This disturbed the nephew so much that he killed himself. This all happened while they were drinking intoxicating liquor. Geronimo, blaming himself for his nephew's death, left the reservation and joined Juh's group, which intended to flee to Mexico. He took with him his own family, he now having two wives as well as another young woman who later also became his wife."

Geronimo's decision seemed to bind Betzinez. "Since Geronimo was now the senior member of our family group, Mother, Sister and I were under compulsion to go with him," Betzinez said. He soon learned that his sister, fifteen years old, had already made up her mind. She had been visiting relatives near the sub-agency, and a report came that she had joined the war party, apparently with a young man. Betzinez's mother, greatly alarmed, said they must find out if the report was true. "I got my rope, butcher knife — my only weapon — and sheet," Betzinez said. "We bid our kinsfolk and friends farewell, and started on foot to the sub-agency fifteen miles to the east. We made such speed that it didn't take us long to get there." They soon learned that the report was indeed true. They met the father of the young man; he was similarly distressed and said he was going after the war party. He would retrieve the boy and Betzinez's sister too.

Betzinez and his mother waited anxiously. After midnight they heard the sound of horses. "It was the man bringing in his son and my sister," Betzinez said. "What joy there was when sister ran into my mother's arms!" He added, "So I narrowly escaped going on the warpath at the age of sixteen."

Instead he went back to Warm Springs. Geronimo's breakout and the violence it produced afforded cover for the Warm Springs band to head back to their previous home. "Under the leadership of Victorio and Loco, we slipped away," Betzinez said. Yet their absence didn't go unnoticed. "Some Indians of other bands, seeing us go, reported it to the authorities. Soon a few soldiers and Indian scouts from Fort Thomas were on our trail. The pursuers, overtaking us, captured several families whom they took back to San Carlos." The others, including Betzinez and his mother and sister, continued toward Warm Springs. Apache scouts were sent to bring them in. "But the Indian scouts, sympathizing with us, stopped and permitted us to go back to our old reservation without further molestation."

For two years they lived at Warm Springs. In 1879, though, the pressure resumed to concentrate the Apaches in one place. "The soldiers and scouts again were sent to return us to San Carlos," Betzinez said. "We were assembled for a conference at which this decision was announced. Chief Loco was willing to go but Victorio and Nanay were not. 'No!' Victorio protested. 'This country belongs to my people as it did to my forefathers. A few years ago the government set aside for us the Warm Springs reservation. Now the white people want it. If you force me and my people to leave it, there will be trouble. Leave us alone, so that we may remain at peace.' "

The agent who heard the speech was unmoved. He had orders. He set the day when all must be ready to depart. Before the day arrived, Victorio and Nanay broke out, with forty warriors and their women and children. Betzinez observed and commented, "I had known both these chiefs since my earliest childhood. They had fought under Chief Roan Shirt (Mangas Coloradas). Victorio, together with Loco, had succeeded to the chieftainship of the Warm Springs band. In our opinion he stood head and shoulders above the several war chiefs such as Mangas, Cochise and Geronimo, who have bigger names with the white people." Betzinez knew Victorio mostly by reputation, but he knew Nanay, his father's first cousin, quite well. "In his youth Nanay was a tall, well-built man, so strong that he could shoot an arrow clear through a steer. I have seen him do it on the Warm Springs reservation even after he was old. He had been a proud, fearless warrior under Mangas and Victorio, a fighter who was able to stand up against anyone who tried to overpower him. He also had a friendly nature, being well liked by our Mexican neighbors near Warm Springs as well as by his own people. Like most of the Warm Springs band he was inclined by nature to be peaceful. This all changed when he went on the warpath with Victorio in 1879. He was filled with a bitter hatred of his enemies, which transformed him into a perfect tiger."

At first Victorio and Nanay and their followers made a base in the Black Mountains south of the Warm Springs reservation. From there they ventured out to raid for guns and ammunition, attacking travelers and pack trains. As their arsenal expanded, so did the scope of their operations. "They extended their range east to the Rio Grande, killing every human being they encountered. For a time they kept returning to the vicinity of the Warm Springs reservation, but soon they headed into the desert and from there south into Mexico. While in Mexico, Victorio's group attacked everyone they saw just as they had in the United States. When pursued by Mexican troops, they turned eastward between Chihuahua and Ciudad Juarez, from the latter area moving north across the river into southwestern Texas, thence westward again into New Mexico. As they went they were fighting almost every day, killing dozens of people, leaving a trail of blood." The violence fed on itself. "The band had to keep on the move day and night. They never thought of surrender, for in addition to the disgrace of such an act, they now knew that their killings would never be forgiven. This made them fight even more desperately, with a continued shedding of the blood of many people."

They came to a bloody end themselves. "A captive Mexican boy with them slipped away and told the enemy that the Indians were out of ammunition," Betzinez related. "The Mexicans, stealing closer, threw dynamite into the pockets and crevices where the Indians had concealed themselves. Soon all had been destroyed." Or not quite all: Betzinez had heard the story from one of the few survivors.

Meanwhile Betzinez and his family and the other Warm Springs Apaches were herded back to San Carlos. The reservation was as dispiriting as ever. "The agency consisted of a few adobe buildings situated on the gravelly flat between the two streams" — the Gila and the San Carlos — "with a few scraggly cottonwoods offering the only shade in a temperature which often reached 110 degrees or higher. Dust storms were common the year round, and in all seasons except the summer the locality swarmed with flies, mosquitos, gnats and other pesky insects. The place was almost uninhabitable, but we had to stay there."

The prisoners — for so they felt themselves — were not allowed to leave the reservation to hunt, and so were entirely dependent on the food rations the agent distributed. Or did not distribute, given the corruption of the

Indian agency. The inmates were told they must farm, but nothing would grow on the desert hardpan. Under the circumstances, Betzinez didn't wonder that the young men found work with the army appealing. "Some of our Apaches enlisted as scouts and went off with the troops to hunt down their fellow tribesmen," he recalled. "They were as happy as bird dogs turned loose in a field full of quail." Yet even this was only temporary. "The rest of the time they lay around their camps, gambling and, when they could get away with it, making and drinking a strong Indian beer made out of fermented corn mash."

Betzinez's mother contrived to distract him from such mischief. "My mother kept my sister and me busy in taking long, fast hikes to keep our muscles like iron, our feet tough, and our hearts and wind in good condition. She knew full well how important that might be if troubled times descended upon us again."

Yet she couldn't fill all his hours, which hung heavily. He listened to stories told by his elders. "Since the Indians had no written language, they kept alive their tribal history, and especially tales of their personal exploits, by recounting these stories over and over again," Betzinez explained. "I think that many white people have the false notion that Indians are silent, taciturn. Nothing could be more erroneous. The Indians, or at least the

Apaches, are great talkers."

He recalled one story session in particular. "It was a mild evening in April of 1882. We had sat up until long after midnight listening to mother and one of her friends exchanging reminiscences. Suddenly we heard a horse approaching on the path leading to our tent. It trotted up to the front of our lodge and stopped. Outside someone spoke in Apache asking for Gil-lee, a member of our Chihenne band. Since Gil-lee lived about five hundred yards southwest of us I ran out to tell the stranger where his tepee was. As he rode away in the darkness the man said, 'Don't be alarmed. We only want to see Gil-lee.'"

But Betzinez, and especially his mother, *were* alarmed. "From his accent, the fact that he was not known to any of us, and from what I had seen of his clothing in the light from our tepee, we knew that the man was a wild Indian from Mexico — a Netdahe. This made us afraid, for we knew that these outlaws had not come for any peaceful purpose. The very fact that this man had sneaked into the reservation and to our camp after dark was ominous. For that is the way of Apaches on the warpath. They avoid being seen. They cover their tracks or disguise them to look like something else. We talked over this threatening visit for some time after the man had gone, wondering what we ought to do or what was going to happen."

The next morning they found out. "Just as the sun was beginning to shine on the distant mountain tops, promising a hot day, we heard shouts along the river," Betzinez said. "Running out of our tepee we saw a line of Apache warriors spread out along the west side of camp and coming our way with guns in their hands. Others were swimming horses across the river or pushing floating logs ahead of themselves. One of their leaders was shouting, 'Take them all! No one is to be left in the camp. Shoot down anyone who refuses to go with us! Some of you men lead them out.' The suddenness of this attack, its surprise effect, and the inhuman order from one of the chiefs calling for the shooting of people of his own blood threw us all into a tremendous flurry of excitement and fear."

Betzinez and the others did as they were told. "We were given no time to look for our horses and round them up but were driven from our village on foot. We weren't allowed to snatch up anything but a handful of clothing and other belongings. There was no chance to eat breakfast."

Betzinez recognized his cousin. "Geronimo, who seemed to be one of the main leaders of the outlaws, was out in front guiding us east along the foot of the hills north of the Gila River." Their escape, or rather capture, didn't go uncontested. "We had only gone a short

549

distance when we heard shooting break out behind us. The chief of the San Carlos Indian scouts and some fifteen of his scouts had ridden up to our deserted camp to investigate the commotion. Some Chiricahuas ambushed the scouts, killing the chief, Mr. Sterling, and one of his men. One of the warriors brought back Sterling's boots. This made me feel badly, because Sterling had been a good friend of ours. He had often visited our camp and once taught me how to make a little wooden wagon. None of our Warm Springs Apaches had weapons. This, with the brutal shooting of the two scouts, convinced us that we were helpless in the hands of the Netdahe."

Betzinez and the others were stunned and puzzled. "We told ourselves that our safety depended on keeping quiet and not trying to escape. We were filled with gloom and despair. What had we done to be treated so cruelly by members of our own race? Our outlook was all the blacker because we realized that the officers at the agency would blame us for the killings which had occurred there and probably would think that we ran away of our own accord. We felt that we could not safely return to the agency even if we could get away from the wild Indians. So the future held for us only hard flight through mountains and desert under constant pursuit by troops."

On they went. "After hustling east along the river for several miles, our column turned northeast into the Gila Mountains," Betzinez said. Reflecting on the flight strategy, he explained, "Apaches on the warpath, especially when accompanied by women and children, move high up in the mountain ranges whenever they can. This way they can see troops approaching, and they avoid many combats by following routes which the soldiers dislike. Troops generally carry their ammunition and supplies by wagon; therefore they follow the flat country." Anticipating events, Betzinez added, "It was only when General George Crook chased the Indians with a column supplied by mule pack trains that the Apaches had a hard time staying out of reach." Betzinez continued, "Also, the Apaches moved mostly in the mountains because they knew of springs and water holes there which were not to be found elsewhere. The Apache knows the secret of how to find water in a dry country where most of the year the stream beds are dry sand. He does not go to a line of green cottonwoods along a creek or river bed to dig for water, for he knows that it is down too deep. In the mountains, especially in a rock basin at the foot of a dry waterfall, he can usually find a little water near the surface by digging with his hands."

But traveling through the mountains took a toll. "As we climbed higher and higher up the rough slopes, over the steep escarpment, many members of our band began to tire out." Betzinez and his mother and sister did better than most. "We were in good shape because of the physical conditioning which mother had been giving us for the past few years."

The logistics of escape had to be fashioned on the fly. "Near sunset we reached a spring just on the other side of the first range where the warriors called a halt to let us rest and have some water," Betzinez said. "But there was nothing to eat. We had had no food since the night before. After a short rest the leaders told us that a night march lay ahead of us. Soon we were again moving east, this time along the ridge. About midnight we came to another spring known to Geronimo, who had been there with his family when they had fled from the reservation in 1878."

Again Betzinez sensed the hand of his cousin guiding events. "It now began to be clear to me that Geronimo was pretty much the main leader although he was not the born chief of any band and there were several Apaches with us, like Naiche, Chatto, and Loco, who were recognized chiefs. But Geronimo seemed to be the most intelligent and resourceful as well as the most vigorous and farsighted. In times of danger he was the man to be relied upon."

Geronimo apparently knew of a sheepherder's camp some distance away. Warriors were dispatched. They rendezvoused with the main party at dawn, after the latter had traveled for several more hours. "Since we had been without food for two nights and a day, and had made a hard trip, we surely were glad to see that our foragers had driven in several hundred sheep." Animals were efficiently prepared for eating. "An Apache kills a sheep by grabbing it by the legs, throwing it on its back, and cutting its throat," Betzinez explained. "Then he throws the carcass, skin and all, on a brush fire. This barbecues the meat while the hide protects it from dirt. Simple; but that roast meat sure tastes good."

While the party ate and rested, Geronimo and the other leaders plotted their next steps. They wanted to avoid battle with the army or with Indian scouts; the women and children made them too vulnerable. And they wanted to get to Mexico, where the international border would protect their rear.

Another foraging party was sent out for horses and mules. The warriors could often travel faster afoot, especially through mountains. But the women and children needed transport. The rustlers returned with a herd of horses. "We spent another day or two in this place while the men broke the animals to be ridden bareback or with improvised saddles," Betzinez said. The saddles were fashioned from bundles of reeds wrapped in cloth or skins; these were then tied around the animals.

The march resumed. Warriors attacked another ranch, for more animals, while the main column skirted around, out of sight and out of gunshot, but not out of earshot of the fighting that ensued.

And then, amid the battle, something unforeseen but not exactly unpredictable brought the column to a halt. "One of the girls with us reached womanhood, so right away her parents arranged the traditional ceremony in her honor, even while the shooting was heard on the other side of the hill," Betzinez recounted. "Since this is one of the most important events in a woman's life the ceremony is never neglected, not even at a time such as this." The girl and her parents — like Betzinez and his sister and mother — had not come along willingly, and they were determined that this significant moment not be sacrificed to the whims of Geronimo and the others. "This girl was a member of the White Mountain Apaches, who with her parents had been living with us at San Carlos and who had been caught in this raid of the Netdahe," Betzinez said. With wisdom of hindsight, Betzinez added, "The ceremony of reaching womanhood marks the time when a girl is ready for marriage. Of course all girls look forward to it eagerly even though if they look around them they should realize that all marriages do not turn out happily." Under ordinary circumstances, the ceremony lasted days; on this occasion it was shortened to hours. "The warriors were in a hurry to start the night march." Yet the fact that it happened at all was significant.

The night march reminded the captives that they were captives. "All through the night we rode close together, so that no one would stray away from the column. The warriors rode on all sides of us in order to keep us together." They weren't entirely successful. "In spite of their watchfulness some members of the Warm Springs band managed to slip away and head north for the Navajo country." Betzinez was in no state for flight. "My mother, my sister and I were riding a big mule. Now and then we could hear the voices of the wild Indians on all sides of us as they called softly to each other in the darkness. Finally I dozed. It is a wonder I didn't fall off the mule but every now and then my mother punched me to wake me up."

He was glad the next day for even the little sleep he got. A company of Indian scouts was searching for Geronimo's band. The Apache sentries spotted the scouts first, and killed one. The scouts set fire to the prairie grass to alert the army and summon help. Geronimo saw the signal and prepared his warriors for pitched battle. "Those of us who were watching the skirmishing from high up on the mountainside were getting restless," Betzinez recalled. "The real old men were hiding behind the rocks, but some of us more adventurous young fellows climbed up where we could see. There was a clear view far to the north, east and south. After about an hour we saw two troops of cavalry approaching from the vicinity of the railroad station. This was the first chance most of us had ever had to see a real battle and we were trembling with excitement."

Betzinez watched the warriors make ready. "When the soldiers had reached a point about a mile from our hiding place, our warriors stripped off their shirts and prepared for action. I heard the leaders calling all able-bodied men to assemble for battle." Betzinez made another observation: "Of course the way Indians fought, this was all voluntary. The chiefs were not able to order any man to fight, as the officers could the soldiers. But the Indians would go into battle to keep from being shamed and to protect their families." Betzinez himself wasn't quite old enough. "I was still considered to be too young to fight, was without experience, and was not given a weapon."

The battle unfolded before his eyes. "We saw our warriors moving down toward a deep U-shaped ravine. The soldiers were approaching up the canyon while our men were on the rim. The fighting began. Three of our men who were wounded were carried back up the mountainside. Maybe some were killed but I didn't see any. The firing grew very heavy, almost continuous. The soldiers fired ferocious volleys. Those of us who were watching were shivering with excitement as our men slowly withdrew under this fire. Finally toward sunset our whole band moved to the southwest side of the mountain and the firing died out."

The army rested after the battle, but the Indians resumed their flight. "The chiefs told us to move very quietly down the mountainside, as they believed that the enemy might still be near." They weren't disturbed by the soldiers, but they had a hard time nonetheless. "A person who has not traveled through these rough mountains at night cannot appreciate how dangerous and unpleasant such a flight can be. In addition to thorns, cactus, yucca, and other spear-like plants to scratch you, you must avoid knife-like rocks that you can't see, holes and crevices in the ground, and cliffs of all kinds." On the night journey, some of the party lost their way and got separated from the main column. But none tried to escape and return to the reservation. "It was too far, and we were now too closely involved with the hostiles in the fight with the troops," Betzinez said.

More of the same lay ahead. "That night we headed southeast through the foothills of the Chiricahua Mountains, crossing and recrossing arroyos and hills. We stayed out of the main mountain range, whose peaks exceed 9,000 feet in elevation, but we had to go through several rough canyons. It was a terrible journey."

But it got them to their first goal: the international border. All breathed more easily, even those who had been forced to come. "After we had crossed into Mexico, we began to feel safe from attack by U.S. troops," Betzinez said. "Since we were under the impression that we were out of danger, there was much cheerful conversation as we packed our horses and mules and prepared to continue our journey. This night march, in contrast to our past hasty and tiresome travel, was a delightful one especially for the young folks. The night atmosphere was cool and dry, the skies bright with stars. So we rode along across the plains, talking, laughing, and singing love songs in low voices — songs our people have long known and liked. Now and then someone would challenge a friend to a race, which of course was only in fun and didn't last long. Here and there riders could be heard calling to companions in the darkness, with answers echoing from the hills and rocks on either side. Several times we came to springs where we stopped to refresh ourselves, then continued on until the sky began to lighten. Finally under a grove of cottonwood trees we came to a fine spring and stream where we pitched our camp and intended to remain for several days."

38

Betzinez and the others soon learned they were wrong in thinking the U.S. troops would not cross the border after them. So vexing had the fugitive Apaches become to Mexicans as well as Americans that William Sherman had been able to negotiate an agreement with the Mexican government letting army units of either country enter the other in pursuit of them. The agreement was quickly put into effect.

"On the third morning I was out at daylight looking for our mule, which had been turned loose to graze and was with the other animals a mile or so from camp," Betzinez recounted. "All at once I heard a gun fired from the foothills east of the camp. I opened my eyes wide in sudden excitement, for there in plain sight south of the horse herd was a troop of cavalry galloping my way. I guess they didn't notice me among the animals or they would have gotten me easily. I ran just as fast as my legs would carry me toward camp." But camp

"As we ran, my mother and I heard Geronimo behind us, calling to the men to gather around him and make a stand to protect the women and children," Betzinez said. Thirty-two answered the call.

But others did not. Betzinez and his mother topped a hill and caught their breath on the far side. "Here we found about fifteen Apache warriors sitting under a tree smoking. These were the men who had ridden ahead that morning and had failed to warn us of the danger they saw. Thus they were partly to blame for our Warm Springs Indians being slaughtered. Here they were sitting well armed and with plenty of ammunition, yet doing nothing. I felt dreadfully ashamed of them. They never fired a shot, while a half mile away beyond the hill their fellow tribesmen and the women and children were being butchered."

Back in the open, Geronimo and the honorable warriors fought for the lives of the women and children, and their own. With the help of the women they dug a hole in the dry creek bed. "Here they made their stand in this rifle pit, in the center of which a little water, mixed with blood from the wounded, seeped in so that they could quench their thirst. The women also dug holes for other warriors in the bank of the little arroyo, around the center strong point. This made a good defensive position from which the men began shooting down the Mexican soldiers as fast as they appeared."

Yet the Mexicans fought bravely, realizing they had cornered Geronimo, the scourge of their country for decades. "Geronimo, this is your last day!" they shouted as they came. But the deadly fire of Geronimo and the warriors held them back. At noon, the firing from the Mexican side ceased. The soldiers disappeared.

Geronimo waited, suspecting a ploy. "Presently a young Indian woman a little way off, who was up in a mesquite tree, called to our men that the soldiers had all gone home," Betzinez said. Neither Geronimo nor the others recognized the woman's voice. One of the warriors wanted to shoot her, as a spy for the Mexicans. But Geronimo said no. In fact he never did discover who she was, or if she was a spy.

The Mexicans returned to the fray, attacking Geronimo's position more fiercely than ever. Yet the Apaches' bullets still kept them at a distance. The stalemate lasted through the afternoon. Finally the Mexicans set fire to the grass, hoping to burn the Apaches out. Things looked bad for Geronimo and the others, Betzinez recalled. "They were surrounded by the prairie fire, the circle of it drawing closer. The warriors asked the consent of the few women who were there to let them choke the small children so that they wouldn't give away their movements by crying." Consent was grimly given. "Then they all crawled through the fire and got away without being seen."

They had survived, barely. "All during the night, in our camp on the cold mountainside, we could hear people mourning and wailing for their relatives who had been killed or captured," Betzinez said. "We lost nearly half our families in this tragedy."

They trudged on. In a few days they reached the main camp of Juh's Netdahes, for whom Betzinez and the other surviving members of the Warm Springs band had no good feelings. "These were the outlaw Indians from whom had come the party who had driven us from the San Carlos reservation," Betzinez reiterated. They caused trouble wherever they went. "When they couldn't find anyone else to mistreat, they fought among themselves."

But in unity lay strength. "Several hundred people were now assembled in this one camp, seventy-five of them being first-line warriors," Betzinez observed. "This was the largest number of Apaches that had come together in many years. Many of the young boys and old men could also have been used as fighters if guns and ammunition had been available, but there were none for them. The older warriors were using single-shot Springfields of the Civil War pattern, while the younger ones were armed with repeating rifles — Winchesters and Marlins. In addition, many of the men had pistols and other miscellaneous firearms which had been taken in raids on the settlements or attacks on travelers on the lonely roads in Arizona and New Mexico."

The camp was high in the Sierra Madre, between formidable ridges to the east and west. It was hard to find, and harder to approach. Sentries kept watch for any pursuit. Finally the fugitives could relax. "For the first time in my life, I witnessed some returning Netdahe raiders perform what they called the Triumph Dance, which old-time Indians used to stage after they had come in from a successful foray," Betzinez said. "The men who had been on the raid got together in the center with the women in a circle around them. Then they sang at the top of their voices some kind of a chant of triumph and rejoicing. Afterwards they all danced for enjoyment." They moved the camp occasionally, as much to find forage for the animals as to evade detection. "We continued to enjoy peace, with no enemy to fear so far. Our group contained Chiricahua, Warm Springs, Mescalero, San Carlos, White Mountain and other Apaches, as well as a few Navajos and even some Mexican and white boys who had grown up to young manhood among the Indians. Some of them had married Indian women and had families. Mostly they were fully Indianized and made good, brave warriors."

Betzinez learned that Geronimo and Juh wanted to talk peace with the Mexicans at Casas Grandes, thirty miles away. Betzinez was skeptical. "I think that Geronimo was largely responsible for this, his motive being to get whisky, that great curse," he said. Yet the overture was made. Geronimo and Juh and some third of the whole band approached Casas Grandes, stopping a few miles outside the town. The leaders sent a woman who spoke Spanish into the town to request a meeting with the *alcalde,* or mayor.

The alcalde assented, and came out with a few soldiers as escort. "The smiling Mexicans told the Apaches that all past troubles were forgotten, there were no hard feelings, and that from now on they would be on friendly terms," Betzinez related. "They assured our leaders that it would be safe for all Indians to come into town to trade and to get acquainted. The town was wide open to them."

Geronimo and the others went into town and got thoroughly drunk. Nothing amiss happened, and they returned the next day. More drinking, and again nothing untoward. "The Indians were now completely off guard, satisfied that all was peace and friendliness," Betzinez remembered. That night most of the Apaches bedded down just outside the walls of the town. "During the night I could hear the drunken Indians in their camp, howling and dancing," said Betzinez, who kept his distance. He was soon glad he did. "Early next morning, while it was still dark, our 'true friends' the Mexicans stole into the camp where the Indians were lying around in a stupor and commenced killing them." Geronimo and Juh sobered up quickly and managed to get away, but many others did not.

Betzinez's swiftness afoot served him well once again. He tarried to help an old woman mount a horse to ride to safety, and consequently didn't make his own start until the Mexican soldiers were all around. "As I ran toward the hills, the bullets were cutting my flying shirt-tails to ribbons," he said. "A Mexican soldier was also running toward the hill trying to cut me off. So I dived into some tall Johnson grass. I had a hard time crawling through the thicket but presently came to a wagon trail which I followed to the river. Here I crossed to the west bank, found a few tracks leading away from the water, and followed them upstream until I finally overtook some other fleeing Apaches." With effort he located his mother and sister. "They were exceedingly glad to find that I had escaped without harm, because from the sound of the yelling and firing at Casas Grandes that morning, they were afraid that no one had gotten away."

Survivors of the Mexican attack at Casas Grandes straggled in for several days. When Geronimo and Juh concluded no more were coming, they decided to move the camp. Game animals had gotten scarce, and the women and children were growing weak from hunger. The band journeyed west and south to the headwaters of the Yaqui River, where a forbidding canyon slashed the mountains. "Our camp was on the eastern edge of this deep gorge, which with its vertical cliffs seemed to be impassable for some distance north and southwest of us," Betzinez said. "We camped on the brink of this canyon for quite a time, far from our enemies and in no danger." Betzinez and most of the others would have been happy to stay there, but Geronimo and Juh had other ideas. "They began to get restless and anxious to move deeper into the mountains. They were like true creatures of the wild, always sensing or anticipating danger." The members of the band, having lost nearly everything they owned, had little to pack. They started down the almost sheer face of the gorge. "We were cautioned especially about not dislodging loose rocks, always a danger to those who were ahead on the trail. The descent was made slowly and in a zig-zag course. It took us nearly a whole day to cross the canyon." But they made it down, and climbed up the canyon's opposite side.

In stages they edged back closer to civilization. Raiding was in Geronimo's blood, and, besides, the larder needed replenishing. There was a cattle ranch not far away.

A big moment arrived for Betzinez. "Geronimo asked me to go with him as his assistant. I decided to do so. I was now old enough to learn to be a warrior, and the way to learn was to go on several raids with an experienced man, taking care of his horses and equipment, standing guard, and cooking his meat for him. That was the Apache custom. No young man was to be trusted with weapons until he had served a long apprenticeship and was judged to be fully qualified. As a result of this system our warriors, though never numerous, were extremely capable and resourceful. They had been fully trained and tested. Now I was to get my chance."

Betzinez remembered his first raid well. "Arriving near the ranch, our warriors sent a small party to scout out the situation and find out if there were any soldiers at the hacienda. They came back to report that there were a great number of soldiers there. So it was decided to let this ranch alone. Just as this decision was made, we saw a whole company of soldiers behind us on a high hill.

We scattered like quail and hid among the briars and rocks. The soldiers marched behind a little knob whereupon we ran to the other side of it. Before we disappeared, the soldiers saw us and opened fire. Though no harm resulted I was filled with great fear and trembling. It made me wonder how many times in the future I would have to run like this with the bullets zipping past. To the wild Indians this was a small incident, just the beginning of a campaign. But I wasn't sure that I was going to enjoy going on the warpath."

Other raids were more successful, and Betzinez grew accustomed to his new responsibilities. A difference of opinion, however, caused a cleaving of the united Apache force. "Chief Juh and some of his people wanted to retreat back into the heart of the Sierra Madres where there was good shelter and refuge," Betzinez said. "Our enemies could scarcely follow us into such almost impassable regions. Chief Juh knew more about those mountains than any other man. A highly capable leader, he was particularly liked by his own band. Therefore he thought that he ought to lead his group, as well as other Indians who had no one to look after them, into that hideout."

Geronimo refused to join him. He wanted to move west, where the raiding was better. "It was admitted that this would be no journey for the weak," Betzinez said. Yet Geronimo drew a following. "The men who sided with Geronimo were mostly our kinsmen, so mother and I decided to go with them," Betzinez said. "Geronimo asked us not to go but we insisted, stating that we preferred hardship to safety. There were about eighty of us — men, women, and children — who chose to go with Geronimo. There were also three or four white boys and Mexicans who had been captured during Victorio's campaign of a few years before and who already had been adopted into the tribe."

Betzinez took pride in his decision. "In my judgment, the warriors who made up our party were the pick of the fighting men of the whole Apache tribe. All of them had seen much action in battle." And now he was one of them, or at least was becoming one of them.

The journey proved as difficult as described. The terrain was rough, the weather was bad, and a crossing of the Yaqui River was dangerous. Each night they tethered the horses and mules a couple of miles from the camp, so that anyone tracking them might find the animals but not them. Finally they transferred the animals' loads onto their own backs, and climbed a steep mountain to a flat place near the top, which was easier to guard against approach. They camped on the mountaintop for several days while Geronimo plotted raids into the southwestern portion of Sonora. Betzinez learned why: "Geronimo, who never forgot what the people of that state had done to his family, carried that bitterness in his heart all his life."

The warriors readied themselves for the campaign. They made new moccasins, sharpened their knives and greased their guns. The women and children were made secure on the mountaintop, with older boys serving as sentries to warn against intruders. If any came, the women and children wouldn't fight but rather disperse. Betzinez and his mother traveled partway with the warriors; their job was to receive cattle from the raiders, slaughter the animals and dry the beef, and transport the meat back to the camp. Within days they were hard at work slaughtering and drying; within a few days more they had delivered enough dried beef to last the band a month.

Although no outsider had detected their presence, Geronimo decided to move the camp again. They passed through a valley thickly populated by deer that seemed never to have encountered a human. "The deer just stood and watched us pass," Betzinez said. Many of the warriors were tempted to shoot the deer for a break from jerked beef. But Geronimo forbade it, lest the report of a gun echo through the mountains and reveal the band's presence. "The men all obeyed

Geronimo and didn't fire a shot," Betzinez said.

Geronimo found another hiding spot. This one would have to shelter the women and children for a month or more, while Geronimo led his warriors back to the United States to replenish the band's ammunition.

Betzinez hoped to be included among the raiders. "I wanted very badly to go along," he said. But he was denied. "The men refused to take any inexperienced young men or boys. It was to be a hard and dangerous trip, the group moving long distances at great speed and in constant danger from the troops. My cousin" — Geronimo — "told me that I would have to stay in camp to look after my mother and sister. Besides, there was a lot of sentry duty and other work to be performed."

The camp couldn't have been more pleasant. "There was plenty of water and abundant supplies of wild fruit," Betzinez said. "We lived here quite contentedly." Yet there was always an edge to the contentment, an underlying anxiety that surfaced, one day, at the sound of a gunshot. "At once the women and children were thrown into a panic. We had no protection and thought the enemy might be coming. Everyone ran from the camp and hid in the hills." From their hiding spots they saw two men approaching the camp. Fortunately these turned out to be two of their own, and calm settled in once more.

Weeks later the warriors returned. The cross-border raid had been brilliantly successful, yielding a large quantity of ammunition and numerous other items. At once preparations were made for a victory dance. "Soon we heard the beating of tom-toms and saw the women and girls gathering on the outer circle," Betzinez said. "The men were singing at the top of their voices rejoicing over their victories. Then the women began choosing their partners for the all-night dance. In the morning the men made valuable presents to their partners, things such as horses, saddles, bridles, blankets, or other useful articles."

A few days after the celebration, Geronimo did something that caused Betzinez and others to believe he had special powers. "Geronimo told us that Mexican soldiers were on our trail," Betzinez recounted. "He prophesied as to the exact moment they would appear. The next morning the women and children were, as usual, on the mountain top while the men were watching the back trail. Sure enough, just as Geronimo had predicted, Mexican soldiers appeared in the very place and at the exact time that Geronimo had foretold."

Uncanny or simply canny, Geronimo's prediction gave the Apaches an edge over the Mexicans, who were quickly routed. "Our men captured all the enemy's horses and did considerable other damage," Betzinez said, with familial pride in Geronimo's powers.

Betzinez and the women and children would have been happy for a break from the fighting and constant movement. But not Geronimo and the other leaders. "The warlike spirit of the Apaches couldn't stay quiet for very long," Betzinez observed. More raids and battles followed.

Betzinez observed Geronimo's style of leadership and remarked that the fifty-three-year-old still commanded by example. One campaign commenced at dawn, with Geronimo going first. "He started to trot, maintaining this pace for miles," Betzinez said. "Every man had to be in good shape to keep up this kind of travel." Geronimo held the pace all morning, inspiring warriors half his age to try to outdo the old man. "A little after noon Geronimo stopped for a breather, while others of us kept on going." Betzinez was pleased at his own performance. "Eight or ten of the younger warriors were running as if they were in a race, but I was right up with them," he said.

Geronimo had another premonition, Betzinez recalled. "Geronimo was sitting next to me with a knife in one hand and a chunk of beef which I had cooked for him in the other. All at once he dropped the knife, saying, 'Men, our people whom we left at our base camp are now in the hands of U.S. troops!

What shall we do?' This was a startling example of Geronimo's mysterious ability to tell what was happening at a distance. I cannot explain it to this day. But I was there and saw it."

At once they started back toward the camp, a hundred miles away. En route Geronimo had another vision. "Tomorrow afternoon as we march along the north side of the mountains, we will see a man standing on a hill to our left," he said. "He will howl to us and tell us that the troops have captured our base camp."

Betzinez continued the story: "We marched quite early the next morning, straight west through a wide forest of oaks and pines. About the middle of the afternoon we heard a howl from the hilltop to our left. There stood an Apache calling to us. He came down through the rocks to tell us that the main camp, now some fifteen miles distant, was in the hands of U.S. troops. General Crook with some cavalry and Indian scouts had taken all the rest of the Apaches into custody." Decades later, Betzinez remarked, "Thus the event which Geronimo had foretold when we were still several days' journey away, and had repeated the last night, came to pass as true as steel. I still cannot explain it."

Geronimo had his own recollection of his last campaign. He placed its beginning in a betrayal years before. "The chief of our tribe, Mangas Coloradas, went to make a treaty of peace for our people with the white settlement at Apache Tejo, New Mexico," he said. The army post at Apache Tejo was Fort McLane. "It had been reported to us that the white men in this settlement were more friendly and more reliable than those in Arizona, that they would live up to their treaties and would not wrong the Indians." Mangas was weary of war, and so with three other warriors he traveled to Fort McLane to hear what the whites had to say.

The commandant and the agent there explained that if Mangas brought in his people, they could live by the fort and receive beef, blankets and other provisions.

Mangas carried the offer back to the band. Geronimo was skeptical. "I did not believe that the people at Apache Tejo would do as they said, and therefore I opposed the plan," he recalled. But others, including Mangas, wanted to give it a try. A compromise was struck. Mangas and those who wanted to go in would do so, while Geronimo and the rest would remain aloof and watch the experiment from a distance. If the whites did what they pledged, Geronimo and the others might join the Mangas group near the fort.

The experiment was a disaster. Mangas was seized and imprisoned for the deaths of several whites killed in previous Apache raids. He was prodded — by hot bayonets, according to later accounts — to attempt escape, and as soon as he moved, he was shot and killed.

The murder confirmed Geronimo's distrust, and caused him to lead his band into the mountains lest a similar fate befall him. "While passing through the mountains, we discovered four men with a herd of cattle. Two of the men were in front in a buggy and two were behind on horseback. We killed all four, but did not scalp them; they were not warriors." They drove the cattle into the mountains, pitched a camp and started slaughtering the animals and drying the flesh.

Word of the killing of the four men got out, and soldiers tracked Geronimo's band and caught them at the camp. "The government troops were mounted and so were we," he said. "But we were poorly armed, having given most of our weapons to the division of our tribe that had gone to Apache Tejo, so we fought mainly with spears, bows, and arrows. At first I had a spear, a bow, and a few arrows; but in a short time my spear and all my arrows were gone. Once I was surrounded, but by dodging from side to side of my horse as he ran, I escaped. It was necessary during this fight for many of the warriors to leave their horses and escape on foot."

They regrouped two days later at an agreed-upon site fifty miles away. For a week they breathed more easily, yet the same soldiers found them again. "The fight lasted all day," Geronimo said. "But our arrows and spears were all gone before ten o'clock, and for the remainder of the day we had only rocks and clubs with which to fight." They held the soldiers off until dark, when they slipped deeper into the mountains. The next morning Geronimo sent out scouts, who determined that the soldiers had gone.

Again Geronimo and his followers caught their breath. But different troops descended upon them and caused another dispersal. "They killed seven children, five women and four warriors, captured all our supplies, blankets, horses, and clothing, and destroyed our tepees," Geronimo recalled. "We had nothing left; winter was beginning, and it was the coldest winter I ever knew."

He decided to join forces with the Warm

Springs Apaches headed by Victorio. "We had always been on friendly terms with this tribe, and Victorio was especially kind to my people," Geronimo said. They made the journey and received a generous welcome. "We stayed with them for about a year, and during this stay we had perfect peace. We had not the least trouble with Mexicans, white men or Indians."

Yet Geronimo couldn't live on the kindness of friends forever. "When we had stayed as long as we should, and had again accumulated some supplies, we decided to leave Victorio's band," Geronimo said. Victorio wouldn't let Geronimo's people depart without a feast. Four hundred Indians ate and danced for four days. "I do not think we ever spent a more pleasant time than upon this occasion," Geronimo said. "No one ever treated our tribe more kindly than Victorio and his band. We are still proud to say that he and his people were our friends."

As part of Ulysses Grant's peace process, Geronimo was invited by General Oliver Howard to Fort Apache for talks. Geronimo was favorably impressed. "He always kept his word with us and treated us as brothers," he said of Howard. "We never had so good a friend among the United States officers as General Howard. We could have lived forever at peace with him. If there is any pure, honest white man in the United States army, that man is General Howard. All the Indians respect him, and even to this day frequently talk of the happy times when General Howard was in command of our post."

Perhaps Geronimo was mistaken at the time, or perhaps he misremembered. Howard was a peace commissioner, not commander of the post or the district. And in the difference lay distress for the Apaches. It was one thing for Howard to make a peace treaty with Geronimo; it was quite another for the promises of that treaty to be carried out by the local commanders and agents.

At first they were carried out, and all was well. "When beef was issued to the Indians, I got twelve steers for my tribe, and Cochise got twelve steers for his tribe," Geronimo remembered. "Rations were issued about once a month, but if we ran out we only had to ask and we were supplied."

The good feeling eroded, though, as the old bad habits returned. The government in Washington got distracted, the agents and traders fiddled with the scales, and the Apaches got shortchanged. Geronimo was growing restless anyway, and he took his band back to Warm Springs in New Mexico.

They had hardly reached their destination when Geronimo and Victorio were summoned to the fort there. "The messengers did not say what they wanted with us, but as they seemed friendly we thought they wanted a council, and rode in to meet the officers," Geronimo said. A council was not on the schedule. "As soon as we arrived in town, soldiers met us, disarmed us, and took us both to headquarters, where we were tried by court-martial. They asked us only a few questions and then Victorio was released and I was sentenced to the guardhouse. Scouts conducted me to the guardhouse and put me in chains. When I asked them why they did this they said it was because I had left Apache Pass."

This was when all the Indians at Warm Springs were being forcibly removed to San Carlos, and Geronimo, in chains, made the same journey. He was eventually released from custody, but not before losing all trust in the word of U.S. officers.

His distrust made him vigilant for any sign of new betrayal. "In the summer of 1883, a rumor was current that the officers were again planning to imprison our leaders," Geronimo said. "This rumor served to revive the memory of all our past wrongs — the massacre in the tent at Apache Pass, the fate of Mangas Coloradas, and my own unjust imprisonment, which might easily have been death to me." An invitation to a council at Fort Thomas arrived. Geronimo and others of his band refused to have anything to do with it. "We did not believe that any good could come of this conference, or that there was any need of it; so we held a council ourselves, and fearing treachery, decided to leave the reservation. We thought it more manly to die on the warpath than to be killed in prison."

This breakout was the one that dragged Betzinez and his mother and sister along. The subsequent time on the run in Mexico made less impression on Geronimo, veteran of many campaigns, than it did on Betzinez, experiencing his first. "We ranged in the mountains of Old Mexico for about a year, then returned to San Carlos, taking with us a herd of cattle and horses," Geronimo summarized.

He was not well received. "Soon after we arrived at San Carlos, the officer in charge, General Crook, took the horses and cattle away from us," Geronimo said, still feeling the resentment he experienced at the time. "I told him that these were not white men's cattle, but belonged to us, for we had taken them from the Mexicans during our wars. I also told him that we did not intend to kill these animals, but that we wished to keep them and raise stock on our range. He would not listen to me, but took the stock."

Geronimo didn't like Crook or trust him. He wasn't surprised, after he left San Carlos for Fort Apache, to learn that Crook had ordered scouts and soldiers to arrest him. "If

I offered resistance they were instructed to kill me," he said, adding, "This information was brought to me by the Indians." He had no choice. "When I learned of this proposed action I left for Old Mexico, and about four hundred Indians went with me. They were the Bedonkohe, Chokonen, and Nedni Apaches. At this time Whoa" — Juh — "was dead, and Naiche was the only chief with me."

Geronimo's band headed for the Sierra Madre. Crook's troops trailed them, but it was the Apache scouts who found them. "We were camped in the mountains west of Casas Grandes," he said. "Here we were attacked by government Indian scouts. One boy was killed and nearly all of our women and children were captured." The captured included Geronimo's family except for one son, a warrior.

Geronimo led his people farther south. But there they ran into Mexican troops. "We skirmished with them all day, killing a few Mexicans, but sustaining no loss ourselves," he said.

The Mexicans persisted. They followed the Apaches and attacked their camp again. "This time the Mexicans had a very large army, and we avoided a general engagement," Geronimo said. "It is senseless to fight when you cannot hope to win."

The Apaches' predicament appeared dire.

"That night we held a council of war. Our scouts had reported bands of United States and Mexican troops at many points in the mountains. We estimated that about two thousand soldiers were ranging these mountains seeking to capture us. General Crook had come down into Mexico with the United States troops. They were camped in the Sierra de Antunez Mountains."

Crook's scouts brought a message saying the general wished to talk. Geronimo still distrusted him, but concluded he had no choice. "When I arrived General Crook said to me, 'Why did you leave the reservation?' "

Geronimo responded, "You told me that I might live in the reservation the same as white people lived. One year I raised a crop of corn, and gathered and stored it, and the next year I put in a crop of oats, and when the crop was almost ready to harvest, you told your soldiers to put me in prison, and if I resisted to kill me. If I had been let alone I would now have been in good circumstances, but instead of that you and the Mexicans are hunting me with soldiers."

Crook denied it. "I never gave any such orders," he said. "The troops at Fort Apache, who spread this report, knew that it was untrue."

Geronimo wasn't convinced, and never would be. "It was hard for me to believe him at that time," he said later. "Now I know that what he said was untrue, and I firmly believe that he did issue the orders for me to be put in prison, or to be killed in case I offered resistance."

Yet he had run out of options. "I agreed to go back with him to San Carlos."

But he changed his mind before he got there. "I feared treachery and decided to remain in Mexico," he said simply. Getting away was easy. "We were not under any guard at this time. The United States troops marched in front and the Indians followed, and when we became suspicious, we turned back." Geronimo felt no pangs of conscience on reneging on his word to Crook. "I have suffered much from such unjust orders as those of General Crook," he said two decades later. "Such acts have caused much distress to my people. I think that General Crook's death" — in 1890 — "was sent by the Almighty as a punishment for the many evil deeds he committed."

Nor was he disappointed to learn that Crook, upon being criticized for letting Geronimo get away, had asked to be relieved of his command. Yet Crook's replacement, General Nelson Miles, was no less determined in pursuing Geronimo, although Miles let his scouts and their officers handle the pursuit's strenuous labor. Mexican soldiers played a part as well. "We had skirmishes every day," Geronimo recalled about the Mexicans. "And so we finally decided to break up into small bands."

Geronimo's band included seven men and four women. He doubled back to the north, reentering the United States and heading for the mountains near Warm Springs. "We passed many cattle ranches, but had no trouble with the cowboys. We killed cattle to eat whenever we were in need of food, but we frequently suffered greatly for water. At one time we had no water for two days and nights and our horses almost died from thirst."

When he supposed that the American soldiers had left Mexico out of discouragement at not finding him there, he went south once more. He admitted engaging in a murder spree. "On our return through Old Mexico, we attacked every Mexican found, even if for no other reason than to kill," he said. "We were reckless of our lives, because we felt that every man's hand was against us. If we returned to the reservation we would be put in prison and killed; if we stayed in Mexico they would continue to send soldiers to fight us; so we gave no quarter to anyone and asked no favors."

Geronimo discovered that the American soldiers had *not* left Mexico but had tracked the other Apache bands, with whom he reunited his own. Skirmishes once more became a daily affair. "Four or five times they surprised our camp. One time they surprised us about nine o'clock in the morning, and captured all our horses, nineteen in number, and secured our store of dried meats. We also lost three Indians in this encounter."

Geronimo concluded that he couldn't win a war of attrition. First he sued for peace with the Mexicans, who stipulated that he and his people go back to the United States and never return. Geronimo agreed.

Then he sued for peace with the Americans. "There seemed to be no other course," he said. He told the Indian scouts he wanted to talk to General Miles. Meanwhile he and his band moved slowly north, toward the American border. The soldiers kept them in sight but did not attack.

Geronimo's offer to talk brought Miles from his Arizona headquarters to the border. He met Geronimo in Skeleton Canyon, just north of the international border.

"I went directly to General Miles and told him how I had been wronged, and that I wanted to return to the United States with my people, as we wished to see our families, who had been captured and taken away from us," Geronimo remembered.

Miles responded, according to Geronimo's recollection, "The President of the United States has sent me to speak to you. He has heard of your trouble with the white men, and says that if you will agree to a few words of treaty we need have no more trouble."

Geronimo's recollection continued: "General Miles told me how we could be brothers to each other. We raised our hands to heaven and said that the treaty was not to be broken. We took an oath not to do any wrong to each other or to scheme against each other. Then he talked with me for a long time and told me what he would do for me in the future if I would agree to the treaty. I did not greatly believe General Miles, but because the President of the United States had sent me word, I agreed to make the treaty, and to keep it."

He asked Miles what the treaty would consist of.

"I will take you under government protection," Miles said. "I will build you a house; I will fence you much land; I will give you cattle, horses, mules, and farming implements. You will be furnished with men to work the farm, for you yourself will not have to work. In the fall I will send you blankets and clothing so that you will not suffer from cold in the winter time. There is plenty of timber, water, and grass in the land to which I will send you. You will live with your tribe and with your family. If you agree to this treaty you shall see your family within five days."

Geronimo had heard such things before. "All the officers that have been in charge of the Indians have talked that way, and it sounds like a story to me," he told Miles.

"This time it is the truth," said Miles.

"General Miles," said Geronimo. "I do not know the laws of the white man, nor of this new country where you are to send me, and I might break their laws."

"While I live you will not be arrested," Miles promised, in Geronimo's recounting.

Geronimo agreed to the treaty. "We stood between his troopers and my warriors," he said. "We placed a large stone on the blanket before us. Our treaty was made by this stone, and it was to last until the stone should crumble to dust. So we made the treaty, and bound each other with an oath."

Miles offered advice. "My brother, you have in your mind how you are going to kill men, and other thoughts of war. I want you to put that out of your mind, and change your thoughts to peace."

Geronimo answered, "I will quit the war-path and live at peace hereafter."

Miles responded by sweeping a spot of ground clear with his hand and saying, "Your past deeds shall be wiped out like this, and you will start a new life."

Miles told his own version of the surrender. "I went down to Skeleton Canyon, near the Mexican line, and there met Lawton's command, with the Indians camped a short distance away," he wrote. "Geronimo came to me to ask what disposition would be made of him in case he surrendered. He said that if they were all to be killed he might as well die fighting at once. He prayed only that we would spare his life and those of his people. He was told that he must surrender as a prisoner of war and accept whatever disposition the government deemed best to make of him and his followers." Yet Miles offered reassurance: "The United States military authorities were not accustomed to kill their prisoners." Beyond that, he could not go. "Their future would depend upon the orders and decision of the President at Washington."

Miles grew more specific with Geronimo. "He was informed that I had directed General Wade to move all the Indians at the Apache Agency in northern Arizona out of the Territory, and that he and his people would be removed," he recalled. He justified the decision: "Indian depredations and atrocities had been endured long enough and must end forever in that country." Geronimo had no choice. "He was in no position to dictate terms. I explained to him the folly of contending against the military, with all its advantages of communication and transportation."

Geronimo observed the communication advantages Miles and the army enjoyed. "While watching a corporal use the heliostat and flash a message in a few seconds by the sun's rays a day's journey for his horse, he was struck with awe and amazement," Miles recalled. "He sent an Indian runner to Natchez" — Naiche — "who remained out in the mountains, to tell him that he was in the presence of a power he could not understand, and told Natchez to come in and come quick. He afterward stated that he had seen these flashes high up on the mountain peaks, but thought they were spirits and not men."

Naiche joined Geronimo shortly. "They then formally surrendered, and placed themselves entirely under our control," Miles said. "Soon after the council a violent thunderstorm swept over the country. As friend and foe were crowded under the very sparse shelter, I explained to Geronimo and Natchez that I hoped it was a good omen, that there was evidently a silver lining to that war cloud, and that the sunshine of peace would bless that land after the turmoil of relentless war."

The next day Miles and an escort of cavalry, with Geronimo and Naiche and four other leaders of the band under guard, set off for Fort Bowie, sixty-five miles away. Captain Lawton followed with the rest of the Apaches. On arrival, Geronimo and the others were informed that they were being sent to Florida. Miles claimed to be thinking of the welfare of the prisoners. "There was quite a demand at the time for the immediate trial and execution of the principal Indians," he said. A fair trial was out of the question. "It would have been impossible to have obtained an unprejudiced jury." Simply getting Geronimo out of Arizona alive wasn't easy. "So intense was the feeling against the Indians in that Territory that it was even suggested that the braces of the railroad bridges be destroyed in order to wreck the train conveying them to Florida," Miles said. "Under all the circumstances, I deemed it best to have all of the Apaches removed to a distant part of the country, not only those who had actually been in the field, but those at the agency, who had given aid and support and furnished supplies, ammunition and recruits with which to continue hostilities." In Arizona he could not guarantee their safety.

Geronimo's departure was a poignant moment, and a crucial one for the history of the Southwest, Miles said. "As they moved out under the escort of the Fourth Cavalry from Fort Bowie, the military band played 'Auld Lang Syne,' an appropriate finale to their departure from the country they had terrified for years." The white residents of the region took heart from Geronimo's banishment. "The capture and removal of all the Apaches from that country, and the establishment of permanent peace, occasioned universal rejoicing with the people of those Territories. Mines that had been closed and practically abandoned were then reopened, and the owners, who had not dared to travel except by night or with a strong escort, were free to go anywhere unmolested. The value of horse and cattle ranches increased fifty per cent."

Miles didn't mind boasting of the gratitude he was shown. "The people of Arizona and New Mexico, with marked kindness and generosity, presented me with a very handsome sword made by Tiffany. The Damascus blade, grip and large India star sapphire are the only parts of the sword and scabbard not solid gold."

■ ■ ■ ■

PART VI
OLD WARRIORS DIE

■ ■ ■ ■

Part VI
Old Warriors Die

40

Geronimo's surrender signaled the end of the war for America — the ten-thousand-year struggle for the territory that became the United States. Of all the tribes that trod the land between the Atlantic and the Pacific, between the Rio Grande and the Lake of the Woods, one had finally conquered, dispersed or outlasted the rest. The invaders from across the eastern ocean had taken four centuries to establish their dominion, but the deed was done. The invaders' diseases, their technology, and their numbers — which now surpassed sixty million, against a quarter million Indians — had been too much for the indigenes to withstand.

The invaders' victory was both more and less than it seemed. The end of the war divided the history of America into profoundly different epochs. During the war, violence had been the arbiter of disputes between peoples that were literally outlaws to each other; after the war, the rule of law —

the victors' law — prevailed. Violence didn't disappear; the end of the war didn't signal the dawn of a new age of human virtue. But where violence had been chronic, now it was sporadic, if sometimes still shocking. A hundred centuries of war gave way to a century — and counting — of peace. And peace made possible developments in the zone of former conflict that fostered the growth of communities that transformed the region beyond recognition.

The invaders' victory was less than it seemed in that though the land was conquered, the Indians retained a certain autonomy. Few of the tribes had vanished, though such a fate had often been predicted. None still controlled all the land they once claimed, but most controlled *some* land. Only in rare cases, involving particular individuals, had the surrender agreements been unconditional; the rest involved negotiation, committing both the government and the tribes to specific actions in the future. In the broadest sense, the war for America had been a struggle of competing tribes to determine how they would get along. That challenge remained.

Most of the war-ending treaties committed the Indians to try to live like white people. The Lakotas would stop their raiding. Geronimo would become a farmer. This commitment made sense — indeed was inescapable — if one accepted the premise that the Indians' traditional way of life was a thing of the past. The reservations were too small, and wrongly sited, for the Indians to support themselves by hunting. The choice was between farming, including ranching, and the government dole. And white voters wouldn't sustain the dole forever.

When efforts to nudge the Indians toward farming failed, the government pushed harder. Henry Dawes of Massachusetts was chairman of the Senate Committee on Indian Affairs; observing the dismal performance of the reservation system, he sponsored a measure to do away with it. The basic problem with the reservations, Dawes reasoned, was that the land there was held by tribes in common. Energetic Indians couldn't claim the fruits of their labors, which had to be shared with the lazy. The reservations practiced a kind of communism, which Americans didn't like even then.

Dawes's idea was to deliver land titles to individual Indians, to foster individual initiative. As approved into law, the 1887 Dawes Act gave each head of an Indian family 160 acres, with another 40 acres for each child. Single adults received 80 acres, as did orphan children. When the allotment process was finished, the reservations would be dissolved and the tribal governments would no longer be recognized by the United States government. The Indians would be ordinary citizens of the United States, subject to its laws and the laws of the states. In the Indian Territory, the de-recognition of tribal governments would allow the establishment of a new state, Oklahoma.

Henry Dawes truly felt for the Indians, as did the many philanthropists who spoke in support of his measure. Perhaps they would have carried the day unaided. Yet the silent support of another group brought additional votes. Simple arithmetic meant that the area of the individual allotments, multiplied by the number of recipients, would total far less than the acreage of the reservations. The land left over would revert to the public domain and become available for white settlement.

The Dawes program didn't work out as advertised. Land was indeed allotted, and the excess opened to settlement. In the Indian Territory, the opening triggered a land rush not unlike the gold rush to California. But prosperity didn't follow, at least not for Indians, who failed to respond like the capitalists-in-waiting they had been assumed to be. Many of the reservations became mired in poverty. During the Great Depression of the 1930s, when conditions reached a nadir, Congress reversed itself, restoring tribal governments and funding the reacquisition of lost lands.

Yet the effort to remake Indians in the image of whites wasn't a total failure. Even decades before the Dawes Act, some Indians had assimilated into white culture. Few rose as far as Ely Parker, Grant's aide and Indian commissioner, but others found their niches. In the case of Parker, he might have assimilated too well. After leaving Grant's administration, he moved to Connecticut, where his neighbors shared their secrets of Wall Street investing. Parker followed their lead, and with many of them was ruined in the financial panic of 1873.

Another Parker — the Comanche Quanah — similarly made the transition to the values and norms of the whites. Whether being the son of a white mother helped is unclear, but in time Quanah Parker became a wealthy rancher in Oklahoma, a pillar of the state respected by Indians and whites alike. Theodore Roosevelt sought out Quanah Parker when visiting Oklahoma; the president picked his brain on Republican prospects there, and invited him along on a wolf hunt.

Other Indians in Oklahoma thrived, too. Many Cherokees understandably held a grudge against the government, but after the trauma of their tribe's forced removal, they rebuilt in the Indian Territory the same kind of progressive, prosperous society they had created in Georgia. Their population rebounded, until by the twenty-first century they were the most numerous of all the tribes in America, with three hundred thousand members, ten times as many as at first contact with whites.

Death came for them all, victors as well as vanquished. John Bourke met Crazy Horse shortly after the Lakota leader's surrender. Bourke was invited to the meeting by a former captive of the Lakotas who had been adopted into the tribe and lately had served as an interpreter for the army. At the approach of Bourke and the interpreter, Crazy Horse remained seated on the ground before his tepee, ignoring them. But when the interpreter addressed Crazy Horse in Lakota and said a few words Bourke didn't understand, his demeanor changed. "He looked up, arose, and gave me a hearty grasp of his hand," Bourke recalled. "I saw before me a man who looked quite young, not over thirty years old" — in fact Crazy Horse was in his early to mid-thirties — "five feet eight inches high, lithe and sinewy, with a scar in the face. The expression of his countenance was one of quiet dignity, but morose, dogged, tenacious and melancholy. He behaved with stolidity, like a man who realized he had to give in to Fate, but would do so as sullenly as possible."

From observing Crazy Horse and hearing about him from others, Bourke inferred his standing among his fellow Lakotas. "All Indians gave him a high reputation for courage and generosity," Bourke said. "In advancing upon an enemy, none of his warriors were allowed to pass him. He had made hundreds of friends by his charity towards the poor, as it was a point of honor with him never to keep anything for himself, excepting weapons of war. I never heard an Indian mention his name save in terms of respect."

Yet Crazy Horse grew restive in the confines of the reservation. Rumors circulated that the Lakotas were going to be sent to the Indian Territory, causing Crazy Horse and others to fear a betrayal of the terms of their surrender. His captors, anticipating trouble, circulated spies — Lakotas themselves — among Crazy Horse's followers. Crazy Horse felt more betrayed than ever. "He found his purposes detected and baffled at every turn," Bourke remarked. "His camp was filled with soldiers, in uniform or without, but each and all reporting to the military officials each and every act taking place under their observation. Even his council-lodge was no longer safe: all that was said therein was repeated by someone, and his most trusted subordinates, who had formerly been proud to obey unquestioningly every suggestion, were now cooling rapidly in their rancor towards the whites and beginning to doubt the wisdom of a resumption of the bloody path of war."

George Crook, having been transferred north from Arizona, called a council of all the Lakota chiefs on the reservation. Crazy Horse declined to attend, apparently believing that the others were conspiring against him.

Whether or not they had been doing so before the meeting with Crook, they certainly did so there. "General Crook informed the Indians that they were being led astray by Crazy Horse's folly, and that they must preserve order in their own ranks and arrest Crazy Horse," Bourke recalled. "The chiefs deliberated and said that Crazy Horse was such a desperate man, it would be necessary to kill him. General Crook replied that that would be murder and could not be sanctioned." He said he had enough troops to deal with Crazy Horse and any of his followers. Yet he reiterated that the Lakotas themselves should make the arrest. "It would prove to the nation that they were not in sympathy with the non-progressive element of their tribe."

Likely Crazy Horse got wind of what the chiefs had said to Crook. And doubtless he reasoned that murder was more in keeping with Lakota ideas of norm enforcement than incarceration. Rather than wait for the murderers to come, he broke away from the reservation.

Crook, prepared for this, ordered pursuit.

Catching Crazy Horse was not difficult, with spies all around. He was arrested and taken to Fort Robinson, near the reservation.

The commandant of the fort filed a report on what happened next. "When he was put in the guardhouse, he suddenly drew a knife, struck at the guard, and made for the door," the report said. "Little Big Man, one of his own chiefs, grappled with him, and was cut in the arm by Crazy Horse during the struggle. The two chiefs were surrounded by the guard, and about this time Crazy Horse received a severe wound in the lower part of the abdomen, either from a knife or bayonet, the surgeons are in doubt which. He was immediately removed, and placed in charge of the surgeons, and died about midnight."

The details of the death raised questions. Was Crazy Horse set up? Could the surgeons really not tell a knife wound from a bayonet thrust? The former presumably would have been inflicted by an Indian, the latter by a soldier. Was Crook sincere in saying murder would not be allowed, or was he speaking simply for the record? Did Bourke, an admirer of Crook, record the meeting with the chiefs accurately? If everything Bourke and the post commandant reported was true, did Crazy Horse simply decide to go down fighting?

No one ever knew for certain. Yet in death Crazy Horse retained the respect he had earned in life. "Crazy Horse was one of the great soldiers of his day and generation," Bourke wrote. "He never could be the friend of the whites, because he was too bold and warlike in his nature." The career of Crazy Horse summarized much of the battle for the northern plains. "As the grave of Custer marked the high-water mark of Sioux supremacy in the trans-Missouri region," Bourke said, "so the grave of Crazy Horse, a plain fence of pine slabs, marked the ebb."

Satanta, the Kiowa chief, met a similar end, except that where Crazy Horse came to consider the Sioux reservation a prison, Satanta's prison was an actual prison. A visitor to the Texas penitentiary at Huntsville described the Kiowa chief, then serving his sentence for the murder of the seven teamsters on Salt Creek. "In the corridor of the penitentiary I saw a tall, finely formed man, with bronzed complexion and long, flowing brown hair, a man princely in carriage, on whom even the prison garb seemed elegant," the visitor said. "His face was good; there was a delicate curve of pain at the lips, which contrasted oddly with the strong Indian cast of his other features. Although he is much more than 60 years old, he hardly seemed 40, so erect, elastic, vigorous was he. When asked if he ever expected liberation, and what he would do if it should come, he responded,

'Quien sabe?' " — who knows? — "with the most stoical indifference."

In fact, Satanta was released, on parole, by Texas governor E. J. Davis, to the disgust of William Sherman. But he violated the terms of the parole, associating with the Kiowas who battled Billy Dixon and the other buffalo hunters at Adobe Walls. As part of the campaign against those Kiowas, Satanta was returned to Huntsville and prison. He lasted four years before the confinement became more than he could bear. "On October 11, 1878, Satanta committed suicide by throwing himself from the second story of the prison hospital, from the effects of which he died within a few hours," reported the superintendent of Texas prisons. No credible evidence surfaced then or later to cast doubt on the report.

Sitting Bull spent the nine years after his surrender living on the Sioux reservation. In the autumn of 1890, James McLaughlin was the agent at the Standing Rock agency, closest to Sitting Bull's village. McLaughlin observed how time had passed the Lakota leader by; a new generation was emerging, with new ideas, leaving the old men behind. "The younger element among the Indians was quite ready to accept the inevitable, to abandon the god of things as they ought to be for the god of things as they are,"

McLaughlin recalled. "The unreconstructed element among the old leaders, who saw their power vanishing in the dawn of the day of the man who works, whose pride of place and chieftainship was being swallowed by Indians who had come to know the meaning of earning their bread by the sweat of their brows — this element was standing for a voiceless and purposeless protest."

But from the Far West came a millenarian cult whose Paiute messiah promised to revive the old ways, and with it the influence of the old men. This cult of the Ghost Dance offered Sitting Bull a chance to become relevant once more. McLaughlin decided to investigate. "I arrived at Sitting Bull's camp about three o'clock in the afternoon," he said. "It was a Sunday, and I was not surprised to see a large gathering of people in front of the houses, six in number, in the center of the camp. Many of the Indians had come on a visit, but they had brought their tents with them as though to make a prolonged stay." The dancing engrossed the gathering; none paid attention to McLaughlin. "The madness of the dance demonstrated the height of distraction to which the dancers had obtained," he observed.

McLaughlin was fascinated. "The sacred pole about which the people danced was set at some distance from the houses," he said. "Around this pole a ring of men, women, boys, and girls, about one hundred in all, were dancing." McLaughlin recognized some of the children as pupils in the reservation schools who had stopped coming to class recently. "The dancers held each other's hands, and all were jumping madly, whirling to the left about the pole, keeping time to a mournful crooning song, that sometimes rose to a shriek as the women gave way to the stress of their feelings." McLaughlin had seen many other Indian dances, and this wasn't like those. "There was nothing of the slow and precise treading which ordinarily marks the time of the Indian religious dance." The dancers had reached the point of exhaustion. "Occasionally a poor creature, overcome by the fatigue of the exciting dance, would fall out of the ring, which was immediately closed up, and the circling to the left continued, the dancers paying no attention to the fallen one."

One woman fell out of the circle and rolled a short distance away. Two Indians, apparently overseers of the dance, picked her up and carried her to a tepee. McLaughlin hadn't particularly noticed the tepee, but he did now. "Within the wide-open flaps of the wigwam, seated on a sort of throne, was my old friend, Sitting Bull," McLaughlin wrote. "He was very much thinner than a few weeks previous." McLaughlin wondered if he was ill. "But the look he gave me showed that his wits were not dulled or his hatred and envy lessened by the rigors of his life." At Sitting Bull's side sat a Lakota named Bull Ghost, elaborately dressed, who acted as Sitting Bull's spokesman to the dancers.

Sitting Bull and Bull Ghost conferred quietly. Then Bull Ghost announced to the dancers that the woman had fallen into a trance and was communicating with the spirit world. The dancing stopped so that dancers might hear any message from that other side. "Sitting Bull performed certain incantations, then leaned over and put his ear to the woman's lips," McLaughlin recalled. "He spoke in a low voice to his herald, Bull Ghost, who repeated to the listening multitude the message which Sitting Bull pretended to receive from the unconscious woman. Sitting Bull had all the tricks of the fake spiritualist. Knowing his people intimately, he knew all about the dead relatives of the woman who had fainted, and he made a tremendous impression on his audience by giving them personal messages from the Indian ghosts, who announced with great unanimity that they were marching east to join their living kinsmen the following spring."

McLaughlin concluded that the Ghost Dance phenomenon would end badly. He realized that the present moment was no time to talk to Sitting Bull, and so he rode off to the home of a friendly Indian, the head of the local Indian police, where he spent the night. He returned the next morning at daybreak. Sitting Bull's camp was quiet. "I entered Sitting Bull's house and found two of his wives and four of his children within," McLaughlin said. The women said Sitting Bull was taking a bath, and offered to get him. McLaughlin told them not to bother; he would come back later. He was just leaving when he encountered Sitting Bull. They shook hands, and McLaughlin asked Sitting Bull to step aside, where they could speak privately.

McLaughlin shared his concern about the direction of things. "I recalled all my connection with him and showed him my friendly inclination," he recounted. "I recalled the time when he had sent word to me from Alberta, Canada, by Bishop Marty, to help him make his peace with the authorities before he surrendered. I reminded him of the talk we had when he was a prisoner on the steamer *General Sherman,* leaving Fort Yates for Fort Randall in September 1881, and how he had been given his liberty through following my advice." McLaughlin recited other evidence of his goodwill toward Sitting Bull and his people. "I went on, Indian-like, through the little list of things I had done for him at various times, and wound up by reproaching him for leading the people astray and setting them back for years, besides making it certain that they would all be punished."

McLaughlin watched Sitting Bull's reaction. "His eyes flashed, but the old man did not break out in a rage as I expected he might," McLaughlin wrote. "On the contrary, he seemed to be impressed." But his attitude shifted when he noticed the crowd that had gathered around. "Then he indulged in a harangue. He spoke only of the new faith, and how he believed in it and the good that it would bring to his people."

"I interrupted him to say that it would bring them all into trouble, and that he well knew it to be rubbish," McLaughlin said.

Sitting Bull said McLaughlin knew nothing about it. He started to get angry. But then he made McLaughlin an offer. "You go with me to the agencies of the West, and let me seek for the men who saw the Messiah, and when we find them, I will demand that they show him to us. And if they cannot do so, I will return and tell my people it is a lie."

McLaughlin shook his head. "I told him that such an attempt would be like catching up with the wind that blew last year," he wrote. He said Sitting Bull should come to the agency and spend the night there, so that he — McLaughlin — could talk sense into him and prevent the disaster that was looming.

Sitting Bull didn't reject the idea outright,

but said he had to consult his people. "I will talk to the men tonight, and if they think it advisable I will go to the agency next Saturday," he said.

"That was the last time I saw Sitting Bull alive," McLaughlin recounted.

Apparently the men did not think it advisable for Sitting Bull to go to the agency. Or perhaps Sitting Bull never consulted them, using them as a dodge to get McLaughlin to go away. In any event, he did not show up on Saturday, and the Ghost Dance fervor intensified. McLaughlin's informants related that Sitting Bull was preparing to leave the reservation. McLaughlin's alarm grew, and it was shared by the army officers in the vicinity. Nelson Miles, now commanding the division that included the Standing Rock agency, sent an order by William Cody — Buffalo Bill — that Sitting Bull should be arrested.

"Such a step at present is unnecessary and unwise, as it will precipitate a fight which can be averted," McLaughlin replied. "I have matters well in hand, and when proper time arrives can arrest Sitting Bull by Indian police without bloodshed."

McLaughlin persuaded the army to stand down. His plan was to wait until a biweekly ration day. Nearly all the Indians would be at the agency, forty miles from Sitting Bull's camp. Sitting Bull would be essentially alone, and could be arrested without trouble.

But before the next ration day, Nelson Miles changed his mind. Rumblings among other Lakotas made him unwilling to risk a breakout that would put Sitting Bull at their head. He ordered the post commander to arrest Sitting Bull. McLaughlin persuaded the commander to let the Lakota police handle the arrest, lest seizing Sitting Bull spark an explosion then and there.

"Thirty nine regular policemen, and four specials, under Bull Head and Shave Head, rode into the Sitting Bull camp the next morning," McLaughlin related. "Some of the men had traveled immense distances to rendezvous at the home of Lieutenant Bull Head, and all were firmly determined to make the arrest." They agreed with McLaughlin that a breakout would bring down the wrath of the army again, and they wanted to do whatever they could to avert it. The camp was quiet, but not deserted as it would have been on ration day. The arrival of the policemen on horseback awakened some of the residents, yet Bull Head directed his men to Sitting Bull's tent without incident.

Bull Head, Shave Head and eight others entered Sitting Bull's tent. Sitting Bull asked them what they wanted. They said they had come to arrest him.

He made no resistance, merely asking time to get dressed. He sent one of his wives to another tent to get his best clothes. He asked that his best pony be fetched.

Whether this was a deliberate play for time, McLaughlin never knew. But when Bull Head and Shave Head escorted Sitting Bull out of the tepee, they encountered resistance. McLaughlin, who doubtless got the story from some of the policemen, described the situation. "It was in the gray of the morning when they came out," he wrote. "They stepped out into a mass of greatly excited ghost-dancers, nearly all armed and crowding about the main body of the police, who had held the way clear at the door."

Still, Sitting Bull himself made no resistance. But one of his sons, Crow Foot, stepped in front of him and denounced him. "You call yourself a brave man," Crow Foot said. "You have declared that you would never surrender to a blue-coat. And now you give yourself up to Indians in blue uniforms."

The taunt struck home. Sitting Bull stiffened and straightened. McLaughlin, speaking secondhand regarding the details of the moment, but firsthand of his knowledge of Sitting Bull, wrote, "The last moment of Sitting Bull's life showed him in a better light, so far as physical courage goes, than all the rest of it. He looked about him and saw his faithful adherents — about one hundred and sixty crazed ghost-dancers — who would have gone through fire at his bidding. To submit to arrest meant the end of his power, and probable imprisonment. He had sure news from Pine Ridge that he, only, was needed to head the hostiles there in a war of extermination against the white settlers. He made up his mind to take his chance, and screamed out an order to his people to attack the police."

Shooting erupted. Bull Head was hit at once, mortally. But as he fell, he turned and shot Sitting Bull in the torso. Another policeman, Red Tomahawk, simultaneously shot Sitting Bull in the face. Sitting Bull was dead by the time his body slumped to the ground.

Before the shooting ended, Shave Head and four other policemen had been killed, along with Bull Head. Eight of the ghost dancers died and several others were wounded.

McLaughlin credited the bravery of the Indian policemen for preventing the deaths of many more of their Lakota kin. "Sitting Bull's medicine had not saved him, and the shot that killed him put a stop forever to the domination of the ancien régime among the Sioux of the Standing Rock reservation," he said.

McLaughlin was right about Sitting Bull's death ending the old regime. But the collateral damage was appalling. The melee at Standing Rock heightened the alarm among army officers in the vicinity, and when soldiers attempted to disarm a camp of Lakotas on Wounded Knee Creek, shooting erupted that didn't end until more than two hundred Lakotas, including many women and children, lay dead in the snow.

The surrender of Joseph caused Sherman to salute Nelson Miles, Oliver Howard and their subordinates for their work in running down the Nez Perce fugitives. It also prompted him to reflect on the accomplishment of those Indians. "Thus has terminated one of the most extraordinary Indian wars of which there is any record," Sherman wrote. "The Indians throughout displayed a courage and skill that elicited universal praise; they abstained from scalping, let captive women go free, did not commit indiscriminate murder of peaceful families which is usual, and fought with almost scientific skill, using advance and rear guards, skirmish lines and field fortifications."

And yet, however brilliant and praiseworthy in its execution, the flight of the Nez Perce could not be condoned. "They would not settle down on lands set apart for them ample for their maintenance, and, when commanded by proper authority, they began resistance by murdering persons in no manner connected with their alleged grievances," Sherman said.

For this reason, he ordered Joseph and the captives sent to Fort Leavenworth in Kansas, where they would be held as prisoners of war until spring. At that time, they should be relocated permanently to the Indian Territory. "They should never again be allowed to return to Oregon or to Lapwai," Sherman said.

Sherman had his way with regard to Joseph. The four hundred who surrendered with him languished in the Indian Territory. To natives of the mountains of the Pacific Northwest, the plains of Oklahoma were intolerably hot and unhealthy. "We were not badly treated in captivity," recalled one of them, Yellow Wolf. "We were free as long as we did not come this way, towards Idaho and Wallowa. We had schools. Only the climate killed many of us. All the newborn babies died, and many of the old people too. It was the climate. Everything so different from our old homes. No mountains, no springs, no clear running rivers." They called their new home the Hot Place. "All the time, night and day, we suffered from the climate. For the first year, they kept us all where many got shaking sickness, chills, hot fever. We were always lonely for our old-time homes."

Joseph campaigned for his people's release. His success in making himself America's favorite Indian eventually won permission for them to return to the Northwest, where they were divided between the Lapwai reservation in Idaho and the Colville reservation in northeastern Washington.

Most of the Nez Perce were given a choice between the two reservations, but not Joseph. He was ordered to Colville, on grounds that the anger hadn't cooled among the Idaho whites whose relatives had been killed at the start of the eastward flight. The Indian Bureau and the army couldn't guarantee his safety, and they didn't want his murder to provoke another uprising.

Joseph lived out his days on the Colville reservation. He died in 1904 of heart failure. Some called it the heartbreak of exile.

Phil Sheridan's heart failed, too. He was still on active duty, at the age of fifty-seven, but the duty didn't keep him from writing his memoirs, which he finished just before suffering a series of heart attacks. The last one killed him, in August 1888. The posthumous publication of his book allowed him, as it were, to tell his side of the controversies of his life, including those relating to the Indian wars, without having to answer to his critics.

George Crook died two years later, also of a heart attack. Ironically, perhaps, he was exercising, lifting weights at his home, when stricken. He was sixty-one, and had Sherman's old position in command of the army of the West. As stern as Crook had been with Indians who did not accept the new order in America, his honesty won the respect of those who did. He fought for better treatment of the Apaches who had assisted him in the pursuit of Geronimo. A fellow officer accompanied Crook on a visit to a crowded military post where some of his former scouts were confined. "A young Indian with long, black hair saw the General, and before we had finished breakfast, Chihuahua was outside, waiting," the officer wrote in his diary. Chihuahua had been one of the scouts. "He seemed overjoyed to see the General. Kaetena joined him, and we walked over to the Indian village, which was just outside the gate of the fort. They live in little log cabins which had been built for them. At the gate was a considerable number of Indians waiting for us. Chato came out, and went up to the General, and gave him a greeting that was really tender. He took him by the hand, and with his other made a motion as if to clasp him about the neck. It was as if he would express his joy but feared to take such a liberty. It was a touching sight. The Apaches crowded about the General, shaking hands and laughing in their delight. The news spread that he was there, and those about us shouted to those in the distance, and from all points they came running in until we had a train of them moving with us."

Regard for Crook extended beyond the Apaches. Red Cloud later reflected on Crook's post-surrender efforts on behalf of the Lakotas, and on the meaning of Crook's death. "General Crook came," said Red Cloud. "He, at least, had never lied to us. His words gave the people hope. He died. Their hope died again. Despair came again."

41

Sherman retired from active duty in 1884.
He had reached the mandatory retirement
age for army officers, sixty-four, and though
he might have petitioned for a waiver, and
doubtless received it, he chose to give his
juniors their chance at the top job.

He might still have become commander in
chief — that is, president. Republicans felt
their grip on the White House slipping, and
they anxiously sought another hero-general
to keep them at the trough of donations and
spoils. The Republican convention that year,
meeting in Chicago, wrangled over potential
nominees until the delegates were worn out.
One of their leaders finally sent a telegram to
Sherman, saying they had no choice but to
nominate him, and he had no choice but to
accept and be elected. Sherman's son Thomas
was with his father in the library of the Sherman home in St. Louis when the telegram
arrived. "Without taking the cigar from his
mouth, without changing his expression,"

Tom Sherman recalled, "while I stood there by his side trembling, my father wrote the answer, 'I will not accept if nominated, and will not serve if elected.' He tossed it over to me to be handed to the messenger, and then went on with the conversation he was engaged in."

Sherman's reply set a standard for political refusals, and it relieved him of the demands of politics once and for all. He had never been shy about speaking his mind, on no subject more than the intersection of politics and military affairs. Addressing the graduates of a military academy in Michigan, Sherman said there would always be need for their talents, unfortunately. Governments pursued peace, safety and happiness for their people, but rarely attained these for long. The United States was no different from other countries in this respect. "Though peace has ever been the controlling genius of our laws and institutions, we are forced to admit that what ministers to the happiness of one class or race often works to the misery of another, and that with Indians, Mexicans, foreign nations and our own people, we have had four great wars and innumerable small ones," Sherman told the graduates. "To accomplish safety in the past, every generation of men since the settlement of this continent has been compelled to take up arms for defense or offense, and it would be foolish to conclude that the future will be different from the past."

War was written into the human soul, Sherman said. "Wars have been, are now, and ever will be as long as man is man. You cannot prognosticate that we are to be wiser and better than those who have gone before us, and that because there is now or in sight no just cause for war, that we are therefore to be forever exempt. Wars do not usually result from just causes, but from pretexts. There probably never was a just cause why men should slaughter each other by wholesale, but there are such things as ambition, selfishness, folly, madness in communities as in individuals, which become blind and bloodthirsty, not to be appeased save by havoc, and generally by the killing of somebody else than themselves. This should not be, but is the fact, and we are no exception to the general rule."

Sherman's grim view of human nature didn't keep him from enjoying humanity's lighter side. He and his wife moved to New York a few years after his retirement, in part so he could indulge his taste for theater and music. He became a regular, and often had to acknowledge the applause of audiences as he entered. Wednesday, February 4, 1891, found him at a special performance of the opera *Poor Jonathan* at the Casino Theatre. Invitations had gone out to all the military officers in the city, and Sherman was pleased to join the group. He sat in a proscenium box with other officers, and again acknowledged the cheers.

But the air was frigid that night, and though he seemed well on going to bed, he awoke on Thursday with symptoms of a cold. He nonetheless attended the wedding of the daughter of a fellow officer.

On Friday he felt worse. He canceled a dinner at the Union League Club, a favorite spot of his. On Saturday his throat was painfully sore and swollen. An army surgeon ordered him to stay in bed. Sunday, Sherman's seventieth birthday, brought consultations with a second doctor, who diagnosed pneumonia and prescribed rest and prayer. Members of the family were summoned. Brother John, the senator, arrived on Monday, along with some of Sherman's children.

The appearance of Senator Sherman alerted reporters that the general was sick, and the death watch commenced. On Thursday Sherman surprised those at his home by rising from bed to take his sole sustenance at this point, whiskey and milk. But he soon returned to bed, and continued to decline. On Saturday afternoon, at two o'clock, Sherman's personal aide stepped to the door of the house and told the crowd that had gathered, "It is all over."

Shortly afterward, a fellow officer told of a premonition Sherman had shared. The two men were talking about the approaching anniversary of the birth of General Grant, in April. Sherman replied, "I shall be dead and buried by that time." The officer tried to treat Sherman's remark as a joke, but Sherman was serious. "Sometimes when I get home from an entertainment or banquet, especially on these wintry nights, I feel as if I were a very sick man," Sherman said. "I suppose that I shall catch cold some night, and I shall go to bed never to leave it."

Sherman's death inspired others to recall other words he had spoken. The saying most often attributed to him was "War is hell." Admirers cited it as evidence of Sherman's acuity, despisers as a signal of his intent. One of the latter, a Confederate veteran, remarked, "General Sherman said, 'War is hell.' Few, if any, did more than William Tecumseh Sherman to make war hell, and if I had to guess, I should say that ere now Sherman knows all about the horrors of both — war and hell."

Sherman himself claimed not to recall saying it. He set a researcher to work to find evidence that he had. The researcher turned up nothing of substance. Neither in his letters nor in his reported speeches did the phrase appear. Yet various people swore they'd heard him say it, during the Civil War or after. The most elaborate memory contended that in his speech to the Michigan cadets, Sherman had extemporized. "I've been where you are now and I know just how you feel," he said, according to one in the audience. "It's entirely natural that there should beat in the breast of every one of you a hope and desire that some day you can use the skill you have acquired here. *Suppress it!* You don't know the horrible aspects of war. I've been through two wars and I know. I've seen cities and homes in ashes. I've seen thousands of men lying on the ground, their dead faces looking up at the skies. I tell you, war is hell!"

Another version had Sherman at the Ohio state fair in 1880, speaking familiarly to Union veterans of the Civil War. "The war now is way back in the past," he told the vets. "And you can tell what books can not. When you talk, you come down to the practical realities just as they happened." He looked at the proud men in their clean uniforms, and remarked the respectful glances they received. "You all know this is not soldiering here. There is many a boy here today who looks on war as all glory, but, boys, it is all hell. You can bear this warning voice to generations yet to come. I look upon war with horror, but if it has to come, I am there."

Geronimo had survived decades of war, and he survived decades of peace. He remembered the transition from the one to the other clearly, and bitterly. "When I had given up to the government, they put me on the Southern Pacific Railroad and took me to San Antonio, Texas, and held me to be tried by their laws," he said. "In forty days they took me from there to Fort Pickens, Florida." Fort Pickens was near Pensacola. "Here they put me to sawing up large logs. There were several other Apache warriors with me, and all of us had to work every day. For nearly two years we were kept at hard labor in this place and we did not see our families until May, 1887. This treatment was in direct violation of our treaty made at Skeleton Canyon."

Geronimo complained, but the authorities who listened cited Nelson Miles's recollection of the surrender agreement, that Geronimo was a prisoner of war. He and the other Apaches were moved to Alabama. "We stayed five years and worked for the government," Geronimo said. "We had no property, and I looked in vain for General Miles to send me to that land of which he had spoken; I longed in vain for the implements, house, and stock that General Miles had promised me." The climate took its toll. "We were not healthy in this place," Geronimo said. "So many of our people died that I consented to let one of my wives go to the Mescalero Agency in New Mexico to live." The government was willing to relocate women and children; the warriors still had to be punished for killing the many settlers who had died at Apache hands.

Eventually, though, the government let Geronimo and the others move to Fort Sill, in the Indian Territory. This was an improvement. "Captain Scott was in charge, and he had houses built for us by the government," Geronimo said. "We were also given, from the government, cattle, hogs, turkeys and chickens." The hogs did the Indians no good, as they didn't like pork and didn't know how to tend the animals. "We did better with the turkeys and chickens, but with these we did not have as good luck as white men do. With the cattle we have done very well, indeed, and we like to raise them. We have a few horses also, and have had no bad luck with them."

Geronimo turned seventy in the Indian Territory. "When General Miles last visited Fort Sill, I asked to be relieved from labor on account of my age," he said. Miles remembered this part of the surrender agreement. "He said I need not work anymore except when I wished to, and since that time I have not been detailed to do any work. I have worked a great deal, however, since then, for, although I am old, I like to work and help my people as much as I am able."

Geronimo and the others re-created at Fort Sill as much of their old life as they could. When his daughter Eva became a woman, he hosted a grand celebration. "Invitations were issued to all Apaches, and many Comanches and Kiowas, to assemble for a grand dance on the green by the south bank of Medicine Creek, near the village of Naiche, former chief of the Chokonen Apaches, on the first night of full moon in September." Preparations included the mowing of a large circle in the grass of the prairie. This would serve as the dancing space. Food was laid in, sufficient for two days of feasting by all the guests.

The event began with a religious ceremony. "First Eva advanced from among the women and danced once around the camp fire; then, accompanied by another young woman, she again advanced and both danced twice around the camp fire; then she and two other young ladies advanced and danced three times around the camp fire; the next time she and three other young ladies advanced and danced four times around the camp fire; this ceremony lasted about one hour. Next the medicine men entered, stripped to the waist, their bodies painted fantastically, and danced the sacred dances. They were followed by clown dancers, who amused the audience greatly."

The dancing space was then opened to all. "The members of the tribe joined hands and danced in a circle around the camp fire for a long time. All the friends of the tribe were asked to take part in this dance, and when it was ended many of the old people retired."

The space was turned over to the young men and women, who began their own dance. "The warriors stood in the middle of the circle and the ladies, two-and-two, danced forward and designated some warrior to dance with them. The dancing was back and forth on a line from the center to the outer edge of the circle. The warrior faced the two ladies, and when they danced forward to the center he danced backward: then they danced backward to the outer edge and he followed facing them. This lasted two or three hours and then the music changed. Immediately the warriors assembled again in the center of the circle, and this time each lady selected a warrior as a partner. The manner of dancing was as before, only two instead of three danced together. During this dance, which continued until daylight, the warrior could propose marriage, and if the maiden agreed, he would consult her father soon afterward and make a bargain for her."

Geronimo was pleased with the celebration for Eva. "Perhaps I shall never again have cause to assemble our people to dance, but these social dances in the moonlight have been a large part of our enjoyment in the past, and I think they will not soon be discontinued, at least I hope not," he said.

In 1904 Geronimo was invited to attend the Louisiana Purchase Exposition in St.

Louis, to commemorate America's great westward leap. The organizers thought Geronimo and other famous Indians would lend authenticity. "When I was at first asked to attend the St. Louis World's Fair, I did not wish to go," Geronimo recalled. "Later, when I was told that I would receive good attention and protection, and that the President of the United States said that it would be all right, I consented." Geronimo was curious to see the fair, and he discovered that the fairgoers were curious to see him. He worked out an arrangement. "I sold my photographs for twenty-five cents, and was allowed to keep ten cents of this for myself." The photographer and the fair split the rest. "I also wrote my name for ten, fifteen, or twenty-five cents, as the case might be, and kept all of that money. I often made as much as two dollars a day, and when I returned I had plenty of money — more than I had ever owned before."

Inconspicuous agents of the Indian Bureau kept watch on Geronimo, lest he get ideas about wandering away. They also kept an eye on fairgoers, lest some hold his history against him.

At Fort Sill, Geronimo converted to Christianity. "Since my life as a prisoner has begun, I have heard the teachings of the white man's religion, and in many respects believe it to be better than the religion of my fathers," he wrote. He said he had always prayed, and believed Providence protected him. But his new faith gave his beliefs new focus. "In our primitive worship, only our relations to Usen and the members of our tribe were considered as appertaining to our religious responsibilities. As to the future state, the teachings of our tribe were not specific, that is, we had no definite idea of our relations and surroundings in after life. We believed that there is a life after this one, but no one ever told me as to what part of man lived after death." This was still something of a puzzle. "I have seen many men die; I have seen many human bodies decayed, but I have never seen that part which is called the spirit; I do not know what it is; nor have I yet been able to understand that part of the Christian religion."

Christianity conveyed a confidence Geronimo's traditional beliefs had not. "We held that the discharge of one's duty would make his future life more pleasant, but whether that future life was worse than this life or better, we did not know, and no one was able to tell us. We hoped that in the future life family and tribal relations would be resumed. In a way we believed this, but we did not know it."

Geronimo said that Christianity would be good for all his people. "I believe that the church has helped me much during the short time I have been a member. I am not ashamed to be a Christian, and I am glad to know that the President of the United States is a Christian, for without the help of the Almighty I do not think he could rightly judge in ruling so many people. I have advised all of my people who are not Christians, to study that religion, because it seems to me the best religion in enabling one to live right."

If Geronimo perceived possible earthly advantages to conversion, besides the heavenly prize that might await him, he would hardly have been the first. It might or might not have been coincidence that the sect he joined was the Dutch Reformed Church, the one to which Theodore Roosevelt belonged. The conversion got Roosevelt's notice, and Geronimo was invited to ride in Roosevelt's inaugural parade in 1905. Geronimo procured an interview with the president. "Take the ropes from our hands," he said. "Take the ropes from the hands of my people and let us go back to the home of our fathers. We are tired of living in a strange country and want to go home."

Roosevelt shook his head. "I cannot do so now," he said. "We must wait a while and see how you and your people act. You must not forget that when you were in Arizona, you had a bad heart. You killed many of my people. You burned villages. You stole horses and cattle." Roosevelt said he was keeping watch on the Apaches. "We must wait a while before we can think of sending you back to Arizona."

Disappointed but not despairing, Geronimo continued to lobby for permission for his people to return to their native country. "There is a great question between the Apaches and the government," he wrote in his memoirs. "For twenty years we have been held prisoners of war under a treaty which was made with General Miles, on the part of the United States Government, and myself as the representative of the Apaches. That treaty has not at all times been properly observed by the Government, although at the present time it is being more nearly fulfilled on their part than heretofore. In the treaty with General Miles we agreed to go to a place outside of Arizona and learn to live as the white people do. I think that my people are now capable of living in accordance with the laws of the United States, and we would, of course, like to have the liberty to return to that land which is ours by divine right. We are reduced in numbers, and having learned how to cultivate the soil would not require so much ground as was formerly necessary. We do not ask all of the land which the Almighty gave us in the beginning, but that we may have sufficient lands there to cultivate. What we do not need we are glad for the white men to cultivate."

The Apaches were currently living on the lands of the Kiowas and Comanches. These lands suited those tribes, but not the Apaches. "Our people are decreasing in numbers here, and will continue to decrease unless they are allowed to return to their native land," Geronimo said. "Such a result is inevitable. There is no climate or soil which, to my mind, is equal to that of Arizona. We could have plenty of good cultivating land, plenty of grass, plenty of timber and plenty of minerals in that land which the Almighty created for the Apaches. It is my land, my home, my fathers' land, to which I now ask to be allowed to return. I want to spend my last days there, and be buried among those mountains. If this could be I might die in peace, feeling that my people, placed in their native homes, would increase in numbers, rather than diminish as at present, and that our name would not become extinct."

Geronimo dreamed of the land of his birth. "I know that if my people were placed in that mountainous region lying around the headwaters of the Gila River, they would live in peace and act according to the will of the President," he said. "They would be prosperous and happy in tilling the soil and learning the civilization of the white men, whom they now respect. Could I but see this accomplished, I think I could forget all the wrongs that I have ever received, and die a contented and happy old man."

For most of his life he had fought for his people's right to live as their fathers had lived. Defeat had compelled him to acknowledge that the matter was beyond his control. And so he had become a supplicant. "We can do nothing in this matter ourselves," he said. "We must wait until those in authority choose to act." He hoped the authorities would act soon. But if not soon, then eventually. "If this cannot be done during my lifetime — if I must die in bondage — I hope that the remnant of the Apache tribe may, when I am gone, be granted the one privilege which they request: to return to Arizona."

Geronimo did not live to see his people returned to their land. He died at Fort Sill in early 1909, of the same malady that felled Sherman. He fell from his horse on a winter night and lay in the cold for several hours before he was found. Pneumonia set in, and carried him off. He was almost eighty at the time of his death.

After his death, his followers at Fort Sill were offered the chance to join the Mescalero Apaches on their reservation in New Mexico. Some accepted the offer; others chose to remain in Oklahoma.

Nelson Miles stayed in the army for two decades after the surrender at Skeleton Canyon, finally succeeding to Sherman's office as commanding general. He retired during the presidency of Theodore Roosevelt, and lived into the presidency of Calvin Coolidge. He reflected on his time in the West, and on the men who had left their mark there. "Geronimo showed a daring and natural military instinct which, developed under favorable conditions, should have accomplished wonders in the field," Miles said. "He is one of the most remarkable men, white or red, I have ever met." Geronimo's visage showed his indomitable character. "His square chin I have only once seen duplicated, in the face of General Sherman." The pairing seemed so obvious that Miles employed it elsewhere, slightly modified. "He was one of the brightest, most resolute, determined-looking men that I have ever encountered," he said of Geronimo. "He had the clearest, sharpest dark eye I think I have ever seen, unless it was that of General Sherman."

SOURCES

Prologue

the war they found in progress there: Lawrence Keeley, *War Before Civilization: The Myth of the Peaceful Savage* (1996), and Stephen Leblanc, *Constant Battles: The Myth of the Peaceful, Noble Savage* (2003), effectively dispel any lingering notions that America was a peaceful Eden before the arrival of the Europeans.

PART I · THE MAKING OF THE WARRIOR

1.

Geronimo's people: James L. Haley, *The Apaches* (1981), affords insight into the history and culture of the Apaches. Robert M. Utley, *Geronimo* (2012), is the best biography of the famous warrior.
"As a babe . . . never seen a white man":

Geronimo's Story of His Life, transcribed and edited by S. M. Barrett (1906), 17–34.

2.

"When I came along . . . number four to six": *Memoirs of General William T. Sherman* (1889 ed.), 1:11–17. There are several good biographies of Sherman; Robert G. Athearn, *William Tecumseh Sherman and the Settlement of the West* (1956), focuses on the general's career in the West.

3.

"Without a timely": Monroe special message to Congress, Jan. 27, 1825, American Presidency Project, presidency.ucsb.edu.
"The condition . . . so great a calamity": Jackson annual message, Dec. 8, 1829, American Presidency Project.
"The evil . . . unavailing": *Speech of Mr. Everett, of Massachusetts, on the Bill for Removing the Indians* (1830), 46.
"In negotiating . . . gratitude and joy": Jackson annual message, Dec. 6, 1830, American Presidency Project.
"We were hedged in": George W. Harkins letter in the Natchez *Weekly Courier,* Dec. 2, 1831.
"John Marshall has made": H. W. Brands, *Andrew Jackson* (2005), 493.

4

"He soon initiated . . . make a good state":
Sherman, *Memoirs,* 1:19–26.

5.

"Being at peace . . . revenge upon Mexico":
Geronimo's Story, 43–46.
"Cochise, their chief . . . scalping the slain":
Ibid., 47–54.

6.

"Everything on shore . . . whole civilized
world": Sherman, *Memoirs,* 1:46–69.
"The white man . . . of men to avert": Peter
Burnett address, Jan. 6, 1851, https://
governors.library.ca.gov/addresses/s_01
-Burnett2.html.

7.

"War is cruelty . . . old homes at Atlanta":
Sherman to James Calhoun et al., Sept. 12,
1864, in J. T. Headley, *The Great Rebellion:
A History of the Civil War in the United States*
(1866), 2:342–44.

8.

"The whites were always trying": Big Eagle in "As Red Men Viewed It: Three Indian Accounts of the Uprising," edited by Kenneth Carley, *Minnesota History,* September 1962, 129–30.

"The war with the South . . . in my place": Ibid., 131–32.

"The daughter of Mr. Schwandt": Judith Kreiger testimony in Charles S. Bryant and Abel B. Murch, *A History of the Great Massacre by Sioux Indians in Minnesota, Including the Personal Narratives of Many Who Escaped* (1872 ed.), 300–301. The most thorough account of the Dakota uprising is Gary Clayton Anderson, *Massacre in Minnesota: The Dakota War of 1862, The Most Violent Ethnic Conflict in American History* (2019).

"Dear Sir": Little Crow to Henry Sibley, Sept. 7, 1862, in *The Rebellion Record: A Diary of American Events,* edited by Frank Moore (1867), 7:247.

"You have murdered": Sibley to Little Crow, undated, in *Rebellion Record,* 7:247.

"Let us exterminate": Sibley report, Sept. 8, 1862, in *Rebellion Record,* 7:248.

"The horrible massacres": Pope to Sibley, Sept. 28, 1862, *The War of the Rebellion: A Compilation of the Official Records of the*

Union and Confederate Armies, series 1, vol. 13 (1885), 686.

"Please forward": Lincoln to Pope, Nov. 10, 1862, *Collected Works of Abraham Lincoln,* edited by Roy P. Basler (1953), 5:493.

"The only distinction": Pope to Lincoln, Nov. 11, 1862, in *Collected Works,* 5:493n.

"I hope": Ramsey to Lincoln, Nov. 10, 1862, in *Collected Works,* 5:493n.

"Anxious to not act": Lincoln to Senate, Dec. 11, 1862, American Presidency Project.

"President in fine spirits": Ramsey diary, Nov. 23, 1864, in Marion Ramsey Furness, "Governor Ramsey and Frontier Minnesota: Impressions from His Diary and Letters," *Minnesota History,* December 1947, 328.

9.

"What shall I do": Evans in Dee Brown, *Bury My Heart at Wounded Knee: An Indian History of the American West* (1970), 79.

"Kill and scalp all!": Testimony of S. E. Brown, *Condition of the Indian Tribes: Report of the Joint Special Committee Appointed Under Joint Resolution of March 3, 1865* (1867), Appendix, 71.

"How many Indians . . . sense of the word": Testimony by John S. Smith, *Condition of the Indian Tribes,* Appendix, 41–42.

"I was aware . . . Colonel J. M. Chivington":

Testimony of James D. Connor, *Condition of the Indian Tribes,* Appendix, 53. The name of the deponent might have been James D. Cannon: the same testimony, almost word for word, was attributed a witness identified as Cannon. Ibid., 57.

10.

"All Indian men . . . toward these Indians": Carleton to Carson, Oct. 12, 1862, *Condition of the Indian Tribes: Report of the Joint Special Committee, Appointed Under Joint Resolution of March 3, 1865* (1867), A100.
"All the other Apaches . . . against the Mexicans": *Geronimo's Story,* 55–65.

PART II · THE CAMPAIGN BEGINS

11.

"The utter destruction": Sherman to Grant, Oct. 9, 1864, *Official Records,* 1:39(3):162.
"My thoughts and feelings . . . fatal to themselves": Sherman, *Memoirs,* 2:411–12.
"There seems to be": Sherman to Grant, May 7, 1866, in *The Papers of Ulysses S. Grant,* edited by John Y. Simon (1967–2009), 16:157.
"Kearny is made up . . . the law allows": Sherman to Grant, May 14, 1866, in *Pa-*

pers, 16:158.

"Some of the posts . . . for existence": Sherman to Grant, June 22, 1866, in *Papers,* 16:162.

12.

"He has thoroughly . . . small garrisons": Sherman to Grant, Sept. 30, 1866, in Senate Executive Document 13, 40th Congress, 1st Session, 3–4.

"I propose . . . herein stated": Sherman to Grant, undated, in Grant to Edwin Stanton, Jan. 15, 1867, in ibid., 17–18.

"The protection of the Pacific railroad": Grant to Stanton, Jan. 15, 1867, in ibid.

"Friends . . . I am for war!" Red Cloud in Charles A. Eastman (Ohiyesa), *Indian Heroes and Great Chieftains* (1918), 14–16. Eastman was an eastern Sioux who recorded the memories of Indians on the plains.

"I have had today . . . butchery beyond precedent": Carrington to P. St. George Crooke, Dec. 21, 1866, Senate Executive Document 13, 40th Congress, 1st Session, 30–31.

"I do not yet . . . of this case": Sherman to Grant, Dec. 28, 1866, in ibid., 27.

"The Indians must be . . . at all hazards": Sherman to Cyrus Comstock, Dec. 29, 1866, in ibid., 28.

"Knowing your anxiety . . . my last letter": Sherman to Grant, Jan. 28, 1867, with extract of letter from unnamed sergeant, in ibid., 34–36.

13.

"All the troops . . . for their conduct": Sherman for Grant (to George K. Leet), Mar. 18, 1867, Senate Executive Document 7, 40th Congress, 1st Session.
"If fifty Indians": Sherman to Edwin Stanton, June 17, 1867, in ibid., 121.
"We the military . . . on their hands": Sherman to Hancock, Jan. 26, 1867, in ibid., 41.
"just right . . . exterminated": Grant to Stanton, Feb. 1, 1867, in ibid., 40–41.
"One of the greatest . . . means of subsistence": Bogy to Orville Browning, Jan. 23, 1867, Senate Executive Document 13, 40th Congress, 1st Session, 18–20.
"That the belt . . . they will yet exist": Ibid.
"My idea . . . during this session": Bogy to Browning, Feb. 11, 1867, in ibid., 39–40.

14.

"Mr. Seward": Arthur C. Parker, *The Life of General Ely S. Parker* (1919), 102–3.
"I am glad to see": Ibid., 133.
"In compliance . . . these purposes": Parker

to Grant, Jan. 24, 1867, in Senate Executive Document 13, 40th Congress, 1st Session, 42–49.

15.

"State to this commission . . . for so doing": *Proceedings of the Great Peace Commission of 1867–1868,* edited by Vine Deloria, Jr., and Raymond Demallie (1975), 10–21.

16.

"The Indians . . . their hearts glad": Henry M. Stanley, *My Early Travels and Adventures in America and Asia* (1895), 1:198–207.
"Friends . . . first of November," Ibid., 208–12.
"Perfect silence . . . absented himself": Ibid., 213–14.

17.

"Over $150,000": Stanley, *My Early Travels,* 257–58.
"Of one thing . . . civil department": *Report to the President by the Indian Peace Commission,* Jan. 7, 1868, House of Representatives Executive Document 97, 40th Congress, 2nd Session, 15–20.

18.

"The commissioners . . . to our own country": *Proceedings of the Great Peace Commission,* 120–24.

"I have now been . . . case admits of": Sherman to John Sherman, June 11, 1868, in *The Sherman Letters: Correspondence Between General and Senator Sherman from 1837 to 1891,* edited by Rachel Sherman Thorndike (1894), 318–19.

"Mr. Tappan": Sherman, *Memoirs,* 2:436.

19.

"General Sherman": *Proceedings of the Great Peace Commission,* 173.

"Red Cloud affected . . . the young braves": Ibid., 173–76.

"Father . . . all lies": *New York Times,* June 1, 1870.

Red Cloud had no better luck: *New York Times,* June 10, 1870.

"My brothers . . . said to you": *New York Times,* June 17, 1870.

20.

"The peace . . . policy today": *Memoirs of General William T. Sherman,* 2:436–37.

"Members of Congress": Ibid., 2:443.

"I never felt so troubled": Sherman to Grant,

Feb. 14, 1868, Ibid., 2:431.

21.

"Our food . . . our six-shooters": *Personal Memoirs of P. H. Sheridan* (1888), 1:27–30.

"They were a pitiable lot": Ibid., 44–46.

"In reply . . . from my memory": Ibid., 86–88.

"Do all the damage": Grant to Sheridan, Aug. 26, 1864, *The War of the Rebellion: A Compilation of the Official Records of the Union and Confederate Armies* (1880), ser. 1, vol. 43, pt. 2, p. 202.

"I have destroyed": Sheridan to Grant, Oct. 7, 1864, in ibid., 308.

"I do not hold": Sheridan, *Personal Memoirs,* 1:487–88.

"Congress had delegated . . . in the campaign": Ibid., 2:285–301.

"The first night out": Ibid., 310–11.

"A ride . . . years of age": De B. Randolph Keim, *Sheridan's Troops on the Borders: A Winter Campaign on the Plains* (1870), 142–50.

"But before going . . . horrible butcheries": Sheridan, *Personal Memoirs,* 2:471–73.

"This party . . . was destroyed": Ibid., 473–74.

PART III · ADOBE WALLS AND LAVA BEDS

22.

"Left San Antonio . . . totally depopulated": Marcy journal, May 2–17, 1871, excerpts in Sherman Papers, Library of Congress.

"I hear": Sherman to Reynolds, May 10, 1871, Sherman Papers.

"I have seen . . . Kiowas to be": Sherman to Reynolds, May 15, 1871, Sherman Papers.

"Of course . . . to stop it": Sherman to Reynolds, May 18, 1871, Sherman Papers.

23.

"This morning": Marcy journal, May 18, 1871, Sherman Papers.

"Five mules lie dead": MacKenzie to Sherman, May 19, 1871, Sherman Papers.

"Passed today": Marcy journal, May 20, 1871.

"Crossed Red River": Marcy journal, May 21, 1871.

"a most benevolent . . . of the fort": Marcy journal, May 23, 1871.

"Yes . . . led it myself": Lawrie Tatum, *Our Red Brothers and the Peace Policy of President Ulysses S. Grant* (1899), 116–17.

"Satanta, seeing" . . . allowed to leave: Marcy journal, May 27, 1871.

24.

"They must not be mobbed": Sherman to commanding officer at Fort Richardson, May 28, 1871, Sherman Papers.

"It will": Sherman to Grierson, June 8, 1871, Sherman Papers.

"I wish to send . . . must die": James Mooney, *Calendar History of the Kiowa Indians* (Seventeenth Annual Report of the Bureau of American Ethnology to the Secretary of the Smithsonian Institution, 1895-96 [1898]), 329–32.

"This is a novel . . . and the entire evidence": Lanham argument in Henry Smythe, *Historical Sketch of Parker County and Weatherford, Texas* (1877), 267–72.

"I cannot speak . . . a big fire": Satanta testimony, in Smythe, 273–74.

"Permit me to urge": Tatum to Sherman, May 29, 1871, in Smythe, 274–75.

"I would have petitioned": Soward to Davis, July 10, 1871, in Smythe, 275–76.

"Knowing as I do . . . worth the experiment": Sherman to Delano, Apr. 23, 1871, Sherman Papers.

"You are in error . . . should be taken": Sherman to Davis, Feb. 16, 1874, Sherman Papers.

25.

"Between Lawrence . . . in marksmanship": *Life and Adventures of "Billy" Dixon,* compiled by Frederick S. Barde (1914), 24–87.

"I always did" . . . on the way back: Ibid., 87–186.

"Choosing a point . . . thriving trade": Ibid., 187–99.

"I spread my blankets" . . . and died: Ibid., 200–33.

26.

"At Fort Hays . . . made productive": Nelson A. Miles, *Serving the Republic: Memoirs of the Civil and Military Life of Nelson A. Miles* (1911), 110–18.

"They believe . . . easily obtainable": Ibid., 119.

"Never . . . be more careful": Ibid., 122–23.

"Leaving camp . . . Adobe Walls": *Life and Adventures of "Billy" Dixon,* 255–78. Years later the government tried to revoke Dixon's Medal of Honor on the grounds that he was a hired scout rather than a regular soldier; he refused to give it back, saying he had earned it.

"The only country . . . best ally": Miles, *Serving the Republic,* 125–28.

27.

"Both are fully competent": Sherman for Secretary of War, Jan. 6, 1873, in *Official Copies of Correspondence Relative to the War with Modoc Indians in 1872-73,* Feb. 10, 1874, House of Representatives Executive Document 122, 43rd Congress, 1st Session, 25.

"Use your authority": Grover to Canby, Dec. 7, 1872, in ibid., 32.

"Aside from": Canby to Grover, Dec. 6, 1872, in ibid., 32.

"I do not think": Canby to Schofield, Dec. 10, 1872, in ibid., 33.

"At this distance": Sherman for Belknap, Jan. 16, 1873, in ibid., 46.

"Colonel Wheaton": Canby for Sherman, Jan. 20, 1873, in ibid., 46.

"This leaves some parts": Canby for Sherman, Jan. 20, 1873, in ibid., 46–47.

"We attacked": Wheaton to Canby, Jan. 19, 1873, in ibid., 50–51.

"I have been": Wheaton to Canby, Feb. 7, 1873, in ibid., 55.

"It is the desire": Sherman to Canby, Jan. 30, 1873, in ibid., 64.

"Let all defensive measures": Sherman to Canby, Jan. 31, 1873, in ibid., 65.

"In late operations": Canby for Sherman, Feb. 4, 1873, in ibid., 67.

"If the authority": Delano to A. B. Meacham,

Feb. 18, 1873, in ibid., 68.

"All parties": Sherman to Canby, Mar. 6, 1873, in ibid., 69–70.

"I sent word": Canby to Sherman, Mar. 8, 1873, in ibid., 70.

"The Modocs": Canby to Sherman, Mar. 11, 1873, in ibid., 70.

"It is manifestly desired": Sherman to Canby, Mar. 13, 1873, in ibid., 70–71.

"The utmost patience": Canby to Sherman, Mar. 14, 1873, in ibid., 71.

"wisdom and discretion": Sherman to Canby, Mar. 14, 1873, in ibid., 71–72.

"The last moment": Canby to Sherman, Mar. 16, 1873, in ibid., 72.

"He is so impressed": Sherman to Canby, Mar. 24. 1873, in ibid., 73.

"Had an unsatisfactory meeting . . . better results": Canby for Sherman, Mar. 24, 1873, in ibid.

"He is of the opinion": Canby to Sherman, Mar. 28, 1873, in ibid., 75.

"We intend . . . it is reasonable": Jeff C. Riddle, *The Indian History of the Modoc War* (1914), 58–61.

"We on our side . . . come to terms": Ibid., 62–67.

"My people, I am old . . . I will do it": Ibid., 69–72.

"Tell the peace-makers . . . in this world": Ibid., 76–79.

"My dear wife": A. B. Meacham, *Wigwam and*

War-Path (1875), 470.
"Good morning . . . in plain view": Riddle, *Indian History*, 79–85.
"My Modoc friends" . . . already gone: Ibid., 87–95.

28.

"I hope to hear": Sherman to Schofield, Apr. 13, 1873, *Official Copies of Correspondence Relative to the War with Modoc Indians*, 77.
"Your dispatch": Sherman to Gillem, Apr. 12, 1873, *New York Times*, Apr. 15, 1873.
"The Indians have murdered": Delano quoted in *New York Times*, Apr. 15, 1873.
"The army has no 'policy' . . . hope for peace": Sherman to Herbert Preston, Apr. 17, 1873, Sherman Papers.
"Thus the tribe": Sherman to Belknap, June 3, 1873, *Official Copies*, 84–85.
"I had already . . . worst of the band": Davis to Schofield, June 5, 1873, in Schofield to Sherman, June 7, 1873, in ibid., 87.
"It is to be regretted": Sherman to Belknap, June 7, 1873, in ibid., 88.

PART IV · BEYOND THE GREASY GRASS

29.

"What do you know . . . again subsided": Sheridan to Sherman, Mar. 25, 1875, *New York Times,* Mar. 27, 1875.

"All Bismarck": *New York Times,* Sept. 4, 1874.

"Although I have . . . the Rosebud": Sheridan to Sherman, Mar. 25, 1875, *New York Times,* Mar. 27, 1875.

"It is very thin . . . avenge his death": Sherman in *St. Louis Globe,* Apr. 21, 1875, reproduced in *New York Times,* Apr. 26, 1875.

"I was born . . . for their dead": She Walks With Her Shawl in *Lakota and Cheyenne: Indian Views of the Great Sioux War, 1876– 1877,* compiled and edited by Jerome A. Greene (1994), 42–46.

"I was a strong young man . . . We will go": One Bull in *Lakota and Cheyenne,* 54–59.

30.

"At 9:25 p.m. . . . be abolished": Reno to E. W. Smith, July 5, 1876, *Annual Report of the Secretary of War, 1876,* 476–79.

"It is time": *Chicago Tribune,* July 7, 1876.

"All through the West": *New York Times,* July 12, 1876.

"an American citizen . . . from our path": Phillips in *New York Herald,* July 19, 1876.

"Several days ago . . . statute law": Sherman to Foster Tappan, July 21, 1876, Sherman Papers.

"I have not . . . Yellowstone country": Sherman in *New York Times,* Aug. 4, 1876.

"I have waited . . . catalogue of heroes": Sherman to Mrs. George A. Custer, August 11, 1876, Sherman Papers.

31.

"On the top . . . accept them": Miles, *Serving the Republic,* 137–59.

32.

"General Sherman": *New York Times,* Apr. 1, 1876.

"I certainly was . . . selling positions": Sherman interview in *St. Louis Republican,* reproduced in *New York Times,* Mar. 6, 1876.

"My friends . . . your mother": Joseph, "An Indian's Views of Indian Affairs," *North American Review,* April 1879, 415–19.

"It was a test case . . . spared nobody": C. E. S. Wood, "Chief Joseph, the Nez Percé," *Century Magazine,* May 1884, 135–42.

"We had no knowledge . . . dead in our hands": Joseph, "An Indian's Views," 428.

"The two old Nez Perces": Wood, "Chief Joseph," 141.

"My people were divided . . . *never would have surrendered*": Joseph, "An Indian's Views," 429.

"Tell General Howard": Wood transcript in *New York Times,* Nov. 16, 1877.

PART V · THE TRAIL TO SKELETON CANYON

33.

"It was a cold . . . for a month": John G. Bourke, *On the Border with Crook* (1892), 2, 5–6, 17–18, 34–37, 107.

34.

"Will the Department Commander": James R. Hastings, "The Tragedy at Camp Grant in 1871," *Arizona and the West* (1959), 1:150.

"A great amount . . . work well done": Paper by William S. Oury, read to the Society of Arizona Pioneers, Apr. 6, 1885, in Thomas Edwin Farish, *History of Arizona* (1915), 2:271–80.

"On my arrival": Testimony by C. B. Briesly, Sept.16, 1871, *Report of the Commissioner of Indian Affairs for the Year 1871* (1872), 72.

"So sudden . . . Papagos and Mexicans": Whitman to J. G. C. Lee, May 17, 1871, in *Report of the Commissioner,* 71.

In time a hundred men: Documents relating to the trial and the Camp Grant massacre generally can be found at Shadows at Dawn, https://www.brown.edu/Research/Aravaipa/index.html, which complements the book *Shadows at Dawn: A Borderlands Massacre and the Violence of History* (2008), by Karl Jacoby.

"that glorious and memorable morning": Oury paper, in *History of Arizona,* 2:282.

35.

"The occupation": Sherman to Belknap, Jan. 7, 1870, in Robert Wooster, " 'A Difficult and Forlorn Country': The Military Looks at the American Southwest, 1850–1890," *Arizona and the West* (1986), 28:339.

"When General Crook . . . the Indian himself": Bourke, *On the Border with Crook,* 108–12.

"How it all . . . on the lower flanks": Ibid., 146–48.

36.

"A great hubbub": Bourke, *On the Border with Crook,* 163–64.

"There the troops": Ibid., 170–71.

"The Indians should be induced . . . over thirty": Ibid., 182, 190–98.

"All in the party . . . became jealous": Ibid., 208–14.

37.

"While I was still . . . age of sixteen": Jason Betzinez, with Wilbur Sturtevant Nye, *I Fought with Geronimo* (1959), 40–48.

"Under the leadership . . . great talkers": Ibid., 49–55.

"It was a mild evening . . . for several days": Ibid., 55–67.

38.

"On the third morning . . . in this tragedy": Betzinez, *I Fought with Geronimo,* 68–75.

"These were the outlaw Indians . . . had gotten away": Ibid., 76–79.

"Our camp was on the eastern edge . . . still cannot explain it": Ibid., 81–115.

39.

"The chief of our tribe . . . killed in prison":
Geronimo's Story, 119–34.

"We ranged . . . back with him to San
Carlos": Ibid., 135–38.

"I feared treachery . . . start a new life": Ibid.,
139–47.

"I went down . . . solid gold": Miles, *Serving
the Republic,* 226–29.

PART VI · OLD WARRIORS DIE

40.

"He looked up . . . marked the ebb": Bourke,
On the Border with Crook, 414–23.

"In the corridor . . . within a few hours":
James Mooney, *Calendar History of the
Kiowa Indians,* 209–10.

"The younger element . . . Sitting Bull alive":
James McLaughlin, *My Friend the Indian*
(1910), 195–207.

"Such a step . . . Standing Rock reservation":
Ibid., 210–21.

"Thus has terminated . . . or to Lapwai":
Sherman to McCrary, Nov. 7, 1877, in
Report of the Secretary of War (1877), 1:15.

"We were not badly treated": *Yellow Wolf: His
Own Story,* edited by Lucullus Virgil
McWhorter (2ed.), 289.

"A young Indian": Lieutenant Kennon diary, Jan. 2, 1890, in *General George Crook: His Autobiography,* edited by Martin F. Schmitt (1960 ed.), 293. The last chapters of this posthumously published work were written by Schmitt.

"General Crook came": Red Cloud comment to Father Craft, in Bourke, *On the Border with Crook,* 486

41.

"Without taking": Rev. Father Tom Sherman address to Society of the Army of the Tennessee, Nov. 17, 1892, in *Report of the Proceedings of the Society of the Army of the Tennessee* (1893), 91–92.

"Though peace . . . general rule": Sherman address in *Pontiac Gazette,* July 4, 1879.

"It is all over . . . never to leave it": *New York Times,* Feb. 15, 1891.

"General Sherman said": W. H. Morgan, *Personal Reminiscences of the War of 1861–65* (1911), 224.

"I've been where you are now": Battle Creek, Michigan, *Enquirer and News,* Nov. 18, 1933, quoted in *Oakland County Book of History,* edited by Arthur A. Hagman (1970), 587.

"The war now": *Columbus (Ohio) Evening Dispatch,* Aug. 12, 1880.

"When I had given up . . . to live right":
   Geronimo's Story, 177–212.
"Take the ropes . . . back to Arizona": *New-York Daily Tribune,* Mar. 10, 1905.
"There is a great question . . . return to Arizona": *Geronimo's Story,* 213–16.
"Geronimo showed": *Army and Navy Journal,* Jan. 26, 1907.
"He was one": *New York Times,* Feb. 18, 1909.

ABOUT THE AUTHOR

H. W. Brands holds the Jack S. Blanton Sr. Chair in History at the University of Texas at Austin. He has written more than a dozen biographies and histories, including *The General vs. the President,* a *New York Times* bestseller, and *Our First Civil War,* his most recent book. Two of his biographies, *The First American* and *Traitor to His Class,* were finalists for the Pulitzer Prize.

The employees of Thorndike Press hope you have enjoyed this Large Print book. All our Thorndike, Wheeler, and Kennebec Large Print titles are designed for easy reading, and all our books are made to last. Other Thorndike Press Large Print books are available at your library, through selected bookstores, or directly from us.

For information about titles, please call:
(800) 223-1244

or visit our website at:
gale.com/thorndike

To share your comments, please write:
Publisher
Thorndike Press
10 Water St., Suite 310
Waterville, ME 04901